Tiepolo

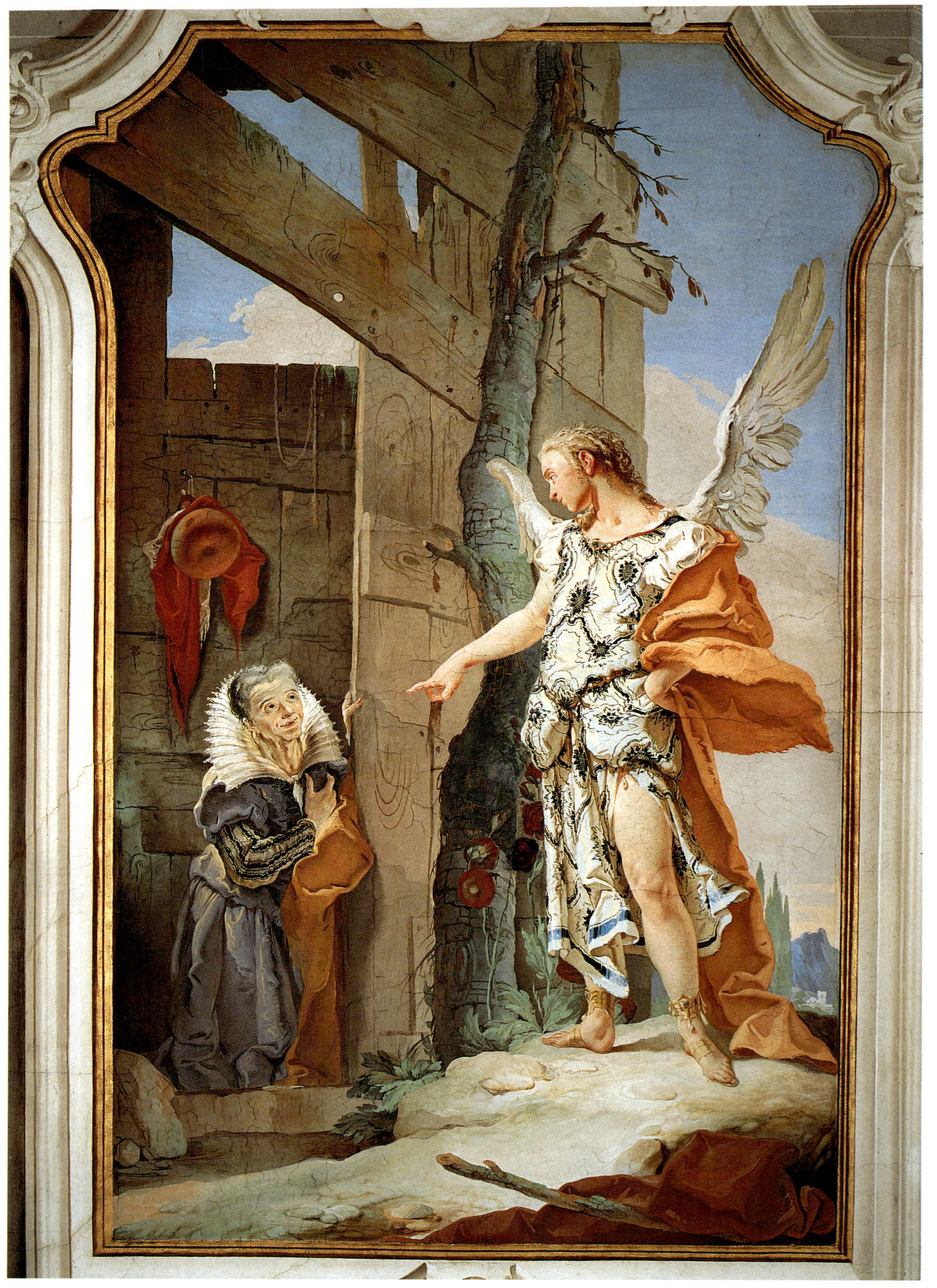

Chantal Eschenfelder

Giovanni Battista

Tiepolo

1696–1770

KÖNEMANN

1 (frontispiece)
The Angel appearing to Sarah, 1726–1729
Fresco, ca. 4000 x 2000 cm
Palazzo Patriacale (now the Archiepiscopal Palace), Udine

Bonner Str. 126, D-50968 Köln

Art Director: Peter Feierabend
Project Manager and Editor: Sally Bald
Assistant: Susanne Hergarden
German Editor: Ute E. Hammer
Assistant: Jeannette Fentroß
Translation from the German: Lena Miller
Contributing Editor: Susan James
Production Manager: Detlev Schaper
Assistant: Nicola Leurs
Layout: Oliver Hessmann
Typesetting: Greiner & Reichel, Cologne
Reproductions: Omniascanners, Milan
Printing and Binding: Neue Stalling, Oldenburg
Printed in Germany

ISBN 3-8290-0256-4
10 9 8 7 6 5 4 3 2 1

Contents

First works in Venice and Udine 1710–1729

2 *Portrait of Doge Marco Cornaro*, ca. 1716
Oil on canvas, 271 x 182 cm
Private collection, Venice

The picture is a posthumous portrait of the Doge Marco Cornaro (ca. 1286–1368). The painting is dominated by the awe-inspiring figure of the Doge, enthroned on a raised podium, several steps high, in front of an architectural backdrop high above the viewer. The work differs from the pictures of the Apostles in Santa Maria dei Derelitti in Venice in the liberal use of warm shades of red. The brisk brushwork and the expressive gesture of the hands is, however, comparable.

Giovanni Battista, called Giambattista, Tiepolo was born on 5 March 1696, in the Venetian district of Castello, and baptized in the church of San Pietro di Castello on 16 April of that same year. His father, Domenico Tiepolo, a merchant and ship owner, died just a year after Giambattista's birth. Orsetta Marangon, his mother, was left the difficult task of providing for the large family in the years that followed under considerable financial hardship. Although Giambattista was raised in a family whose main involvement was in the world of commerce, in around 1710 he began an apprenticeship in the workshop of the artist Gregorio Lazzarini (1655–1730), a painter generally forgotten today, but very successful in Venice at that time. Giambattista probably worked in Lazzarini's studio until 1717. That year, Tiepolo's name appeared in the registers of the Venetian painters' guild, the *fraglia*, marking the start of his career as an independent artist.

There has been much speculation about Lazzarini's influence on Tiepolo's artistic development. As well as teaching the rudiments of form and technique such as drawing, perspective and the composition of large groups of figures, the master's first priority was to familiarize his pupils with the traditions of 16th century Venetian art, through the works of Jacopo Tintoretto (1518–1594), Paolo Veronese (ca. 1528–1588) and Palma Giovane (1548–1628). Although Tiepolo's earliest works differ greatly from the classicizing tendencies of his master, Lazzarini was still a decisive influence. His eclectic method of uniting different stylistic stimuli in the one composition led the young Tiepolo to study the works of other artists closely, right from the beginning of his career. In this way he collected a rich fund of pictorial motifs and techniques of representation, which he could later vary at will and adapt to his own mode of expression.

One of Giambattista's first commissions was to make graphic reproductions of a number of works by 16th century artists – Tintoretto, Francesco Bassano (1549–1592) and Giuseppe Salviati (1520–1575) – for the *Gran Teatro delle pitture e prospettive di Venezia*, a collection of engravings published by Domenico Loviso in 1717. This lowly work as a copier gave him the opportunity to gain inspiration from the works in question, allowing him to appropriate their essential elements and compositional structures.

Tiepolo's early works differ very clearly from the more academic orientation of his master in the rapid brushwork and in the dramatic play between light and shade. In 1715/16, Tiepolo produced five canvases depicting apostles for a series of *Apostles and Prophets*, which were hung in the lunettes over the side arches in Santa Maria dei Derelitti – the church of the Ospedaletto – in Venice (ills. 3, 4). Tiepolo's paintings are characterized by very dark tones of color and an expressive handling of light, reminiscent of the Tenebrist school of painters of the late Baroque period, in particular of Federico Bencovich (1677–1756) and Giambattista Piazzetta (1682–1754).

The twenty-year-old appears already to have gained access to influential circles in society and to have been introduced to important clients towards the end of his apprenticeship. In 1716, he became artistic advisor and painter to Giovanni Cornaro (1647–1722), who reigned as doge of Venice from 1709 to 1722. Amongst others works which Tiepolo created for the Cornaro family palace were the *supra porte* portraits of the Doges Giovanni and Marco Cornaro (ill. 2) – the latter, an early 14th century ancestor of the patron. In contrast to the depictions of the *Apostles*, these portraits are dominated by reddish tones and characterized by a lighter and warmer coloring, which appears to have been inspired more by Sebastiano Ricci (1659–1734).

In the same year, his oil sketch *The Crossing of the Red Sea*, a design presumably intended for the decoration of the church of Santi Cosma e Damiano on the island of La Giudecca in Venice, was exhibited in public, to great applause, on the Feast Day of St. Roch.

In 1716, with the *Assumption of the Virgin* in Santa Maria Assunta in Biadene, Tiepolo created his first ceiling fresco. Tiepolo's extraordinary talent for decorating interior spaces is evident in the frescoes which he produced for Giambattista Baglioni in Padua in 1719/20. This wealthy publisher had just recently bought his way into the Venetian nobility, and, in order to demonstrate his new social status, had the main salon of his country villa in Massanzago near Padua decorated with *The Triumph of Aurora* (ill. 5) on the ceiling and

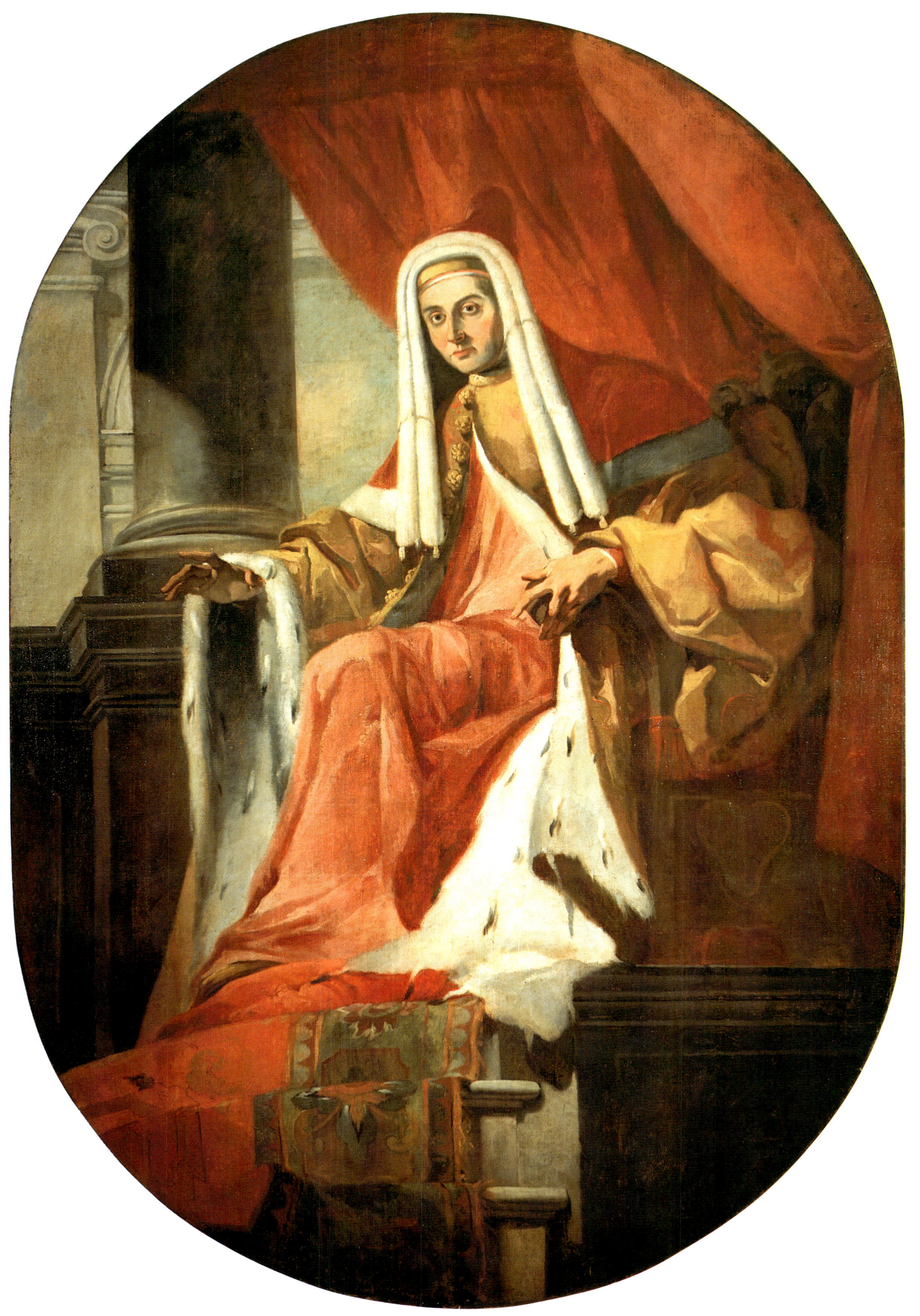

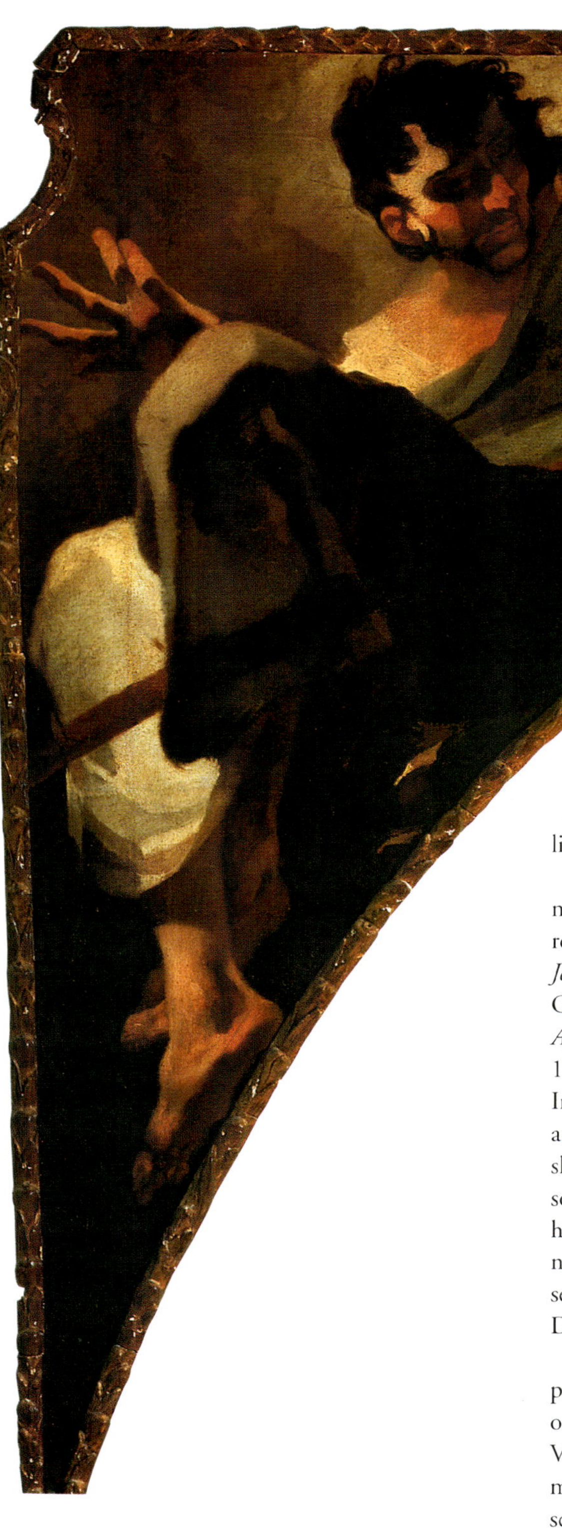

3, 4 *The Apostles Thomas and John*, 1715/16
Oil on canvas, 205 x 390 cm
Santa Maria dei Derelitti (Ospedaletto), Venice

The Apostles Thomas, on the left, and John, on the right, can be recognized by their attributes. The lance refers to the martyrdom of Thomas, and the chalice to the beaker of poison from which, according to legend, John is said to have drunk without coming to any harm. The book is an allusion to John the Evangelist, who is equated with the Apostle of the same name. The expressive gestures of the figures and the dark tones of the picture are characteristic of Tiepolo's early works, as is the dramatic play between light and shade.

scenes from the myth of Phaethon on the walls. The frescoes take up the whole room, creating the illusion that the walls open out onto an unbounded space – a scheme of decoration to which Tiepolo would return time and again and which was particularly valued by his clients. In contrast to his works on canvas, the lightened and radiant coloring of the frescoes is striking.

In the period which followed, Tiepolo received numerous commissions to execute frescoes – mainly on religious subjects. Thus he completed the fresco *St. Jerome pointing at the Cross* in the sacristy of San Giovanni Crisostomo, probably in 1721, as well as the *Apotheosis of St. Theresa*, which dates between 1722 and 1730, in Santa Maria, the church of the Scalzi, in Venice. In both these works, the strong modelling of the figures and the great use of *chiaroscuro* effects – i. e. of light-and-shade painting – bring to mind the formulations of the somewhat older Giambattista Piazzetta. On the other hand, the 1722 fresco in the parish church in Vascon near Treviso, *The Glory of St. Lucy*, now badly damaged, seems inspired more by the French painter Louis Dorigny (1654–1742).

As well as the great fresco decorations, Tiepolo also produced numerous canvases on religious, mythological or historical subjects. The Gallerie dell'Accademia in Venice now houses the series of four identical-sized mythological canvases, dated 1720–1722, depicting scenes from Ovid's "Metamorphoses". They are: *The Rape of Europa*, *Diana and Actaeon* (ill. 6), *Diana and Callisto* (ill. 7) and *Apollo and Marsyas*. The most impressive aspect of these works is the way the groups of figures are placed in the landscape, arranged rhythmically along diagonal lines which correspond from one picture to another.

Arising from an instruction in the will of the patrician Andrea Stazio in 1722, Tiepolo was commissioned alongside eleven other famous artists of the day, including Sebastiano Ricci, Piazzetta, Giovanni Antonio Pellegrini (1675–1741), Antonio Balestra (1666–1740) and Lazzarini, to execute a cycle of canvases depicting episodes from the lives of the twelve apostles for the church of San Stae in Venice. Originally intended for the nave, the pictures were later transferred to the presbytery, where they still hang today. Each artist was to contribute the portrayal of one apostle to the cycle and Tiepolo was assigned the *Martyrdom of St. Bartholomew* (ill. 8). The dark tones of the picture and the dramatic composition look back to his earlier works, although the handling of the figures shows signs of greater maturity.

The small canvas, *The Glory of St. Dominic*, now in the Gallerie dell'Accademia in Venice, was executed in 1723. Tiepolo entered this *modello* in a competition to fresco the ceiling of the chapel dedicated to St. Dominic in Santi Giovanni e Paolo in Venice – a contest won, in the end, by Piazzetta.

At the same time, Tiepolo was engaged on one of the most important works of his early period, the canvas *Our Lady of Carmel* (ill. 9). Commissioned by the apothecary Giacomo Tonini, he probably commenced work on the large canvas for one of the side chapels in the church of San Aponal in Venice as early as 1721, but did not complete it till 1727. It was taken down in 1810 and is now in the Pinacoteca di Brera in Milan. The unusual composition, in which the Madonna has been moved from the center to the right of the picture, takes into consideration both the fact that it was originally to be hung on a side wall and the particular lighting conditions in the chapel. The picture for the Carmelite brotherhood deals with their belief in eternal life and in the veneration of the Virgin Mary as the way to salvation. It demonstrates Tiepolo's ability to render traditional Counter-Reformation themes in a dramatic pictorial language.

Another large-scale painting stems from the same period (1722–1725) and was likewise executed for a rich apothecary: the *Crucifixion* in San Martino on the island of Burano. The distinctly lighter coloring, compared to *Our Lady Of Carmel*, was already apparent in a cycle of paintings which Tiepolo produced sometime before 1725 for a room in the Ca' Zenobio in Venice, and which mark a definite step in Tiepolo's artistic development towards a significantly lighter palette of colors. The cycle of canvases depicting scenes from the life of Queen Zenobia contains four pictures, which were removed and sold in 1817. *Queen Zenobia*

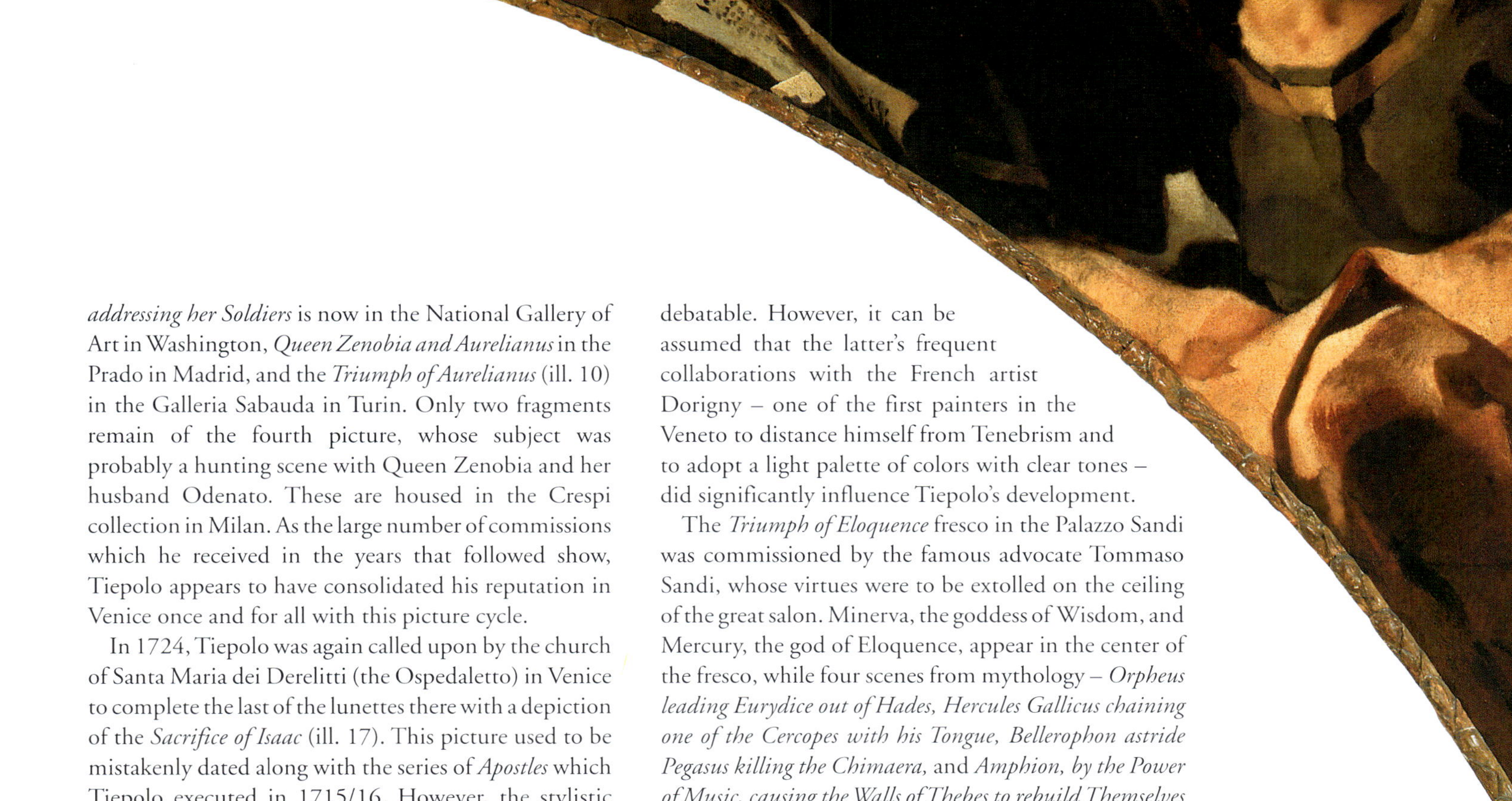

addressing her Soldiers is now in the National Gallery of Art in Washington, *Queen Zenobia and Aurelianus* in the Prado in Madrid, and the *Triumph of Aurelianus* (ill. 10) in the Galleria Sabauda in Turin. Only two fragments remain of the fourth picture, whose subject was probably a hunting scene with Queen Zenobia and her husband Odenato. These are housed in the Crespi collection in Milan. As the large number of commissions which he received in the years that followed show, Tiepolo appears to have consolidated his reputation in Venice once and for all with this picture cycle.

In 1724, Tiepolo was again called upon by the church of Santa Maria dei Derelitti (the Ospedaletto) in Venice to complete the last of the lunettes there with a depiction of the *Sacrifice of Isaac* (ill. 17). This picture used to be mistakenly dated along with the series of *Apostles* which Tiepolo executed in 1715/16. However, the stylistic resemblance of the *Sacrifice* to works such as the *Martyrdom of St. Bartholomew*, along with a piece of documentary evidence, verify the later dating of 1724.

The second project for this church marked the beginning of a most productive working partnership between Tiepolo and the Ticinese architect Domenico Rossi (1657–1737). Rossi was in charge of renovation work at the Palazzo Sandi in the parish of San Angelo in Venice, where Tiepolo executed the fresco *The Triumph of Eloquence* (ills. 11, 12) on the ceiling of the large principal salon in 1724/25. He also worked in the cathedral at Udine, where Giambattista had frescoed the chapel of the Holy Sacrament (1726). And the architect from Ticino was also responsible for the renovation of the Udinese Patriarchal Palace, where Tiepolo worked on his famous fresco decorations between 1726 and 1729. Also attributed to Rossi is the alteration work in the Ca' Dolfin Palace in Venice, for which Tiepolo delivered ten canvases with episodes from Roman history at the same time as he was working on the frescoes in Udine.

These large decorative projects occupied Tiepolo throughout the late 1820s, a period of activity in which the artist unquestionably turned towards the lighter, brighter shades of color which would continue to characterize his work in the 1830s. The extent to which the architect Rossi was involved in this development is debatable. However, it can be assumed that the latter's frequent collaborations with the French artist Dorigny – one of the first painters in the Veneto to distance himself from Tenebrism and to adopt a light palette of colors with clear tones – did significantly influence Tiepolo's development.

The *Triumph of Eloquence* fresco in the Palazzo Sandi was commissioned by the famous advocate Tommaso Sandi, whose virtues were to be extolled on the ceiling of the great salon. Minerva, the goddess of Wisdom, and Mercury, the god of Eloquence, appear in the center of the fresco, while four scenes from mythology – *Orpheus leading Eurydice out of Hades, Hercules Gallicus chaining one of the Cercopes with his Tongue, Bellerophon astride Pegasus killing the Chimaera,* and *Amphion, by the Power of Music, causing the Walls of Thebes to rebuild Themselves* – are portrayed along each of the picture's four sides. The contrast between the light-filled center and the rather darker colors of the scenes around the edges gives rise to a dramatic composition.

The structure of the fresco is strongly reminiscent of famous examples of 17th century Baroque ceiling decorations, particularly the frescoes in the Palazzo Medici-Riccardi in Florence by Luca Giordano (1643–1705). Tiepolo's creations for the Palazzo Sandi show that, at this stage of his career (the mid-1820s), he had already fully developed the compositional structure of his later decorative projects: groups of figures are positioned around the edges of the fresco, while mythological figures, heroes or saints occupy the cloud-filled and brilliantly lit skies in the center. But there is another reason why the Palazzo Sandi frescoes represent an important example with regard to the artist's stylistic development: For the first time, he demonstrably falls back upon the example of Veronese, his great 16th century predecessor, not only in the lightened palette of colors, but also in his use of a technique typical of that artist – the colored shadow. Veronese's influence can also be seen in the three mythological canvases, *Odysseus discovering Achilles among the Daughters of Licomedes, Apollo flaying Marsyas,* and *Hercules and Anteus,* which Tiepolo executed for the same room, and which are currently in private ownership in Castelgomberto.

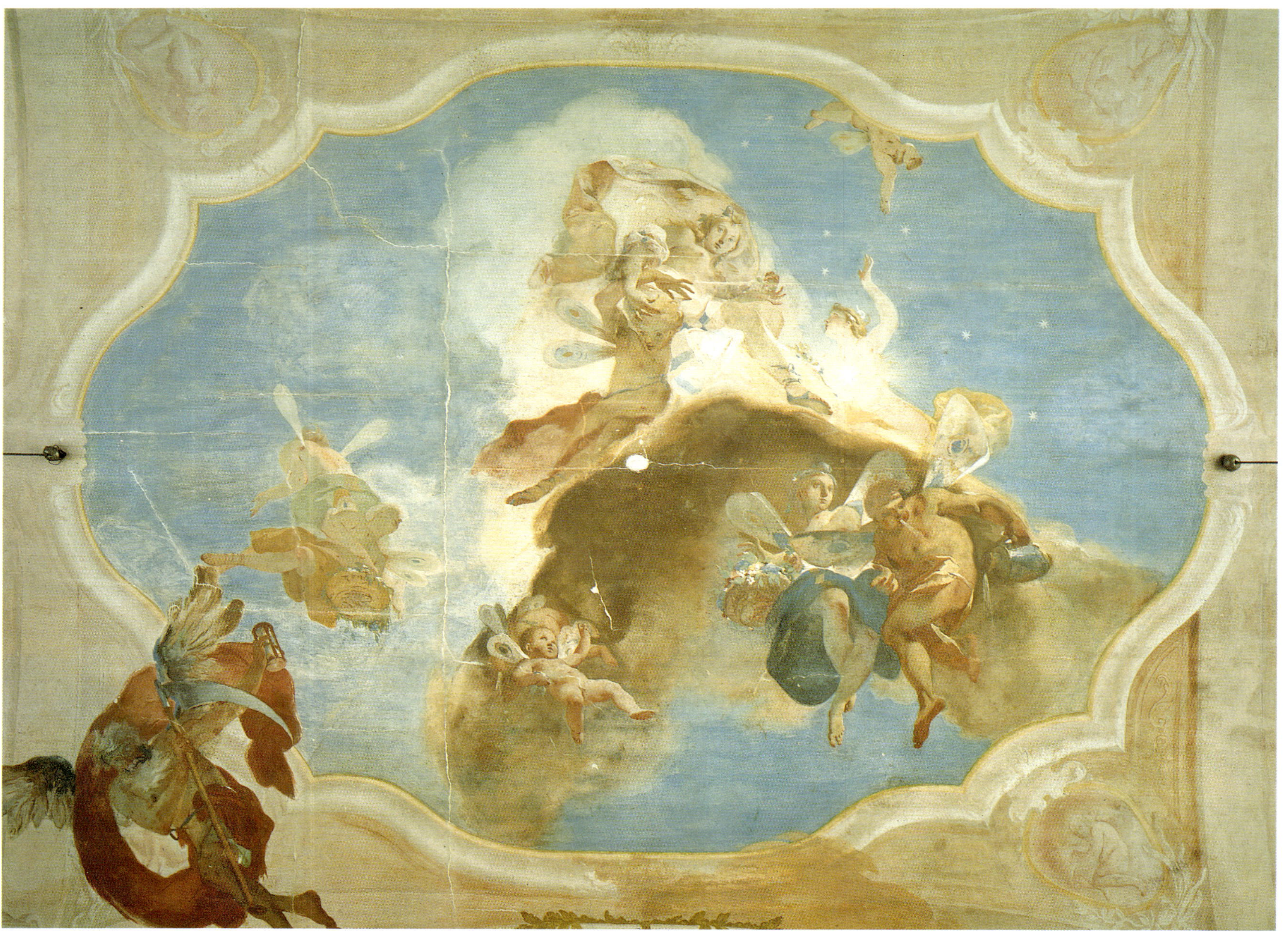

5 *The Triumph of Aurora*, 1719/20
Ceiling fresco
Villa Baglioni, Massanzago, Padua

The ceiling fresco, conceived as if we were looking up at open skies, shows the goddess of the dawn, Aurora, enthroned on a cloud *di sotto in sù*. She is accompanied by Zephyr and Flora and a handful of *putti*, while, in the bottom corner, outside the painted frame, a bearded elderly man, the personification of Time, raises his hourglass in admonishment. In comparison to other works from Tiepolo's early period, the light and clear colors make an impression.

Having finished work at the Palazzo Sandi, Tiepolo went on to execute his first major commissions outside Venice in 1726. In June of that year, he began decorating the chapel of the Holy Sacrament in the cathedral at Udine, for the brotherhood of the Holy Sacrament, with depictions of *The Sacrifice of Isaac*, *Abraham's Dream* and figures of angels on the vault. The chapel is built in semi-octagonal form, thus representing an exceptional compositional challenge, since the resulting compartmentalization of the surface of the walls and vault left little scope for decoration.

In the same year, Tiepolo began work on the frescoes in the stairwell and in the rooms on the *piano nobile*, or first floor, of the Patriarchal Palace (now the Archiepiscopal Palace) at Udine. This important project had been commissioned by Dionisio Dolfin (1663–1734), a member of a Venetian patrician family, who had held the office of patriarch of Aquileia since 1699. In the center of the stairwell ceiling, Tiepolo frescoed the Fall of the Rebel Angels, which he surrounded with eight monochrome scenes from the book of Genesis. He then went on to decorate the Gallery, the so-called Sala Rossa, or Red Room, (at that time, the seat of the ecclesiastical tribunal), and the Throne Room on the *piano nobile.* The Gallery features scenes from the lives of the Old Testament patriarchs, likewise inspired by the book of Genesis. The three main episodes, *The Three Angels appearing to Abraham* (ill. 13), *Rachel hiding the Idols from her Father Laban* (ill. 14) and *The Angel appearing to Sarah* (ill. 1) are each surrounded by a *trompe-l'œil* frame. They are hung alternately with monochrome portraits of prophetesses, which create the illusion of being statues in niches along the walls. On the ceiling, a depiction of *The Sacrifice of Isaac* (ill. 17) occupies center position, flanked by smaller oval compartments portraying *Hagar in the Wilderness* (ill. 15) and *Jacob's Dream* (ill. 16). Tiepolo was aided in the realization of this famous ensemble by the *quadratura* specialist from Ferrara, Girolamo Mengozzi Colonna (1688–1766), with whom he

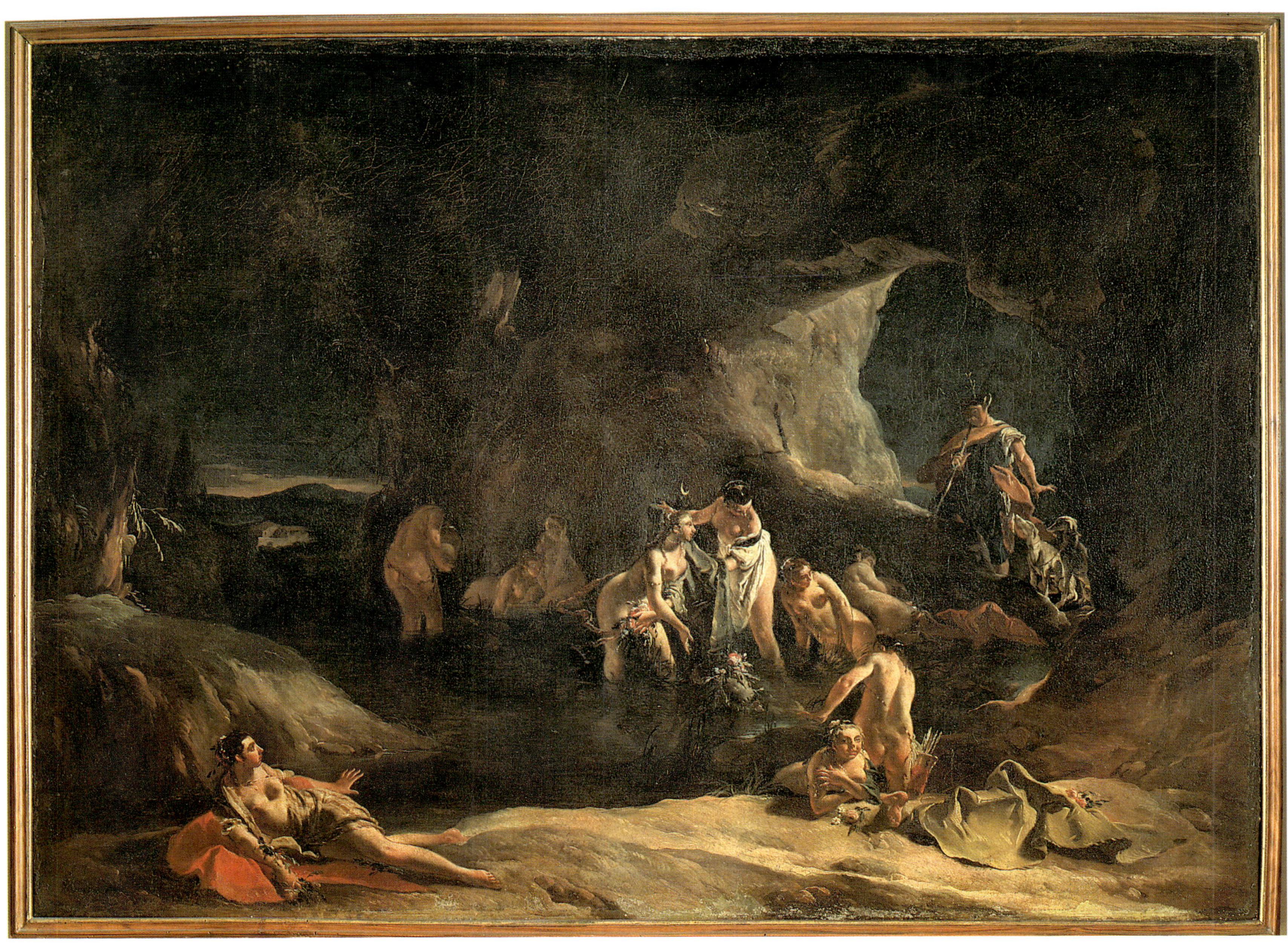

continued to work closely during the years that followed. On the ceiling of the Sala Rossa, Tiepolo painted *The Judgement of Solomon* (ill. 19), surrounded by portraits of the prophets *Isaiah* (ill. 18), Jeremiah, Ezekiel and Daniel – a theme appropriate to a room used both as a civil and ecclesiastical tribunal. Finally, there are portraits of Old Testament patriarchs in the Throne Room, but these have deteriorated badly, and not all are by Tiepolo himself.

The ambitious pictorial program of the overall decoration was probably conceived by Dionisio Dolfin himself, with the help of his theological advisers, including Francesco Florio, his vicar-general. The subjects chosen for the pictures were intended to reinforce the legitimacy of the ruling patriarchy, which at that time found itself at the center of a fierce politico-ecclesiastical struggle between Venice and Vienna. The decoration of the Patriarchal Palace in Udine unquestionably represents the high point in Tiepolo's early career. By portraying figures in 16th century dress, and placing them in landscapes bathed in sun and light, he recalls the magnificently staged scenes of Veronese. The decisive element in this project must be his sense of the theatrical, where the respective subject matter of the picture is presented in a dramatically staged scene. Each figure is assigned a primary or secondary role and the relationships between the protagonists are elucidated by means of a masterly handling of color. Tiepolo thus transformed the revival of Veronese's art, also favored by his contemporaries, from a mere stylistic fashion into a pictorial language that was to confirm his own reputation as a representative of the Venetian tradition.

In 1726–1729, at the same time as he was working on the Udinese frescoes, and probably during the winter months, Tiepolo produced ten canvases for the Reception Room in the Ca' Dolfin palace in Venice. Tiepolo's patrons were the brothers of the patriarch Dolfin, Daniele III (1654–1729) and Daniele IV (1656–1729), who both played an important role in the political life of the Venetian Republic, the former as a

6 *Diana and Actaeon*, 1720–1722
Oil on canvas, 100 x 135 cm
Gallerie dell'Accademia, Venice

Inspired by Ovid's "Metamorphoses", the picture illustrates the tale of the young hunter Actaeon, who was transformed by Diana, the goddess of the hunt, into a stag after he had watched her bathing. He was subsequently torn to pieces by his own hounds. Tiepolo has transposed the scene to a mysterious, bizarre grotto setting, in which the brilliant bodies of the bathing nymphs form a dramatic contrast with the dark waters and cliffs.

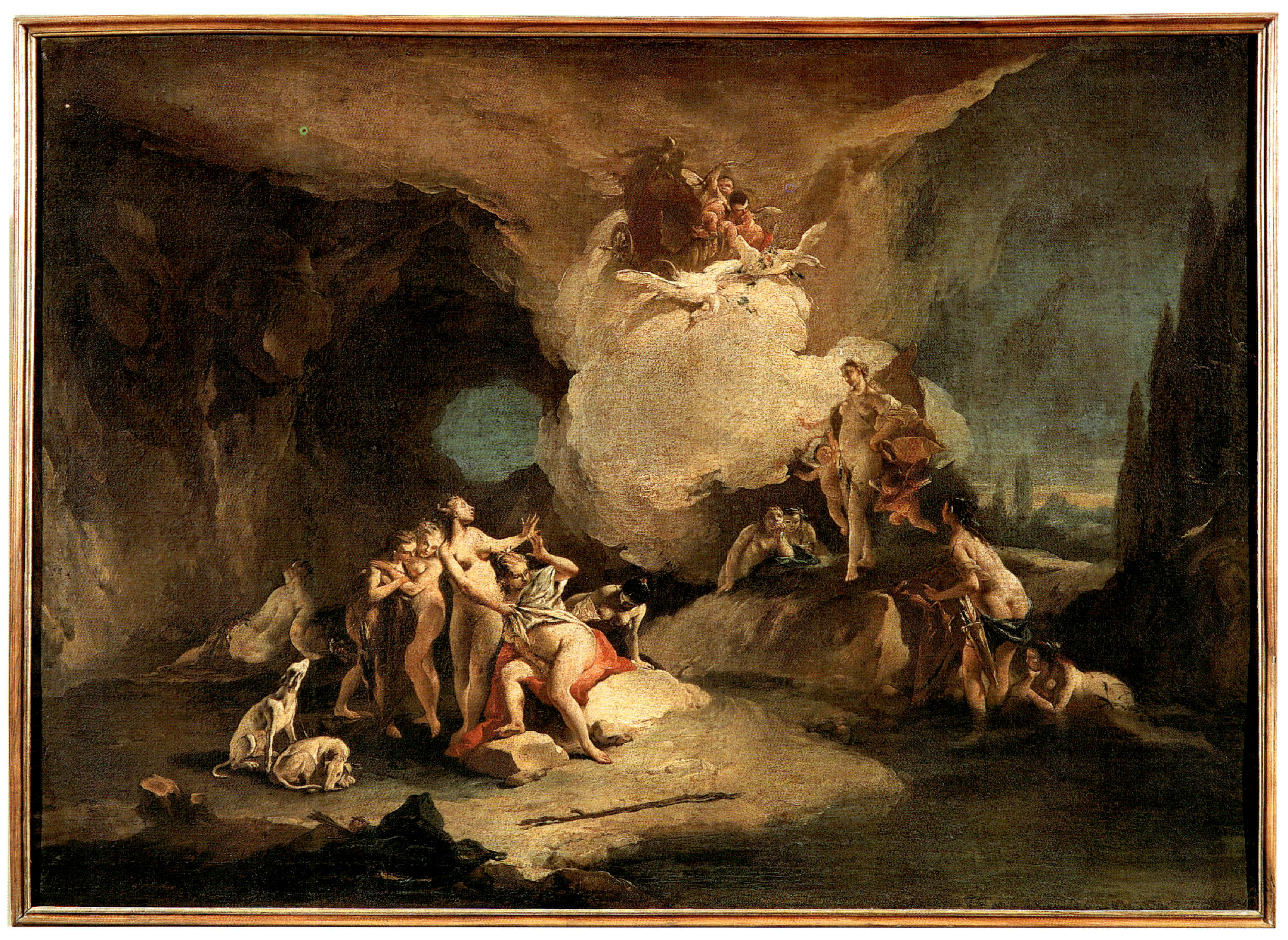

7 *Diana and Callisto*, 1720–1722
Oil on canvas, 100 x 135 cm
Gallerie dell'Accademia, Venice

In his "Metamorphoses", Ovid narrates the story of the nymph Callisto, whose pregnancy – she has been seduced by Jupiter – is discovered by the other nymphs in the huntress Diana's entourage as they bathe. As a punishment, Diana subsequently turns Callisto into a bear, who is later killed by her own son during the hunt. In the picture, the goddess has descended from her heavenly chariot and stands high up on a rockface in the midst of an unreal, bizarre, craggy landscape while passing judgement. Here, too, Tiepolo builds the picture up dramatically with strong contrasts of light and dark in the coloring.

diplomat, the latter as an army commander in the war against the Turks. The picture cycle illustrates episodes from the history of the Roman republic, based on Lucius Annaeus Florus' text "Epitomae de Tito Livio bellorum", and was intended to celebrate the patriotic devotion of the two brothers. The individual works are currently housed in the Kunsthistorisches Museum in Vienna, the Metropolitan Museum of Art in New York and the Hermitage in St. Petersburg (ill. 20). They are notable for the skillful use of complementary colors, and their diffuse lighting demonstrates Tiepolo's more mature sense of color.

Alongside these grand commissions, Tiepolo also created a number of pictures on a smaller scale, of which *Apelles painting Campaspe* in the Museum of Fine Arts in Montreal is particularly worthy of mention. Tiepolo painted the famous painter of antiquity in his own likeness, while endowing Campaspe with the features of his wife, Cecilia Guardi, whom he had married in 1719. As well as representing a homage to his wife, this picture can be interpreted as a testimony to the awareness of his own standing as an artist, which Tiepolo had developed by the end of his apprenticeship.

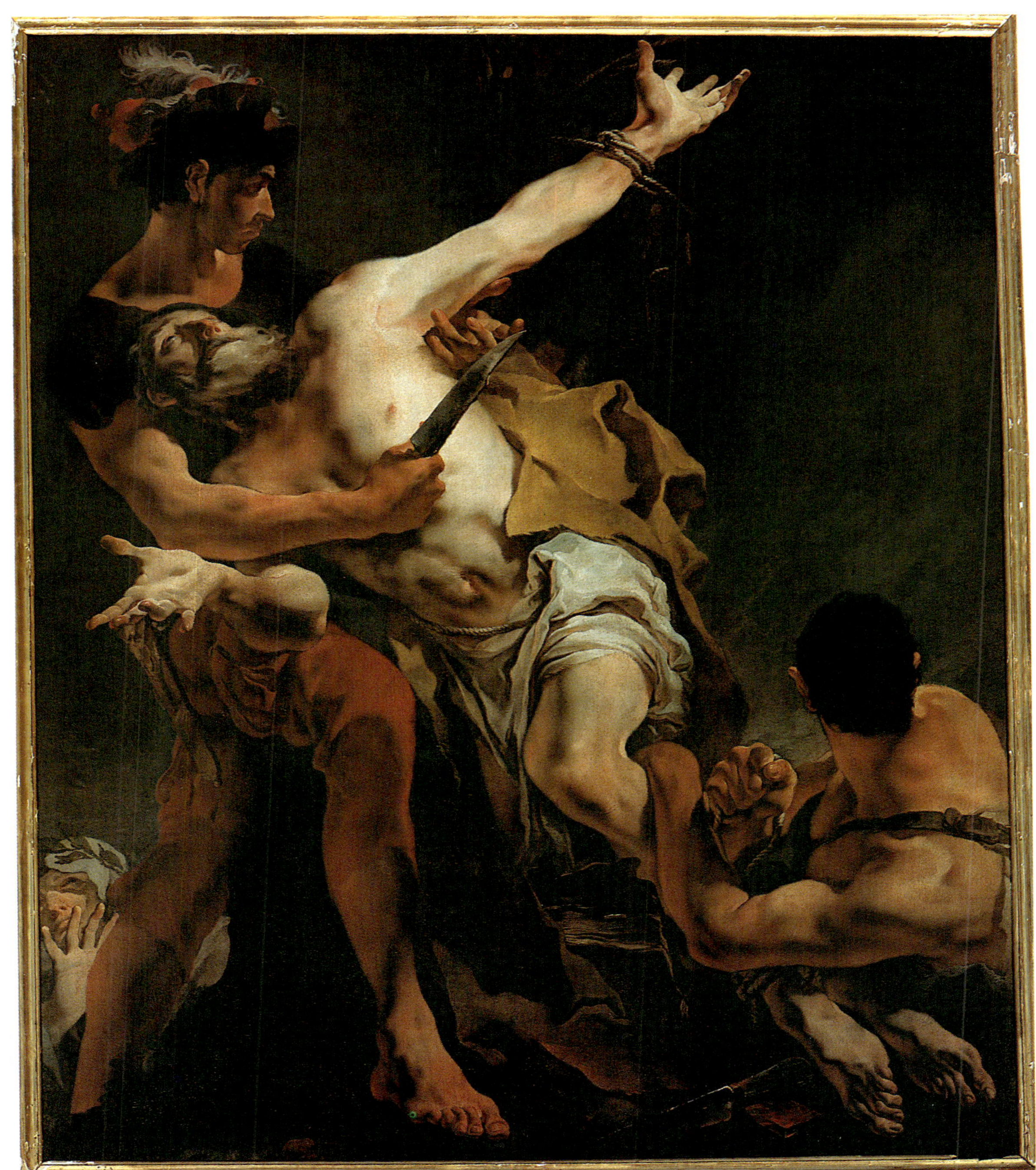

8 *The Martyrdom of St. Bartholomew*, 1722
Oil on canvas, 167 x 139 cm
San Stae, Venice

The subject of the painting is the martyrdom of St. Bartholomew, whose tormentors are on the point of flaying him alive. The awfulness of the scene is matched by the extremely powerful composition which places the writhing body of the saint along the diagonal between the two henchmen. The eerie contrast between light and shade makes the scene all the more vivid. The expressive gesture with which the despairing saint stretches his arm heavenward transforms the picture into a wonderful depiction of divine grace, the existence of which is already signalled by the bright light emanating from above.

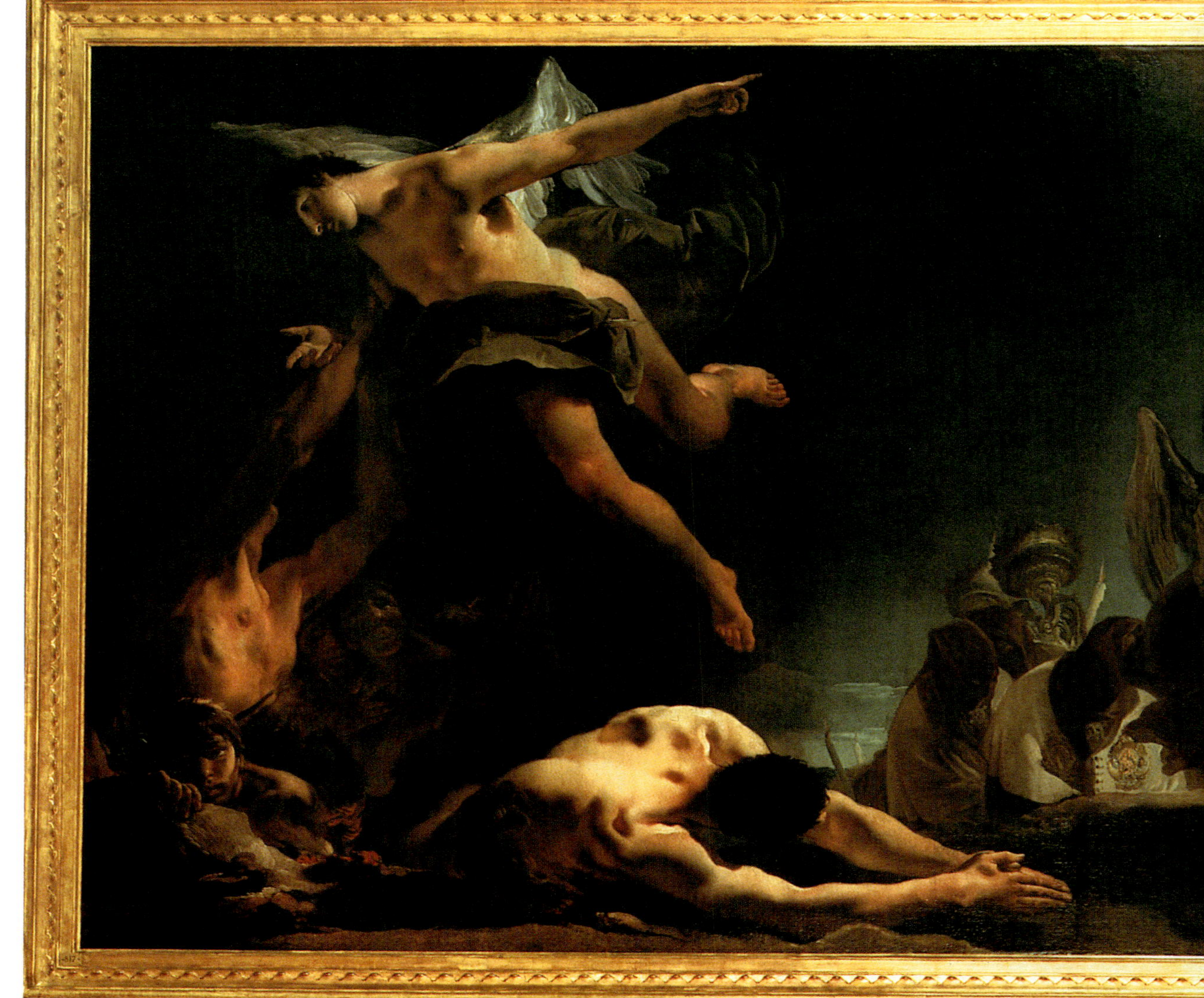

9 *Our Lady of Carmel*, 1721–1727
Oil on canvas, 210 x 650 cm
Pinacoteca di Brera, Milan

The picture takes as its subject the Roman Catholic cult of the scapular, which dates from the late Middle Ages, and popular belief in its capacity to save the soul from the eternal fires of Hell. On the left, an angel is showing souls that the way to salvation lies in the adoration of the Virgin Mary, as portrayed in the center of the canvas. There, Mary and the Christ Child are engrossed in a *Sacra Conversazione* with the beatified Patriarch Albert of Jerusalem, Simon Stock and St. Teresa of Avila. On the right, in a reference to the Old Testament, the prophet Elijah appears at prayer, accompanied by angels, with Mount Carmel in the background. The bright light behind Mary contrasts with the dark figures that surround her and can be understood as an allusion to the divine message of salvation.

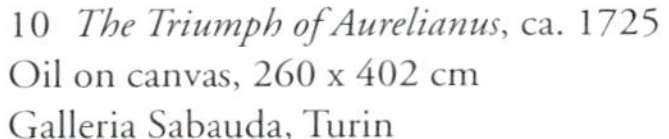

10 *The Triumph of Aurelianus*, ca. 1725
Oil on canvas, 260 x 402 cm
Galleria Sabauda, Turin

This canvas is a depiction of the triumphal procession of the Roman emperor Aurelianus following his conquest of the kingdom of Palmyra in AD 272. The victorious Emperor stands in the center of the picture aboard his triumphal chariot, drawn by white horses, and gazes into the distance. Queen Zenobia of Palmyra walks in front of the chariot, chained and bound, a prisoner of the Emperor.

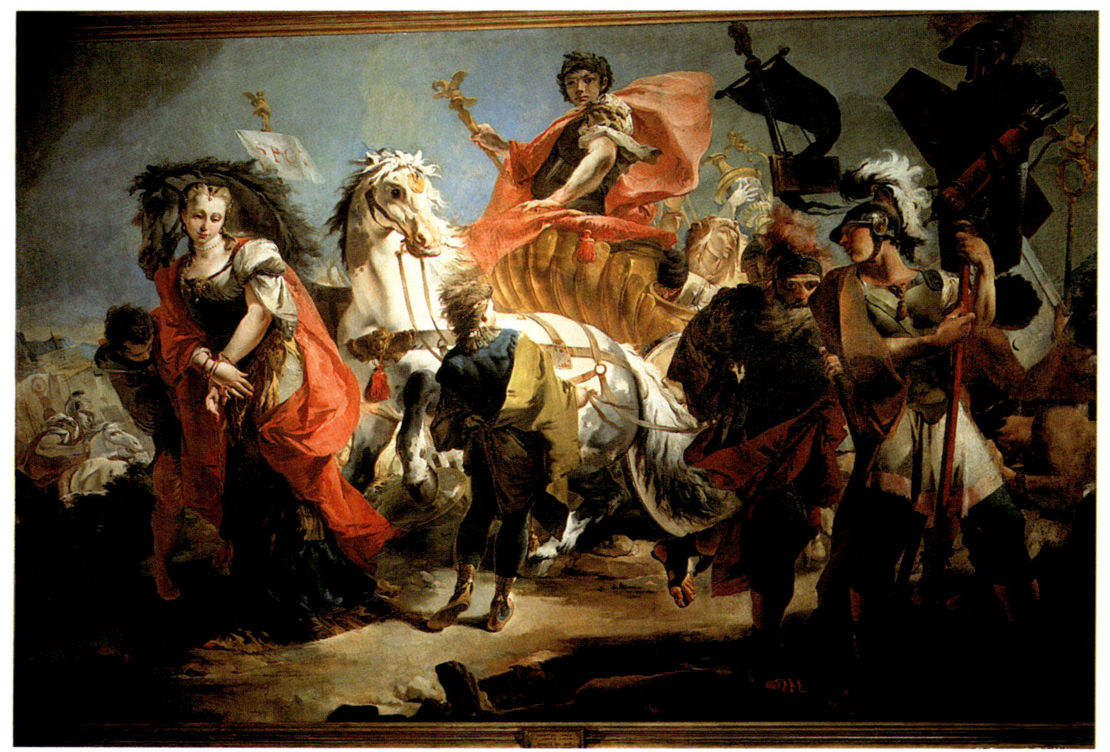

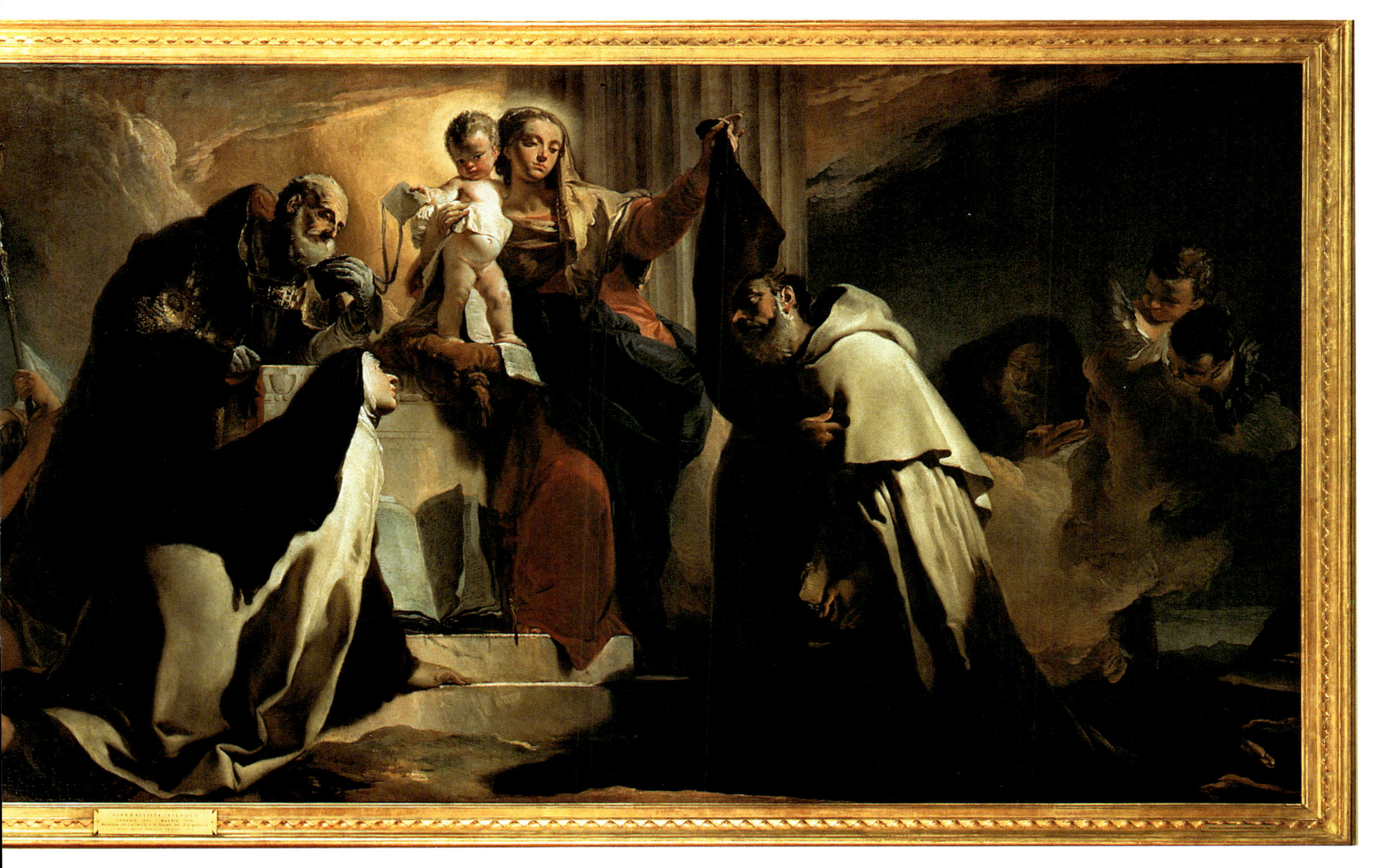

11 (following double page, left) Detail of *The Triumph of Eloquence*, 1724/25
Fresco, ca. 650 x 1070 cm
Palazzo Sandi, Venice

On the lower edge of the picture, Amphion plays on his lyre, whose music, according to myth, caused the walls of Thebes to erect themselves. Above him, Minerva, the goddess of wisdom, floats on a cloud. The surface of the heavens is largely free of figures, but activated with yellow and mauve banks of clouds. Their circular arrangement at the center of the fresco lends the painting a certain dynamic. To the left, Bellerophon appears on the winged steed Pegasus, battling with the Chimaera. At the very top, a part of the Underworld from the Orpheus episode is visible, as are the three Fates, spinning the thread of life.

12 (following double page, right) Detail of *The Triumph of Eloquence*, 1724/25
Fresco, ca. 650 x 1070 cm
Palazzo Sandi, Venice

Mercury, the god of eloquence, hovers above the left-hand side of the picture. Below him we see the remaining part of the walls of Thebes, which are building themselves to the sound of Amphion's music. The representation of Hercules on the right of the picture is likewise an example of the power of words, symbolized by the chains which bind his mouth to the ear of the Cercope. A little higher up is Orpheus, embracing his wife Eurydice, who he has just reclaimed from the Underworld. Amor, whose blindfolded eyes suggest that they are "blinded by love", hovers over them.

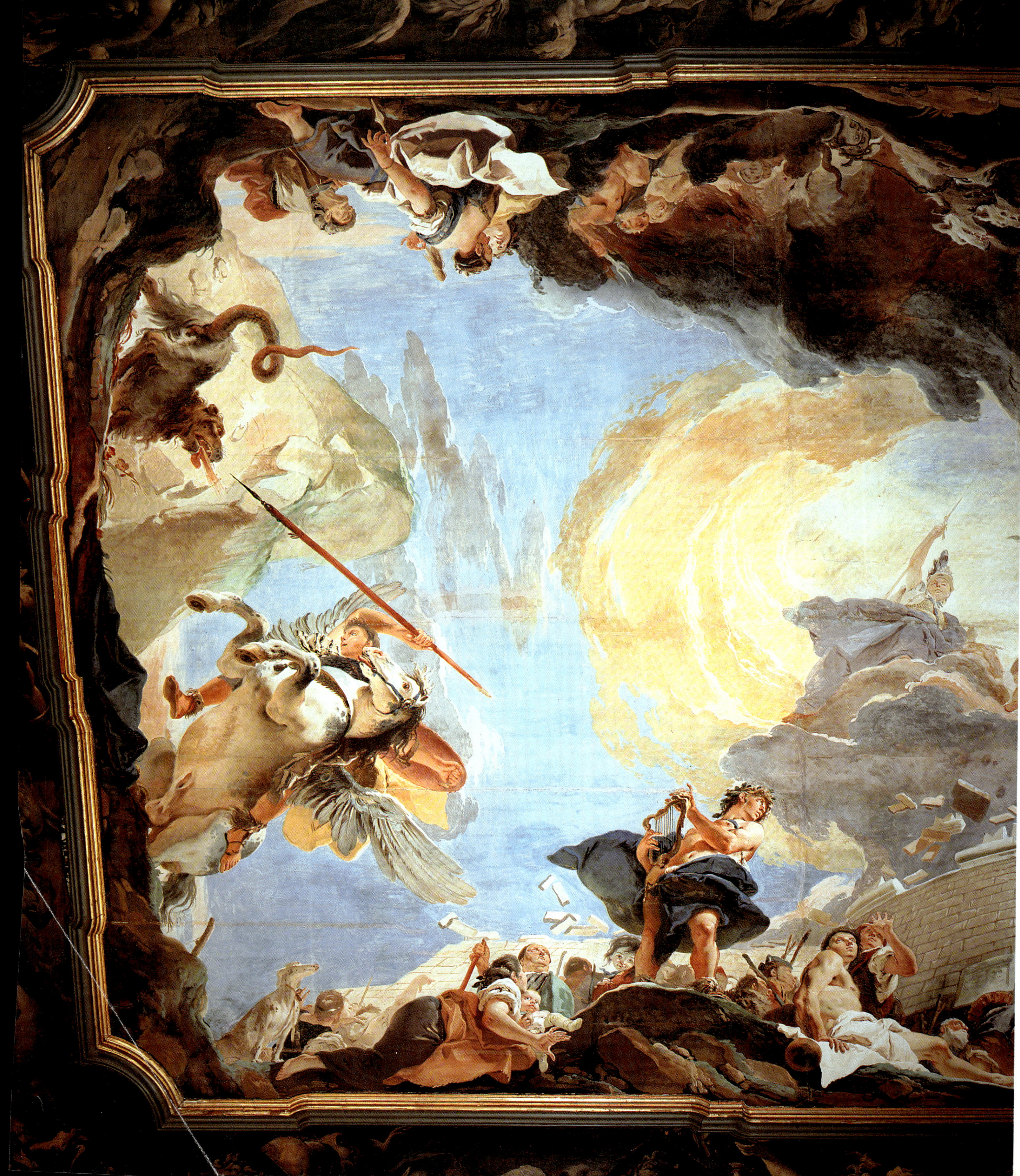

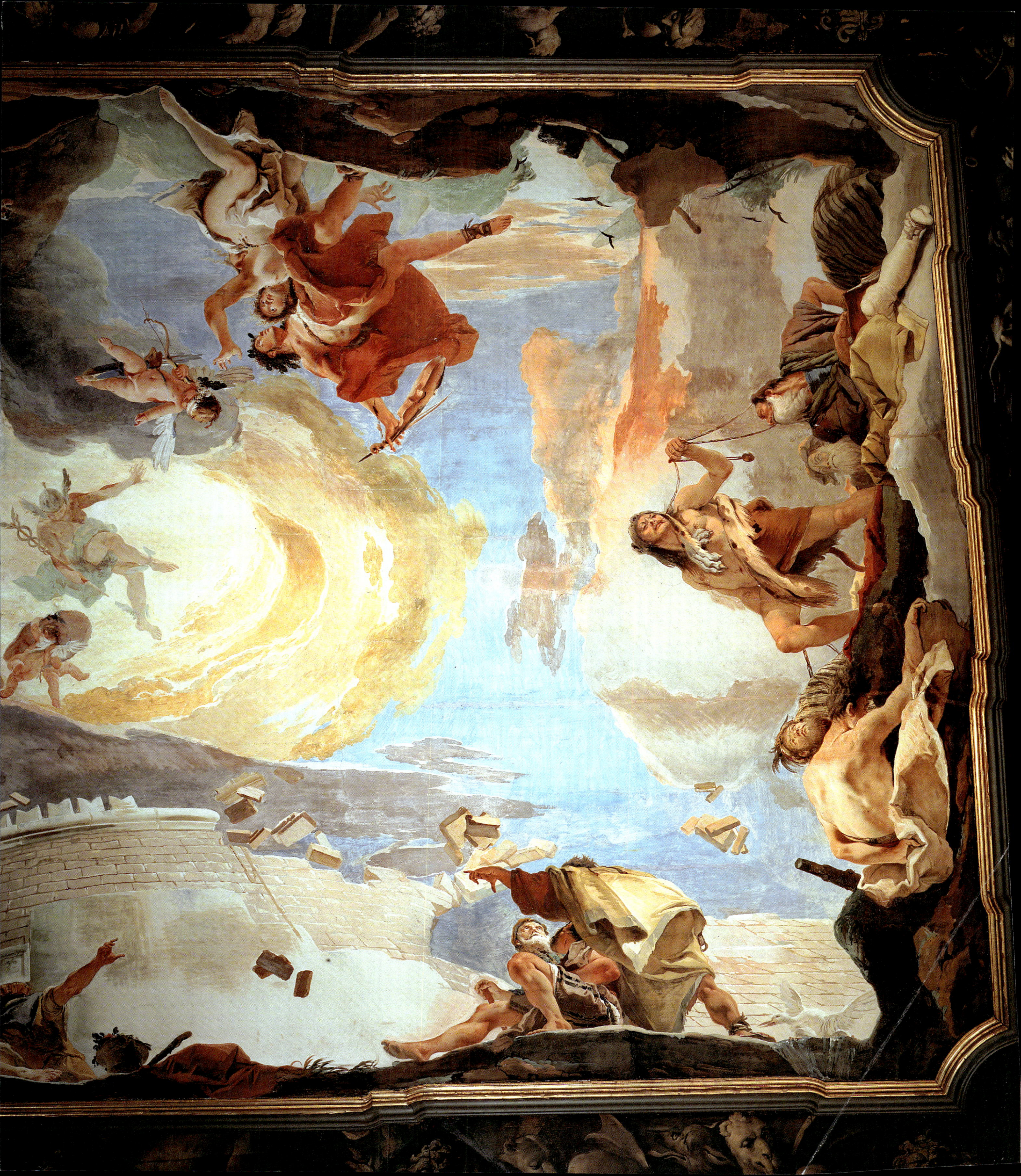

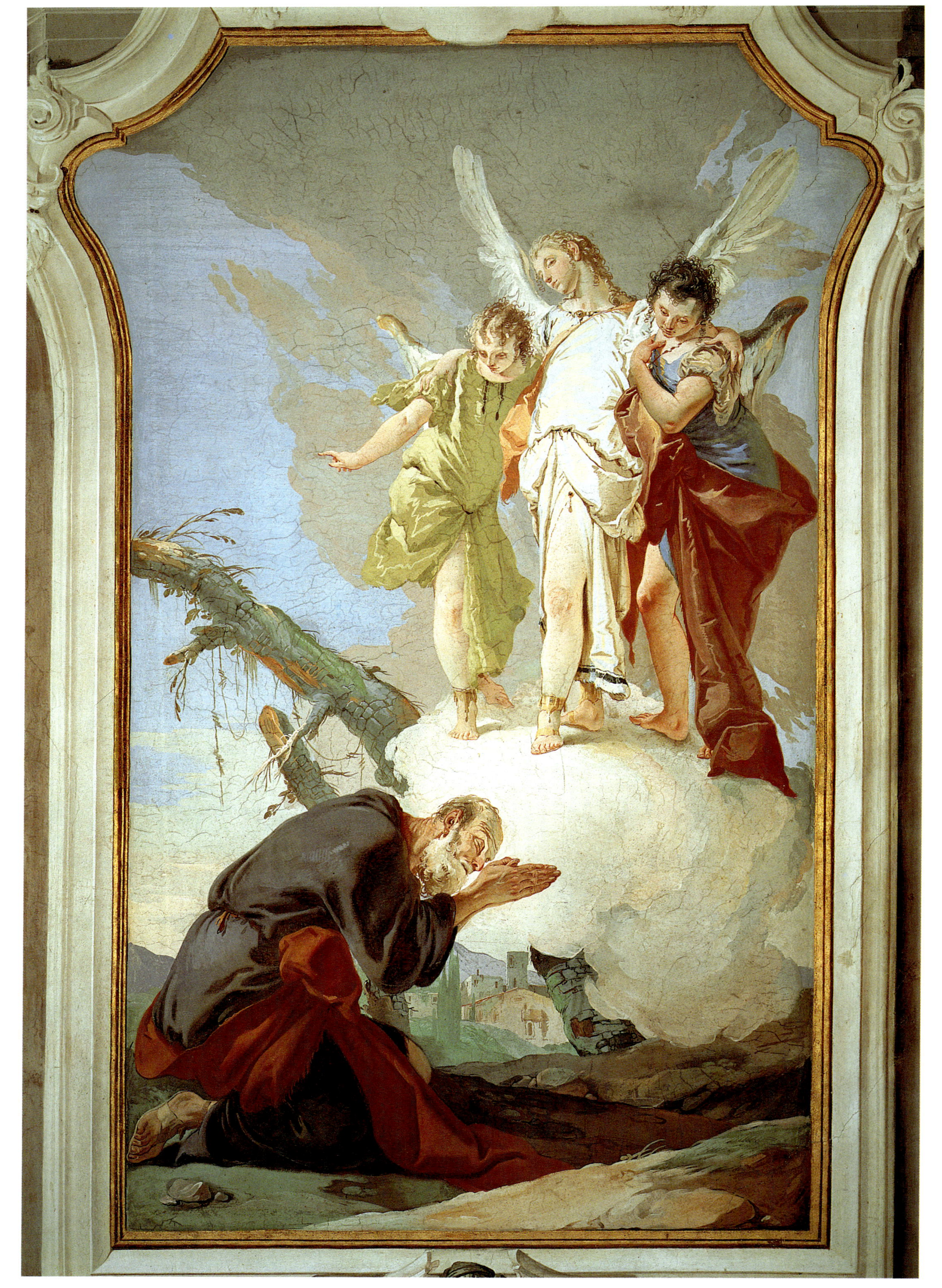

13 (opposite) *The Three Angels appearing to Abraham,*
1726–1729
Fresco, ca. 4000 x 2000 cm
Palazzo Patriarcale (now the Archiepiscopal Palace), Udine

Abraham kneels in prayer, awed by the appearance of the three angels, who float on a very solid-looking white cloud. The scene illustrates both the promise to make Abraham "a father of many nations" and the favor shown by God towards him, as described in the book of Genesis. Although the divine origin of the angels is made clear by their being placed in the upper portion of the picture, Tiepolo has portrayed them with very human features.

14 (below) *Rachel hiding the Idols from her Father Laban,*
1726–1729
Fresco, ca. 4000 x 5000 cm
Palazzo Patriarcale (now the Archiepiscopal Palace), Udine

The aged Laban stoops over his daughter and demands that she hand over the graven images that she has stolen. She refuses to do so. The action takes place in the encampment where Jacob's caravan rests on its way to Canaan. The staged character of the composition, imaginatively enriched with scenes from everyday life, obscures its Old Testament subject matter, reducing the latter to the status of a vague vision.

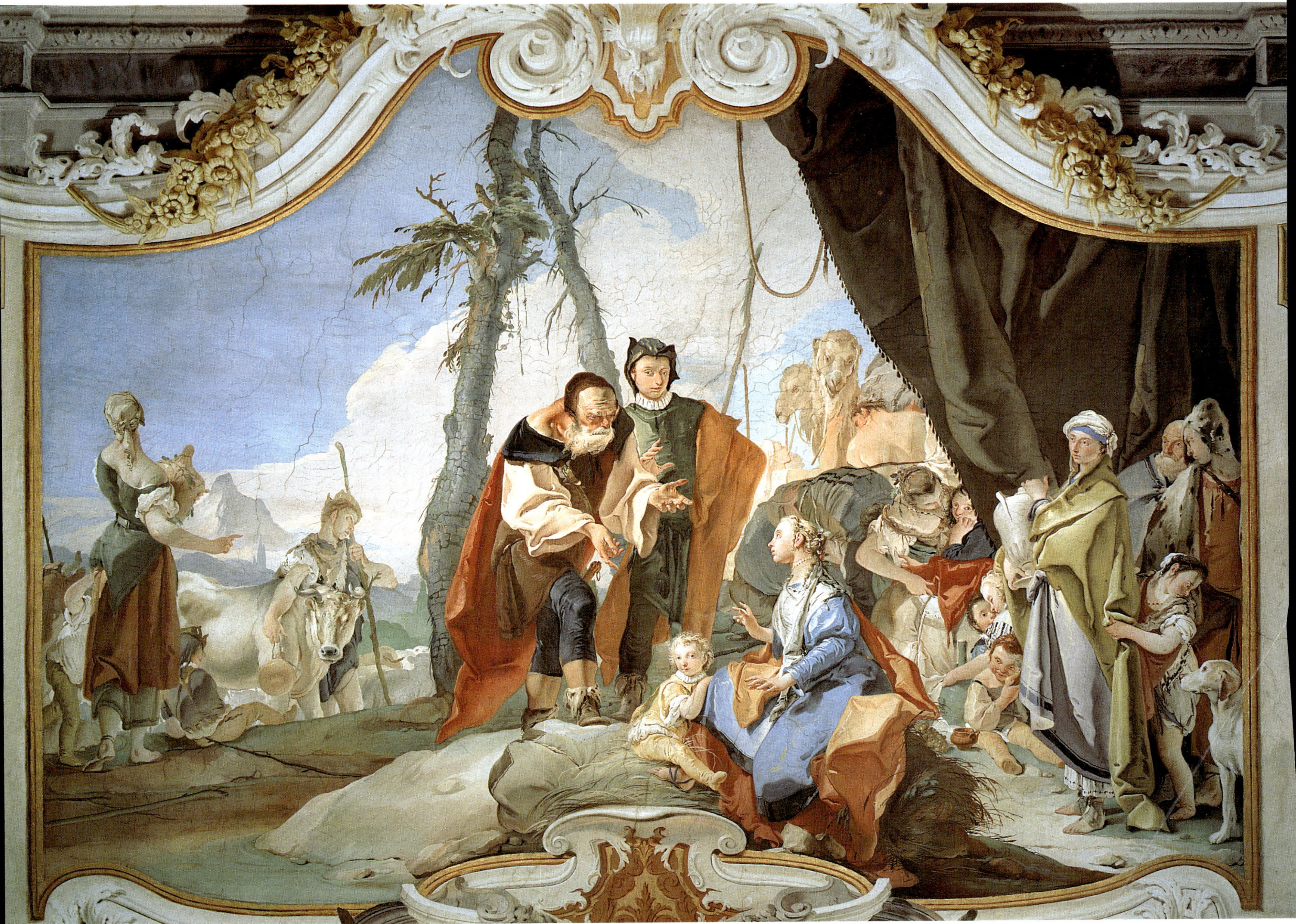

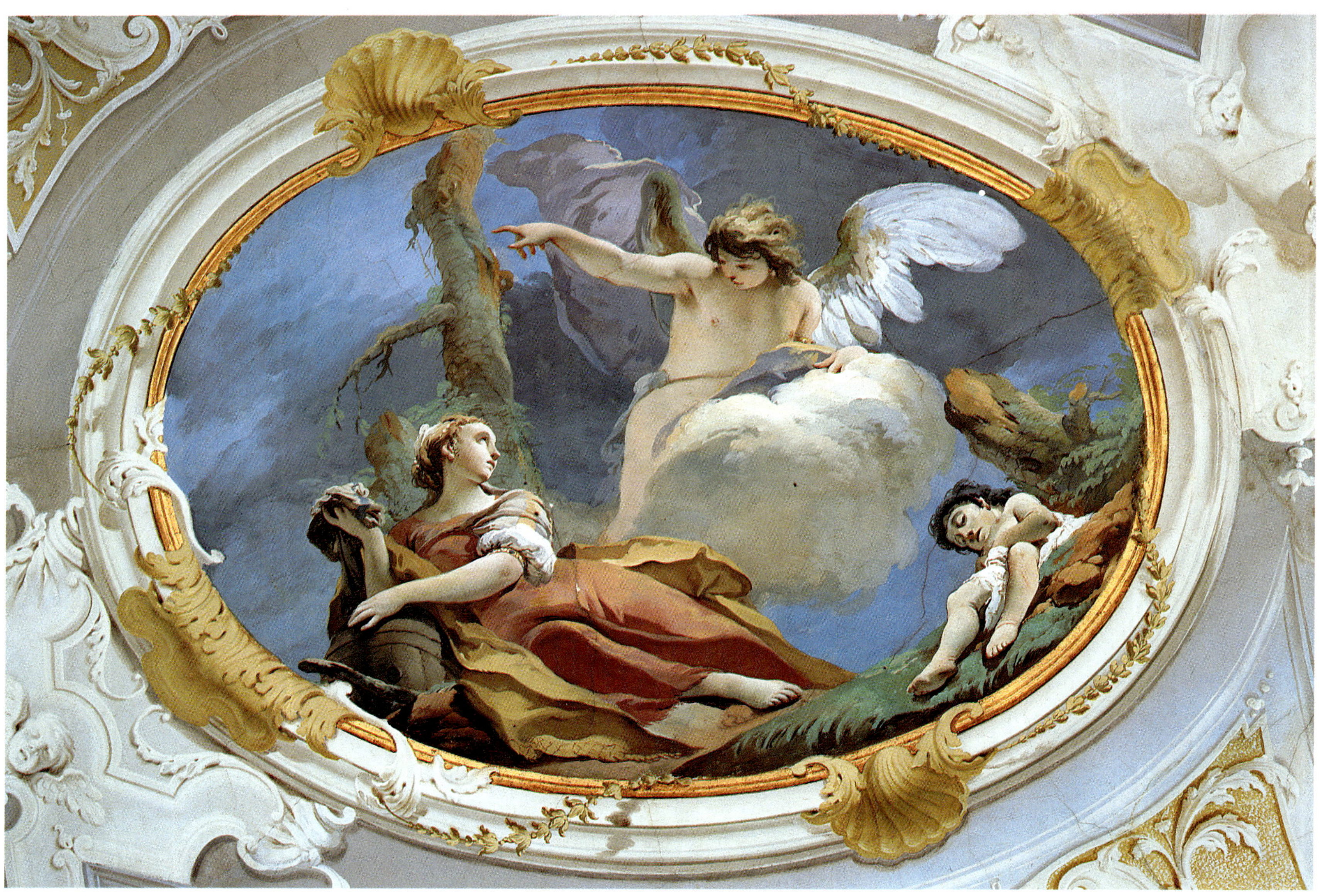

15 *Hagar in the Wilderness*, 1726–1729
Fresco
Palazzo Patriarcale (now the Archiepiscopal Palace), Udine

Hagar, Abraham's handmaiden, with whom he had conceived the illegitimate son Ishmael, had been driven from the house by Sarah. The theme of this representation is the appearance of the angel, who saves the completely exhausted Hagar, leaning against an empty barrel in the desert, and her son from dying of thirst, and who prophecies that Ishmael shall be made the "father of many nations". With an energetic gesture he points out the way, which, in reference to the central ceiling painting *The Sacrifice of Isaac*, leads away from the divine light. This symbolizes the biblical belief that the Arab nations derive from Ishmael's line of descendants, who, unlike the children of Isaac, will not inherit the divine Jerusalem.

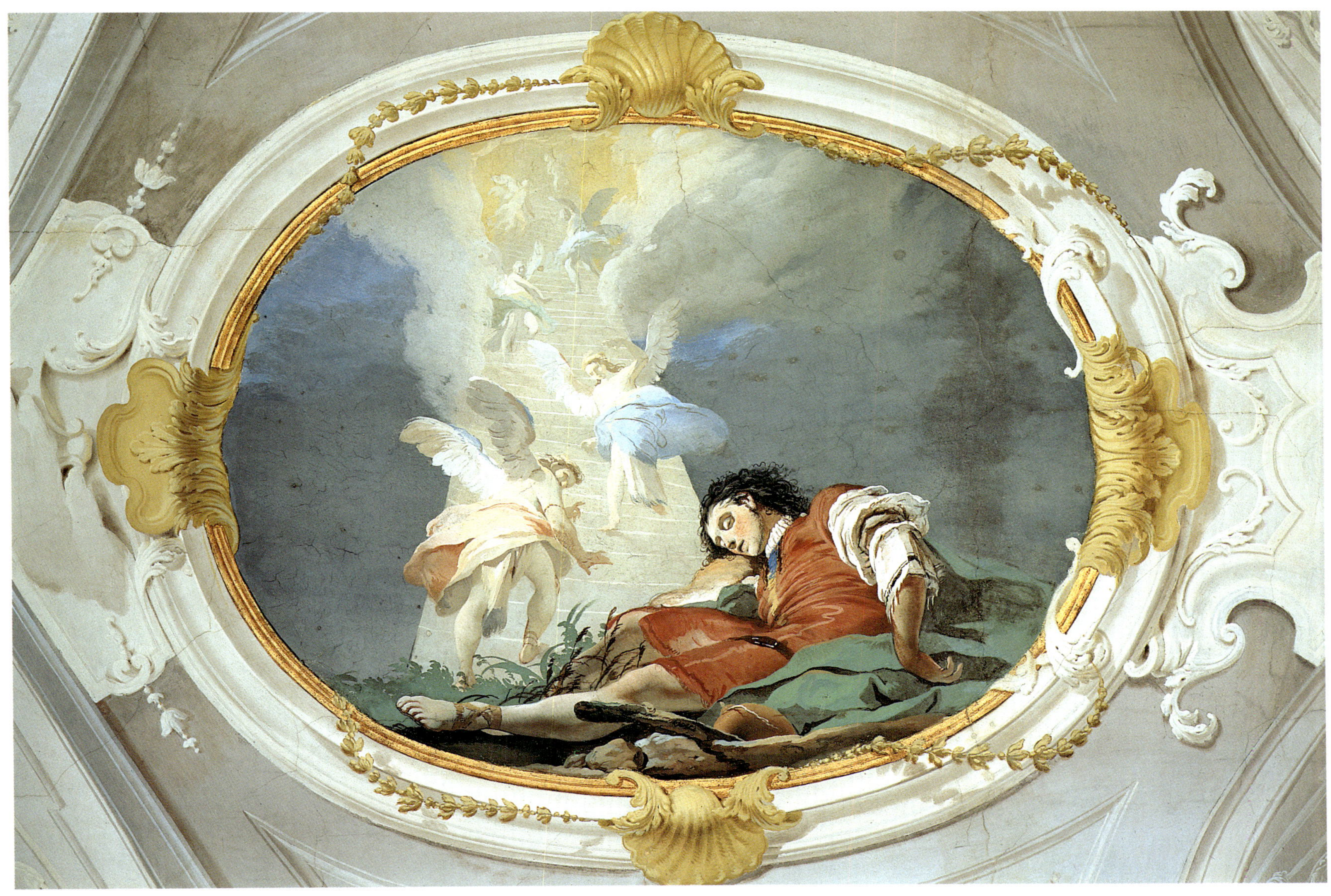

16 *Jacob's Dream*, 1726–1729
Fresco
Palazzo Patriarcale (now the Archiepiscopal Palace), Udine

The fresco illustrates Jacob's dream of the ladder to heaven. The artist has moved the ladder, seen ascending into the divine light, from the center of the picture slightly towards the left. The sleeping Jacob sees in his dream the vision of a divine prophecy, in which he is promised numerous descendants and safe arrival in the land of Canaan under the protection of God himself. In form and content, Jacob represents the antithesis of Hagar and Ishmael, since his line leads directly to Christ. This is reflected compositionally in the way the figure of Jacob is aligned towards the central fresco, *The Sacrifice of Isaac*.

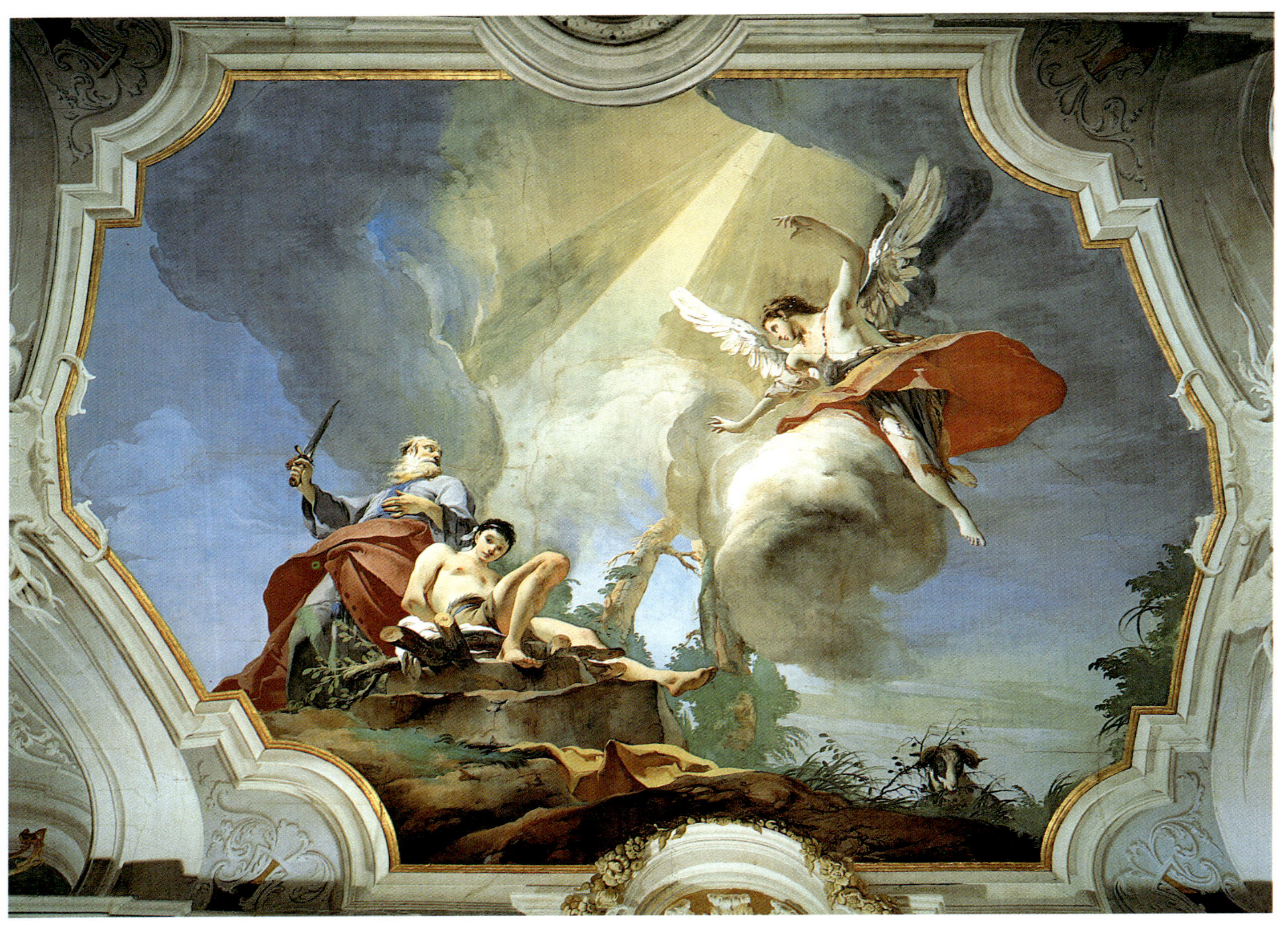

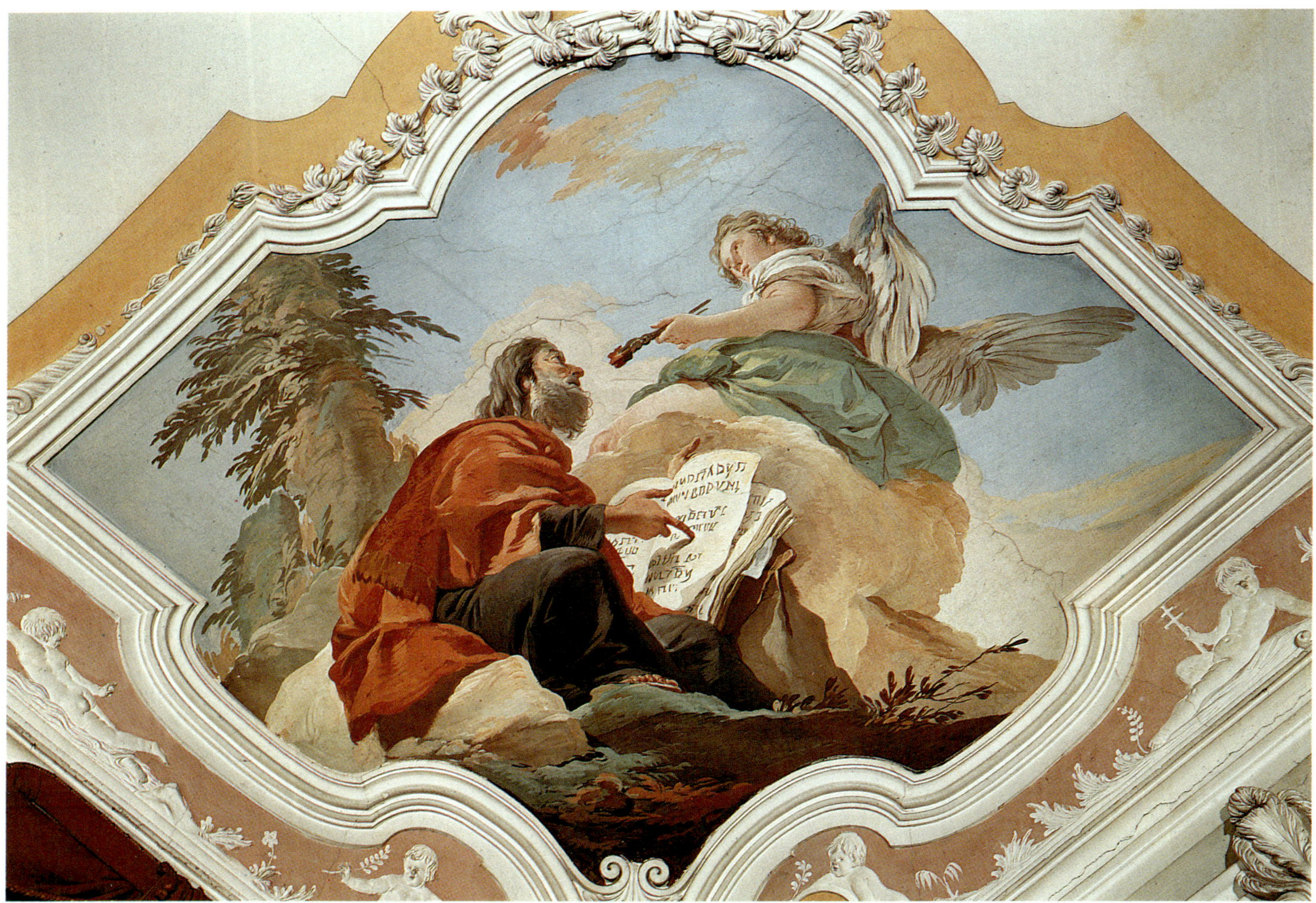

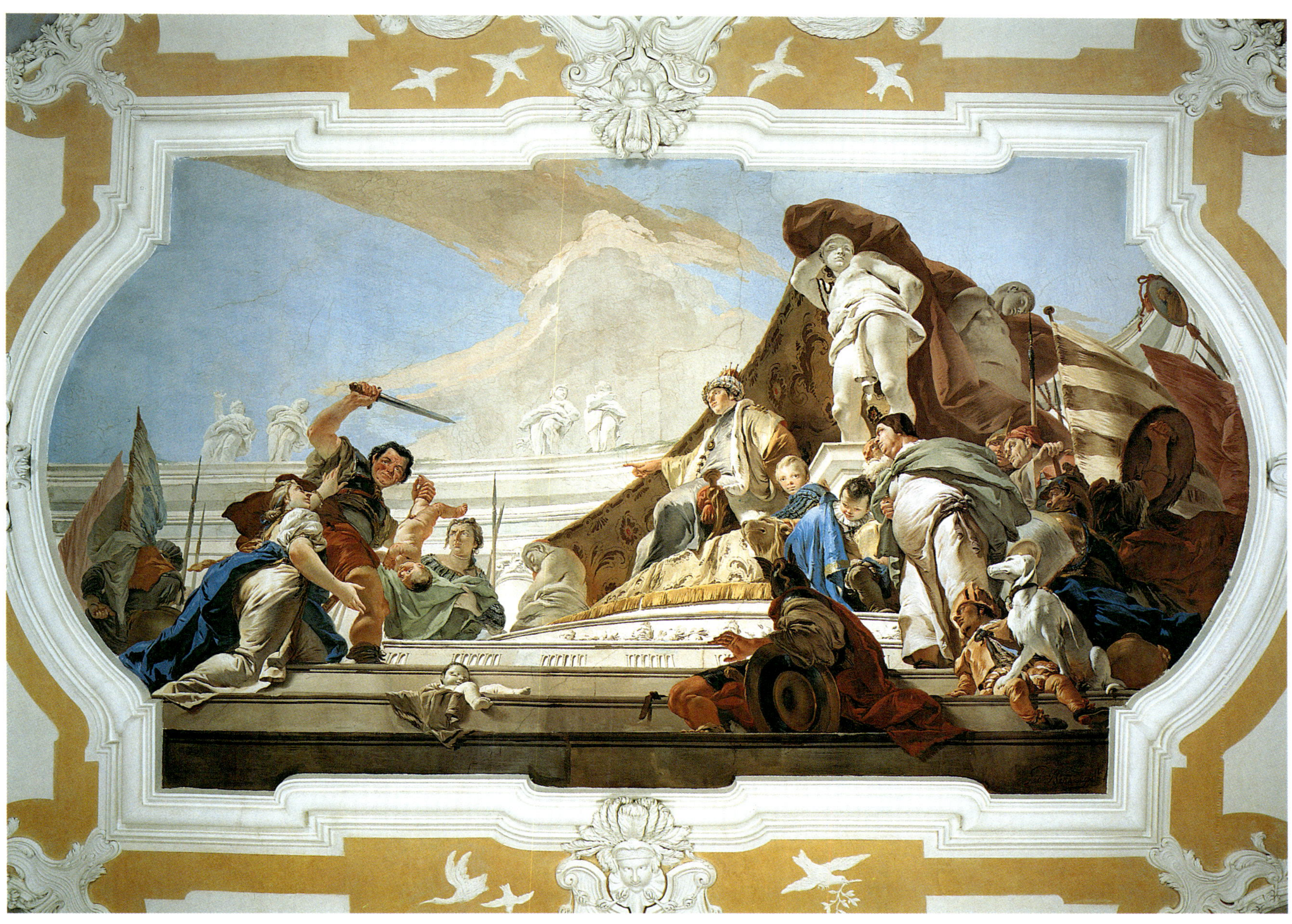

17 (opposite, above) *The Sacrifice of Isaac*, 1726–1729
Fresco, ca. 4000 x 5000 cm
Palazzo Patriarcale (now the Archiepiscopal Palace), Udine

The central ceiling painting depicts the sacrifice of Isaac. Accompanied by a shaft of divine light, an angel floats down on a cloud to stay Abraham's hand just as he is about to slay his son as commanded by God. The ram, which is to be sacrificed in Isaac's place can already be seen on the lower edge of the picture.

18 (opposite, below) *The Prophet Isaiah*, 1726–1729
Fresco, ca. 200 x 250 cm
Palazzo Patriarcale (now the Archiepiscopal Palace), Udine

The painting depicts the prophet Isaiah at the moment where he is called to prophecy. The approaching angel holds a piece of burning coal to his lips with tongs and so brings about the forgiveness of his sins. Isaiah hears the voice of the Lord and agrees to his mission.

19 (above) *The Judgement of Solomon*, 1726–1729
Fresco, 360 x 655 cm
Palazzo Patriarcale (now the Archiepiscopal Palace), Udine

The large oblong painting in the center of the ceiling shows a wide flight of stairs, seen from below at an oblique angle, on which King Solomon is enthroned in front of a canopy of cloth, acting in his capacity as a judge. The moment in which the true mother is revealed is re-enacted here. Contrary to what it says in the Bible, a crowd of onlookers, including a dog and a dwarf, are present as Solomon makes his judgement that the child shall be "divided equally" by the sword. The true mother prevents the awful deed in order to save her child, while the dead infant of the false mother in the foreground is a reference to the cause of events.

20 *The Triumph of Scipio*, ca. 1729
Oil on canvas, 546 x 322 cm
Hermitage, St. Petersburg

On a chariot drawn by two elephants, Scipio approaches the viewer frontally as his triumphal procession draws near. The throng of applauding people is dominated by the figure of the victorious hero of Carthage, majestically enthroned in his chariot high above the others. The brilliant colors of the robes and banners, along with the balanced composition of the figures, bathed in the light of the evening sun, make the scene so vivid, you almost think you can hear the noise of the drums and the fanfares.

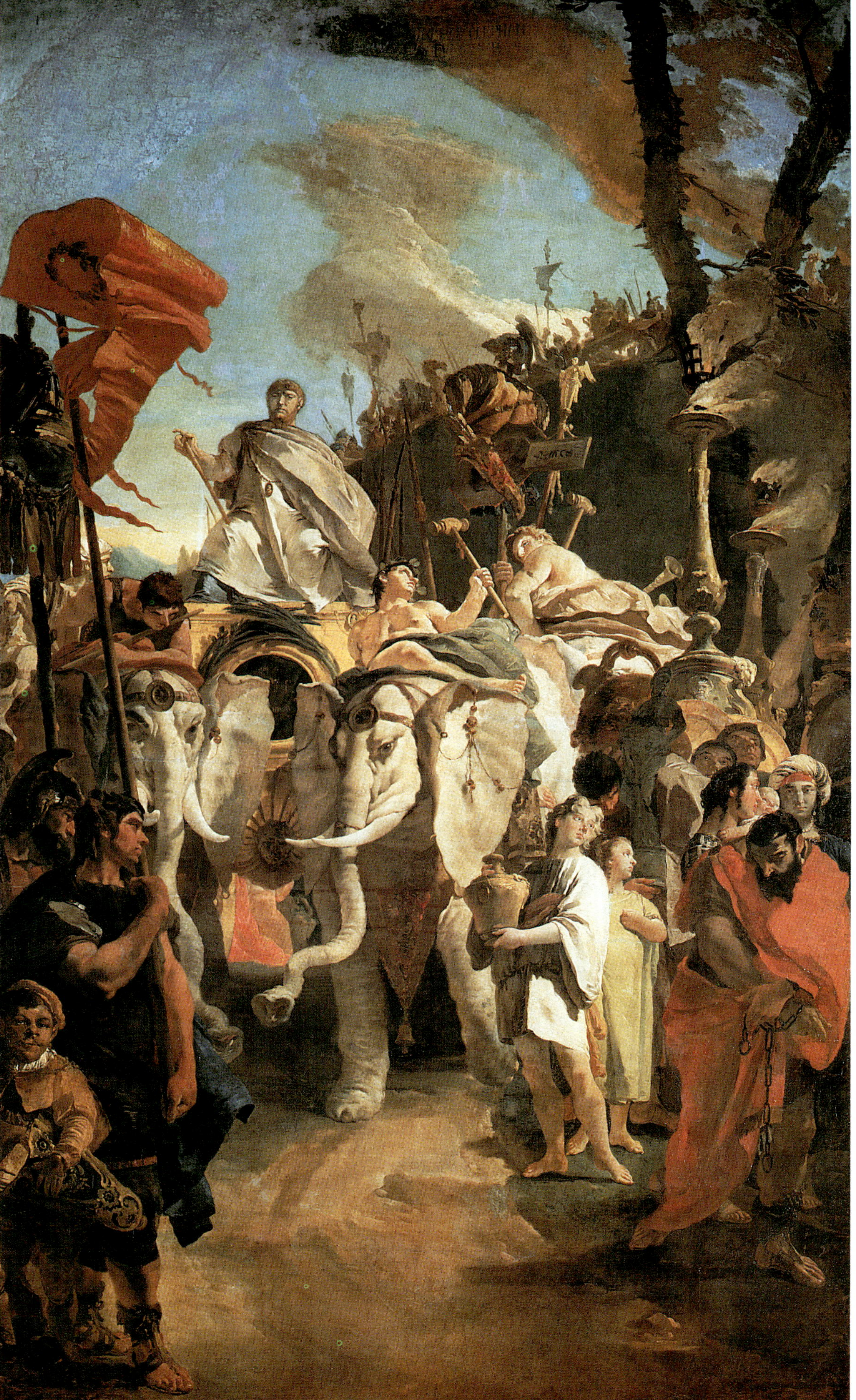

Commissions in Lombardy and the Veneto 1731–1737

In the meantime, Tiepolo had gained a reputation as an eminent artist in the Veneto region, thus bringing him commissions outside his native city. In 1730, he was called to Milan, most likely through the intercession of the Veronese scholar Scipione Maffei (1675–1755), where he worked first of all in the Palazzo Archinto. There he painted five ceiling frescoes, a representation of the *Triumph of Apollo* in the main salon, and four smaller mythological and allegorical scenes in other rooms. Unfortunately, these works were all but destroyed in a bomb attack in 1943. He then went on to fresco the walls and ceiling in the principal salon of the Palazzo Casati in Milan with scenes from the life of Scipio as an *exempla virtutis*. These decorations are just as badly damaged and convey very little of the original quality of the coloring.

On his return to Venice he created, in 1732, his first important and large-scale altarpiece, the *Education of the Virgin Mary* (ill. 21), executed for the Church of Santa Maria della Consolazione, known as della Fava. The strong *chiaroscuro* contrast in the lighting reminds us vaguely of Tiepolo's earlier works, but it is now the bright, rich color which dominates the overall impression. Tiepolo's painting corresponds to the Venetian preference for altarpieces in which a celestial vision in the upper portion of the picture appears to burst the frame, a device derived from the Roman and Emilian artists of the Baroque period such as Reni (1575–1642), Lanfranco (1582–1647) and Guercino (1591–1666), and which Tiepolo's contemporaries Ricci, Pittoni (1687–1767) and Piazzetta were also happy to borrow.

Another large-scale altarpiece depicting the nativity was created in the same year for the church of San Giuliano (Zulian) in Venice and is currently housed in St Mark's basilica. Two small oil paintings which can presumably be dated to the same period – *The Angels appearing to Abraham* (ill. 23) and *The Angel succoring Hagar* (ill. 22) in the Scuola Grande di San Rocco – bear stylistic comparison with the two altarpieces, above all in the rendering of the faces and the dynamics of the gazes. The thirteen meter long canvas, *The Miracle of the Bronze Serpent*, also stems from this period. Originally installed under the choir in the church of Santi Cosma e Damiano on the island of the Giudecca, it now hangs in the Gallerie dell'Accademia. Although the work is badly damaged, we can still guess at the exceptional quality of the unusual composition – its coloring dominated by shades of silver and blue.

From 1732 to 1733 Tiepolo worked in the cathedral at Bergamo, painting the Colleoni Chapel. Parts of the original decoration were painted over in the 19th century, but three frescoes remain in good condition: *John the Baptist preaching* (ill. 25), *The Baptism of Christ* and *The Beheading of John the Baptist* (ill. 26). *The Martyrdom of St. Bartholomew* and *Mark the Evangelist* appear on the lunettes, with the Virtues Justice, Faith, Love, and Wisdom represented on the pendentives. The sketches on canvas of scenes from the life of St. Jerome (ill. 24), now in the Art Institute of Chicago, the Staatsgalerie in Stuttgart and the Poldi Pezzoli Museum in Milan, were probably executed during work on the Colleoni Chapel frescoes. We do not know for whom they were originally intended, but may suppose that they were part of an extensive decorative project dedicated to St. Jerome.

The dramatic way in which the subject matter of the pictures in Bergamo is formulated, especially in the portrayal of *The Beheading of John the Baptist*, stands in stark contrast to the frescoes Tiepolo painted a short time afterwards in the Villa Loschi outside Vicenza. There he was asked by Count Niccolò Loschi to fresco the stairwell and the main salon of the villa with an ambitious and scholarly programme of allegorical themes taken from Cesare Ripa's "Iconologia". First published in Rome in 1593, the work is a collection of abstract terms and ideas, each of which is meant to be expressed by means of a human figure, equipped with the various attributes appropriate to their characteristics. The themes of the pictures in the Villa Loschi, such as *Marital Concord* (ill. 27), *Virtue crowning Honor* (ill. 28) or *Generosity bestowing her Gifts* (ill. 29), themselves convey a noble and somewhat formal atmosphere, also expressed by the classicist style of painting, previously untypical of Tiepolo. The figures, dressed in antique costume and often positioned frontally, seem inert and distant like classical statuary, their gestures mostly restricted to the holding of their

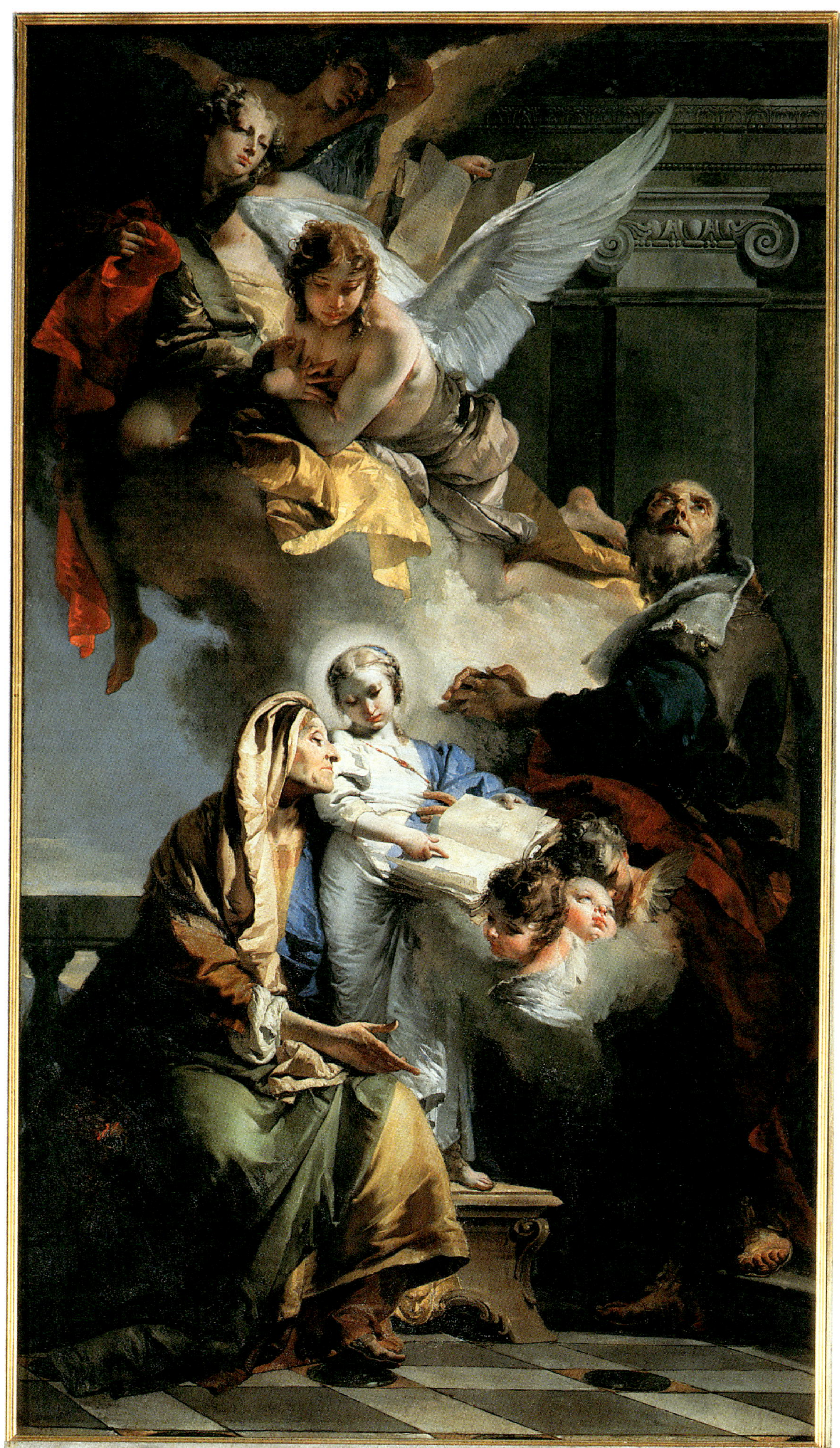

21 *The Education of the Virgin Mary*, 1732
Oil on canvas, 362 x 200 cm
Santa Maria della Consolazione (Fava), Venice

In the center of the representation, in front of a magnificent architectural backdrop, stands Mary as a young girl, reading from an open book, and instructed by her mother, who sits next to her. Her father, standing to her right, is deep in prayer and has his eyes raised towards Heaven. What is striking about the composition, is the diagonal line which runs from the three angels' heads beneath the book to the three large angels above Mary, and which symbolizes the way to the Kingdom of Heaven.

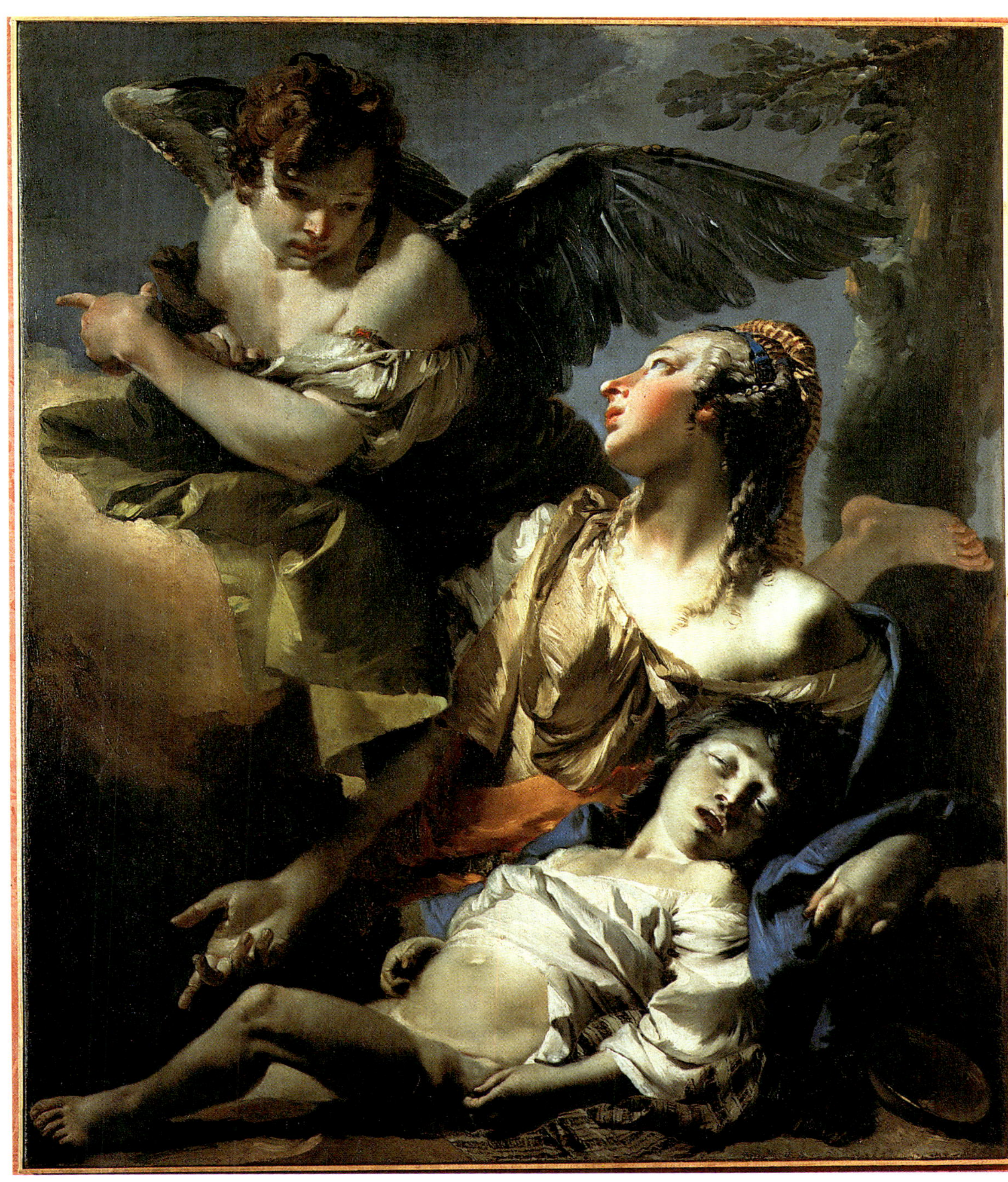

22 *The Angel succoring Hagar*, 1732
Oil on canvas, 140 x 120 cm
Scuola Grande di San Rocco, Venice

The picture shows Hagar with her son, who has almost expired with thirst, in the foreground. The angel above them points the way to water and sustenance. In comparison to the fresco of the same name in Udine, it is the affliction of the mother and son which is given prominence. This is emphasized by the close-up presentation of the scene and the graphic depiction of the dying boy.

attributes. Any attempt to introduce tension to the composition is avoided. Architecture and landscape are also reduced to a minimum, and the light appears subdued in an atmosphere which gives the impression of being almost windless. The logical consistency with which Tiepolo pursued the translation of the respective subject matter into pictorial images offers proof of his flexibility, of his ability to meet the demands of his patrons, whose cultural milieu and taste in art had to be expressed in appropriate pictorial terms.

The altarpiece *The Virgin in Glory with Saints* (ill. 30) for the high altar in the parish Church of the Ognissanti in Rovetta, a small town in the hills above Bergamo, was also painted in 1734. The picture shows the Virgin, accompanied by angels, ascending towards Heaven on a cloud above a group of male saints, clustered around a column in the foreground. The figure of Mary is absent from the oil sketch for this picture in the Poldi Pezzoli Museum in Milan, indicating that it was originally intended as an All Saints painting, in keeping with the patronage of the church. The composition of the Saints is unusual for an 18th century artist, especially the

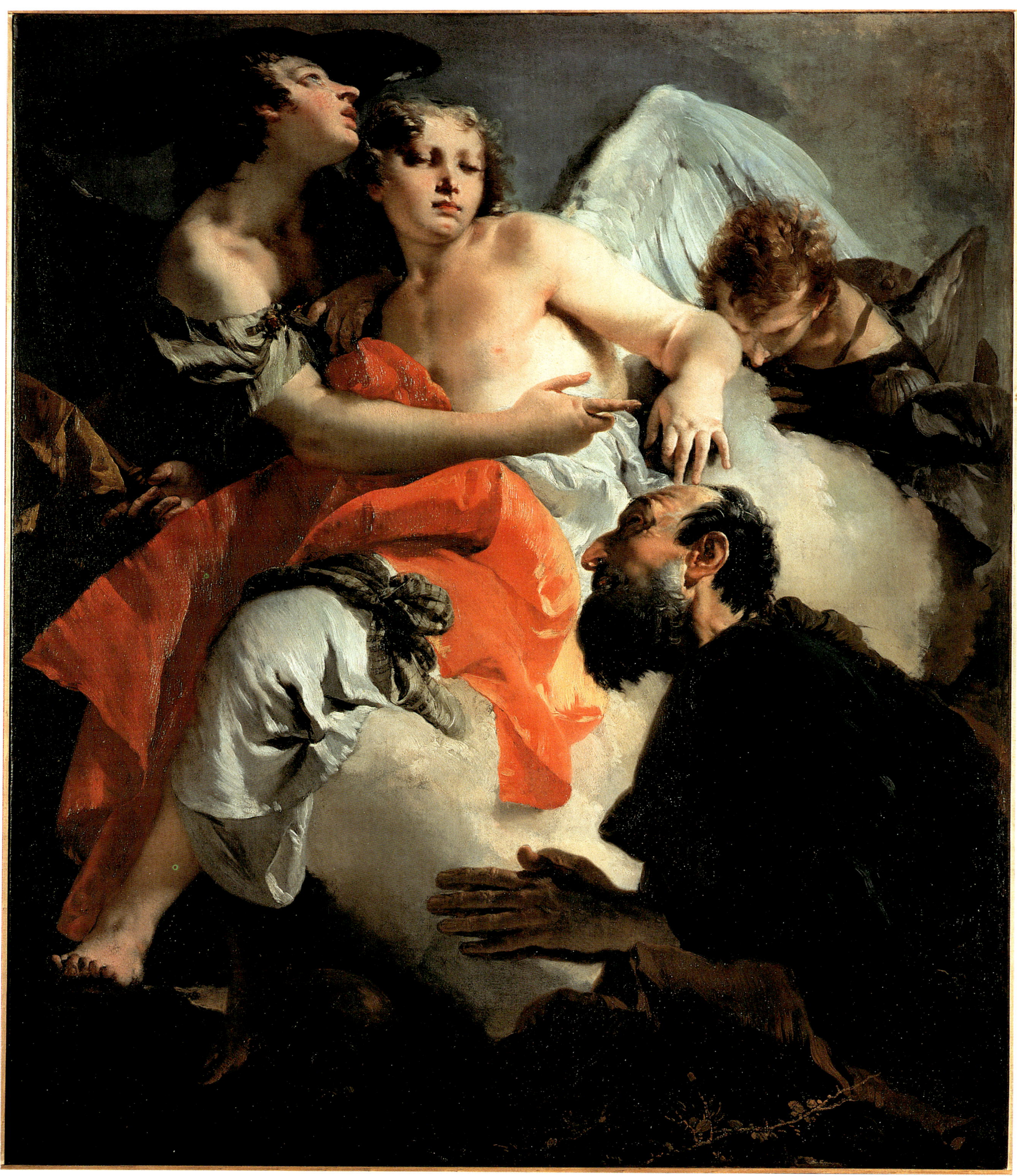

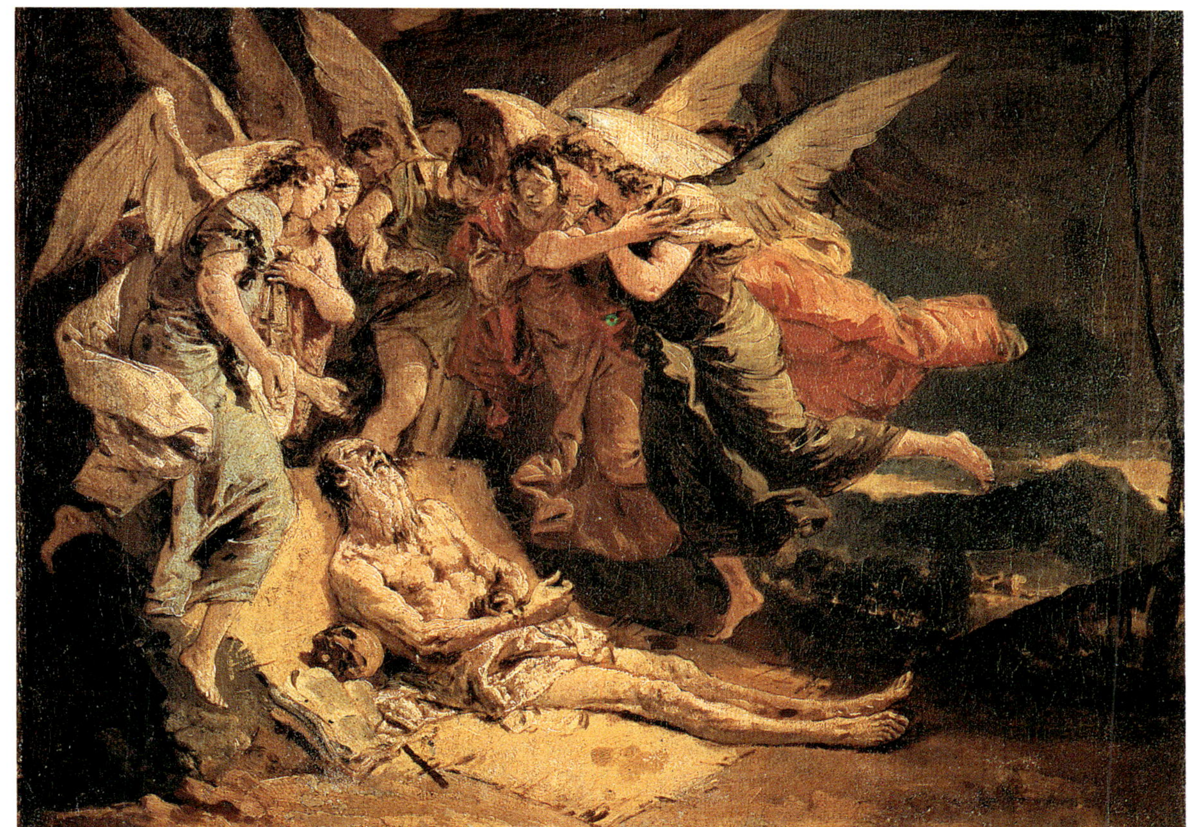

24 (right) *The Death of St. Jerome*, 1732/33
Oil on canvas, 33 x 44.2 cm
Museo Poldi Pezzoli, Milan

In the foreground, and in front of a panoramic landscape, the corpse of Jerome is laid out on a mat, together with the few possessions from his hermetical existence: the skull, the cross, the Holy Scriptures and a rosary. Seven angels, grouped in a semi-circle, hover above his head and mourn the Father of the Church. The rapid brushwork and the barely executed faces of the angels point to the fact that this is an oil sketch for an unidentified work of the same name.

23 (opposite) *The Angels appearing to Abraham*, 1732
Oil on canvas, 140 x 120 cm
Scuola Grande di San Rocco, Venice

Here, too, Tiepolo has chosen the same close-up viewpoint in re-enacting the three angels' promise of a son to Abraham. The composition of the three angels before Abraham, who appears in profile, and the directions in which he has the figures look is unusual. While the angel on the right, who leans over towards Abraham, can hardly be made out, the one in the middle reclines somewhat indifferently – half on the cloud, half in the lap of the third angel – and looks down. The latter, on the other hand, to the very left of the picture, has his eyes raised towards Heaven as an allusion to the origins of the divine prophecy.

frontal position of St. Peter in the foreground, who appears to be descending towards the faithful congregated in the church. In a demonstrative gesture, he raises his key as a reminder of the way to salvation. The picture's composition seems inspired by Venetian All Saints paintings of the late 15th and early 16th centuries. These are more hierarcically structured and derive from the Byzantine tradition, which continued to have an effect on Venetian art for a very long time. The scene is bathed in a bright light and the robes of the figures gleam in brilliant hues of red, blue and yellow which have almost completely replaced the dark shadows of the early pictures.

Tiepolo produced another altarpiece at the same time: the depiction of *The Immaculate Conception* for the church of Santa Maria dell'Aracoeli in Vicenza, at the behest of the Franciscan Order of the Poor Clares. The picture originally hung opposite Piazzetta's painting *St. Francis in Ecstasy*. It shows the Virgin standing on top of a globe, wrapped in a shimmering silver and blue cloak, and apparently transformed from an earthly being into a hallucinatory vision. Distant and untouchable, she embodies the belief that she is untouched by original sin – symbolized by the snake beneath her feet –, a dogma widely preached by the Carmelites and Franciscans at that time.

The ceiling painting *The Triumph of Zephyr and Flora* (ill. 31), which Tiepolo probably created contemporaneously with the altarpiece at Rovetta in 1734 for one of the rooms in the Palazzo Pesaro in Venice, represents a quite different kind of commission. The work now hangs in the Ca' Rezzonico Museum. The association of the wind-god Zephyr with the goddess of flowers Flora was a widely represented subject in 18th century art and, with its allusions to spring and fertility, might have been intended to represent an allegory of marriage. The airy composition is an example of Tiepolo's extraordinary talent for illusionistic ceiling painting, for which he also offered evidence in other large decorative projects where he populated ceilings, vaults and high walls – apparently effortlessly – with figures flying through the sky, and in so doing extended the room into boundless depths.

By 1736, Tiepolo seems to have achieved the status of an artist of international renown. The Swedish Count Tessin had travelled to Venice to engage Tiepolo to fresco the ceiling of the Royal Palace at Stockholm. However, the project was never realized, since the fee did not meet Tiepolo's expectations. Instead, Tessin acquired both the oil sketch for the *Beheading of John the Baptist* painting in Bergamo and the small portrait of *Danae* (ill. 33), now in the collection of the University of Stockholm. Here, Tiepolo had created a cabinet work suffused with wit and eroticism by maintaining an ironic distance to the mythological version of the story of Jupiter and Danae. Once again he had demonstrated his ability to meet the needs of the respective clients. Both the architectural backdrop of the scene, arranged in tiers like theatrical wings on a stage, as well as the humorous tone of the episode, in which the myth is treated as farce, suggest that Tiepolo was inspired by contemporary theatre culture.

At the behest of the Cornaro family another cabinet piece was executed in 1737, *The Finding of the Infant*

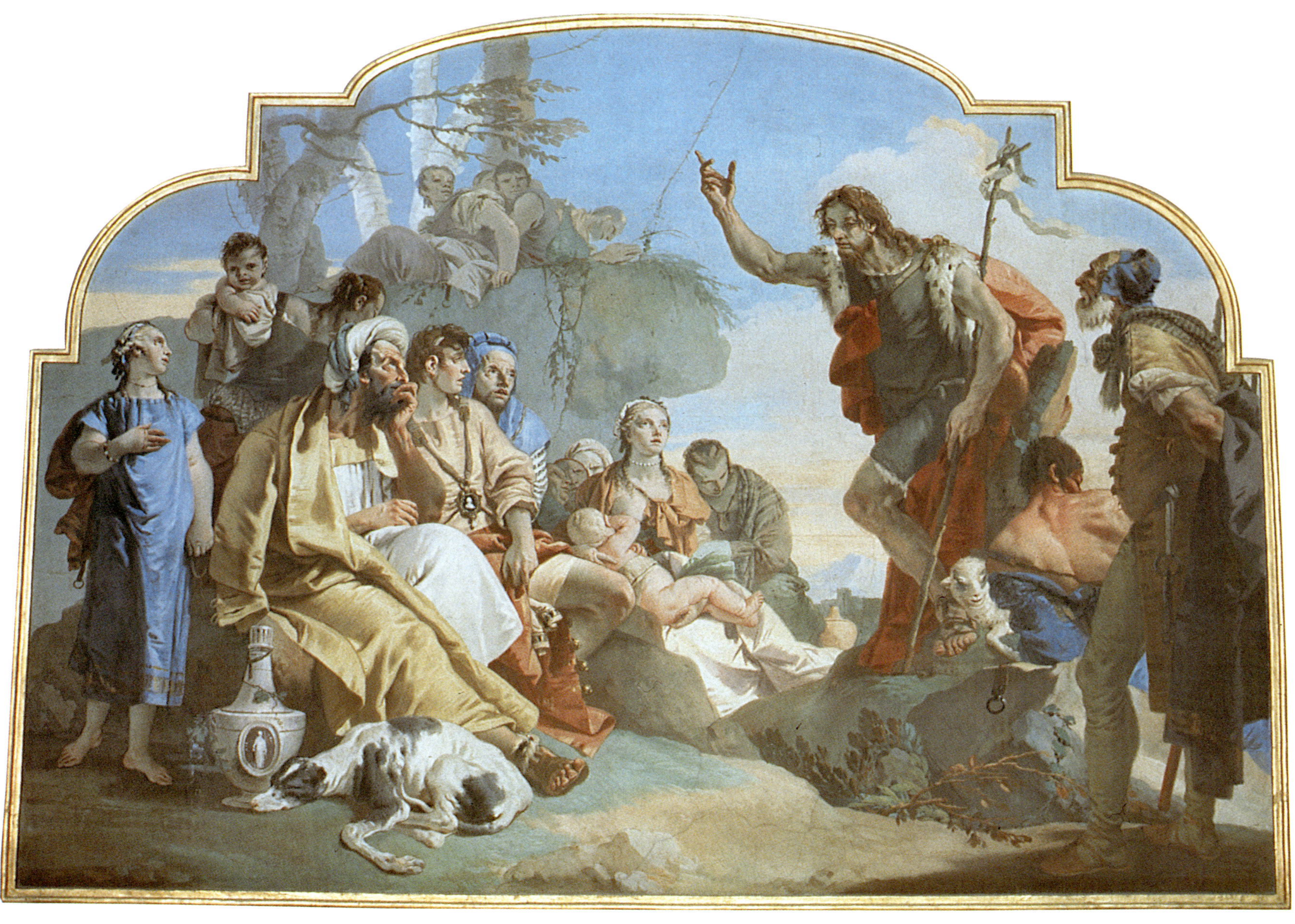

25 *John the Baptist preaching*, 1732/33
Fresco, 350 x 300 cm
Cappella Colleoni, Bergamo

The impressive figure of John the Baptist, delivering his sermon with raised forefinger from the top of a rock in the landscape, dominates the right-hand side of the picture. His cross staff and the lamb at his feet refer to the fate of Christ. The left-hand side of the picture is almost completely taken up by men, women and children, who listen spellbound to the sermon. The young woman placed in the very center of the picture breast-feeding her child, who thus conforms to the standardized portrayal of the Madonna and Child, can be understood as an allusion to the birth of Christ, which is the subject of John's sermon.

Moses, which deals with an Old Testament subject, and which was destined for the Palazzo Corner della Regina in Venice. The pictorial motif is based on a work by Veronese of the same title and has an unusually asymmetrical composition in which the main action is concentrated on the left-hand side, while, to the right, the view opens out into the landscape, bordered only by the isolated figure of a halberdier. Once again, we are dealing with an original, ironic interpretation of the biblical text, in the manner of a *capriccio*, which met the high expectations of learned patrons of the arts in the 18th century. However, at a later date, the picture was obviously deemed to contain an imbalance and the right-hand side with the halberdier was promptly removed. The latter is currently in a private collection in Turin, while the scene of *The Finding of the Infant Moses* is in the National Gallery in Edinburgh.

In that same year, Tiepolo worked for several clients outside Venice. He painted a large canvas with the *Martyrdom of St. Agatha* for the church of Sant'Antonio in Padua, and three large frescoes in the basilica of Sant'Ambrogio in Milan at the behest of Cardinal Erba Odescalchi: *The Martyrdom of St. Victor*, *The Demise of St. Satyrus* and the now destroyed *Apotheosis of St. Bernard*.

The monumental altarpiece *Pope St. Clement adoring the Trinity* (ill. 32) also dates from this period (between 1737 and 1738). It was commissioned by Prince-Bishop Clemens August of Cologne (1700–1761), the brother of the Bavarian Elector Karl Albrecht (Elector from

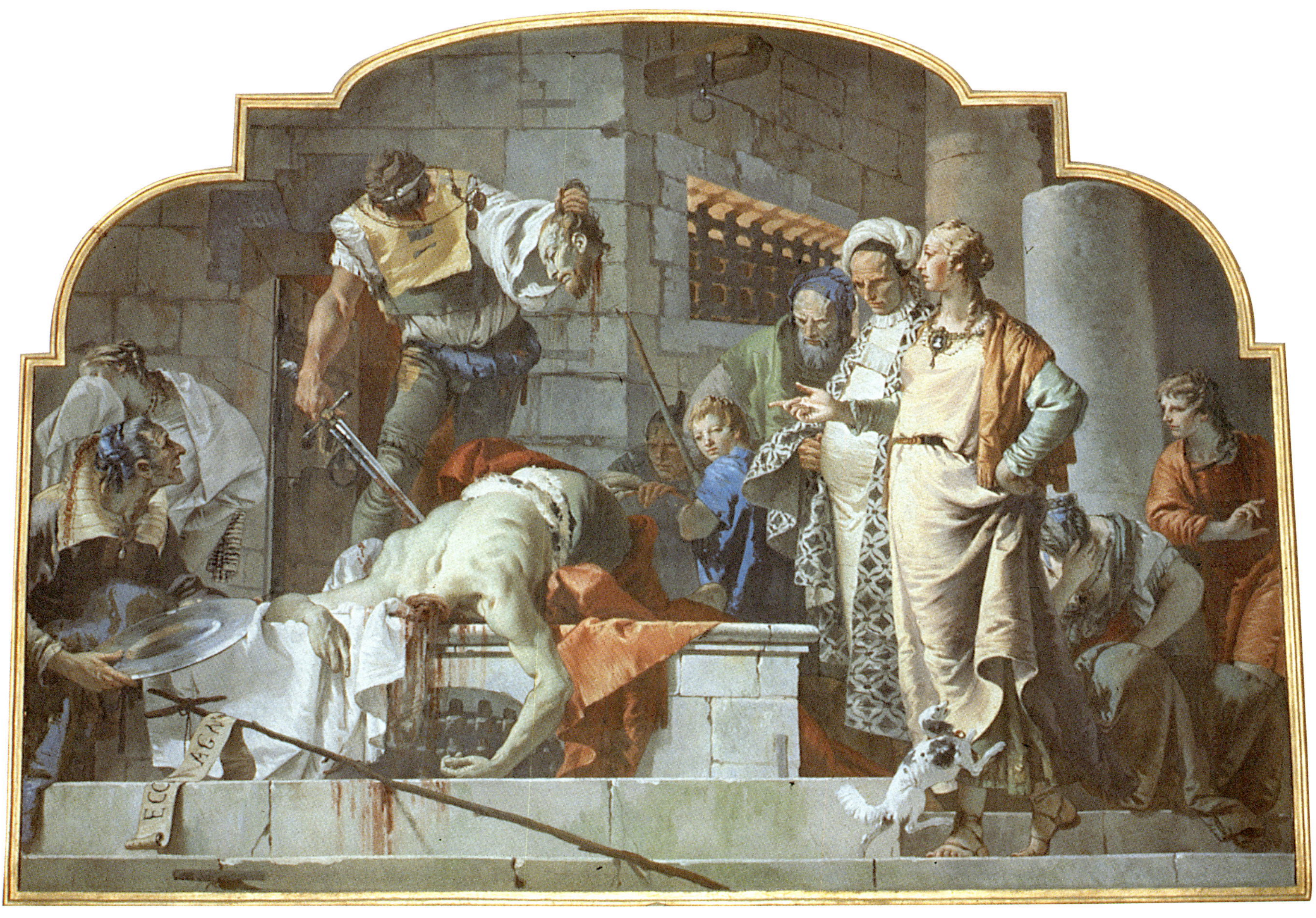

26 *The Beheading of John the Baptist*, 1732/33
Fresco, 350 x 300 cm
Cappella Colleoni, Bergamo

Tiepolo presents us with a particularly graphic depiction of the beheading of John the Baptist, which takes place in a stone dungeon. The torso of the beheaded man lies on a raised stone podium, the blood dripping down the few steps which lead to it, while the executioner, who stands over him, holds up the severed head. To the left, a female servant approaches with a salver. Behind her, a young woman turns from the scene in horror. On the right-hand side, Salome, who has ordered the murder, stands in elegant robes, surrounded by Herod and members of the royal court.

1726 to 1745), for the high altar in the convent church in the Nymphenburg palace. However, it was not installed there until 1739 following the consecration of the church. The charm of this work lies mainly in the highly illusionistic nature of the scene, which has the miracle of the manifestation appear to take place in the space occupied by the viewer. Here Tiepolo differs from his Venetian colleagues, who always emphasized how distanced was the world of the saints. A further large-scale altarpiece which Tiepolo delivered to Bavaria was *The Martyrdom of St. Sebastian*, not painted until 1739, for the church of the Augustinian Monastery in Dießen on the Ammersee.

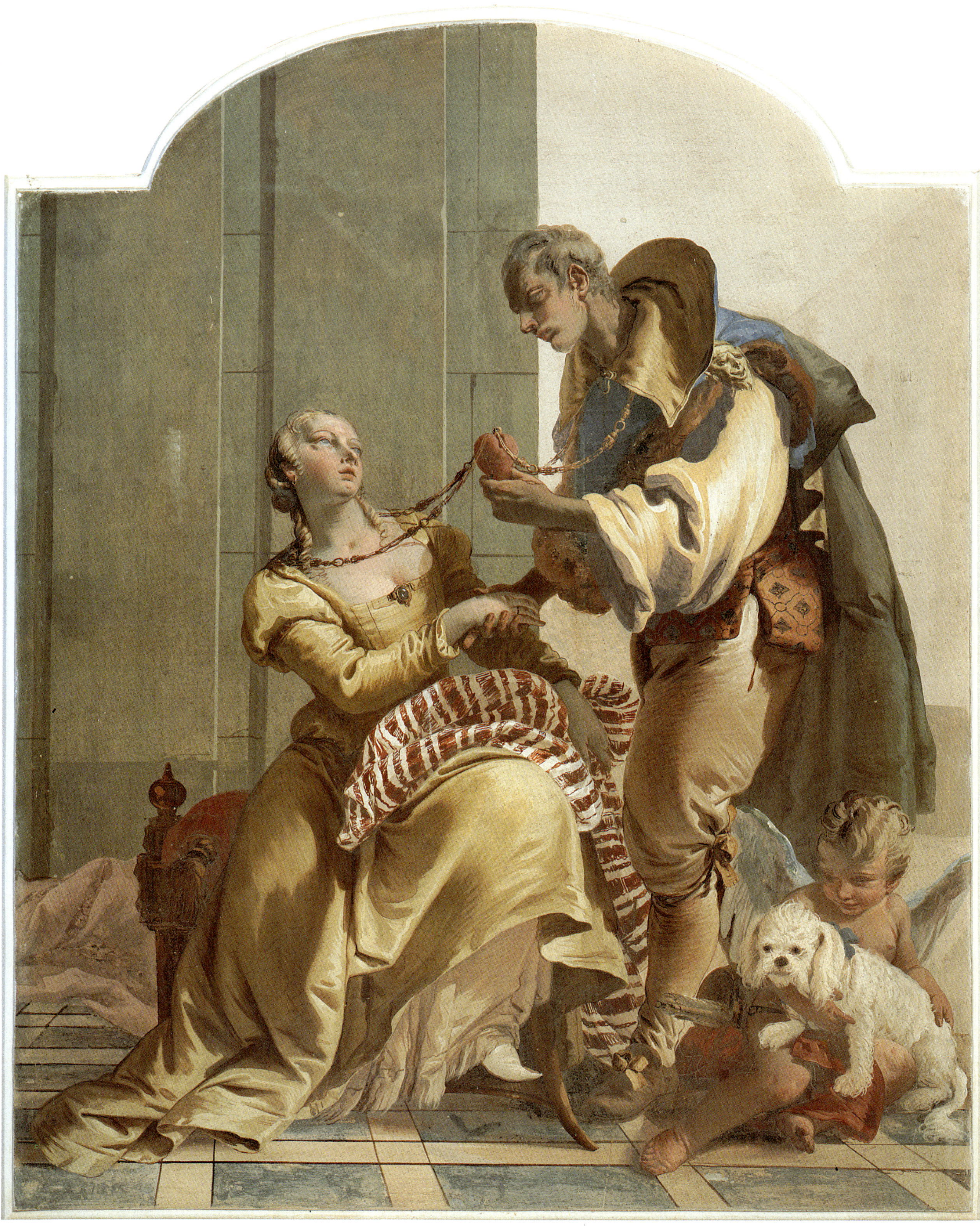

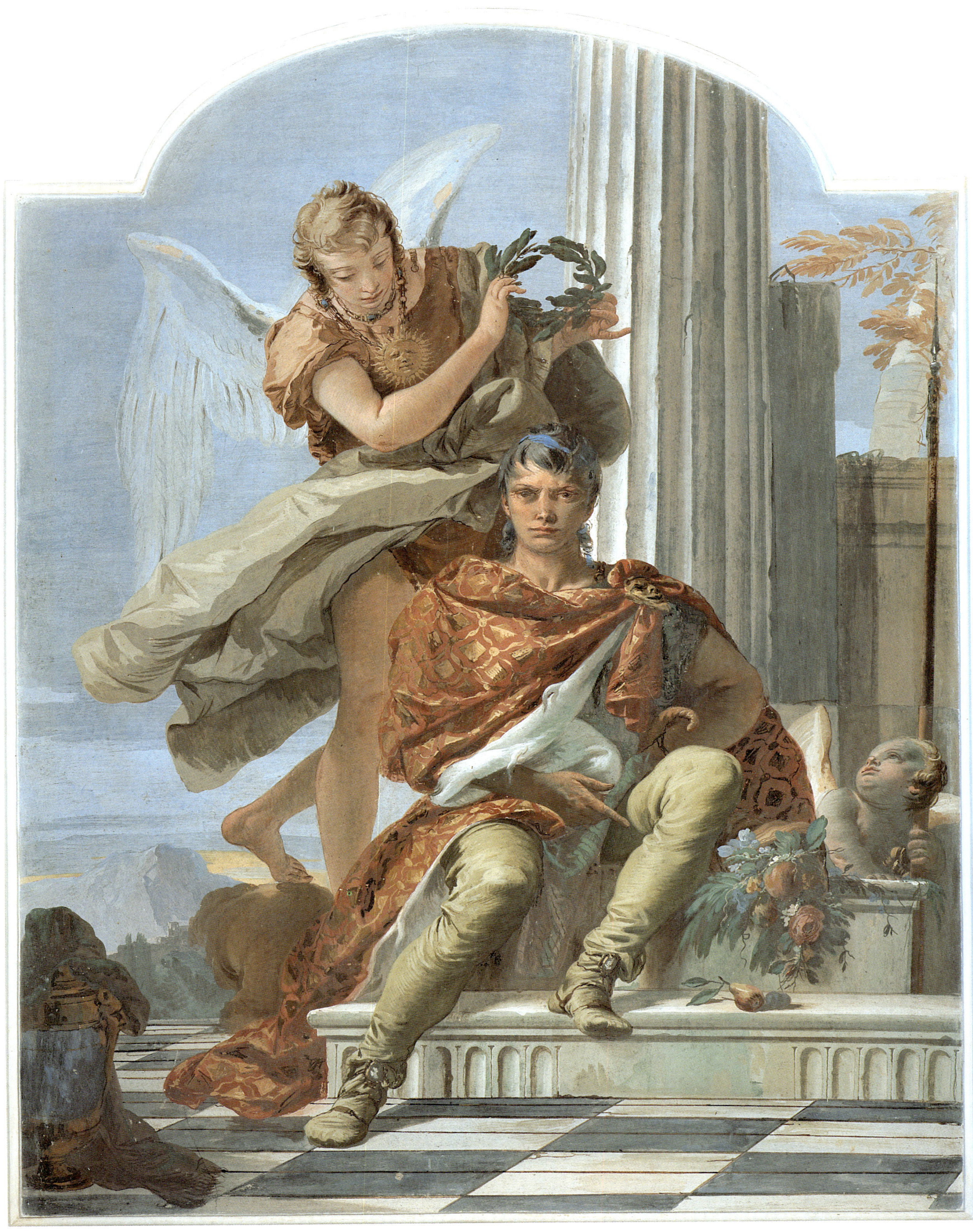

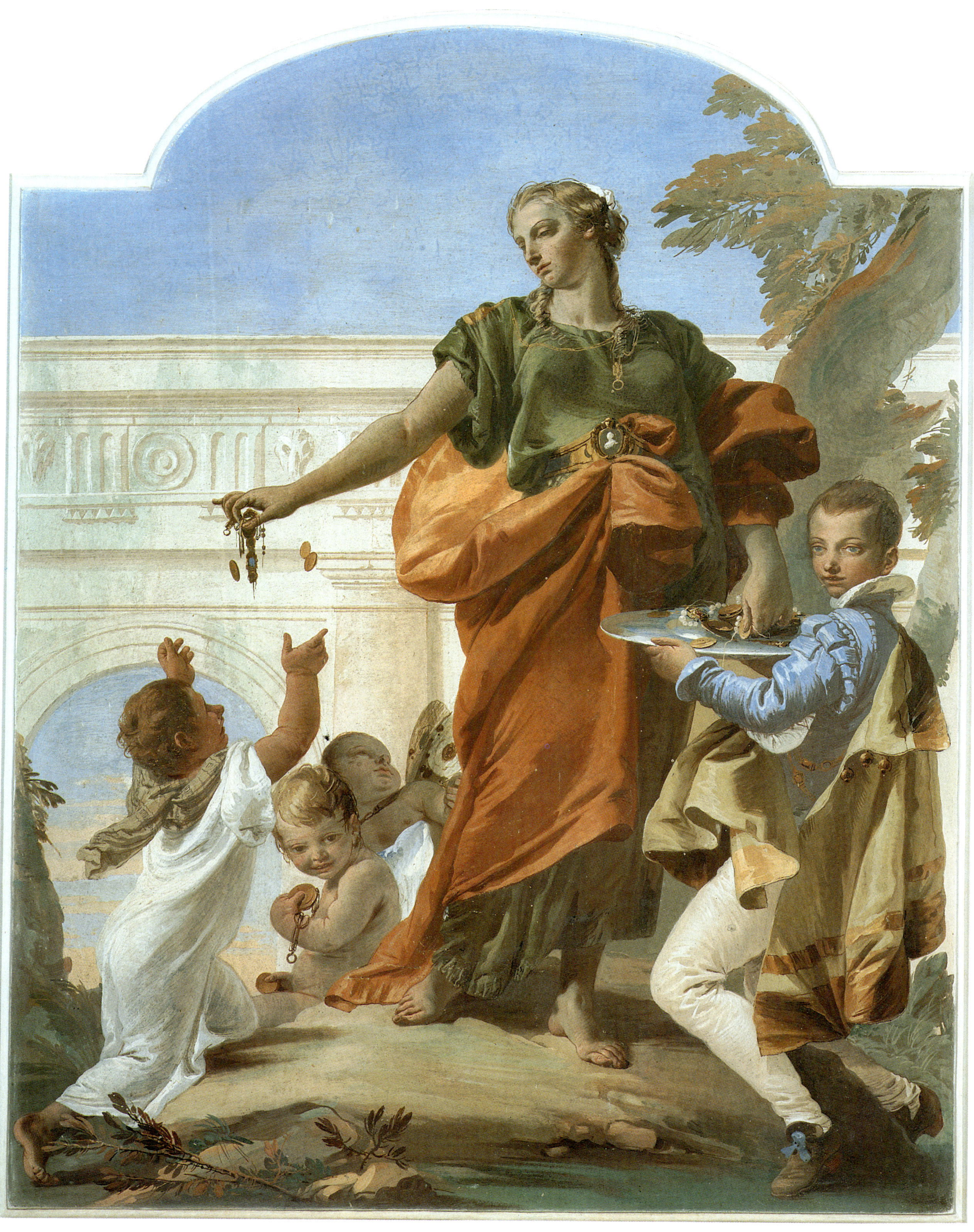

27 (previous double page, left) *Marital Concord*, 1734
Fresco, 230 x 180 cm
Villa Loschi Zileri dal Verme, Biron, Vicenza

Using a simple composition and very dull coloring, unusual for Tiepolo, the fresco shows the allegory of Marital Concord. It is symbolized by a young couple holding hands. A heart in between the two, from which one chain is placed around the woman's neck, the other around the man's, expresses the attachment between husband and wife.

28 (previous double page, right) *Virtue crowning Honor*, 1734
Fresco, 230 x 180 cm
Villa Loschi Zileri dal Verme, Biron, Vicenza

Here, too, the static placement of the figures and the austere structuring of the architectural background determine how the allegorical theme is rendered. Honor is personified by a young man seated majestically in front of the viewer and facing him directly. His toga-like robes vaguely recall the clothes of the Roman emperors. Above him, the winged personification of Virtue hovers and crowns him with a laurel wreath.

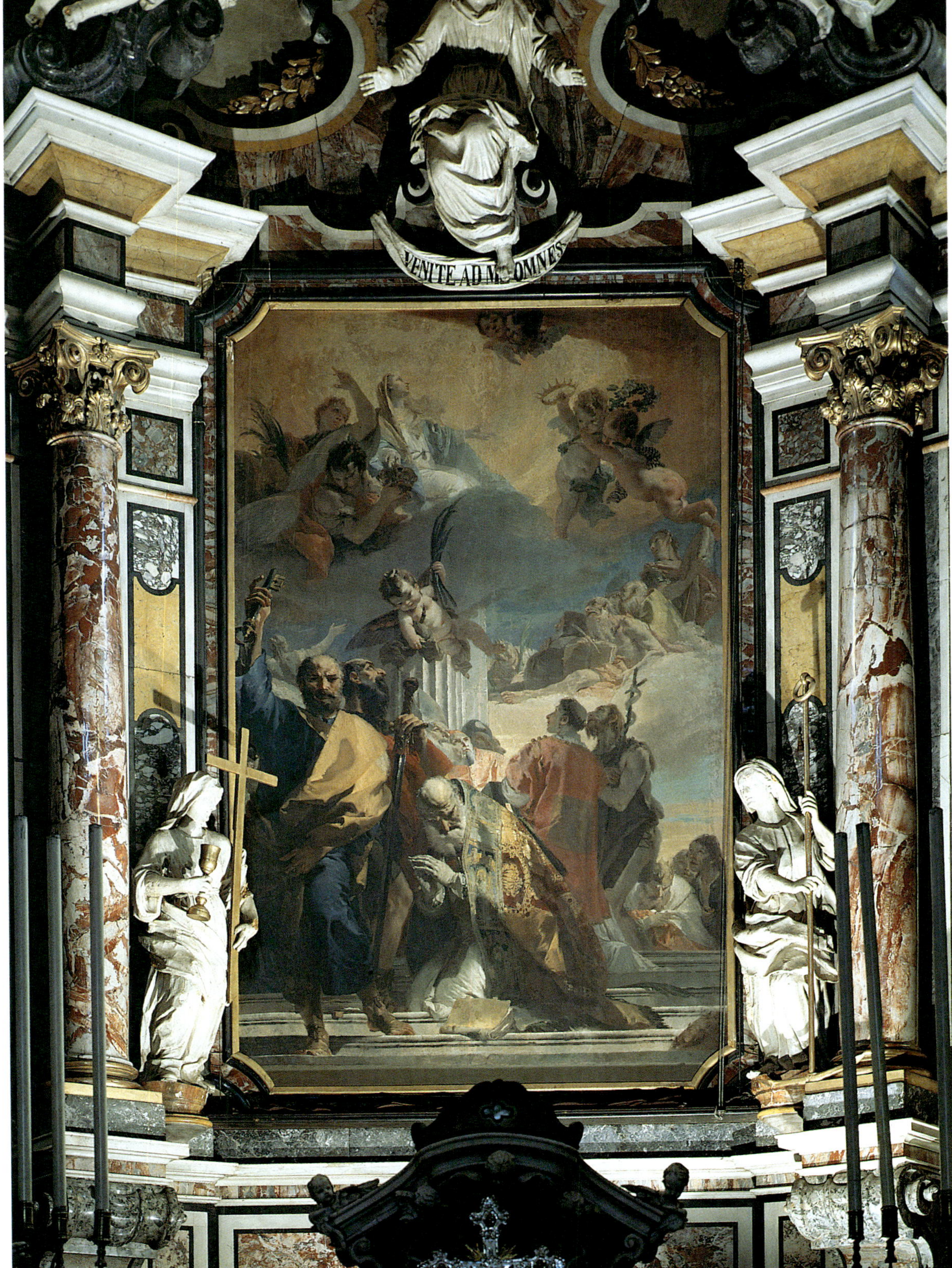

29 (opposite) *Generosity bestowing her Gifts*, 1734
Fresco, 230 x 180 cm
Villa Loschi Zileri dal Verme, Biron, Vicenza

This fresco is one of the most lively in design of the decorations in the Villa Loschi. Generosity is symbolized by a woman bestowing coins and jewelry on the children who surround her. The portrayal of the page boy in the foreground, holding the tray bearing Generosity's valuables, is typical of Tiepolo. His contemporary dress, and the way he looks out of the picture, make him definitely appear to belong to the world of the viewer.

30 (right) *The Virgin in Glory with Saints*, 1734
Oil on canvas, 378 x 234 cm
Chiesa di Ognissanti, Rovetta

The picture exalts the Virgin Mary, who rises on a cloud, accompanied by angels, through the heavens, which are bathed in a golden light. She rises directly above a white column, where a *putto* hovers with palm leaves, and around which are grouped a large number of male saints. Peter appears on the far left in the foreground, demonstratively holding up his key to show the faithful that the way to salvation lies in following the example of the saints gathered around him. Paul is behind him, and John the Baptist can be made out on the right-hand side. The crowned figure to his right is most likely King David. The bishop who kneels in a prominent position in the foreground has not been identified.

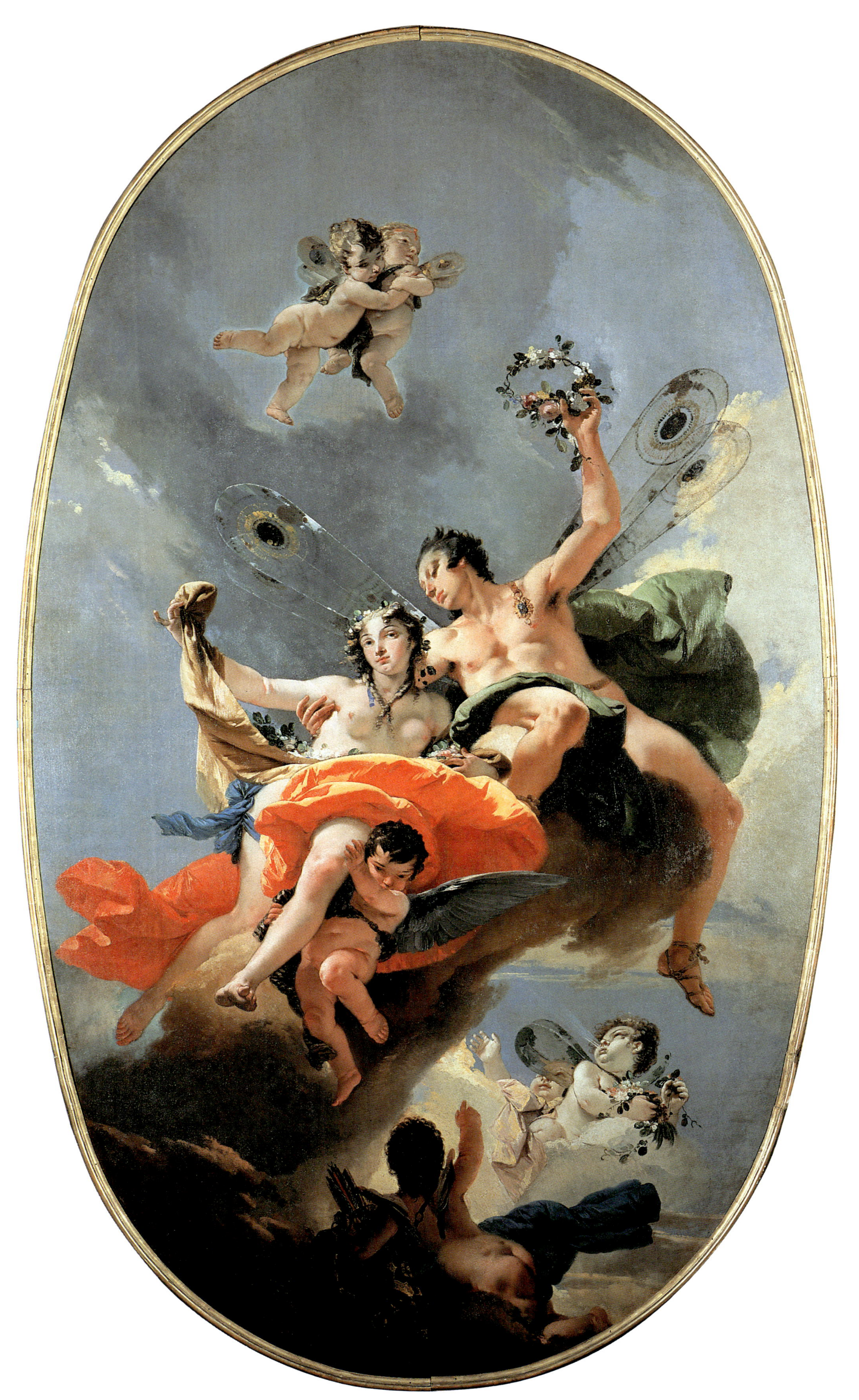

32 (right) *Pope St. Clement adoring the Trinity*, 1737/38
Oil on canvas, 488 x 256 cm
Bayerische Verwaltung der Staatlichen Schlösser, Gärten und Seen, on loan to the Alte Pinakothek, Munich

The painting shows Pope Clement I at prayer, in an ecclesiastical architectural setting which cannot be identified more closely, before a vision of the Holy Trinity. The lively facial expressions suggest a conversation between Clement and God the Father, which is further dramatized by the strong *chiaroscuro* contrasts. In an allusion to the particular connection between the donor and his famous patron saint, Tiepolo lends the portrait of the Pope a private character: the tiara and crosier, symbols of his power, have been laid aside and placed in the keeping of a *putto*.

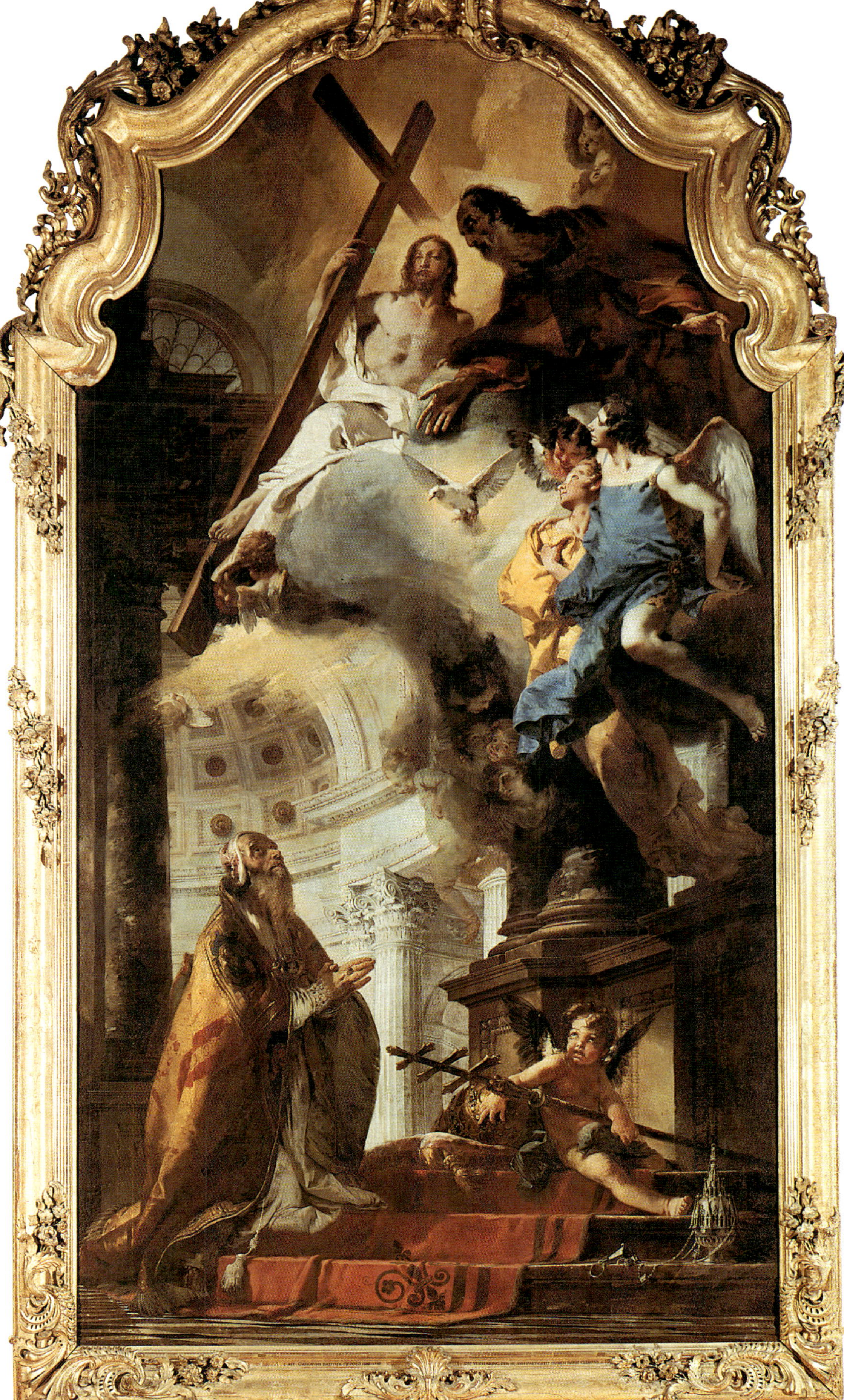

31 (opposite) *The Triumph of Zephyr and Flora*, 1734/35
Oil on canvas, 395 x 225 cm
Museo del Settecento Veneziano di Ca' Rezzonico, Venice

As an allegory of Spring, this picture brings together the god of the spring winds, Zephyr, and the goddess of all that blooms, Flora. Accompanied by several *putti*, they hover on a cloud in the sky, while on the lower edge of the picture, the god of love, Amor, seems to be showing them the way. The brilliant coloring of the robes, the successful modelling of the bodies and the dynamic depiction of the multicolored cloud formations, full of contrasts, make the picture one of Tiepolo's masterpieces.

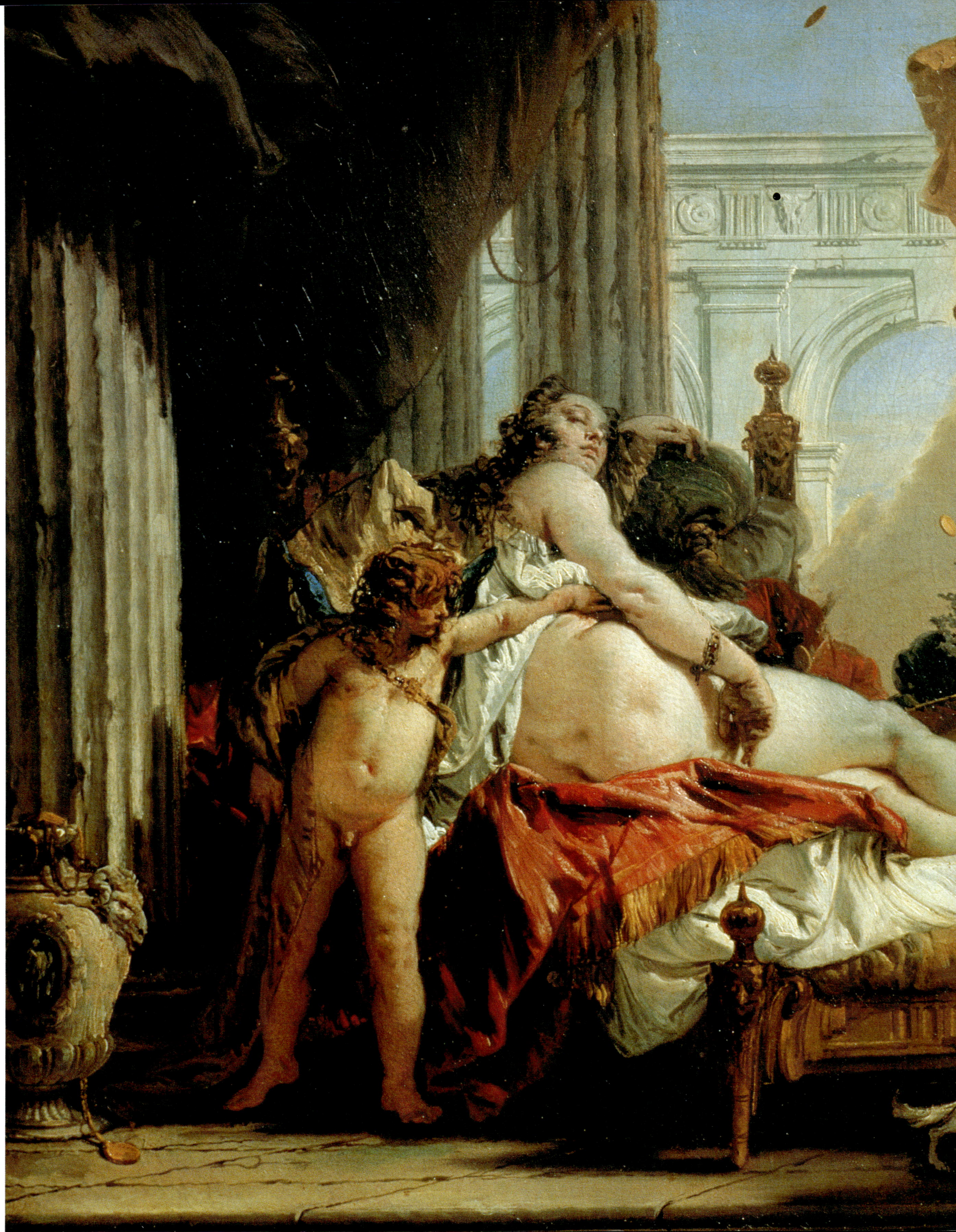

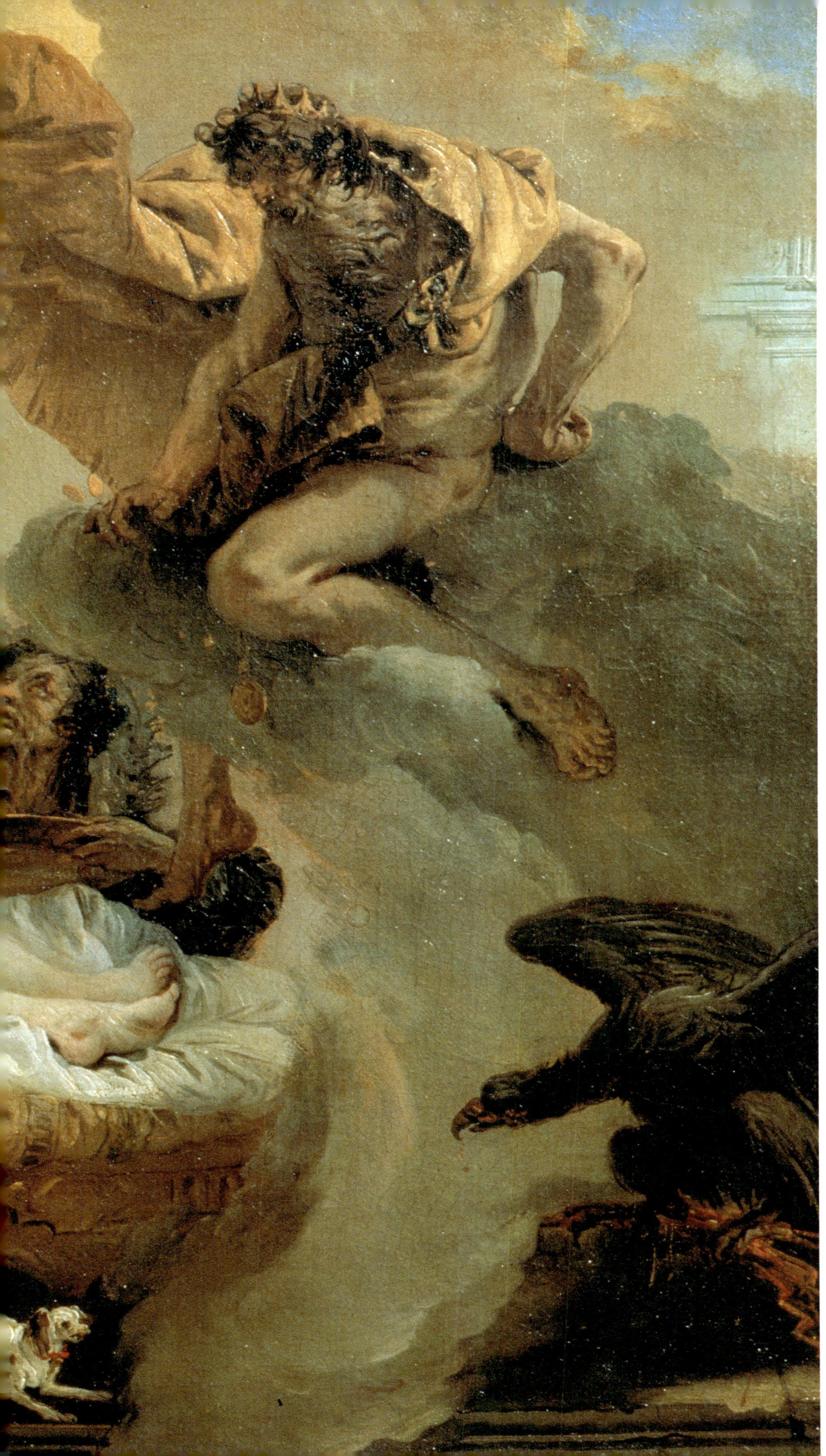

33 *Danae*, 1736
Oil on canvas, 41 x 53 cm
Universitet Konsthistoriska Institutionen, Stockholm

Based on the story of Danae as narrated by Ovid in his "Metamorphoses", Tiepolo here presents an ironic version of the subject matter and shows the less than graceful Danae lying on her magnificent bed, completely unimpressed by the meager shower of gold of a Zeus who already appears somewhat aged. Another humorous addition is the fight about to take place between the lap dog in the foreground and the eagle – the attribute of the king of the gods, which should normally inspire awe. The scene does not take place indoors, as is usual, but in front of an architectural backdrop arranged like theatrical wings on a stage, and where the balanced handling of light bolsters the action.

The Great Decorations 1737–1750

34 (opposite) *The Institution of the Rosary*, 1737–1739
Fresco, ca. 1200 x 450 cm
Santa Maria del Rosario (Gesuati), Venice

The fresco is the largest version of this subject in European art, and it combines two different iconographic traditions: in the upper part of the picture, the Rosenkranzbild, in which Mary gives the Rosary to mankind, and, in the lower part, a depiction of the beneficence of the Rosary on earth, represented by St. Dominic. As well as the Madonna of the Rosary, the fresco also extols St. Dominic, the founder of the Dominican order, to whom the dog is a reference (lat. *domini canes*, God's hounds). All manner of people are portrayed – represented among others by the Doge, a Turk, a nun, and a mother and child, a symbol of Christian charity – so that the viewer, whether rich or poor, could identify with them.

Shortly before he created the altarpieces for Bavaria, Tiepolo had signed an important contract with the Dominican order in Venice, agreeing the decoration of the church of the Gesuati (or Jesuits), Santa Maria del Rosario, built in 1720 – the artist's first great ceiling frescoes for a church interior in Venice. Beginning in 1738, Tiepolo created a total of 40 frescoes of varying dimensions within the very short period of twelve months. Three large frescoes cover the center of the vault of the Jesuit church: *The Glory of St. Dominic, The Institution of the Rosary* (ill. 34) *and The Virgin appearing to St. Dominic.* Medallions portraying the fifteen mysteries of the Rosary decorate the rest of the ceiling. On the wall above the main entrance, is a portrait of Pope Pius V, kneeling before an altar. The symbols of the four Evangelists are represented over the high altar, a medallion of King David playing the harp, surrounded by the prophets Isaiah, Jeremiah, Ezekiel and Daniel, hangs over the choir's central bay, with a further medallion of the Holy Trinity placed on the choir wall. All the decorations, apart from the three frescoes on the vaulted ceiling, are executed in *grisaille*, or grey monochrome. The organization of the ceiling follows the Venetian tradition in ceiling painting, in the same manner as Veronese's famous decoration in the Sala del Collegio in the Doge's Palace in Venice. Tiepolo's decoration benefits from the brightness of the church's interior, which is lit by six large windows, and his frescoes harmonize in an extraordinary fashion with the architecture of the vault. The light and clear style of painting also contributes to the legibility of the frescoes, and translates the Dominican rhetoric into images anyone can understand.

Contemporaneously with his decoration of the Jesuit church and at the request of Alvise Cornaro (1675–1766), Tiepolo created three canvases of scenes from Christ's passion for the church of Sant'Alvise in Venice. A large-scale *Christ Carrying the Cross* (ill. 37) and two smaller pictures, *The Flagellation* and *The Crowning with Thorns*, suggest that the paintings were meant to be displayed as a triptych, but we have no further proof that this was so. The visibly darker coloring and the dramatic realization of the scenes point to the work of Tintoretto, from whom Tiepolo had here drawn inspiration.

In 1740 Tiepolo payed a final visit to Milan, having been invited by the Marchese Giorgio Antonio Clerici to decorate the great hall of his palace in preparation for his intended marriage to Fluvia Visconti the following year. The fresco *The Course of the Chariot of the Sun* (ills. 35, 36, 39, 40) was the artist's first mature, monumental decoration on a secular theme for a noble client and it established his reputation as a specialist in palace decoration. The great commissions which followed – for the Residence in Würzburg, the Villa Valmarana in Vicenza or the Royal Palace in Madrid – would have been inconceivable without the Palazzo Clerici. The starting point for this ceiling decoration was the decorative principle of the illusionistic opening of the heavens, which Tiepolo had developed earlier in the Palazzo Sandi in Venice. In the Palazzo Clerici, however, this has been conceived in a less static and much more lively fashion. Various groups of figures are arranged irregularly against a multicolored sky, dominated by different layers of clouds, so forcing the viewer to wander round the room, constantly changing direction, in order to appreciate the painting as a whole. In the center of the ceiling, Apollo's sun-chariot, bathed in brilliant light, is surrounded by individual mythological figures and the gods of Olympus, while the four continents, the sea and the rivers are portrayed along the cornice in an impressive overall scheme which represents a masterly solution to the considerable architectonic difficulties posed by the long dimensions of the room.

Tiepolo's reputation as a painter of religious subjects had grown steadily over time, yet his commissions were mostly restricted to northern Italy. It is therefore astonishing that, on his return from Milan in 1740, the artist received a commission for an altarpiece in the small town of Camerino in the Marches, where he executed *The Virgin appearing to St. Philip Neri* (ill. 38) for the chapel of the Foschi family in the Oratorian church of San Filippo Neri. Unusually for Tiepolo, the scene is placed in an elaborate architectural setting, which clearly refers to the late-Baroque architecture of the newly erected church.

In 1740, Tiepolo was commissioned to paint two monumental altarpieces for the parish church of Verolanouva near Brescia. However, *The Gathering of*

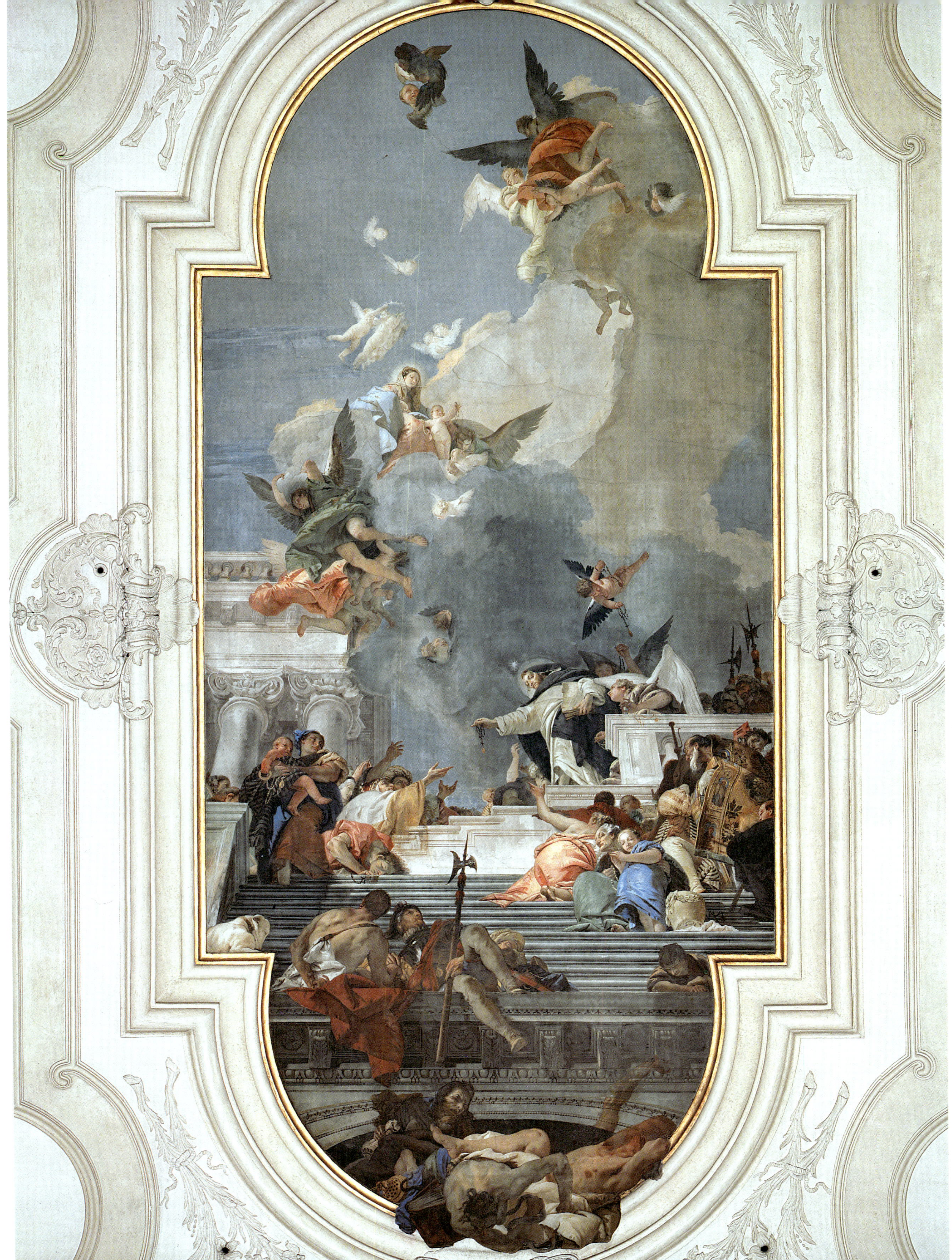

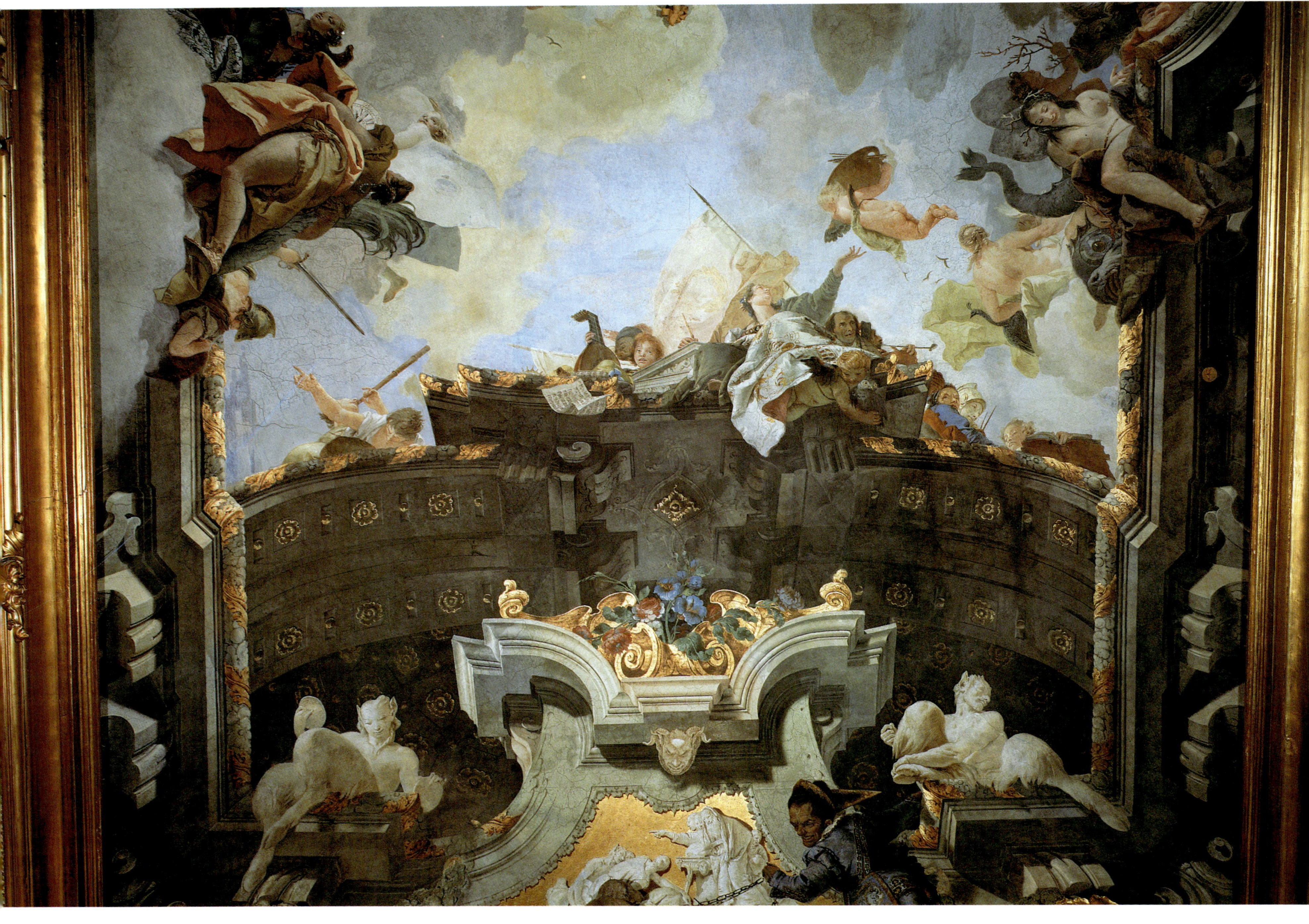

35 Detail of *The Course of the Chariot of the Sun*, 1740
Fresco, 220 x 540 cm
Palazzo Clerici, Milan

The detail shows how the fresco is incorporated into its simulated architectural framework, how the border of the actual picture dissolves into the illusionistic portrayal of the open heavens. Juno, on the left of the picture, above a coral-studded sea god, can be recognized by her attribute, the peacock. At the bottom, we see the continent of Europe, symbolized by the flourishing arts of music and painting.

Manna (ill. 41) and *The Sacrifice of Melchizedek* (ill. 42), were not completed and installed on the side walls of the Chapel of the Holy Sacrament until 1742.

In 1743, Tiepolo began work in Venice on the ceiling of the chapter room of the Scuola Grande dei Carmini, a commission he had received back in 1739 and which was to occupy him until 1749. At the same time – and also in Venice – he painted the ceiling of the great salon of the Palazzo Pisani-Moretta with a fresco depicting *The Apotheosis of Admiral Vettor Pisani* (ill. 45), an ancestor of the patronness, Chiara Pisani. The work was to celebrate the Admiral's victory in the war against the Genoese at Chioggia.

Two portraits – a genre in which Tiepolo seldom worked – can also be dated to the year 1743. *The Blessed Ladwyna* (ill. 44) is an idealized representation of the Dutchwoman Ladwyna di Schedam (1380–1433), who died at the beginning of the 15th century and was later beatified. She is portrayed here as a young girl in winter clothing. This depiction conforms to the standardized portrayal of a suffering Saint, a genre often encountered in the 17th century, and this lends it the air of a picture intended for private devotion. The *Portrait of Antonio Riccobono* (ill. 43) is also a posthumous representation of a scholar from Rovigo, who held the Chair of Rhetoric at the University of Padua in the 16th century. The work was part of a series of portraits of famous members of the Accademia dei Concordi di Rovigo, to which Piazzetta and Pittoni also contributed. The scholar's features are based on

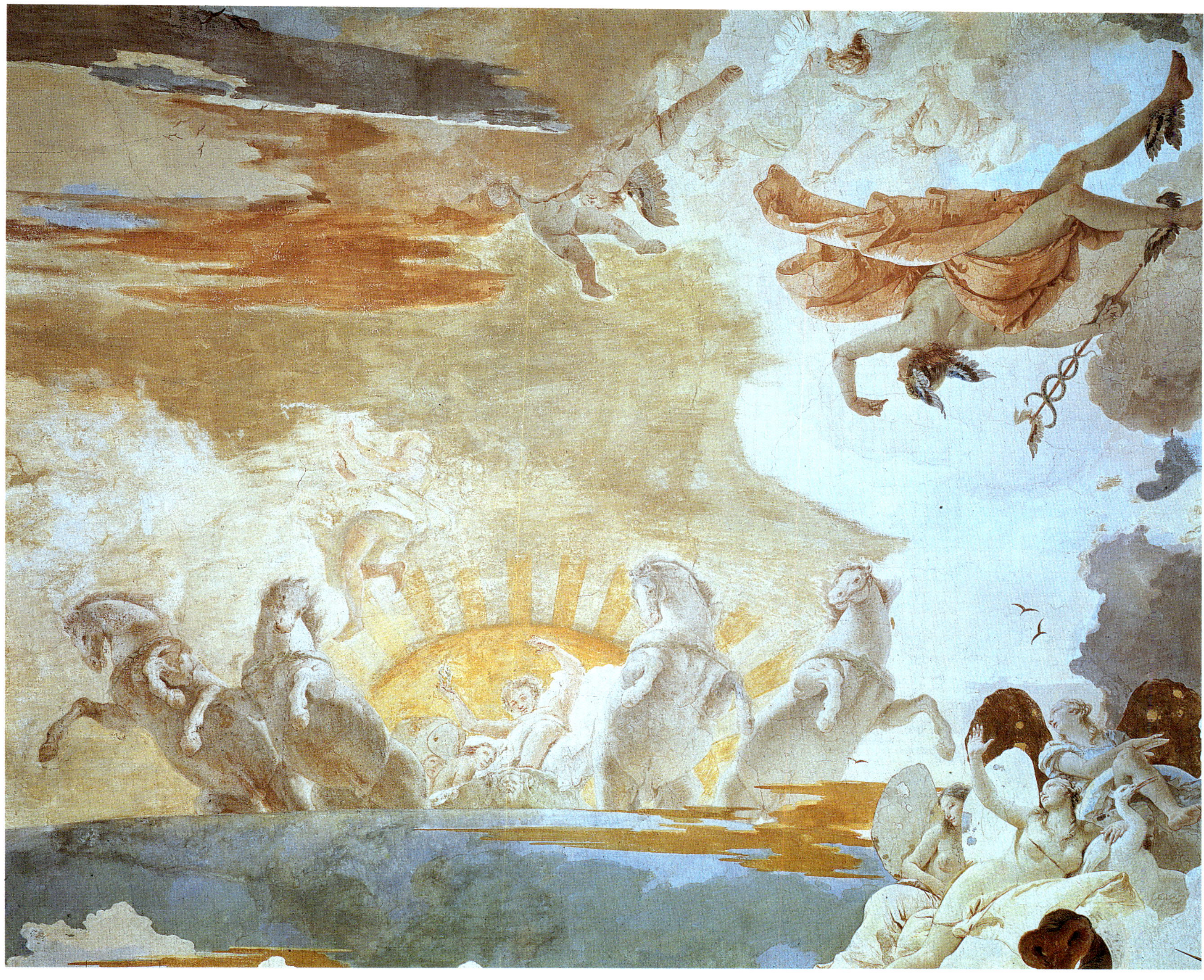

contemporary sources. However, the extremely vivid portrayal, with its speedy brushwork, seems to have been inspired by the late-period portraits of Titian (ca. 1490–1576), such as the *Portrait of Jacopo Strada* in the Kunsthistorisches Museum in Vienna.

The canvas ceiling painting *St. Helena discovering the Cross* (ill. 46), which Tiepolo created for the church of the Capuchins in the Castello district of Venice, is probably from the same year (1743). In a bold piece of illusionism, it shows the triumphant Helena, in the midst of soldiers and other figures, with the cross which soars up into the heavens. An oil sketch for this picture survives, but it differs greatly from the finished version, suggesting that alterations were proposed by the clients.

In May 1743, Francesco Algarotti (1712–1764), art advisor to Augustus III (1696–1763), Elector of Saxony and King of Poland, returned to his native city of Venice to acquire works by old and new masters for the royal collection of art in Dresden. Three works by Tiepolo were included in those chosen – the two smaller canvases *Maecenas presenting the Arts to Augustus* and *The Triumph of Flora*, along with the large-scale *Banquet of Cleopatra* (ill. 47), now in the National Gallery in Melbourne. Francesco Algarotti was an interesting personality: he had travelled widely, was an outstanding connoisseur of contemporary Roman, Bolognese and French painting, and a collector with access to the leading social circles in Europe. In addition, he was extremely well-educated and disseminated the theories of Newton (1643–1727)

36 Detail of *The Course of the Chariot of the Sun*, 1740
Fresco, 220 x 540 cm
Palazzo Clerici, Milan

Highlighted by the glowing light of the rising sun, Apollo's sun-chariot appears in the center of the fresco, drawn by four galloping white horses. The chariot itself can hardly be seen due to the strongly distorted perspective, which emphasizes the upward direction in which the quadriga is moving. The three winged figures at the lower right are the Horae, daughters of Zeus and goddesses of fertility, who also appear as symbols of the seasons. Along the upper edge are Mercury and several *putti* (rotated through 180°). The largely empty sky is otherwise animated only by the multicolored layers of cloud.

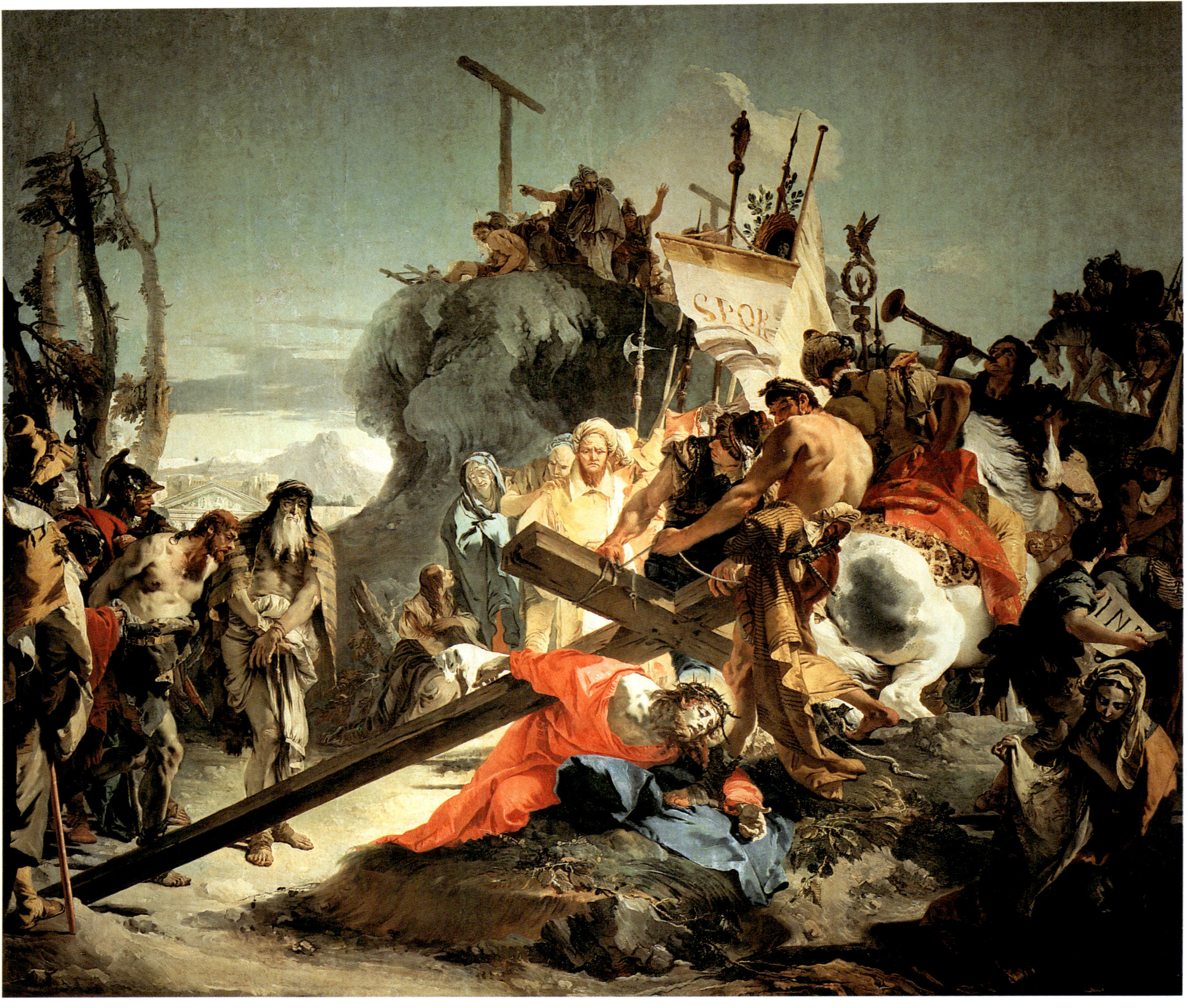

37 *Christ Carrying the Cross*, 1737/38
Oil on canvas, 450 x 517 cm
Sant'Alvise, Venice

The subject of the painting is Christ's carrying of the cross to the hill of Golgotha, which rises up in the center of the picture as a tall rock, the crosses already erected upon it. Directly beneath it in the foreground we see Christ in a flame red robe. He has collapsed under the heavy weight of the cross. To the right, Veronica, holding the sudarium, turns away from the dramatic scene, visibly moved. To the left, the two thieves likewise condemned to crucifixion are being led forward. In the exact center of the picture, between Christ's cross and the hill of Golgotha, and directly facing the viewer, are the figures of Jesus' disciples, together with Mary and Mary Magdalene. Brightly illuminated, they stand out symbolically from the other figures.

on light and colour in Venice. His acquaintance with Algarotti, which over time developed into a true friendship, was of great importance to Tiepolo's development. Through Algarotti, he could not only benefit from introductions to important European clients, but he also came into contact with the new trends in Classicism emanating from France.

The Banquet of Cleopatra is Tiepolo's first attempt at a subject to which he would return a short time later in the Palazzo Labia in Venice. The overall composition of the picture, the architectural framework and the splendid costumes of the figures are all clearly inspired by Veronese's opulent banqueting scenes, such as *The Feast in the House of Simon* (ill. 48), now in the Galleria Sabauda in Turin. Tiepolo has been criticized again and again for borrowing motifs and stylistic quotations from Veronese. But we must bear in mind the fact that references to the Venetian pictorial tradition of the 16th century were decidedly popular amongst 18th century collectors, and that the artist could thus reach a greater market.

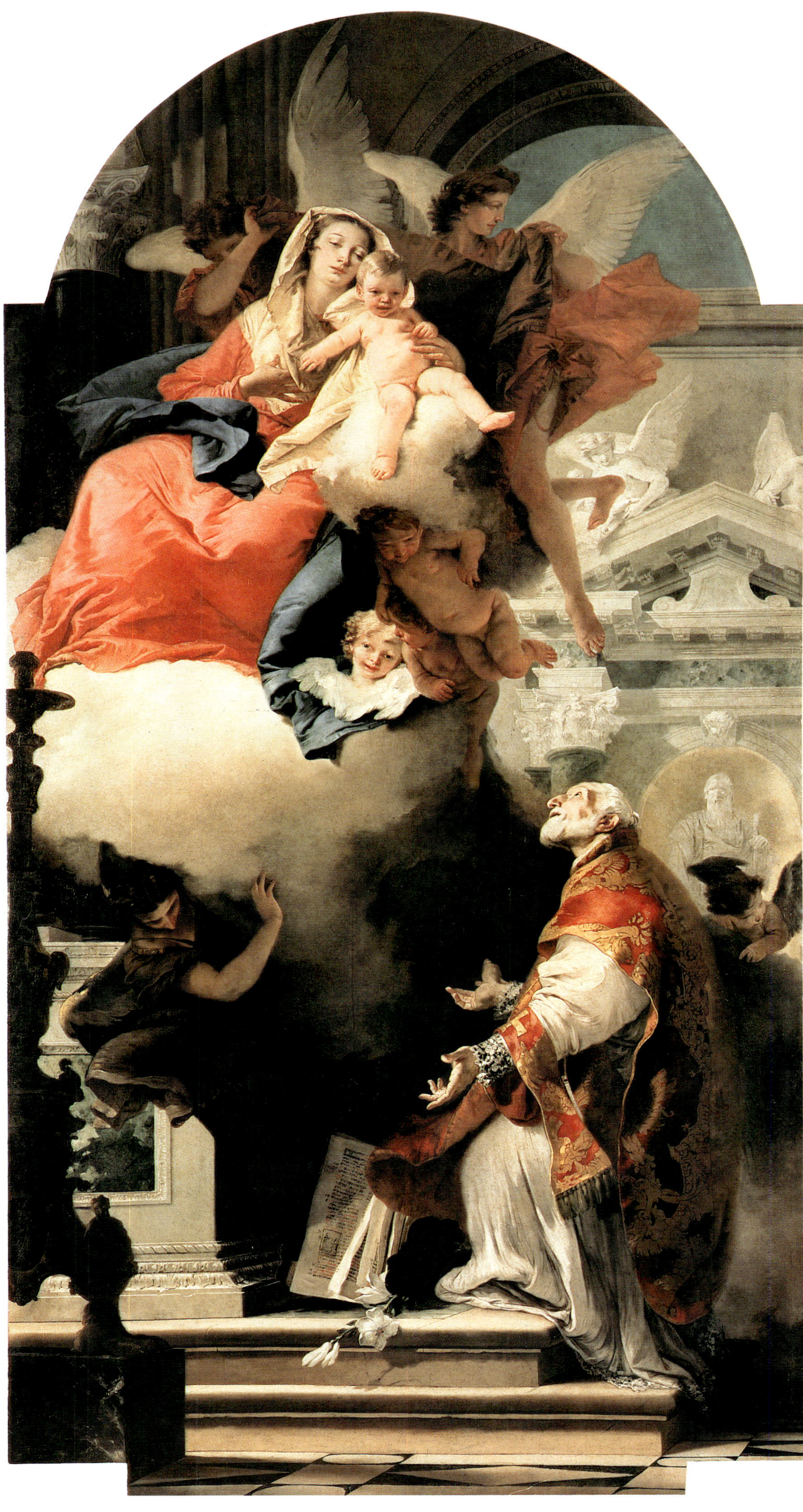

38 *The Virgin appearing to St. Philip Neri*, 1740
Oil on canvas, 360 x 182 cm
Museo Diocesano, Camerino

The saint stands in profile at the steps of an altar in front of a highly-developed architectural background. His gaze diverted upward in astonishment, he experiences the manifestation of the Mother of God and her Child, who appear to float in the interior of the church on a cloud, accompanied by angels. The rendering of the material of the robes is particularly impressive, as is the mist-like quality of the cloud, which almost turns the vision into an actual happening.

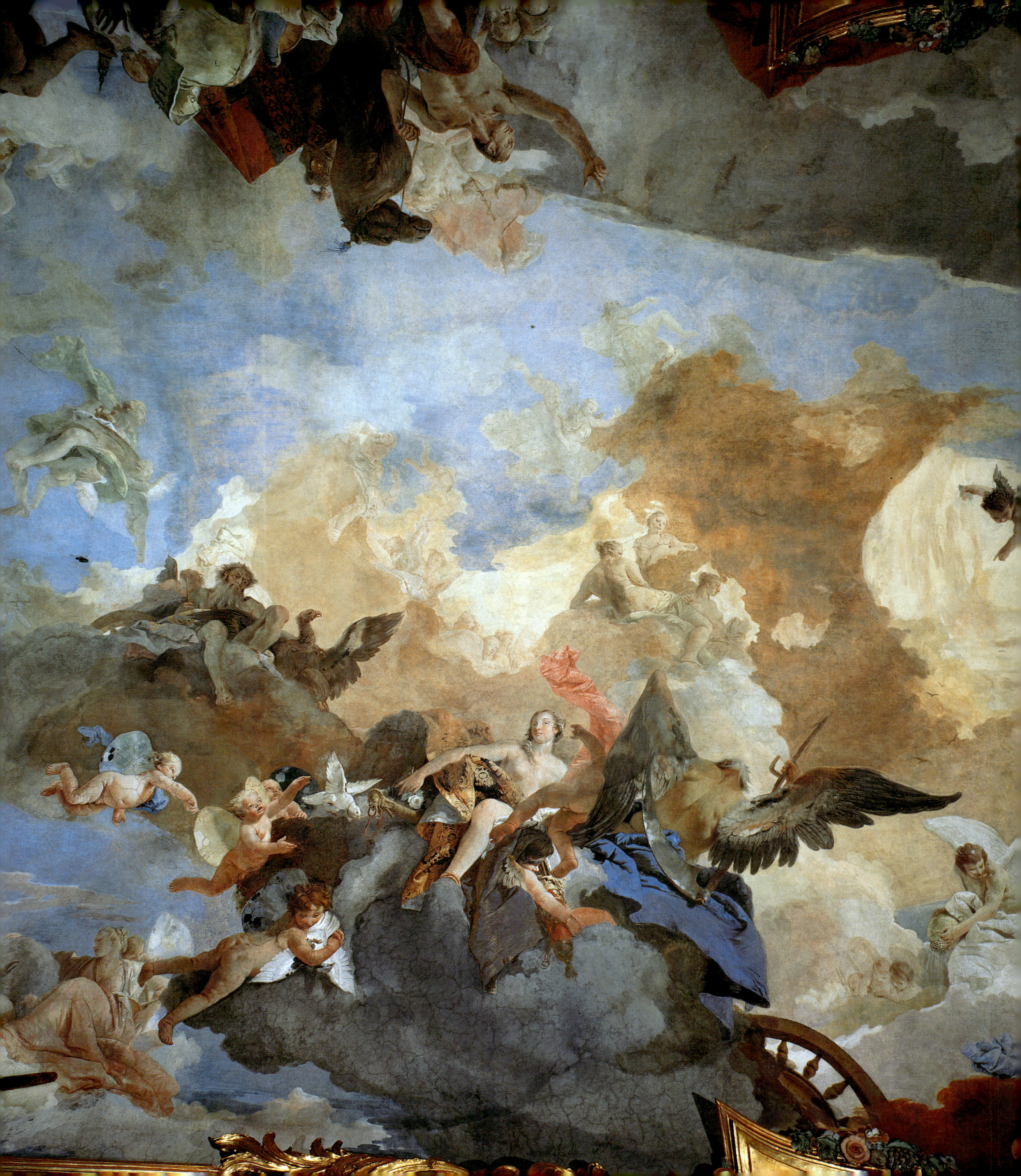

39 (opposite) Detail of *The Course of the Chariot of the Sun*, 1740
Fresco, 220 x 540 cm
Palazzo Clerici, Milan

This section of the fresco, perhaps the most beautiful, shows various deities of Olympus in the midst of a heavenly landscape dominated by variously-colored cloud formations. Venus sits on a dark cloud in the foreground, surrounded by *putti* and white doves. Amor, clutching his quiver of arrows, rests at her feet, while the winged personification of Time can be seen to his right, his back turned towards the viewer. To the left and a little above, Jupiter is enthroned, beside him an eagle, his attribute. Other gods populate the layers of cloud above, bathed in brighter light and, therefore, more difficult to make out. This device creates a strong impression of spatial depth. A part of the continent of Africa can be seen along the upper edge of the picture.

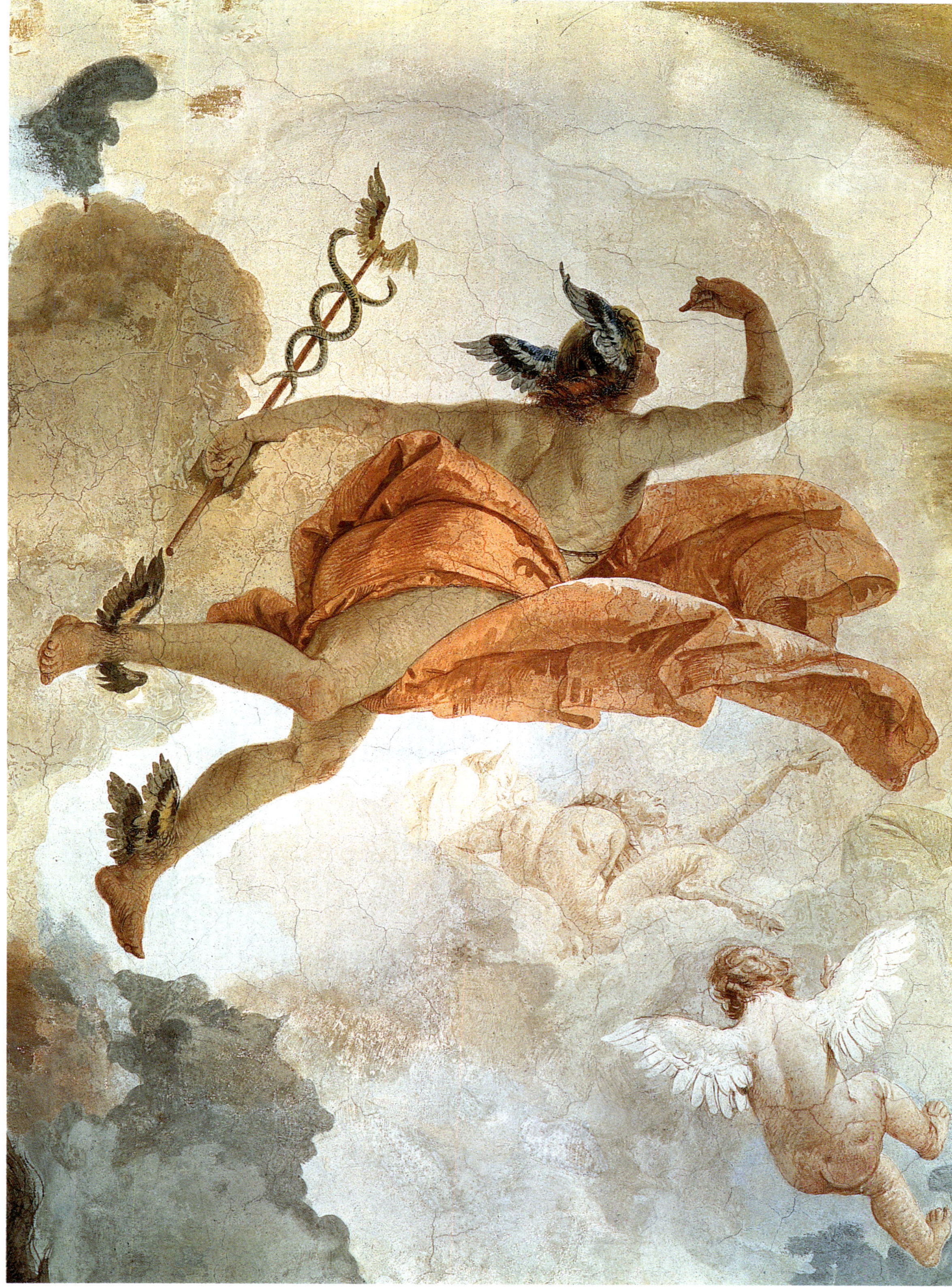

40 (right) Detail of *The Course of the Chariot of the Sun*, 1740
Fresco, 220 x 540 cm
Palazzo Clerici, Milan

The detail shows Mercury, the messenger of the gods, recognizable by his attributes: the winged helmet, the winged sandals and the caduceus. The billowing robes and the twisted posture emphasize the idea of his flying.

41 (following double page, left) *The Gathering of Manna*, 1740–1742
Oil on canvas, 1000 x 525 cm
Parrocchiale, Verolanuova

The altarpiece shows Moses standing on a rocky outcrop, with outspread arms, his gaze raised towards Heaven, which has already heard his prayers. An angel pours bread from a large vase down to earth, where the hungry Israelites scurry around on the ground to collect it. The strict division of the composition into two different areas – the spheres of heaven and earth – is broken by the figure of Moses, who is placed dead center, and so is characterized as a mediator between the two spheres.

42 (following double page, right) *The Sacrifice of Melchizedek*, 1740–1742
Oil on canvas, 1000 x 525 cm
Parrocchiale, Verolanuova

The *Sacrifice of Melchizedek* is shown here as a pendant to the *Gathering of Manna*. The Priest-King of Salem brings Abraham bread and wine on the evening following the Battle of the Kings, and blesses him. Abraham, who kneels before him in armor, and the army to the right are a reminder of the battle which went before. To the left, we see the civilian population, including women, children and the elderly, while a triumphal procession is already approaching from behind the altar.

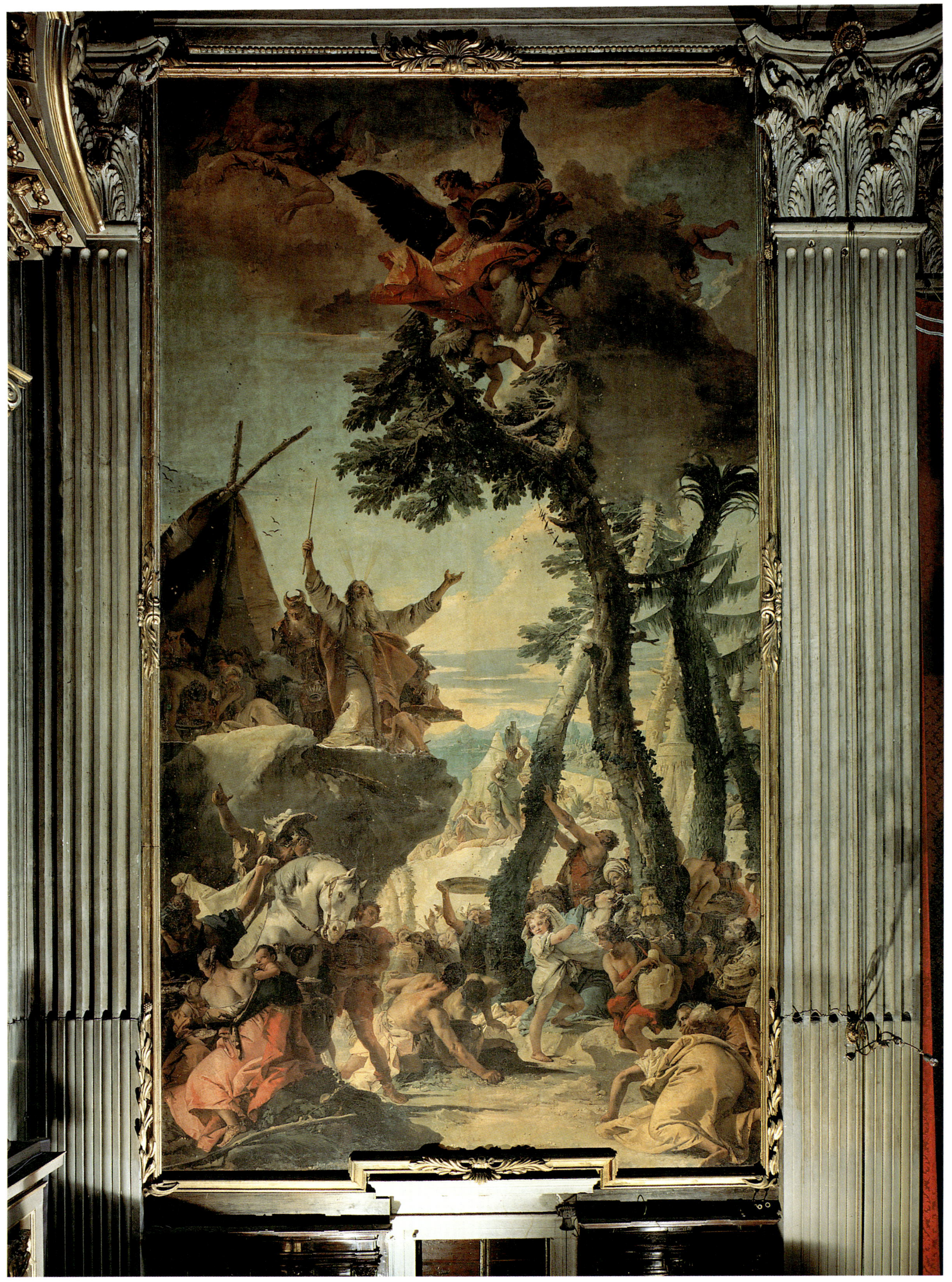

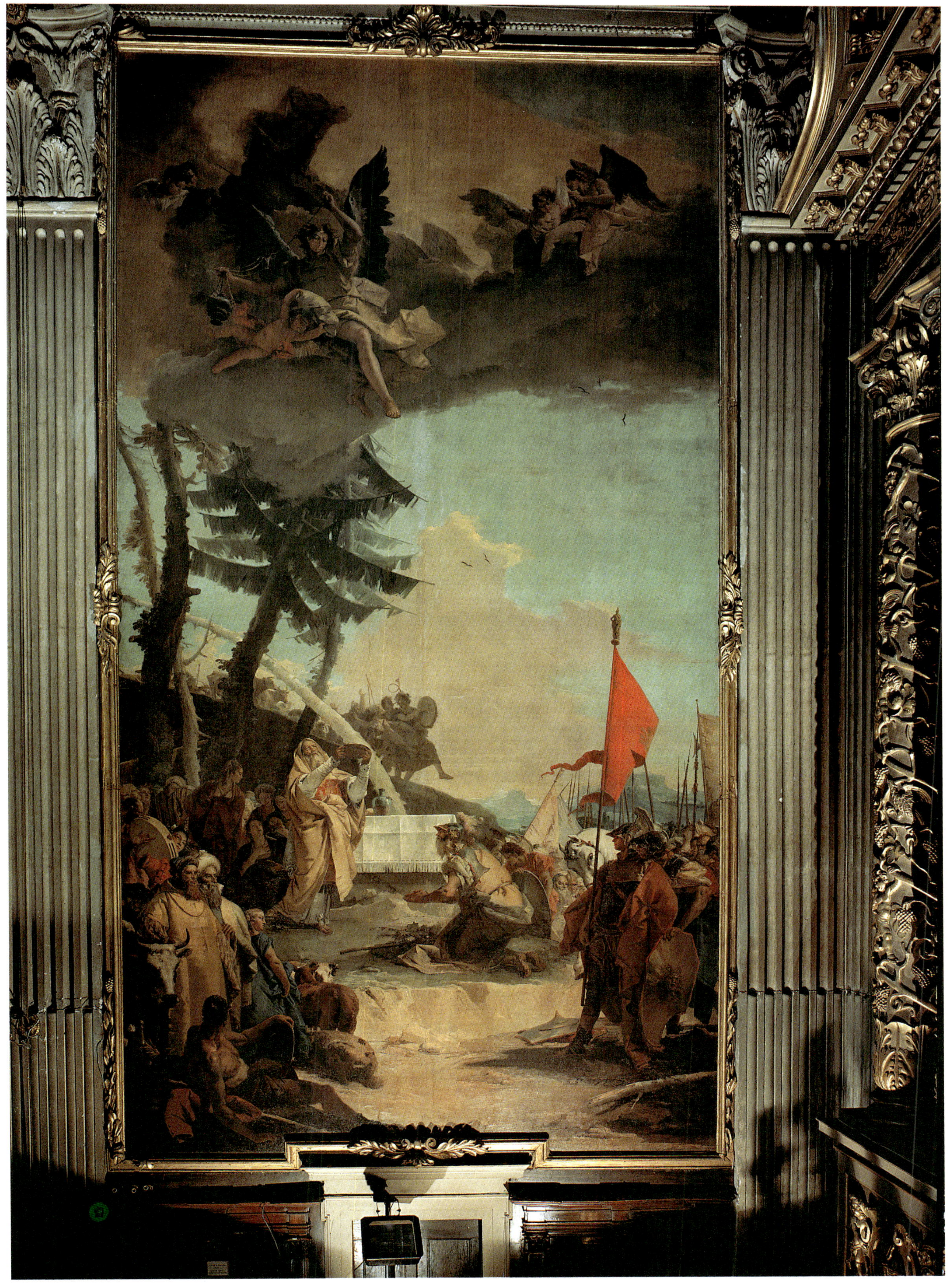

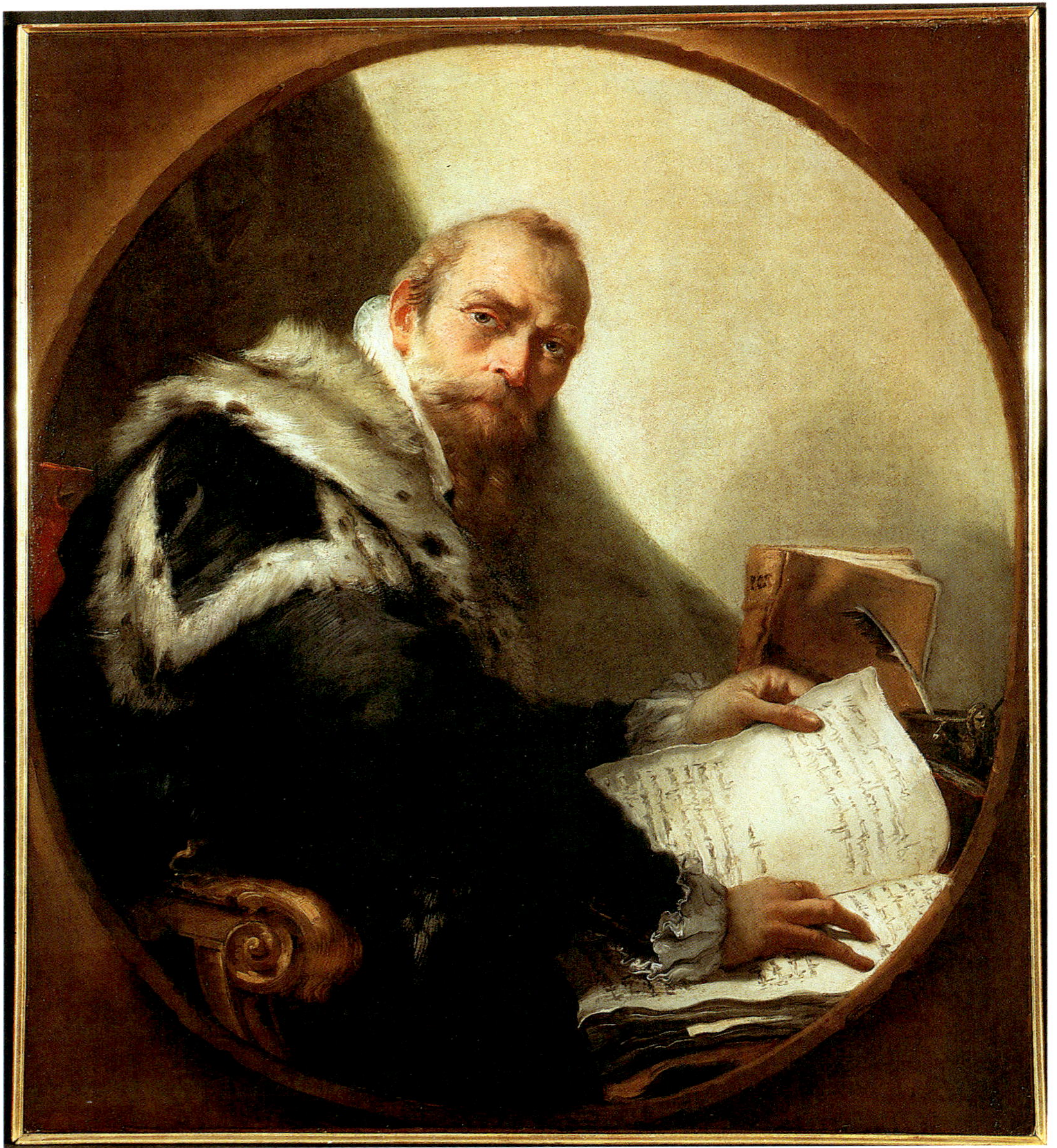

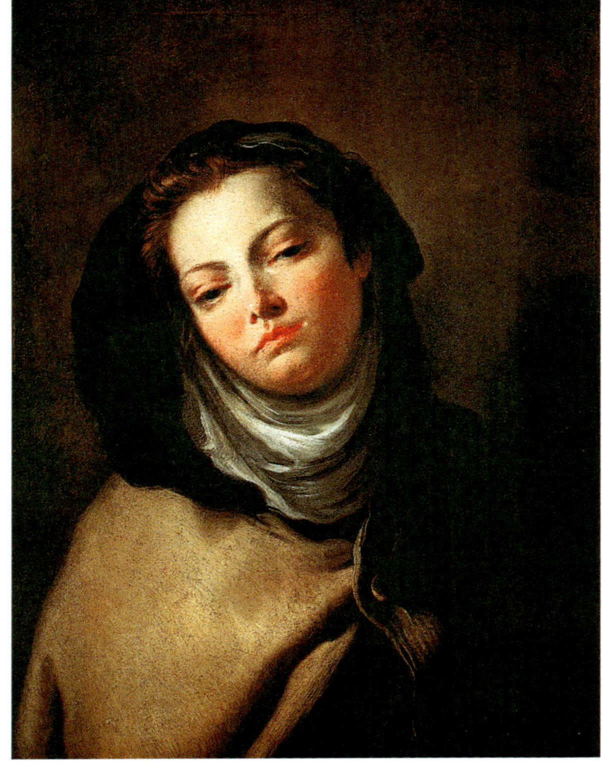

43 *Portrait of Antonio Riccobono*, 1743–1745
Oil on canvas, 102 x 90 cm
Pinacoteca dell'Accademia dei Concordi, Rovigo

The posthumous portrait depicts the scholar, dressed nobly in furs, in front of an opened book in his study, thus conforming to the traditional genre of the portrait of the man of letters. However, the alert gaze of the protagonist, whose eyes almost seem to fix firmly on the viewer, along with the dynamic brushwork, lend the picture a great deal of vitality.

44 *The Blessed Ladwyna*, 1743
Oil on canvas, 65 x 48 cm
Collection Stanley Moss, Riverdale on Hudson, New York

This simple picture, with its gently executed brushwork, is a posthumous portrait of the blessed Ladwyna, who fell seriously ill following an accident at the age of sixteen. The painting gives prominence to the girl's suffering. Patiently borne, it can be seen in the gentle, yet pain-racked facial expression, and is emphasized by the dull and dark coloring of the background.

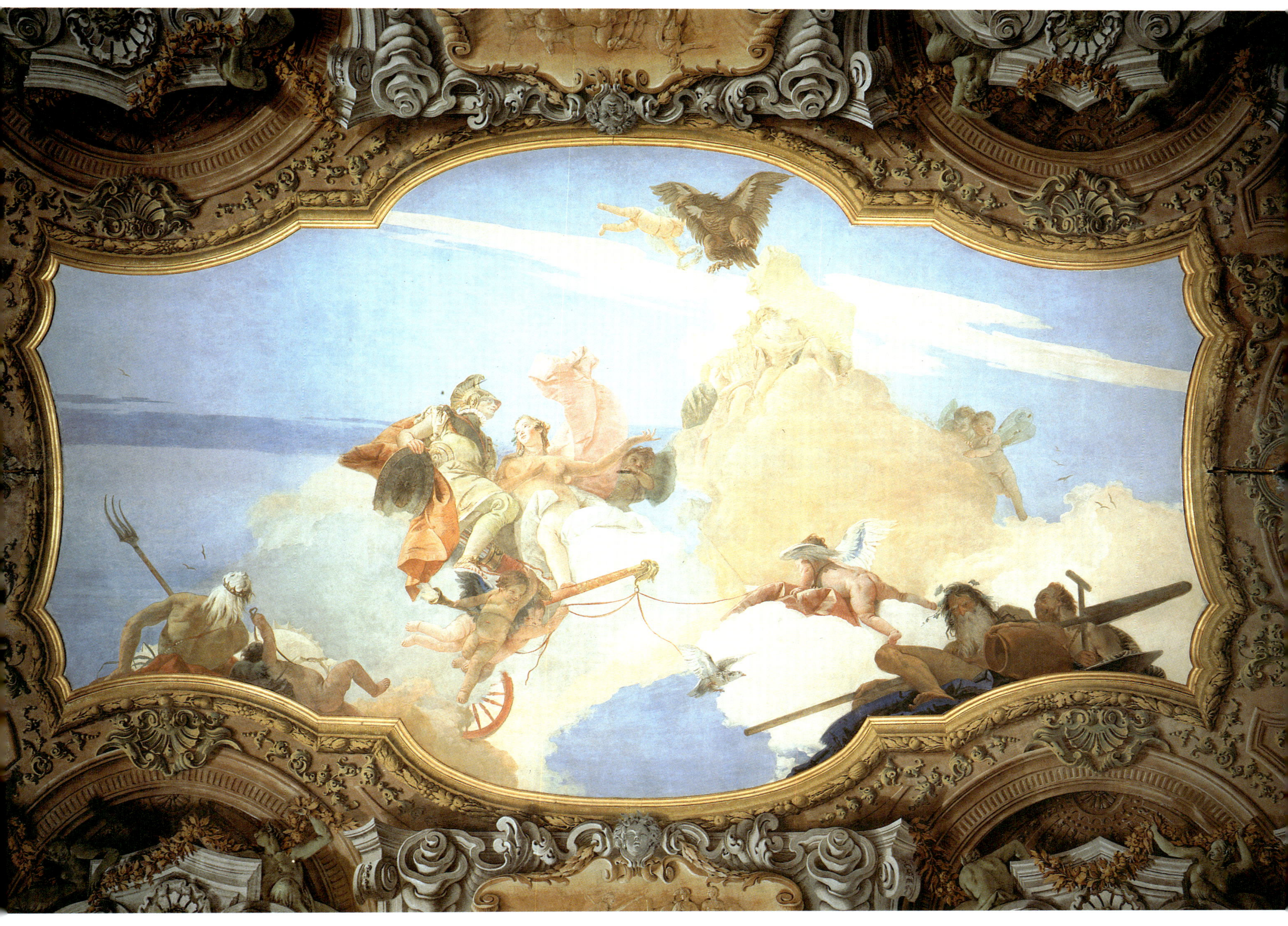

45 *The Apotheosis of Admiral Vettor Pisani*, 1743
Fresco
Palazzo Pisani-Moretta, Venice

The fresco shows the apotheosis of Admiral Vettor Pisani *di sotto in sù*. He is portrayed as a warrior in armor and floats in the company of Venus and Amor on a cloud in the sky. Further up, on top of Mount Olympus, sit Jupiter and Mars, waiting to receive the honored admiral, while the eagle of the king of the gods and a *putto* bearing a laurel wreath appear at the top of the picture. Neptune, at the bottom left, and a river god at bottom right symbolize mastery over the sea.

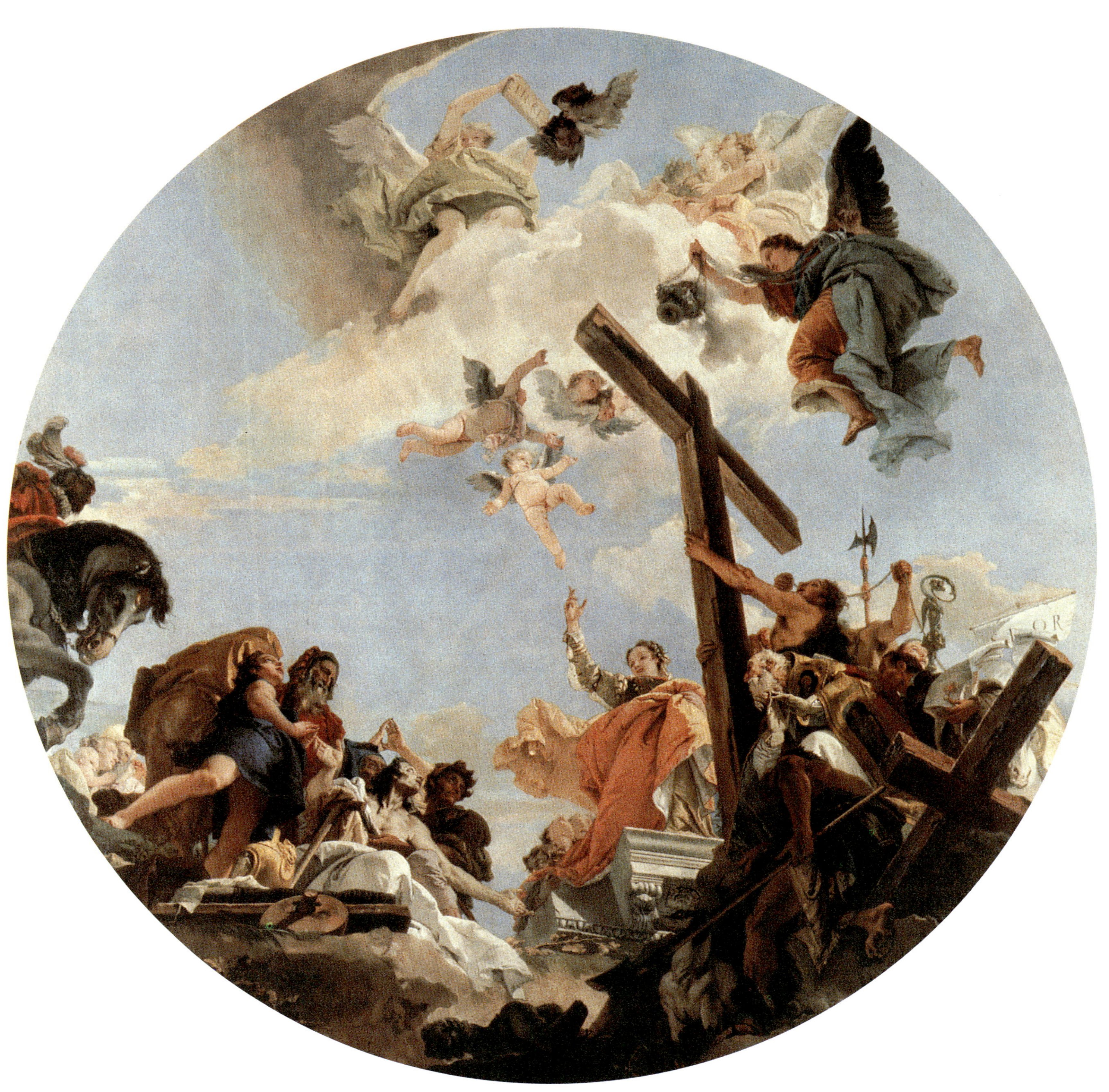

46 (opposite) *St. Helena discovering the Cross*, ca. 1743
Oil on canvas, 486 cm diameter
Gallerie dell'Accademia, Venice

According to legend, St. Helena, the mother of Constantine the Great, discovered the True Cross on a pilgrimage to Jerusalem. Tiepolo portrays the saint, in daring foreshortening from below, making a triumphal gesture in front of the Cross, which towers up into the sky. She is surrounded by the usual retinue of soldiers, holy men, the old and the young, women and children, commonly used by Tiepolo as extras in his paintings. A number of angels hover over the scene, carrying a thurible and a tablet bearing the name of Christ, looking down on the miracle of the discovery of the cross.

47 (below) *The Banquet of Cleopatra*, 1743/44
Oil on canvas, 249 x 346 cm
National Gallery of Victoria, Melbourne

Magnificent, brightly lit palace architecture is the setting for Cleopatra's banquet. However, the historical event of the meeting between the Queen of Egypt and the Roman Anthony takes second place to the creation of an opulent banqueting scene in the manner of Veronese. It is therefore the sumptuous costumes, the magnificent receptacles and the rich variety of foods which draw most attention as they are proffered by the servants of the court, who include moors, a dwarf and a dog – a collection of elements typical of the work of Veronese.

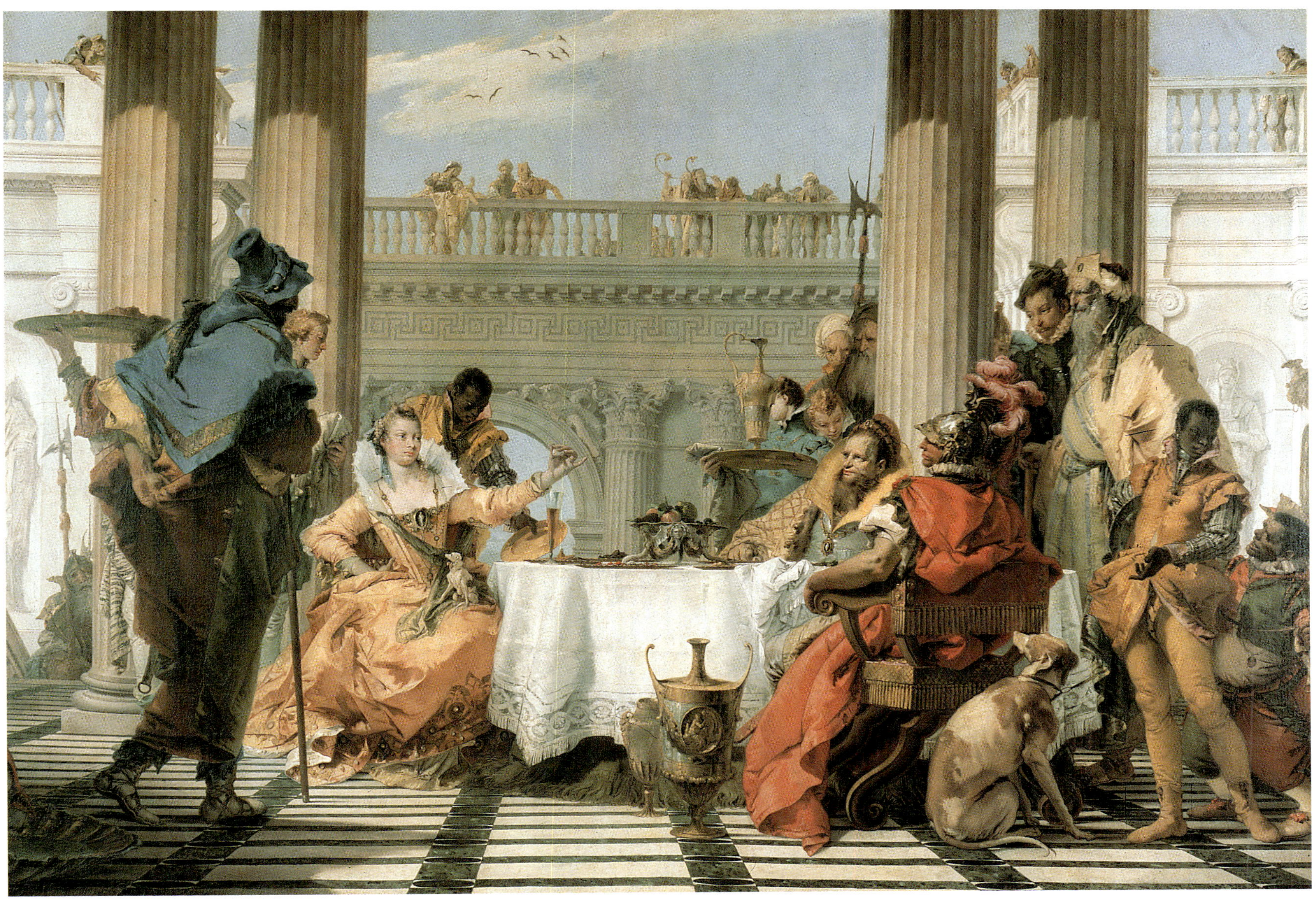

48 Paolo Veronese
The Feast in the House of Simon, 1560
Oil on canvas, 315 x 451 cm
Galleria Sabauda, Turin

The subject of the picture is the feast in the house of the Pharisee Simon, at which Mary Magdalene comes to Jesus, washes his feet with her tears, anoints them and finally dries them with her hair. The portico with the balustrade full of onlookers, the diversity of characters, the dog in the foreground and the festive setting are elements which can also be found in Tiepolo's pictures.

In 1740, in a poem celebrating his frescoes in the Palazzo Clerici in Milan, Tiepolo was already being hailed as an *imitatore*, or emulator, of Veronese. We have long known the extent to which he looked to the paintings of his 16th century predecessor for stimulation. The revival of Veronese's art was indeed a widespread phenomenon in the 18th century, however, Tiepolo was the artist most deserving of the title of "successor". Veronese's influence is most noticeable in Tiepolo's works in the borrowing of pictorial motifs, in the particular use of color, in the figures and in the pictorial architecture. Various of Veronese's typical figures – of differing gender, age, physiognomy, dress and posture – can be found in Tiepolo's paintings, as can the rendering of magnificently shimmering robes. The various animals – the shorn dogs and the monkeys – are another recurring motif. The motif of the tabularium in the background architecture, often used as a balustrade for spectators or as part of a loggia, is another of Veronese's models. There are close parallels in the themes of the paintings, too. The representation of the *Banquet of Cleopatra* derives from Veronese's opulent banqueting scenes such as *The Feast in the House of Simon* (ill. 48), now in the Galleria Sabauda, Turin. It was also Veronese who led the way in the radical foreshortening of the steps and of the architecture in the ceiling paintings. We can see similarities in the composition of the landscapes, in the setting of the scenes. Both artists preferred to hint at, rather than to specify, the scene of the action. By depicting fragments of arches, columns and other pieces of architecture, they evoke the idea of noble buildings and so establish a splendidly decorative pictorial order. As far as coloring is concerned, Veronese's light palette and his

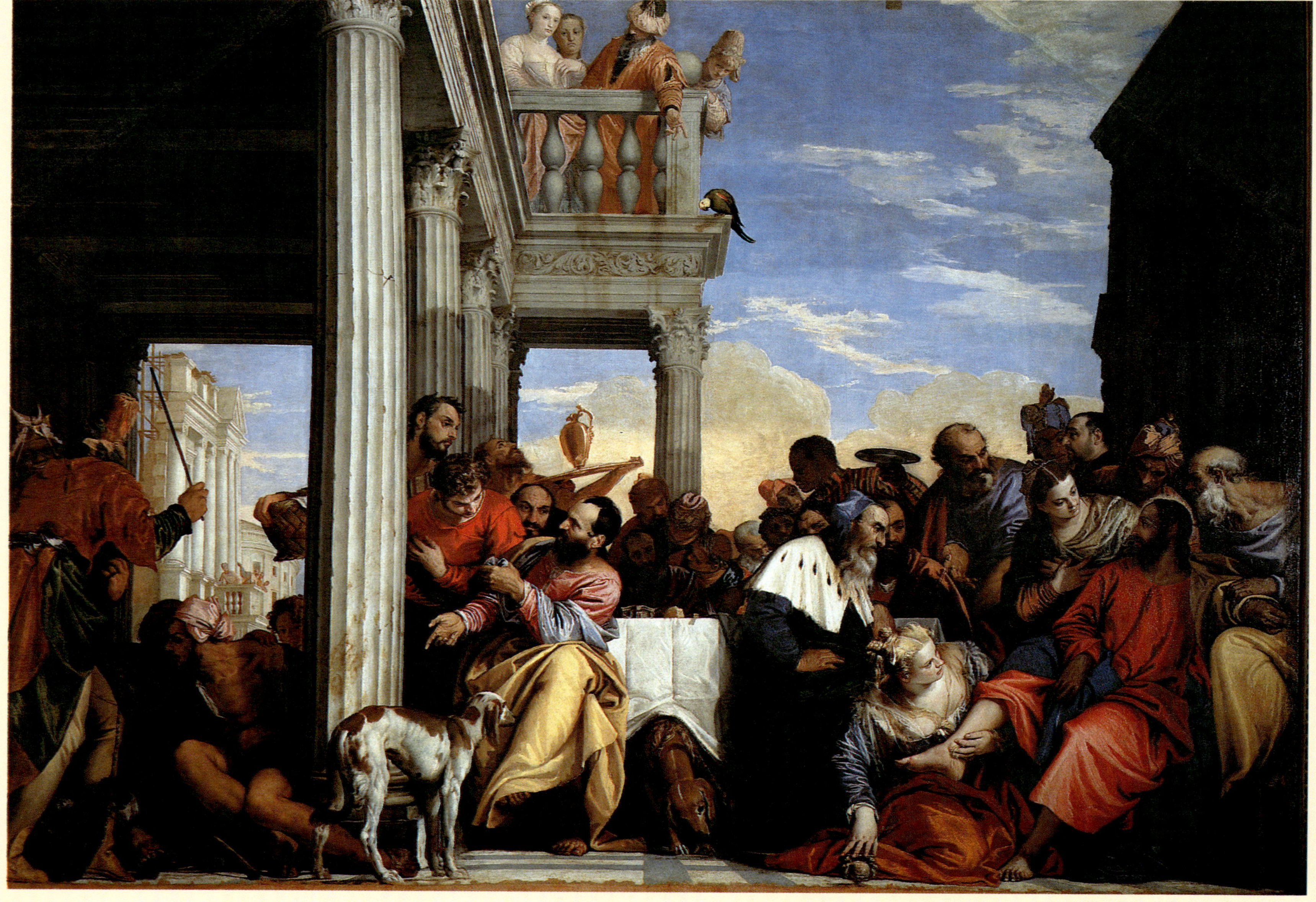

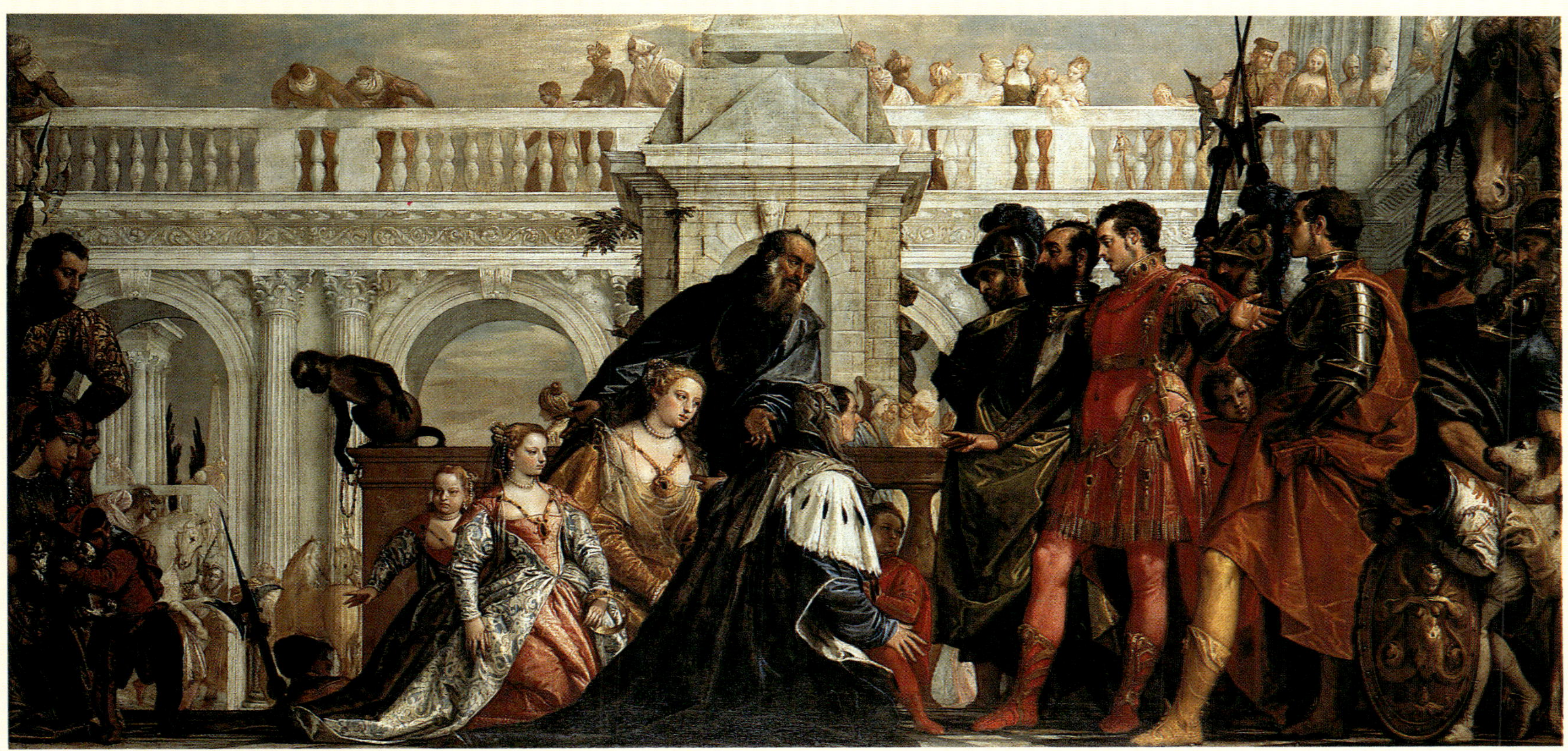

preference for strong, richly-contrasting bright colors already clearly distinguished him from his contemporaries such as Tintoretto, and represented a particular incitement to Tiepolo to turn away from the light-and-shade painting of Tenebrism. As an example, we can point to Tiepolo's fresco in the Villa Cordellina in Montecchio Maggiore, *The Family of Darius before Alexander* (ills. 50, 51), which obviously imitates Veronese's famous work of the same title, now in the National Gallery (ill. 49). But despite all these similarities, there are still differences in the mode of representation of the two artists. Tiepolo's cast of characters is much less ordered and clear: he preferred stereotypes and the standardized representation of period figures. The differences are most obvious in their representations of people. Veronese's men and women are still distinguished by natural variety and individuality, while Tiepolo is more interested in outward appearances and in demonstrating his predilection for humor and frivolous exaggerations. In spite of Tiepolo's numerous borrowings from Veronese, it cannot be overlooked that two hundred years separate the two men – a period during which ideas about art had changed fundamentally.

49 Paolo Veronese
The Family of Darius before Alexander, ca. 1565
Oil on canvas, 93 x 187 cm
The National Gallery, London

Alexander receives the family of Darius, whom he had just defeated in the battle of Issos, and shows clemency towards the prisoners. The scene is represented in the foreground: Alexander and his retinue, still in their armor, are on the right, while the finely-dressed members of Darius' family kneel before him to his left. Although Veronese adds in secondary figures who have nothing to do with the plot, such as the monkey on the wall, the servant with the dog, or even the bystanders on the balustrade in the background architecture, the main action is still easily recognizable and the framework of characters clearly structured.

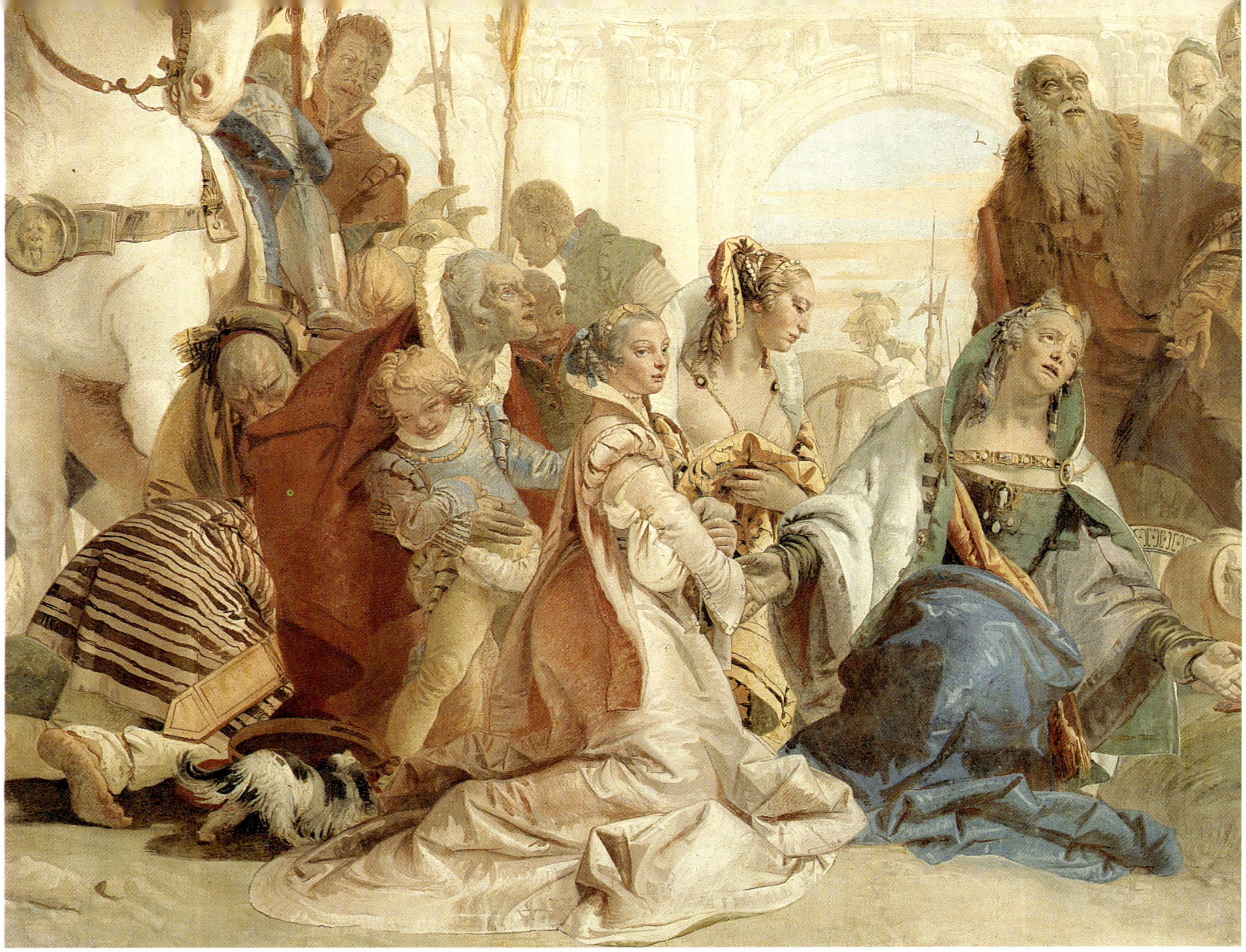

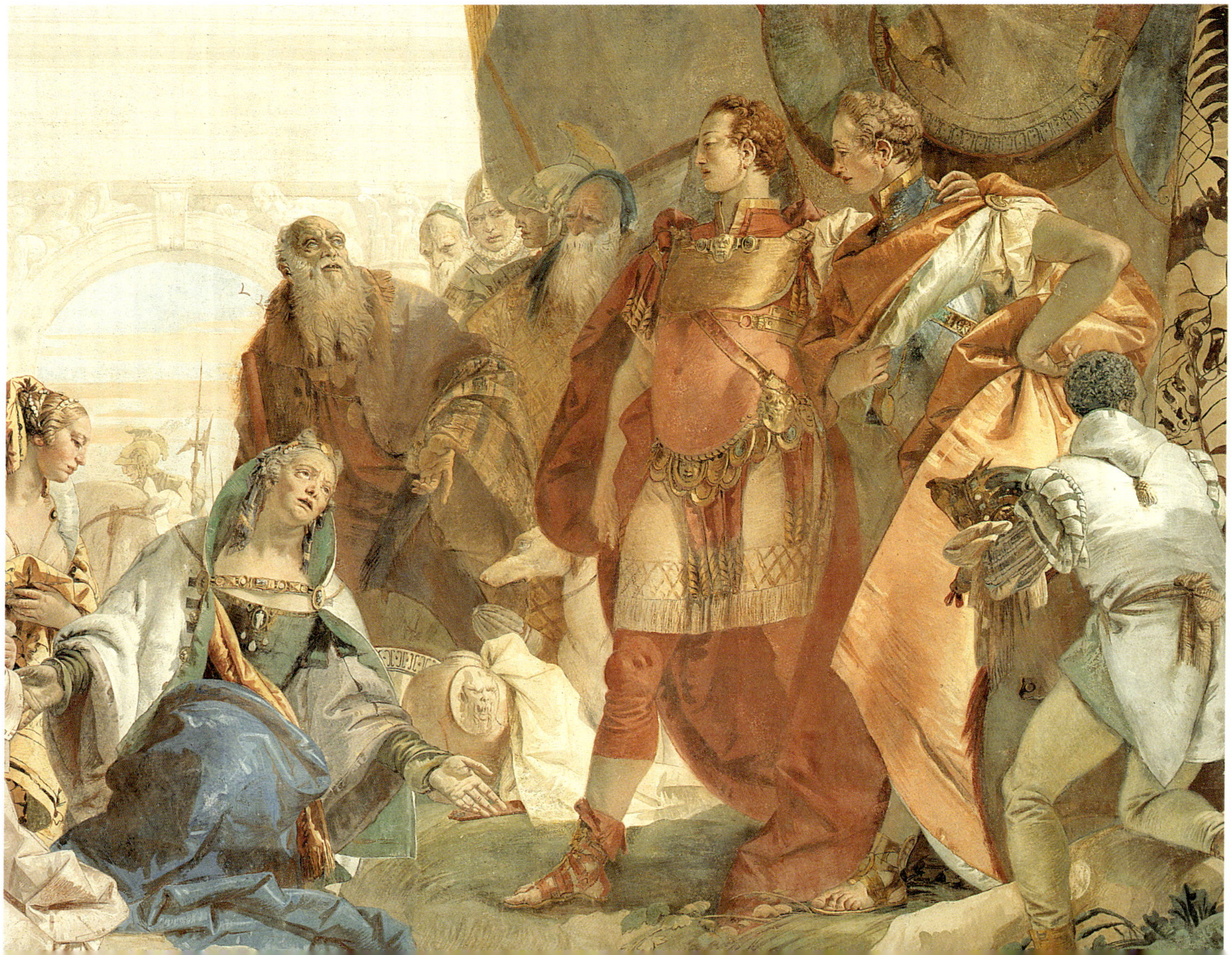

50, 51 (opposite, above and below) *The Family of Darius before Alexander*, 1744
Frescoes, 490 x 550 cm
Villa Cordellina, Montecchio Maggiore

Tiepolo's version of the same subject may borrow a number of motifs from Veronese's representation, yet the arrangement of figures is less well-ordered in his presentation of the scene. Alexander stands out clearly beneath an enormous, baldachin-like tent, but it is difficult to tell which of the figures around him belong to his retinue and which are mere extras. The same is true of the family of Darius. While the adult women plea for mercy with sorrowful faces, the son laughs and plays with a dog, caricaturing the gravity of the situation. No meaningful explanation can be found for the man, viewed from behind, crawling along the earth in the foreground. This appears to be a simple case of the artist playing around.

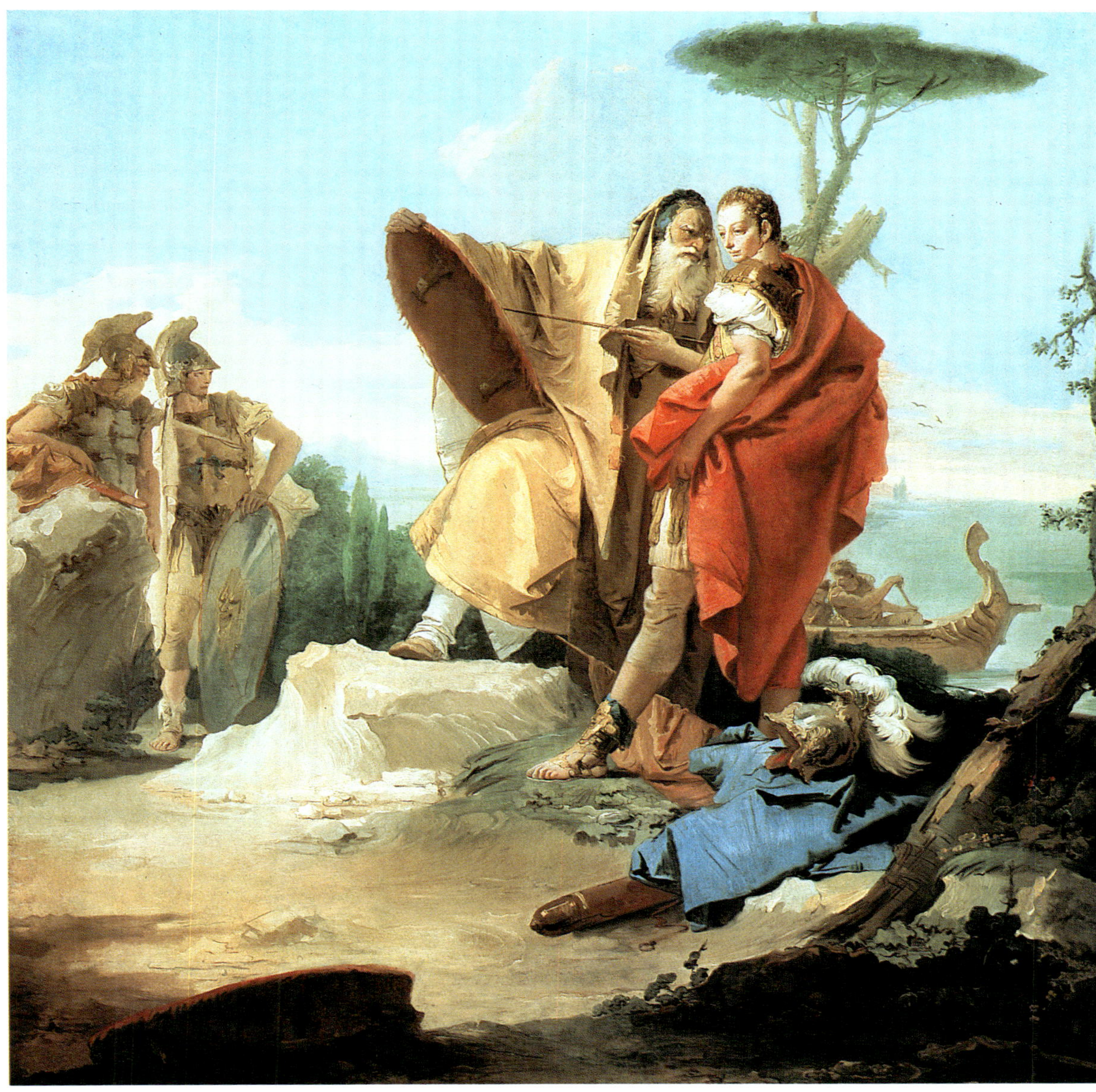

52 (right) *Rinaldo and the Magus of Ascalon*, 1743
Oil on canvas, 186.9 x 214.7 cm
The Art Institute of Chicago, Chicago

The meeting of Rinaldo and two of his companions with the Magus of Ascalon following their arrival in Palestine is set before a tree, visible in the background. The Magus is showing Rinaldo a shield, on which the latter recognizes the coat of arms of his ancestors. Fired up by this example, Rinaldo finally declares himself ready to fight against the heathen enemy and to serve the Christian cause, and, in so doing, to fulfill his destiny. Tiepolo shows us a hero conscious of his responsibilities and of the military tasks which face him. This is emphasized by the positioning of his helmet and quiver in a central position in the foreground.

The decorations in the Palladian Villa Cordellina in Montecchio Maggiore, which Tiepolo completed in October 1743, were just as strongly influenced by Veronese. The work had been commissioned by Carlo Cordellina (1703–1794), a successful lawyer whose expertise in international jurisprudence certainly played a decisive role in the choice of subject matter. Both *The Magnanimity of Scipio*, a wall fresco, and *The Family of Darius before Alexander* (ill. 49: Veronese; ills. 50, 51: Tiepolo) deal with the clemency shown by a head of state towards foreign captives. The scenarios extol the private virtues of Generosity and Compassion in a most vivid manner which attempts to engage the sympathy of the viewer. In addition to these two frescoes, ten monochrome representations of the Continents and allegorical figures (Politics, War, Poetry, Art, Music, Merit, Counsel) complete the decoration of the salon. The ceiling shows the dramatic scene *The Apotheosis of Virtue*.

Tiepolo also created a series of canvases in that same year (1743) for an unidentified patrician palace in Venice. Eight pictures from the cycle survive – four in the Art Institute in Chicago and four in the National Gallery in London (ill. 52). The paintings illustrate scenes from Torquato Tasso's "Gerusalemme liberata", a masterwork of Italian literature first published in 1581 (written between 1570 and 1575). The epic poem tells of the heroic deeds of the Knights of the Cross during the First Crusade to free Jerusalem from the Saracens in 1099. The subplot contains many episodes which have continued to inspire painters since the 16th century. The story of Rinaldo and Armida in particular has been

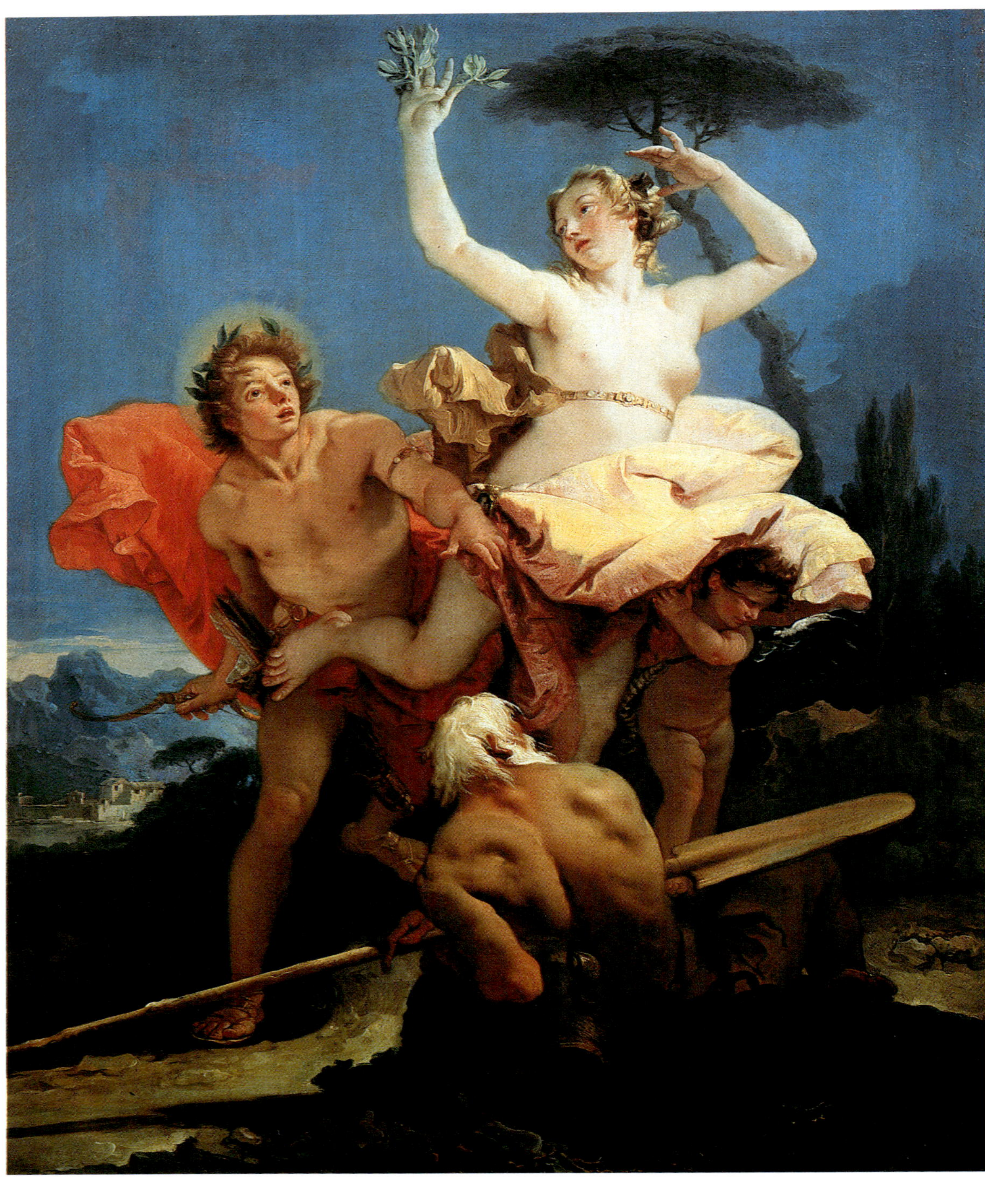

53 *Apollo and Daphne*, 1744/45
Oil on canvas, 96 x 79 cm
Musée du Louvre, Paris

The dramatic episode of Apollo and Daphne, as narrated by Ovid in the "Metamorphoses", is staged in front of an almost Alpine backdrop. Daphne escapes the attentions of Apollo, who has fallen madly in love with her, by turning herself into a tree. The moment in which the transformation begins is represented: Apollo is hard on her heels and Amor, too, is attempting to hold her, but her hands have already turned into foliage. The backward-facing figure of a river god in the foreground marks the end of her desperate flight. The strong contrast between the brilliant yellow and red robes and the dark blue shades of the background brings to mind works of French art.

54 (opposite) *The Miracle of the Holy House of Loreto* (oil sketch), 1744/45
Oil on canvas, 124 x 85 cm
Gallerie dell'Accademia, Venice

The oil sketch shows, in *di sotto in sù* perspective, the house of the Virgin Mary in the center of the picture, borne through the skies by a host of angels, with the Virgin herself on the roof, her arm raised in the direction of travel. In the banks of cloud above, angels play musical instruments. One of them holds the crown over Mary's head. In the background, God the Father and Jesus with the Cross can be vaguely made out, and it is probably the archangel Michael who is portrayed at the very top of the picture with an olive branch. The earthly zone at the lower edge of the picture is dominated by unbelievers, symbolized by soldiers and the falling figure of Lucifer. Top right is Italy, welcoming the arrival of the relic with fanfares.

55 (following double page, left) *The Meeting of Anthony and Cleopatra*, 1746/47
Fresco, 650 x 300 cm
Palazzo Labia, Venice

The arrival of Anthony and his entourage is staged as an illusionistic vista within a feigned architectural framework. While the sails of the Roman fleet can still be glimpsed in the background, the magnificently costumed figures move off towards Cleopatra's palace in the manner of a triumphal procession. In the foreground, Anthony and Cleopatra lead the way, already portrayed as a couple. Tiepolo ironically plays around with different levels of reality by having Anthony point to the entrance of the palace, which is at the same time the room in which the viewer stands, and to which the steps in the picture also seem to lead down.

56 (following double page, right) *The Meeting of Anthony and Cleopatra* (detail ill. 55), 1746/47

This section shows Cleopatra and Anthony in the middle of a group of men of all ages in Oriental dress, the latter presenting a large variation of different types of figure. The main actors are emphasized by their magnificent costumes. Cleopatra's robes bring to mind the bridal dress for a royal wedding, like the one Tiepolo would eventually execute in his Würzburg frescoes.

the subject of paintings by von Agostino (1557–1602) and Annibale Carracci (1560–1609), Poussin (1594–1665) and Guercino (1591–1666), among others. Tiepolo's cycle is his first version of the subject, anticipating the famous decoration in the Villa Valmarana in Vicenza. It is significant that, in this cycle, Tiepolo sets the scenes in an Arcadian landscape which does not feature in the original text.

The small picture *Apollo and Daphne* (ill. 53), now in the Louvre in Paris, was probably executed in 1744/45. Here, too, a landscape forms the background against which the mythological story takes places. However, the coloring – significantly stronger, compared to the Tasso cycle – and the physiognomy of the figures are greatly reminiscent of works of French art.

In the summer of 1745, Tiepolo frescoed the nave of the church of the Scalzi in Venice with a representation of *The Miracle of the Holy House of Loreto*, a commission he had received back in 1743. The fresco was destroyed by a firebomb in 1915. However, two preparatory oil sketches in the Gallerie dell'Accademia in Venice (ill. 54) and the National Gallery in London have survived, and they document the process of working on this important decoration. The subject matter is the miracle of the Holy House of the Virgin Mary, which, according to legend, was carried by angels, following the invasion of the Holy Land by the infidels in 1291, from Nazareth to Loreto in Italy, where it is still venerated as a Marian relic. There are fundamental differences between the version which was realized and the oil sketch in Venice.

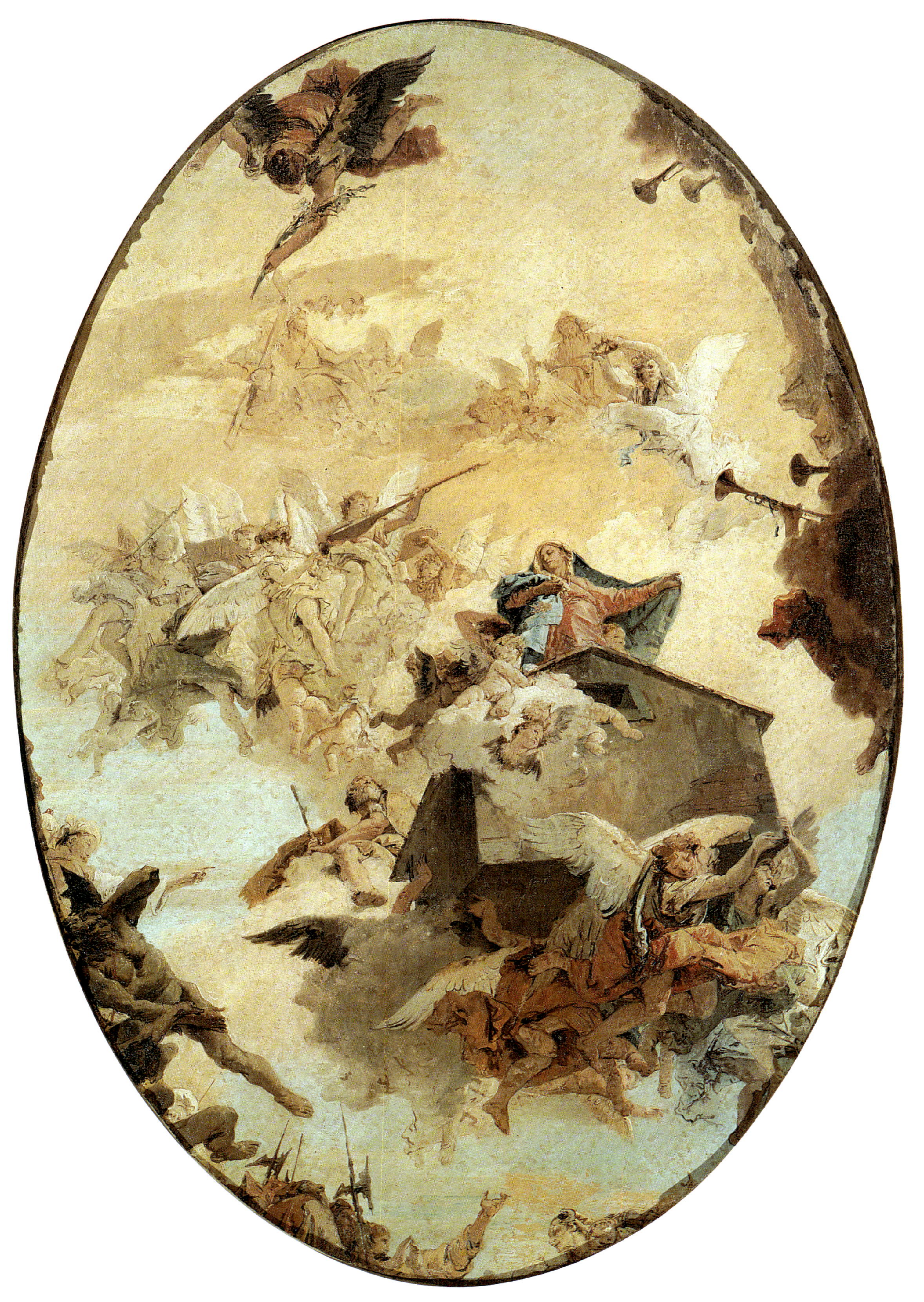

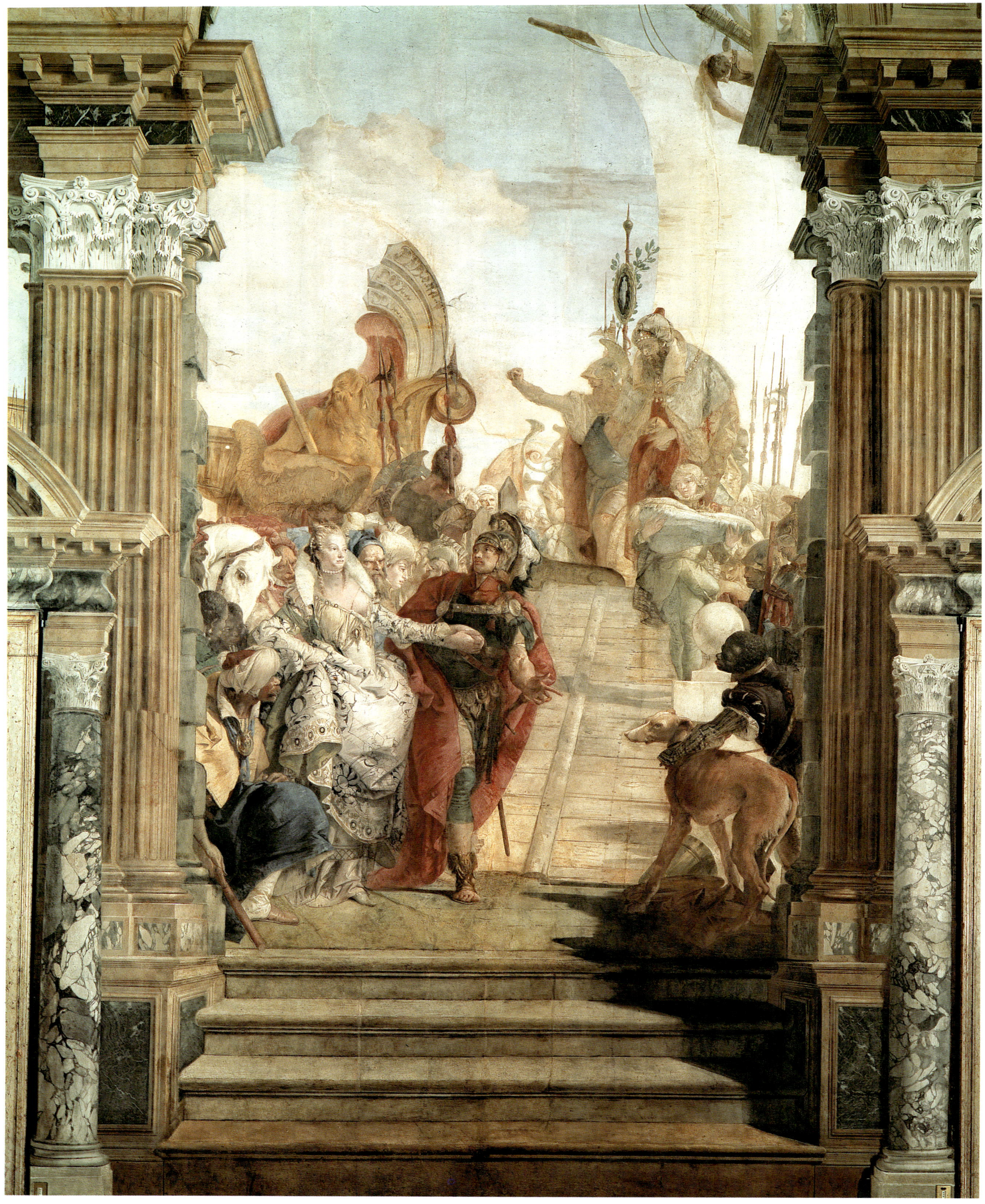

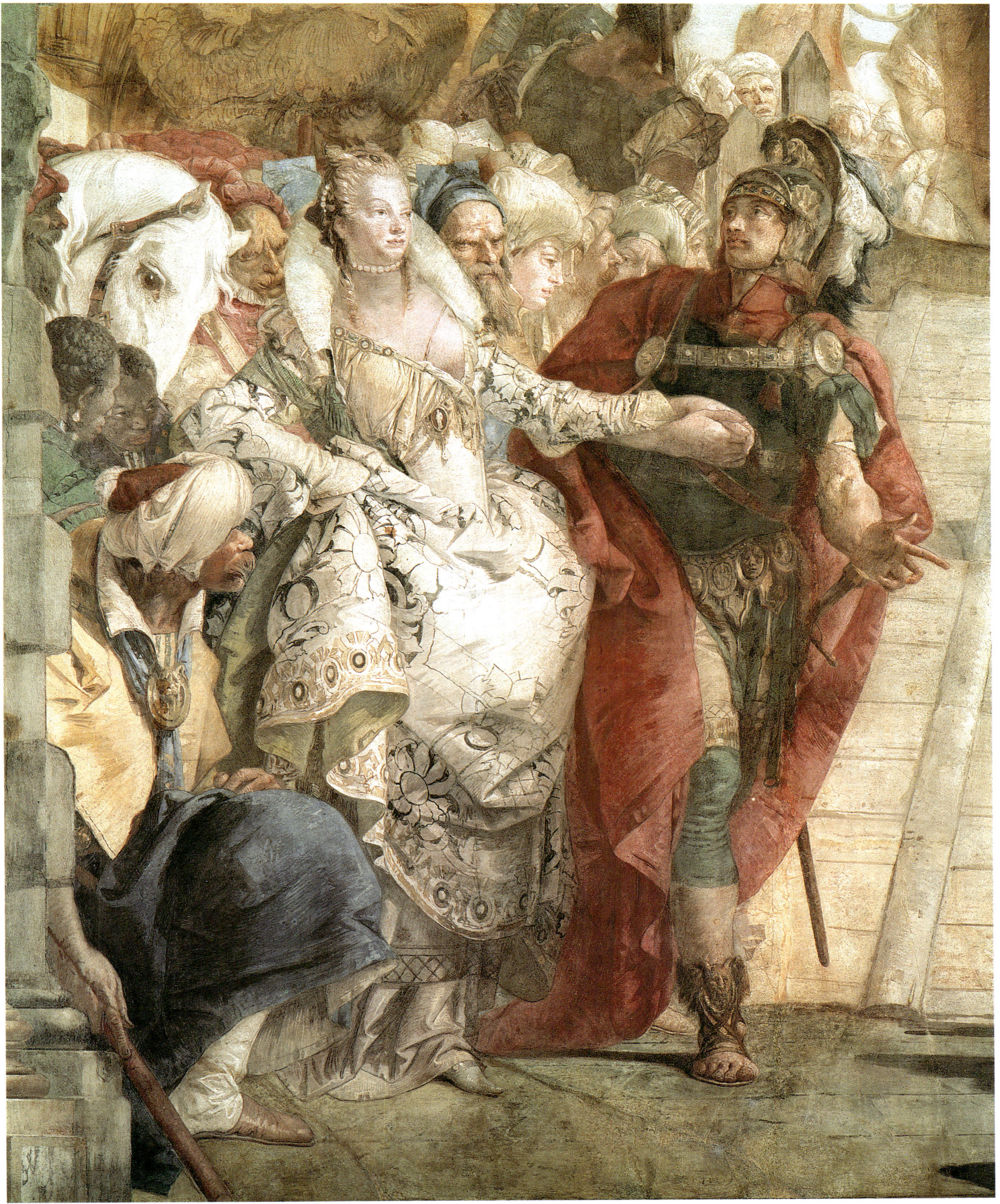

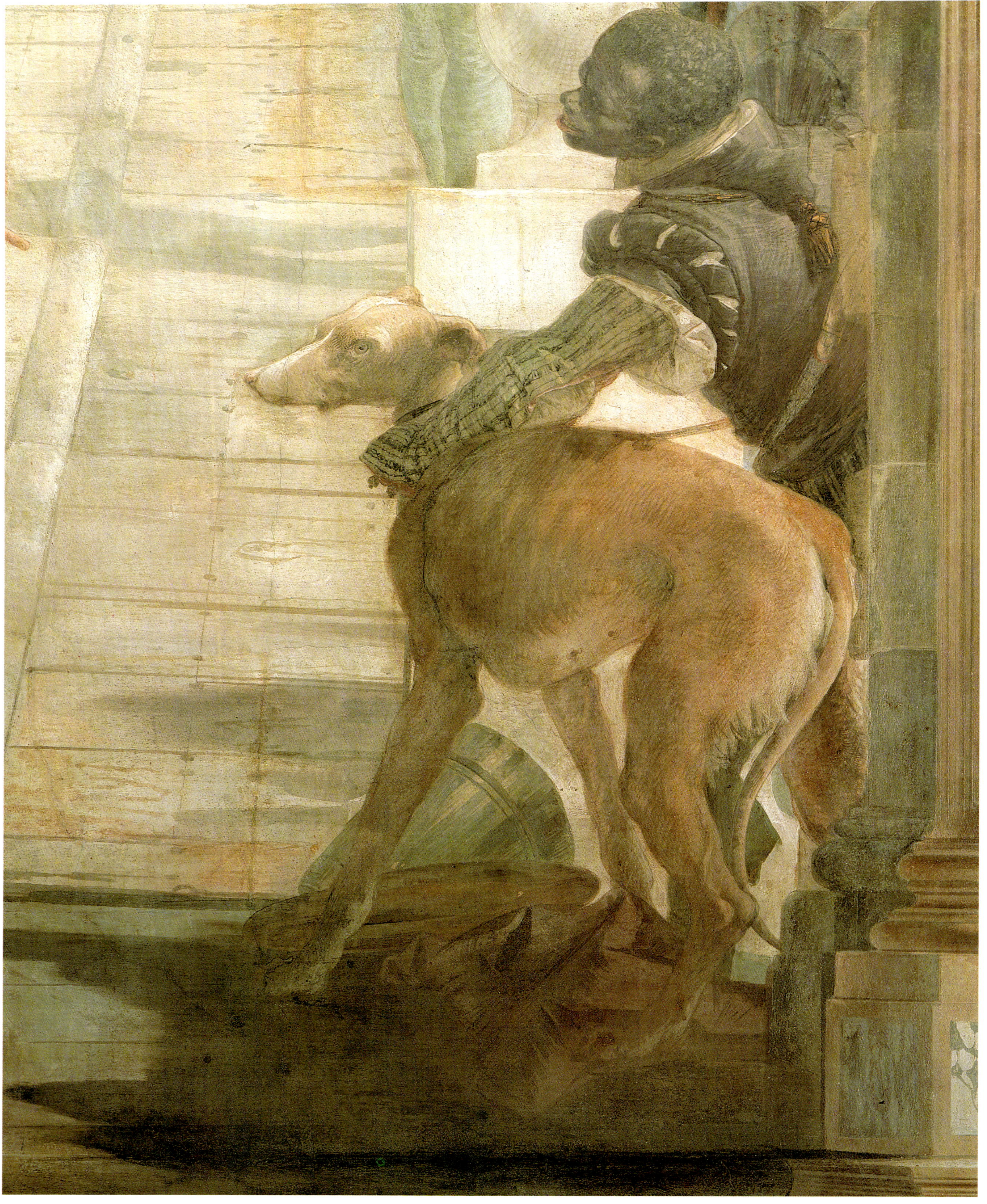

57 (opposite) *The Meeting of Anthony and Cleopatra* (detail ill. 55), 1746/47

The moor with the dog portrayed in the foreground belongs to the usual cast of characters of the history pictures of both Tiepolo and Veronese. He is more important from a compositional point of view than he is content-wise, and is intended to add to the diversity of the figures represented.

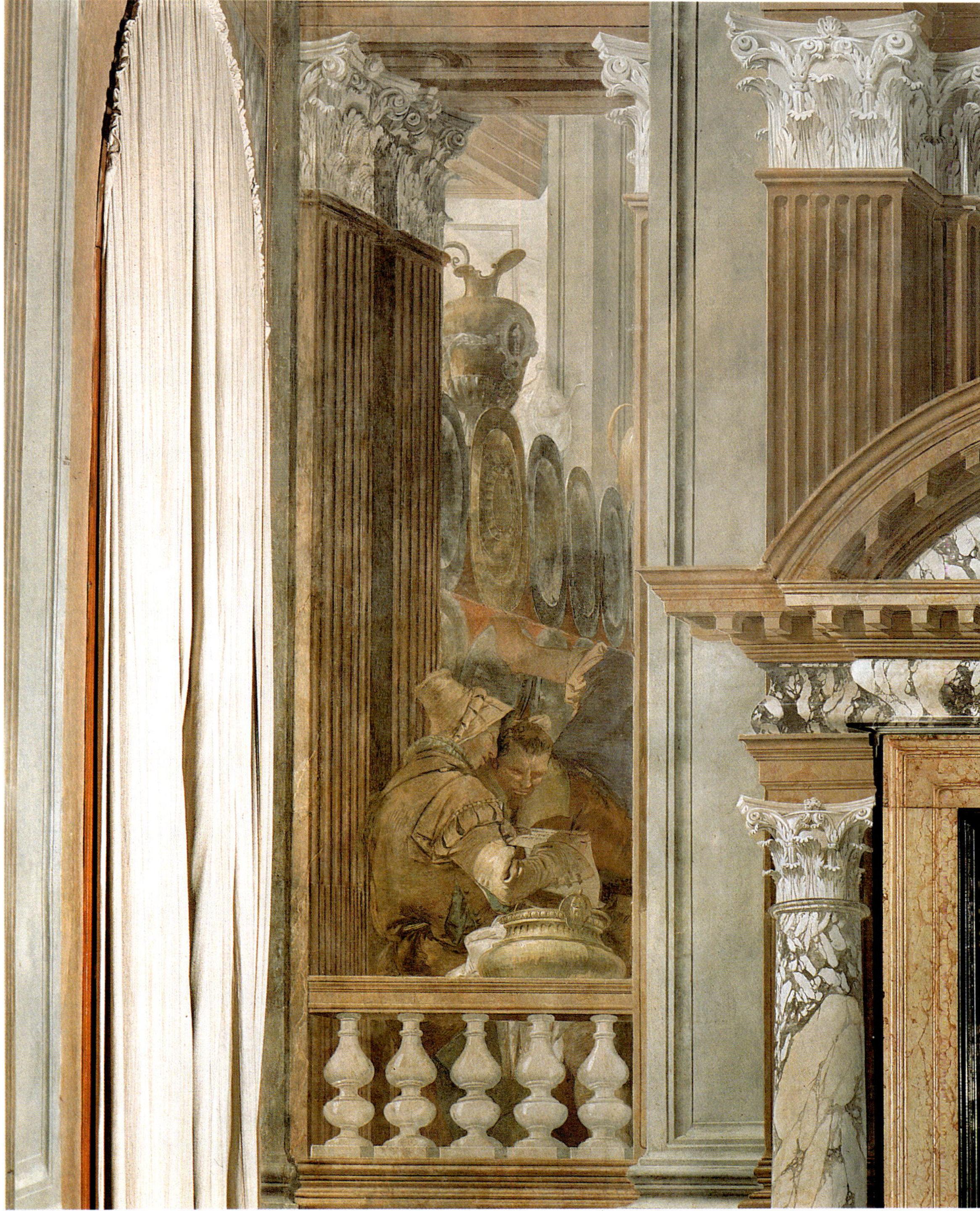

58 (right) *The Entourage of Cleopatra* (detail of the whole wall), 1746/47
Fresco
Palazzo Labia, Venice

The simulated architecture offers apparent glimpses into other rooms in the palace, giving the viewer the impression that he can watch the servants at work. This genre-like scene is related to the historical banquet as far as content is concerned, but the manner in which it is portrayed is more in keeping with the contemporary festivities in the Palazzo Labia.

The house has been moved to the left, the divine orchestra to the right, and several groups of figures have been added to the latter. In the fresco itself, the composition was expanded to an even greater extent. It shows a clear tripartite organization, with the heretics in the lower portion of the picture, the miracle in the center and the heavenly host at the very top. This makes the fresco easier for the viewer to read, and is almost certainly a concession to the clients, the Carmelites from the convent adjoining the church.

That same year, Tiepolo consigned the monumental altarpiece *The Martyrdom of St. John, Bishop of Bergamo* to the cathedral at Bergamo. The work had been commissioned two years earlier, but Tiepolo was not able to complete it until later due to the huge number of projects on which he was working simultaneously.

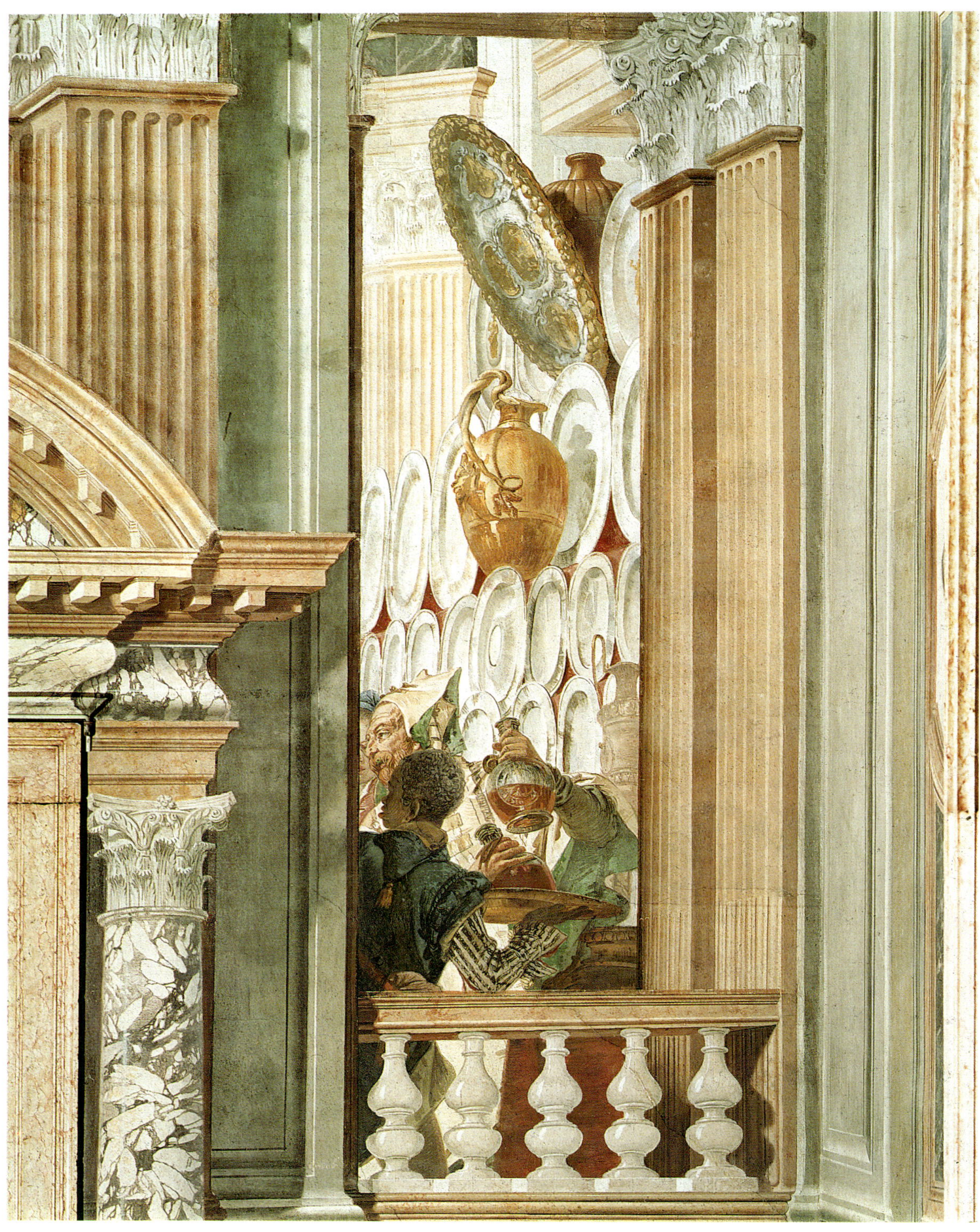

59 (left) *The Entourage of Cleopatra* (detail of the whole wall), 1746/47
Fresco
Palazzo Labia, Venice

Here, too, Tiepolo plays with different layers of reality with the aid of the fictive architecture and the contemporary appearance of the servants, so that the viewer is bound up with the events.

60 (opposite) *The Banquet of Cleopatra*, 1746/47
Fresco, 650 x 300 cm
Palazzo Labia, Venice

The table for Cleopatra's banquet is laid out in front of a portico, behind which the sails of the Roman fleet are visible. The somewhat static ordering of the main figures is relaxed by the ironic positioning in the foreground of the little dog and the dwarf, who drags himself with difficulty up the steps towards the table. Cleopatra's exposed décolleté is meant as a reference to the by now advanced stage of her relationship with Anthony. In contrast to the Melbourne picture (ill. 47), the erotic and witty interpretation of historical events is given prominence over the festive setting itself.

It is assumed that some of the secondary figures were executed by Tiepolo's eldest son, Giandomenico (1727–1804). Giandomenico worked in his father's studio and, from about 1745, became one of Giambattista's most intimate collaborators, supporting him and accompanying him on all his working trips.

One of the most important commissions carried out by Tiepolo in the 1740s was, without a doubt, the decoration of the Palazzo Labia in Venice. The Labia family were of Spanish origin and had only recently joined the Venetian patriciate. Tiepolo's frescoes reflect the family's great desire to create an impression: they are the greatest secular decoration he ever produced in Venice. The great hall of the palace, which rises up two

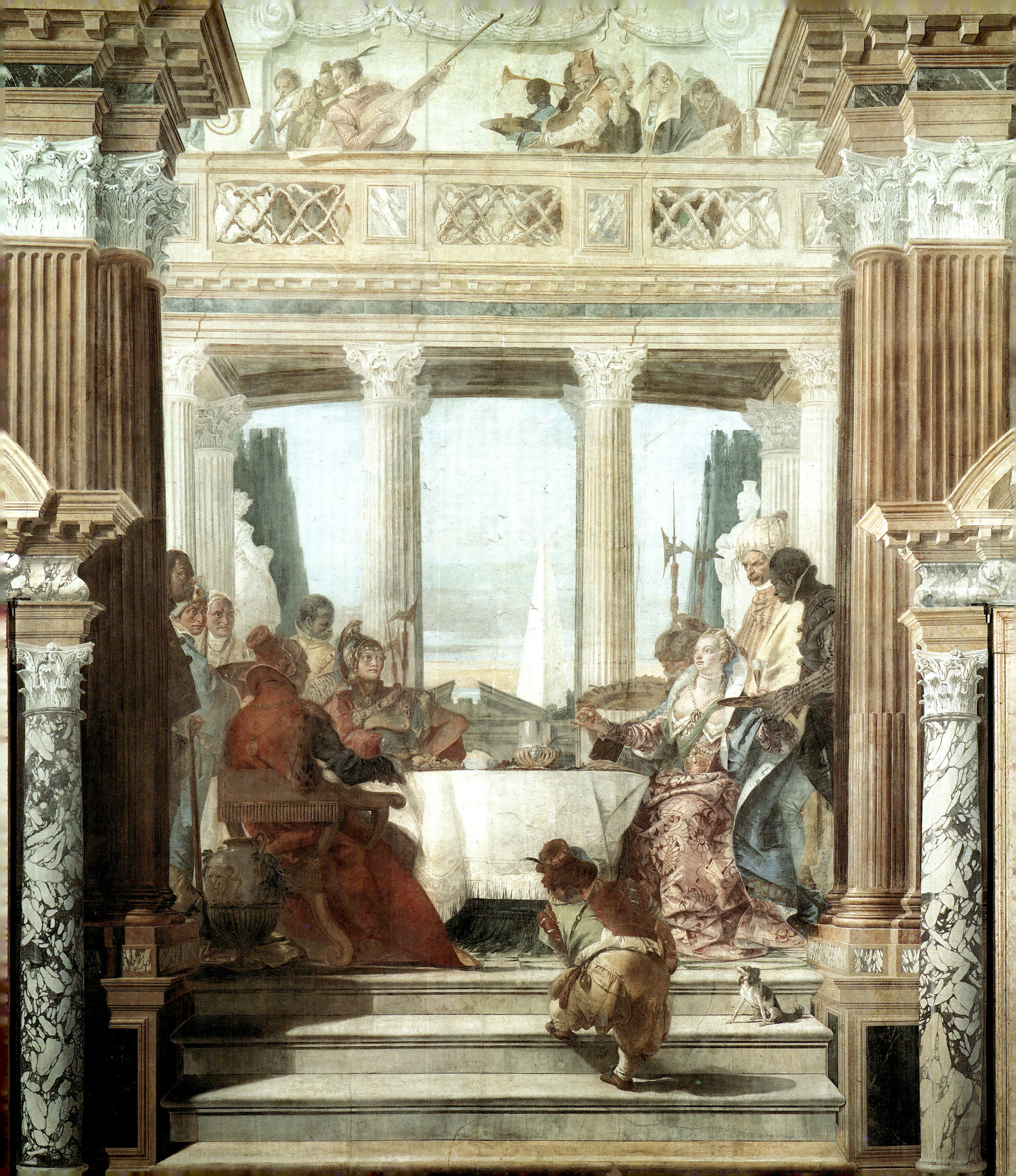

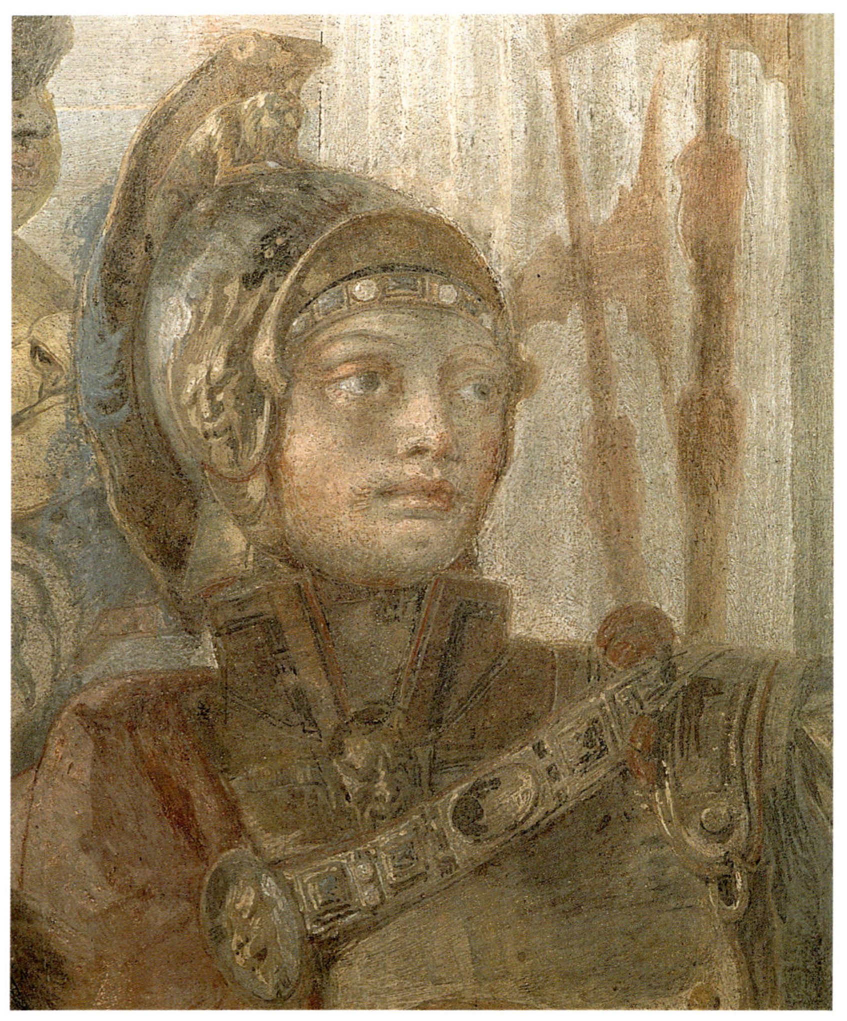

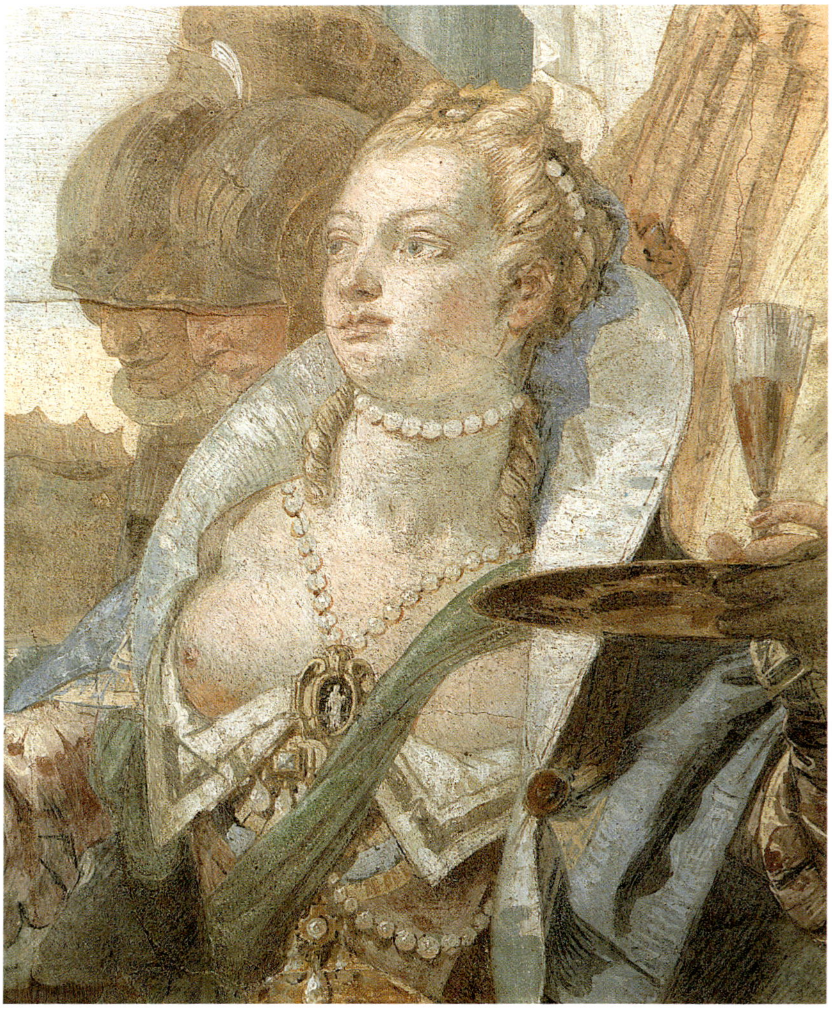

61 *The Banquet of Cleopatra* (detail ill. 60), 1746/47

For the face of Anthony Tiepolo fell back on a type of portrait which he often used in other contexts, e. g. for the god of war, Mars. This section lets us see the detailed rendering of the ornamental decoration on the armor and helmet, thus demonstrating the importance Tiepolo assigned to such apparently insignificant details.

62 *The Banquet of Cleopatra* (detail ill. 60), 1746/47

This section of the fresco shows the care Tiepolo lavished on details such as jewelry, costume and tableware.

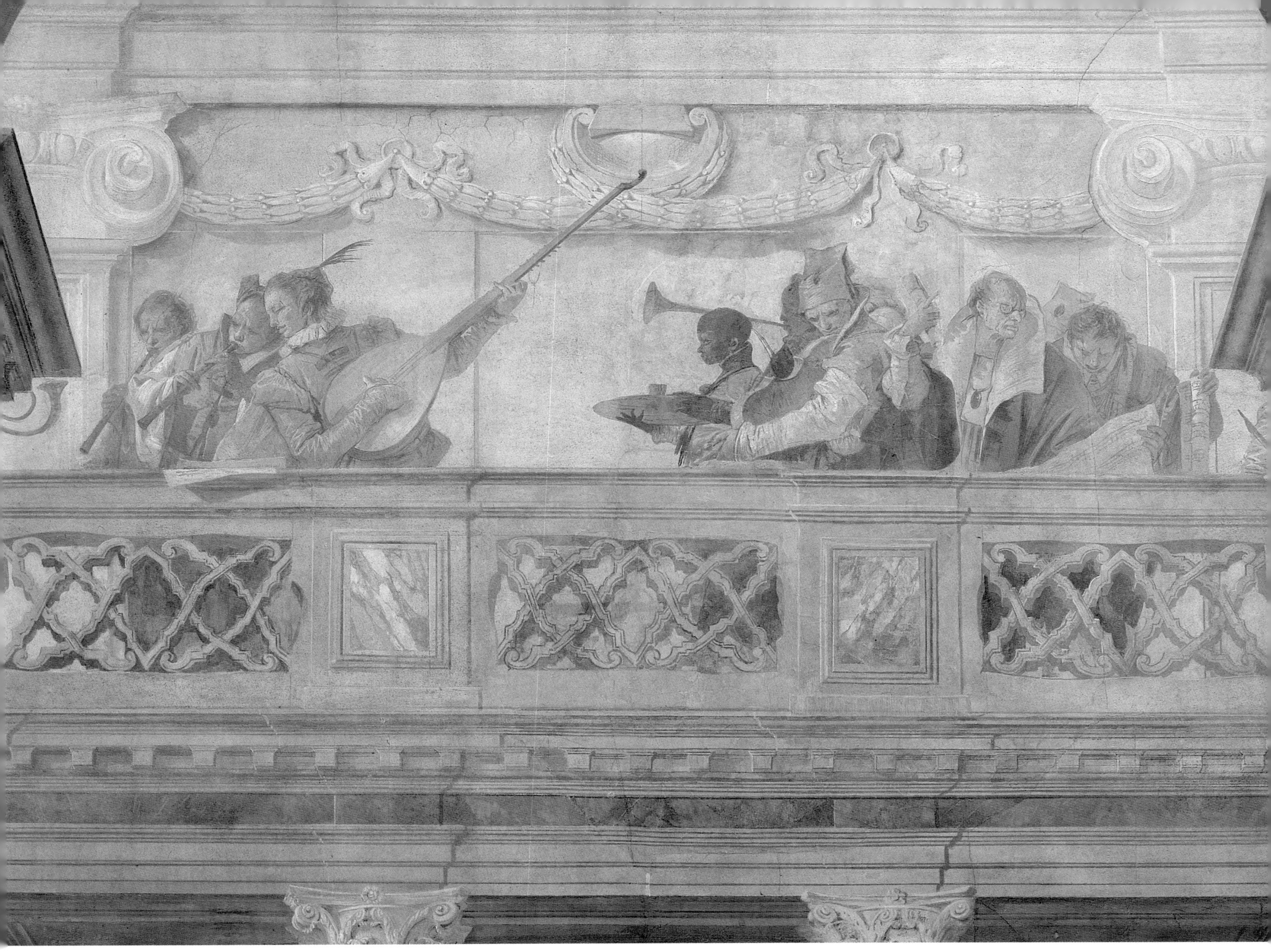

storeys, is entirely covered by frescoes, which Tiepolo executed in collaboration with Girolamo Mengozzi Colonna, the *quadratura* specialist to whom we referred earlier. The walls of the room have been opened up by an illusionistic simulated architecture, into which the real doors and windows have been integrated. In this way, a multilayered system of fictive interior and exterior spaces has been created, supported by a massive architectural framework of multicolored painted marble. Tiepolo's scenes, *The Meeting of Anthony and Cleopatra* (ills. 55–57) and *The Banquet of Cleopatra* (ills. 60–63), are staged within this illusory architecture, the scenic framework lending them a theatrical character. Tiepolo's method of representation, characterized by wit and irony, is enriched by many narrative details. Servants, soldiers, musicians and other figures on rostrums and balconies populate the room in so natural a manner, that the viewer begins to doubt whether they belong to Cleopatra's entourage or to the real staff of the palace (ills. 58, 59, 63–66). The central ceiling fresco depicts *The Triumph of Bellerophon over Time* (ills. 67–70), flanked by four monochrome scenes of mythological and allegorical characters (ill. 71). The adjoining Hall of Mirrors was also decorated with the ceiling fresco *The Triumph of Zephyr and Flora*.

It was not until he had finished work on the Palazzo Labia that Tiepolo was able to complete the ceiling fresco in the chapterhouse of the Scuola Grande dei Carmini in Venice, which he had begun in 1743. The canvas *The Virgin Mary presenting the Scapular to St. Simon Stock* (ill. 72) occupies the center of the ceiling. The picture shows the Virgin Mary bestowing the scapular on Simon Stock, an Englishman who created the Third Order of the Carmelites in the 13th century

63 *The Banquet of Cleopatra* (detail ill. 60), 1746/47

On the one hand, the musicians on the balcony in the background are an extension of the banqueting scene. Yet, like the fictive architecture, they could just as well be part of the courtly celebrations taking place in the Palazzo Labia itself. They belong to the group of figures used by Tiepolo to establish a connection between the historical representations and the real world of the viewer.

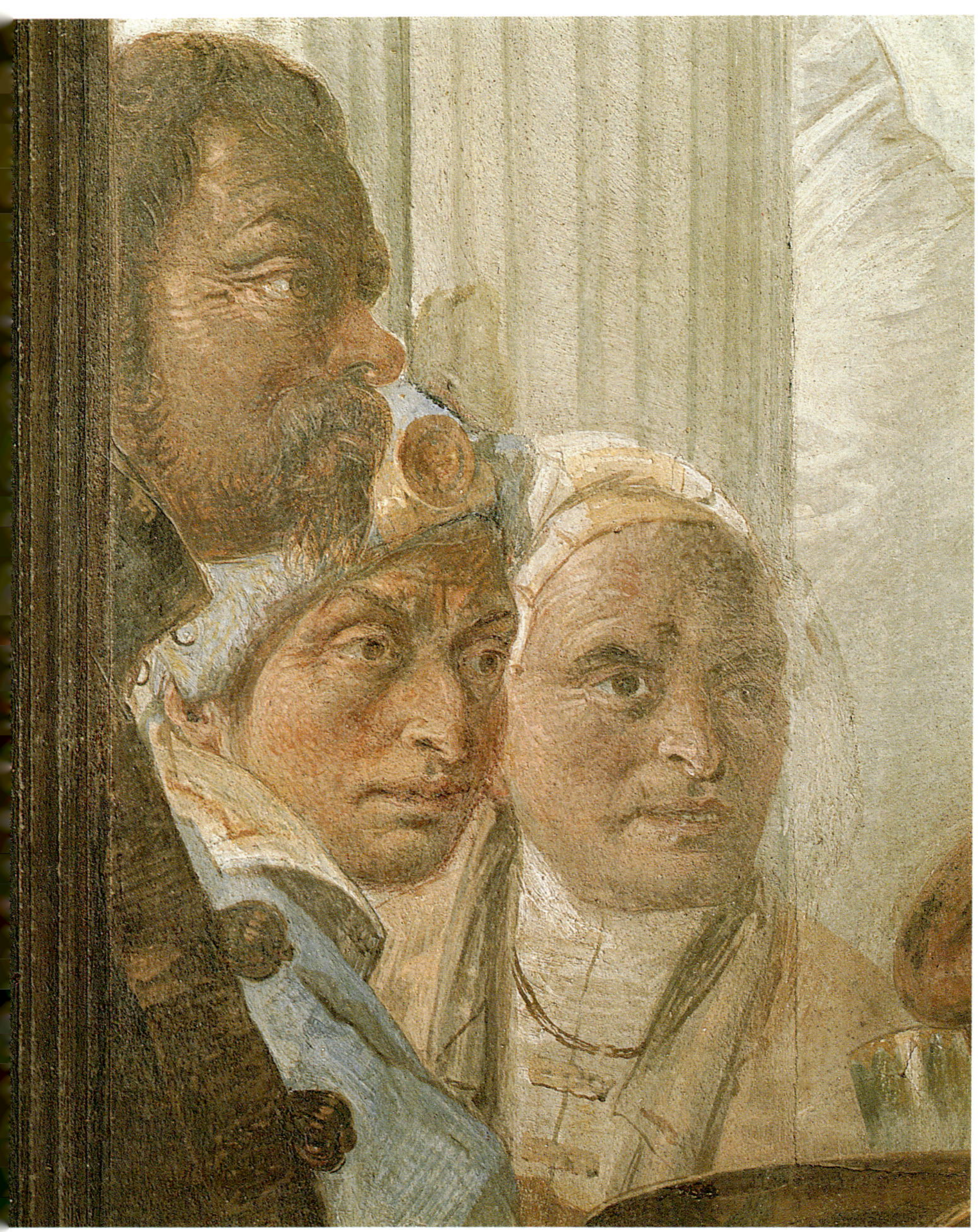

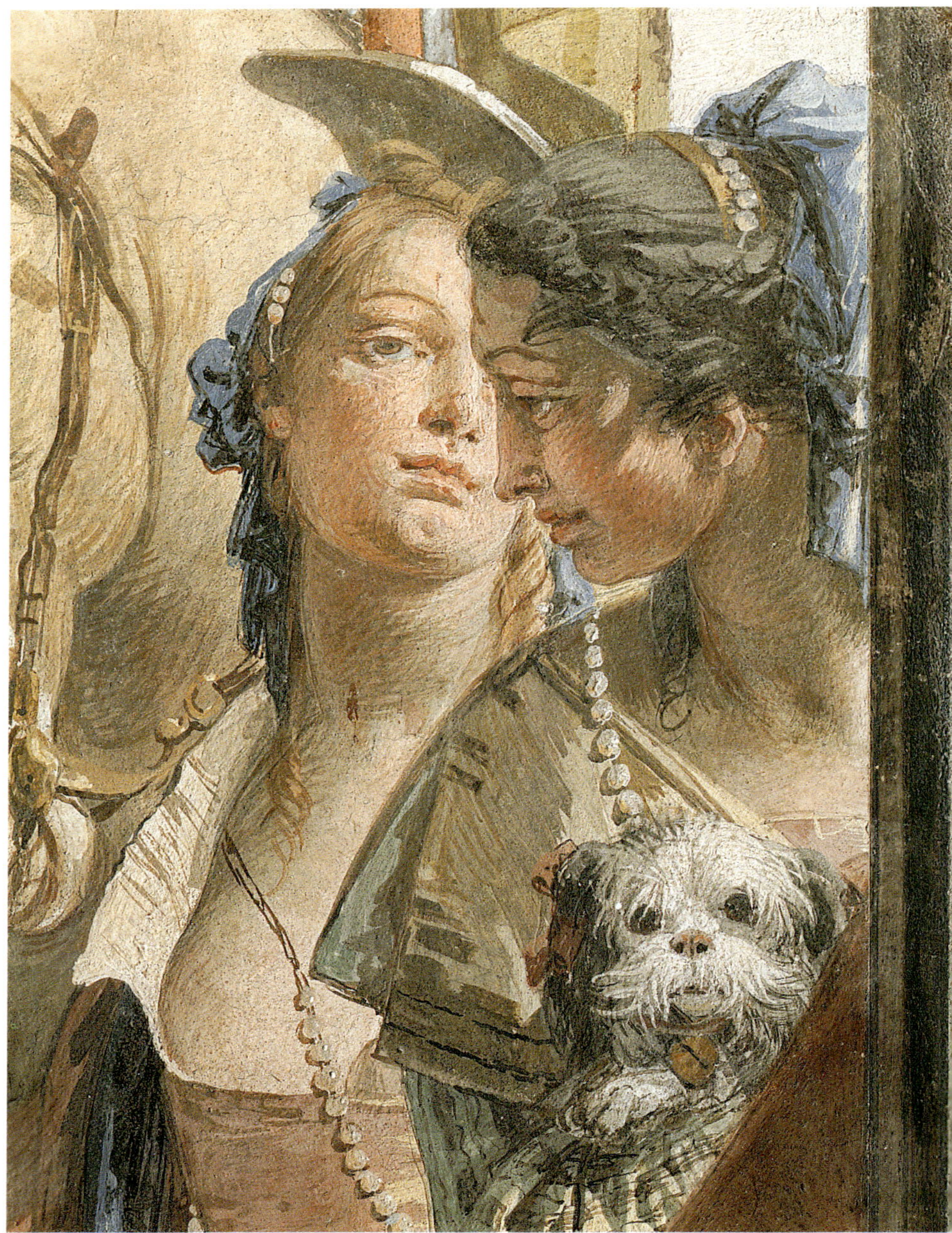

64 (above left) *The Banquet of Cleopatra* (detail ill. 60), 1746/47

This section shows the faces of three of Anthony's companions and demonstrates the careful rendering of the physiognomies.

65 (above right) *The Entourage of Cleopatra* (detail of the whole wall), 1746/47
Fresco
Palazzo Labia, Venice

The two female servants with the dog are typical secondary figures, used time and again by Tiepolo in numerous works to enrich the main action. The special way in which the faces have been rendered impresses here. The one to the fore is in half shadow, the one behind brilliantly lit, thus creating a spatial gradation.

and founded monasteries in Cambridge, Oxford, Paris and Bologna. The perspectival composition of the painting presents the figures *di sotto in sù* and takes into account the relatively low ceiling of the room. Around the central picture, Tiepolo grouped smaller canvases of different shapes and sizes representing the angels, with objects relevant to the scapular, and the Virtues. The nine canvases are set in a white and gold stucco decoration.

The altarpiece *The Virgin Mary with Saints Catherine, Rose of Lima and Agnes of Montepulciano* (ill. 73) for the Jesuit church of Santa Maria del Rosario in Venice, commissioned in 1739, was only now completed and installed above the first altar on the right of the entrance to the church in 1748. The church is dedicated to the Virgin Mary, St. Dominic and the Rosary, and Tiepolo was meant to contribute, as part of its overall programme, a representation of three female saints of the Dominican Order, who, in their visions, hold the Christ Child in their arms. The brilliant accents of red, blue and golden yellow in the figure of the Virgin, the crystal clear rendering of the robes, and the particular beauty of the faces of the saints: all of these are striking. The latter element was later deemed inappropriate to the religious subject matter and Tiepolo was criticized for having placed the main emphasis in his portraits on worldly attributes.

The bright coloring of this work stands comparison with the altarpiece *The Last Communion of St. Lucy* (ill. 74) which was executed at roughly the same time (1747/48) for the Cornaro chapel in the Church of the Apostles in Venice. The painting depicts the last communion of the saint before her martyrdom against an imposing architectural background. In the foreground, a bloodied knife and a platter with the gouged-out eyes already point to her gruesome fate.

In the course of 1750, shortly before his departure for Würzburg, Tiepolo created a few more works worthy of mention. The *Portrait of Procurator Captain Dolfin* (ill. 75), now in the Fondazione Querini Stampalia in Venice, is a masterpiece of portraiture. It is a posthumous portrait of the Dolfin Daniele IV (1656–1729)

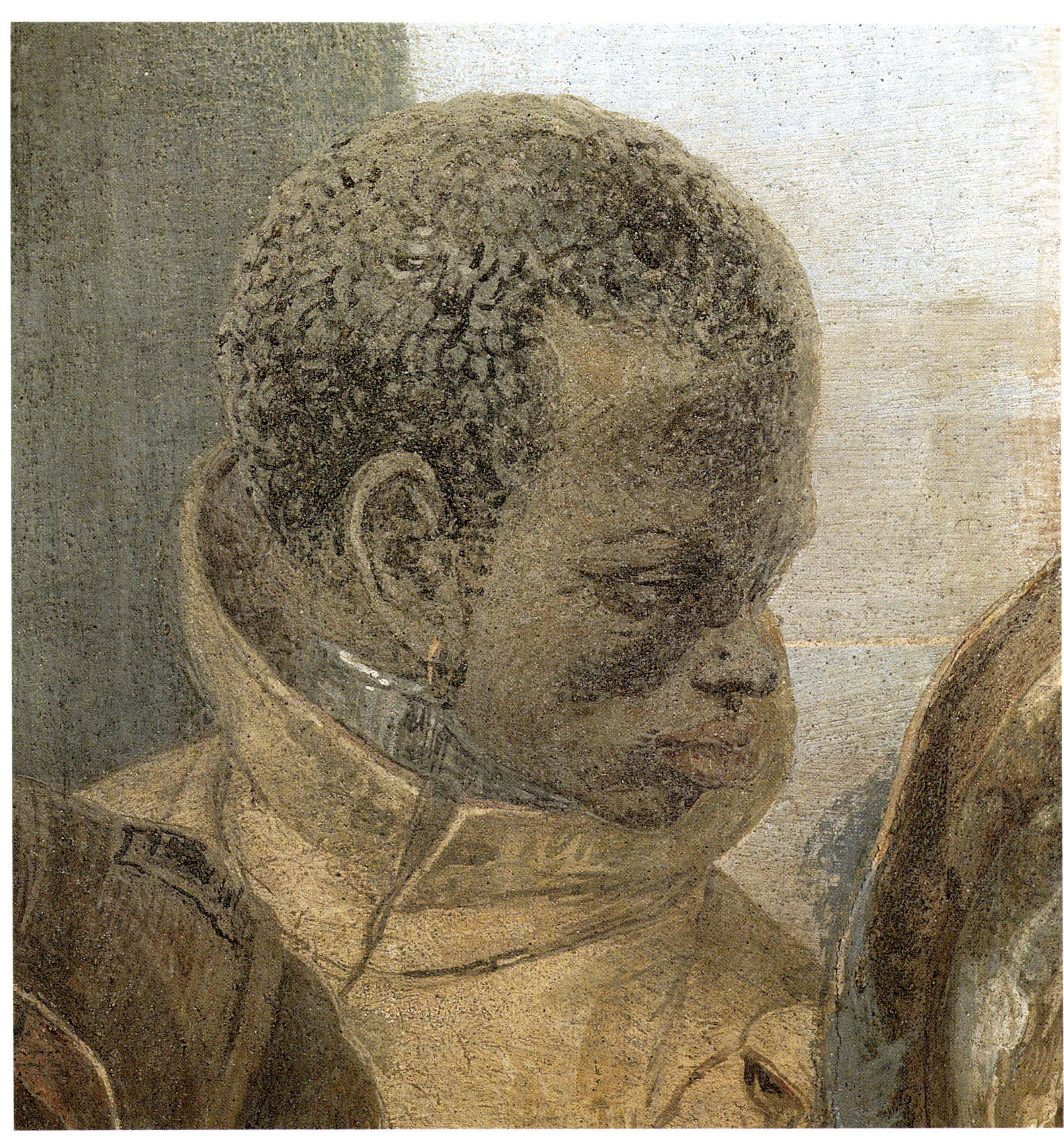

66 *The Banquet of Cleopatra* (detail ill. 60), 1746/47

Moorish servants already belonged to Veronese's typical cast of characters for a banqueting scene. Tiepolo also made frequent use of this pictorial motif.

and depicts the hero of the Venetian fleet in the war against the Turks in awe-inspiring pose way above the viewer's vantage point. The rich costume of red brocade and furs especially stands out against the neutral, dark background.

During this period, Tiepolo was also working on the canvases for the decoration of the Palazzo Barbaro in Venice, to which Antonio Zanchi (1631–1722), Sebastiano Ricci and Giambattista Piazzetta also contributed works. In addition to the great ceiling fresco *The Apotheosis of the Barbaro Family* (now in the Metropolitan Museum in New York), the artist delivered four *supra porte* paintings depicting episodes from the lives of famous women of antiquity. These can now be seen in the Städtische Kunstsammlungen in Augsburg, in the Necchi Collection in Pavia, in the Royal Museum of Fine Arts in Copenhagen and in the National Gallery of Art in Washington.

Tiepolo painted the likeness of *St. James of Compostella*, the Spanish patron saint, for the Spanish ambassador in London, Ricardo Wall. It is now housed in the Szépmüvésteti Múzeum in Budapest. The dramatic effect of the scene derives from the picture's strong chromatic contrasts. It portrays the Apostle as a victorious warrior in the struggle against the Moors rather than as a holy figure, directly facing the viewer on his white steed in a most impressive fashion. The work clearly refers to the 16th century tradition of equestrian portraits. Together with the monumental canvas *The Patron Saints of the Crotta Family* (now in the Städelsches Kunstinstitut in Frankfurt), *St. James of Compostella* was one of Tiepolo's last works before his departure for Würzburg.

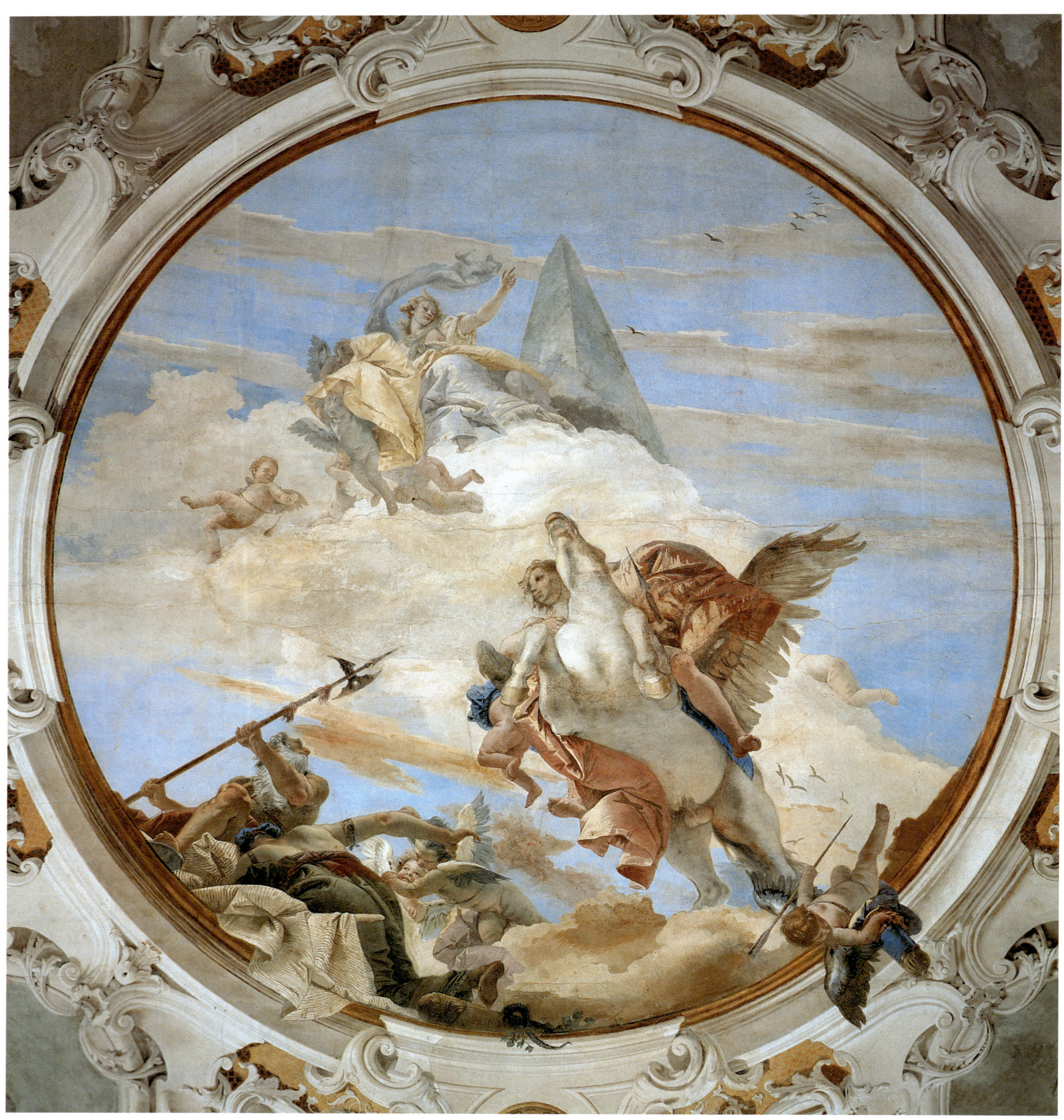

67 (opposite) *Bellerophon on Pegasus*, 1746/47
Fresco, ca. 600 cm diameter
Palazzo Labia, Venice

The ceiling fresco is conceived as an illusionistic view of the heavens, where Bellerophon rides upon the white winged-steed Pegasus towards Glory, untroubled by the old man with the lance at the bottom of the picture, who can no longer harm him. Glory is personified by a female figure in golden yellow robes, floating on a cloud next to a pyramid, the traditional symbol of eternity.

68 (right) *The Winds* (detail), 1746/47
Fresco
Palazzo Labia, Venice

This section shows two wind gods, whose exaggerated blowing gesture and faces distorted with effort demonstrate Tiepolo's sense of exaggeration and droll style of portrayal.

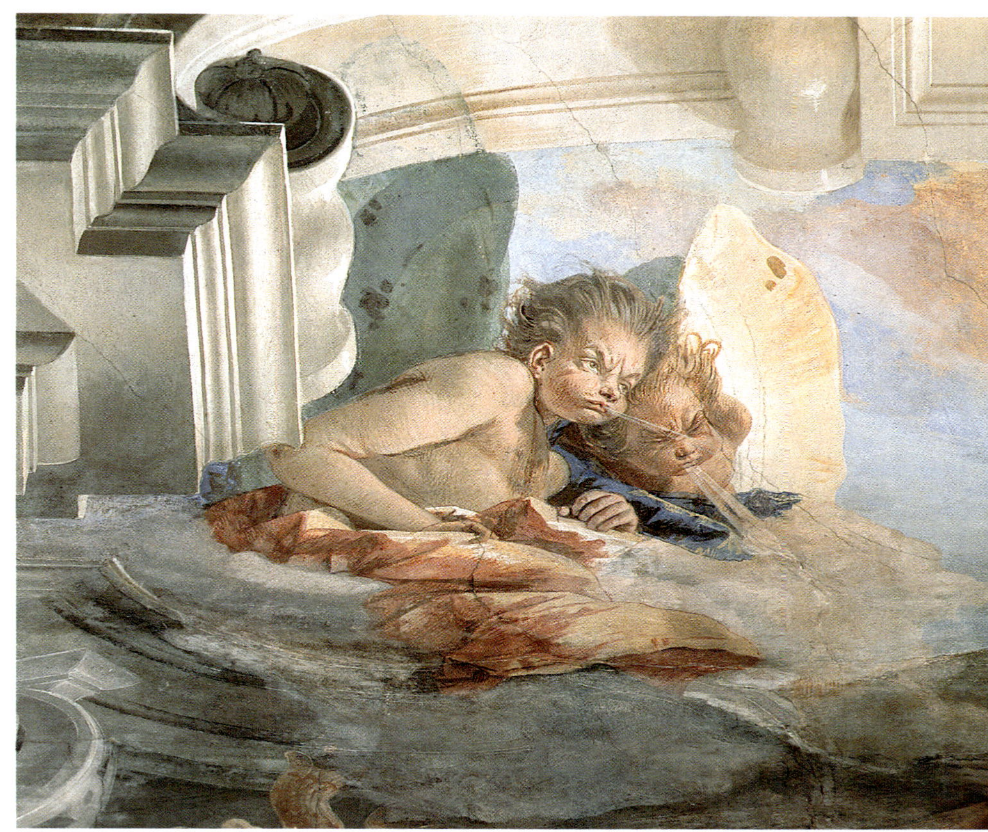

69 (below) *Bellerophon on Pegasus* (detail ill. 67), 1746/47

In contrast to the turbulent figural grouping of Bellerophon on Pegasus, the portrayal of Glory next to the pyramid, accompanied by several *putti*, represents an oasis of peace in the overall composition, in keeping with her thematic meaning of timeless Eternity.

70 (below right) *Bellerophon on Pegasus* (detail ill. 67), 1746/47

This section illustrates the daring compositional structure and the extreme perspective in which Pegasus and Bellerophon appear. These devices further reinforce the idea of the horse galloping forward, and this is given additional emphasis by the figure of Amor who almost tumbles out of the picture, head over heels, at its lower edge.

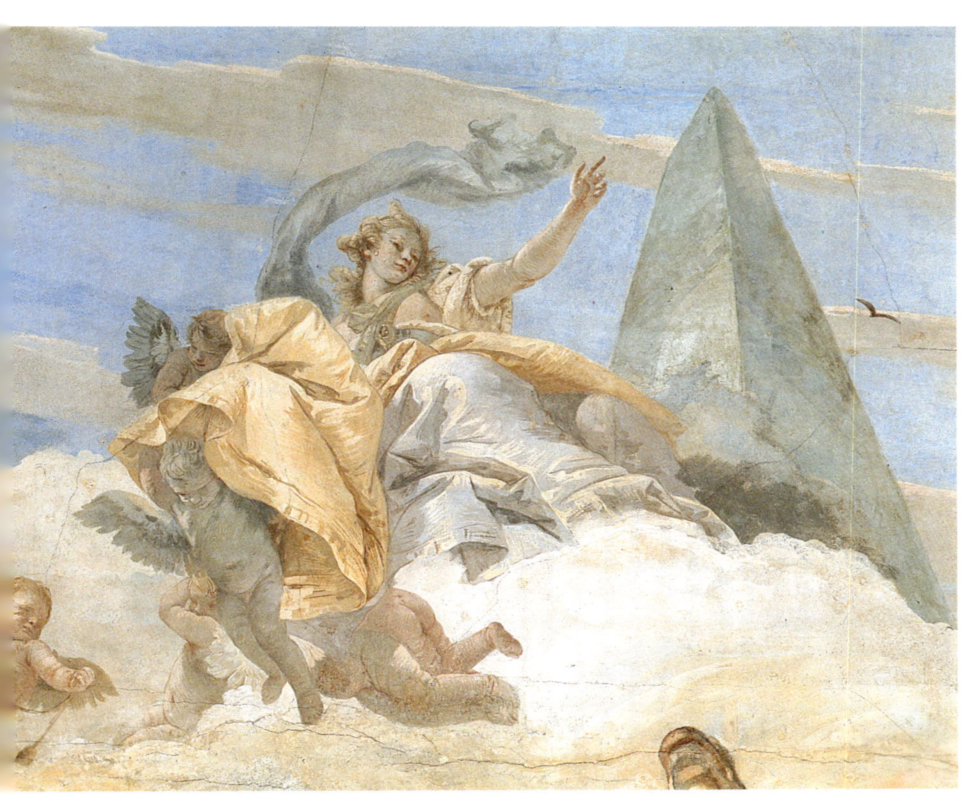

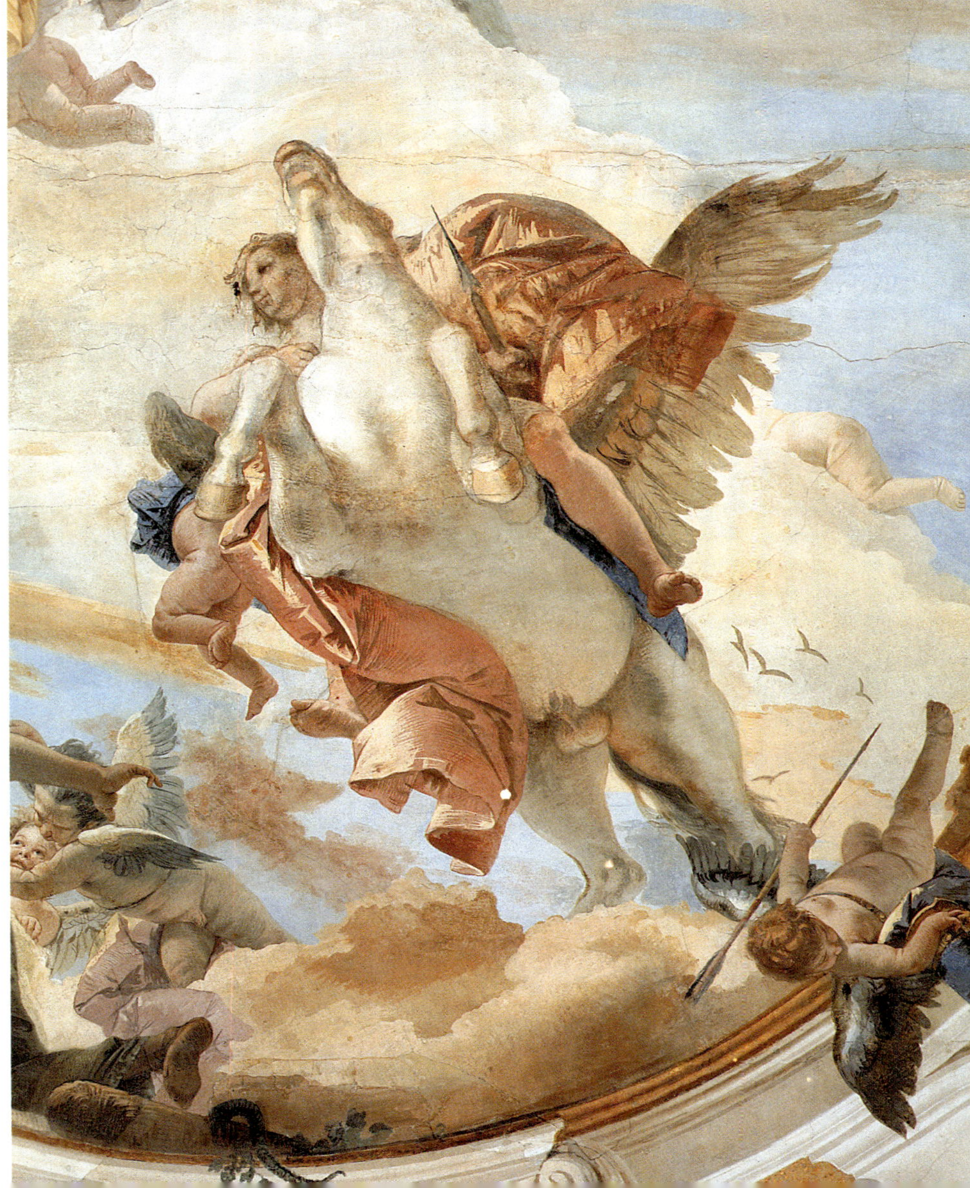

72 (right) *The Virgin Mary presenting the Scapular to St. Simon Stock*, ca. 1748/49
Oil on canvas, 533 x 432 cm
Scuola Grande dei Carmini, Venice

The picture shows the gift of the scapular to St. Simon Stock. The saint kneels in profile on a stone pedestal before the manifestation of the Virgin Mary, borne by a host of angels, while receiving the scapular from an angel behind him. Beneath the pedestal, a burial ground is indicated in dismal colors. According to Christian tradition, the Marian scapular promised those wearing it a reduced punishment in Purgatory. The cult of the scapular began in 1322 following a papal bull, and achieved great popularity during the Counter-Reformation.

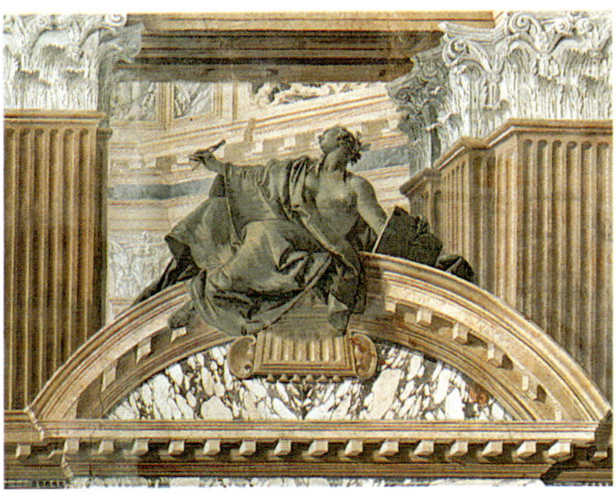

71 (above) *Allegory of Architecture*, 1746/47
Fresco
Palazzo Labia, Venice

The personification of Architecture appears above the door, recognizable by the slab of stone and the compasses. This representation belongs to the monochrome allegorical and mythological figures who are integrated into the simulated architecture.

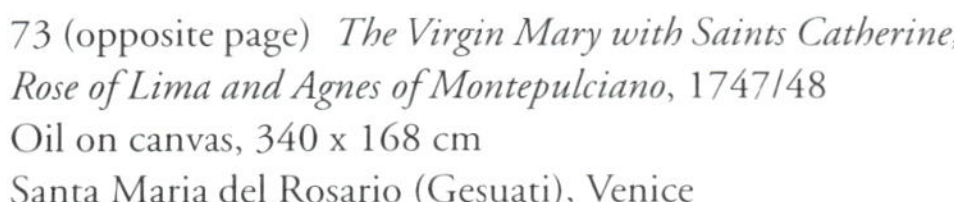

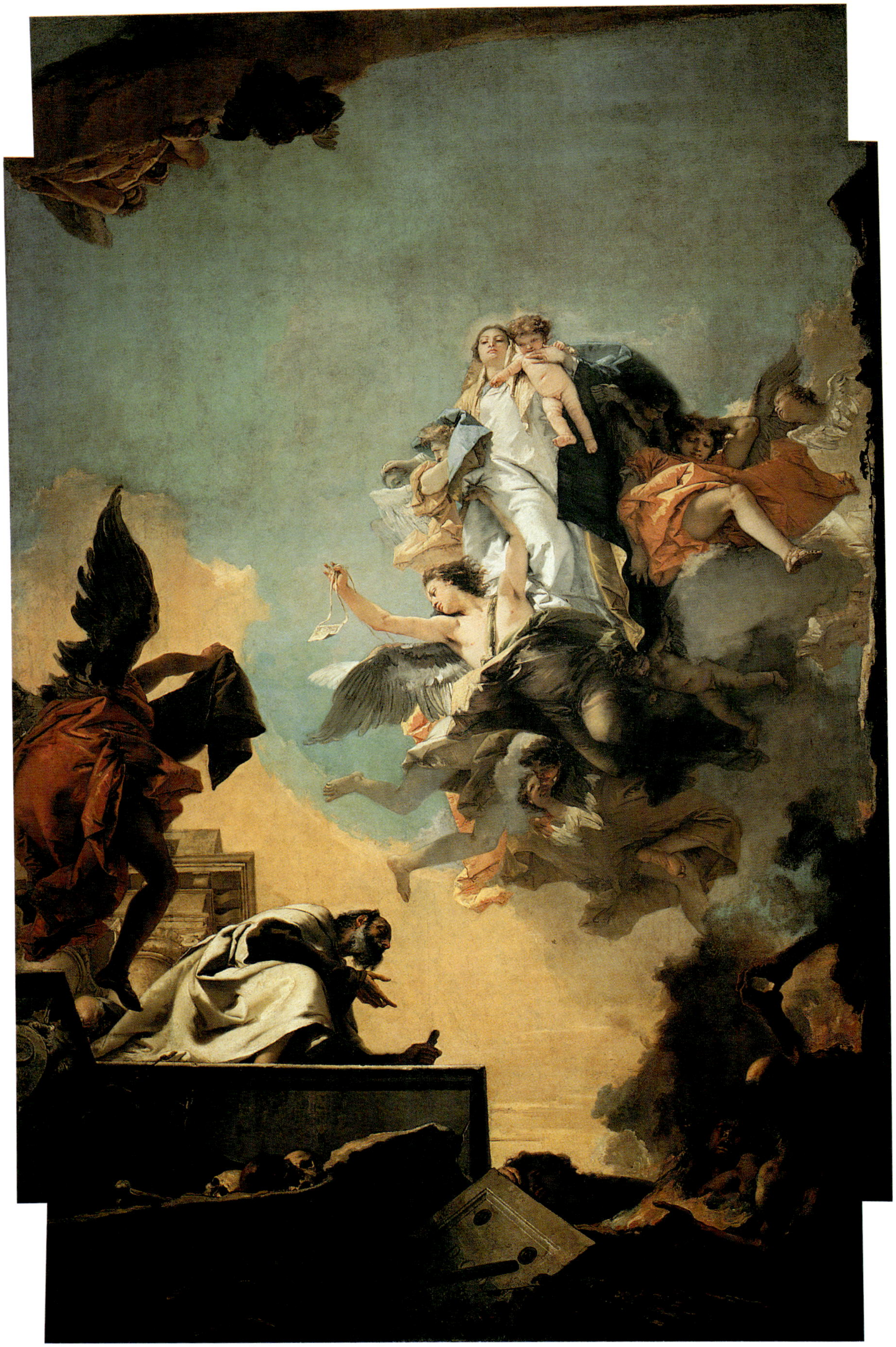

73 (opposite page) *The Virgin Mary with Saints Catherine, Rose of Lima and Agnes of Montepulciano*, 1747/48
Oil on canvas, 340 x 168 cm
Santa Maria del Rosario (Gesuati), Venice

The Virgin Mary hovers on a throne-like golden yellow cloud beneath a baldachin in front of Renaissance architecture, dressed in brilliant reds and blues and accompanied by angels. In the foreground are the three saints, all members of the Dominican order. Agnes of Montepulciano (1274–1317) sits at the front and meditates over a small crucifix. Her robes illusionistically jut out into the viewer's space. To her left stands St. Catherine of Siena (1347–1380) with a crown of thorns and a crucifix, and St. Rose of Lima (1586–1617), holding the Christ Child in her arms.

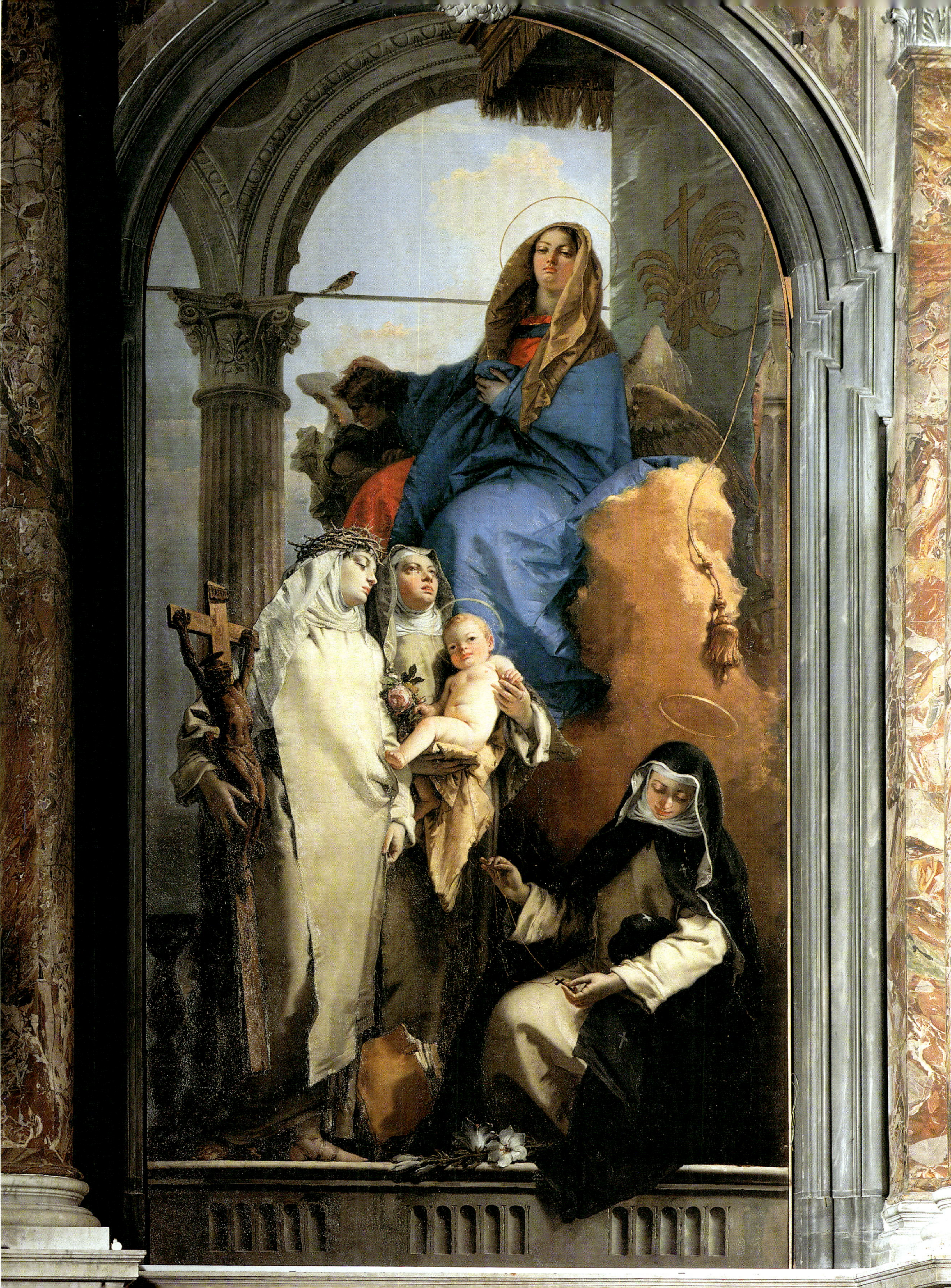

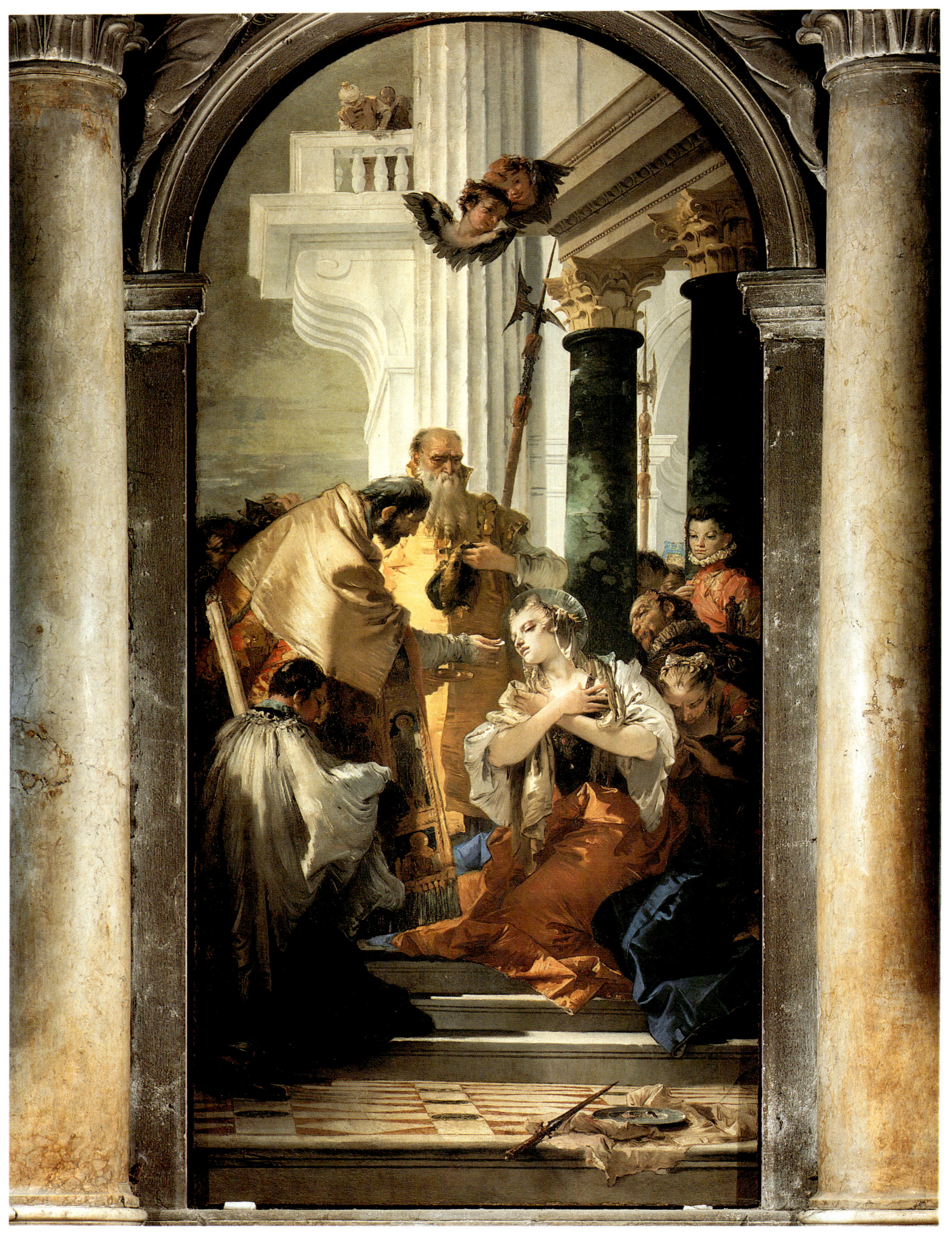

74 (opposite) *The Last Communion of St. Lucy*, 1747/48
Oil on canvas, 222 x 101 cm
Santi Apostoli, Venice

With arms crossed, St. Lucy kneels before a priest to receive the last communion. Her half-closed eyes and the elegiac expression on her face hint at her later fate. The priests and secular dignitaries who surround her wear magnificent robes, whose beautifully rendered material and brilliant colors are of particular intensity. The scene takes place in front of an imposing palace, upon whose balustrade Tiepolo has again placed spectators. While the bloody knife and the platter with the gouged-out eyes in the foreground are a drastic reminder of the impending martyrdom, the heads of angels which hover over the saint announce her entry into the Kingdom of Heaven.

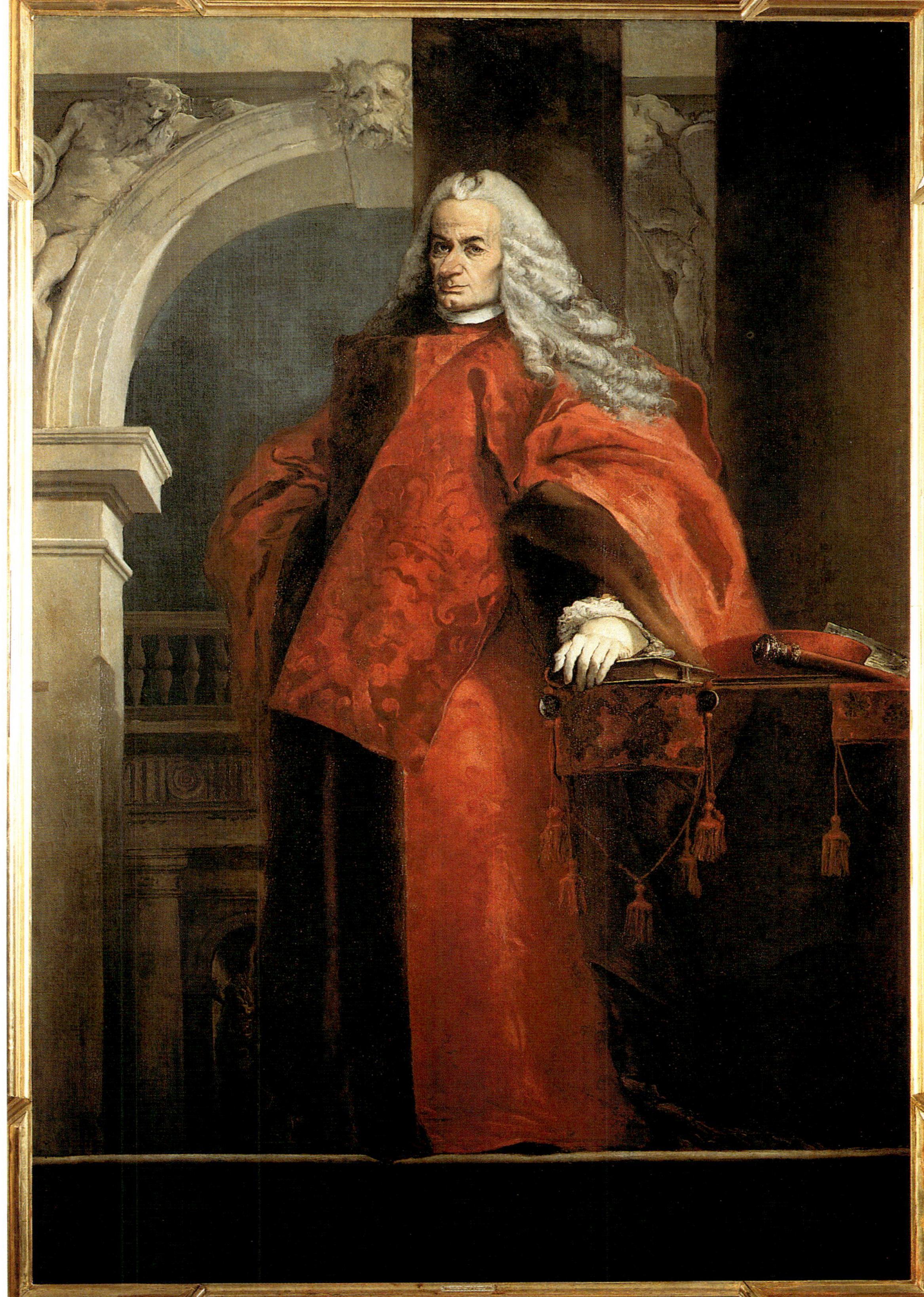

75 (right) *Portrait of Procurator Captain Dolfin*, 1749/50
Oil on canvas, 235 x 158 cm
Fondazione Querini Stampalia, Venice

The posthumous portrait shows the 17th-century war hero of the Venetian fleet as an imposing presence in red, fur-trimmed silk brocade and white periwig. His hand rests on a book as he presents the insignia of his office as procurator. The dark background architecture, executed in dull colors, provides an especially effective contrast to the subject of the portrait.

The Würzburg Years 1750–1753

76 *Apollo leading Beatrice of Burgundy toward the Genius Imperii* (detail ill. 77), 1751

Seen in daring foreshortening from below, Apollo's wildly galloping steeds powerfully draw the chariot of the sun up through the skies. The bride, Beatrice of Burgundy, sits at the front of the chariot, dressed in white silk and accompanied by *putti* and a female figure. Apollo towers over her from behind as he turns upwards with outstretched arms, the rising sun shining behind him.

77 (following double page)
Apollo leading Beatrice of Burgundy toward the Genius Imperii, 1751
Fresco, 900 x 1800 cm
Imperial Hall of the Residenz, Würzburg

The personification of Burgundy, in the shape of Princess Beatrice on the right-hand side, is conducted by the sun-god Apollo towards the Genius Imperii (the Genius of the Holy Roman Empire of the German Nation), who is enthroned on a high stone podium on the left-hand side in the form of a youthful ideal figure. The goddess Fame hovers above him, while a winged putto to his right hands him the Franconian sword. The personification of Religion appears at the foot of the throne, and the Genius of Franconia, with the red and white Franconian flag, kneels to the left above the river-god Main and a nymph. The figure of Hymen, the god of marriage, who hovers, torch in hand, above the horses that draw the sun-chariot, is a further allusion to the union of the two main protagonists.

In December 1750, Tiepolo, accompanied by his sons Giandomenico and Lorenzo (1736–1776), arrived in Würzburg where, at the invitation of Prince-Bishop Carl Phillip von Greiffenclau, he was to fresco the large dining room – known as the *Kaisersaal*, or Imperial Hall – in the newly-built Residence of the Prince-Bishops designed by the architect Balthasar Neumann (1687–1753). Both native and Italian artists worked on the decoration of the room, including the Lombardian stucco artist Antonio Bossi (died 1764), who was responsible for the gold and white stucco decoration on the ceiling. Prince-Bishop von Greiffenclau had originally intended the Swabian Johann Zick (1702–1762) to create the frescoes, but instead gave the commission to Giuseppe Visconti from Milan. The latter began work on the fresco *The Marriage of the Emperor Frederick Barbarossa to Beatrice of Burgundy* in October 1749, but the Prince-Bishop disliked his style of execution so much that he soon began looking around for another artist. Thanks to the intervention of Lorenz Jacob Mehling, a merchant who had long been resident in Venice, the Prince-Bishop finally succeeded in gaining the services of Tiepolo. While still in Venice, the arist received a plan of the room and of the decorative programme worked out by the Jesuit fathers Seyfried and Gilbert back in 1735, along with the promise of a handsome salary – three times as much as he had received for painting the ceiling of the church of Santa Maria di Nazareth (Scalzi) in Venice.

The decorative programme of the Imperial Hall comprizes the central ceiling fresco – an allegorical portrayal of the Genius Imperii (ills. 76, 77), towards whom Apollo is conducting the Burgundian bride – and two historical scenes, *The Marriage of the Emperor Frederick Barbarossa to Beatrice of Burgundy* (ill. 81) and *The Investiture of Herold as Duke of Franconia* by Emperor Frederick Barbarossa at the Imperial Diet in Würzburg in 1168 (ill. 82), on either side of the room. Representations of mercenary footsoldiers and courtiers under the windows, monochrome allegorical scenes in the lunettes and *supra porte* paintings by Tiepolo's son Giandomenico complete the decoration of the room. Tiepolo had begun preparatory sketches as soon as he arrived in Würzburg; the ceiling fresco was then painted in the spring of 1751 and the two lateral wall frescoes were completed the following year.

The magnificently-decorated Imperial Hall is the highpoint of the ceremonial sequence of public rooms in the Residence. The room is high and wide, well-lit by tall windows on three sides, and is situated in the central axis of the Residence overlooking the garden. It rises from the ground plan of an elongated octagon and is vaulted by an imposing oval cupola with ten, for the most part windowed, lunettes. Having passed through the White Room, with its neutral white stucco decoration by Antonio Bossi, the visitor enters the Imperial Hall someway down its length and is at first overwhelmed by the polychromatic variety of its decoration: by the walls with its divisions of half-columns in red stucco marble, by the white and gold stucco decoration of the vault, by the areas of shellwork, by the sculptures and, not least, by Tiepolo's frescoes. In the Imperial Hall, architecture, ornamental structuring and painted decoration form an incomparable unity and so create one of the most beautiful secular rooms of the Baroque period (ill. 80).

Tiepolo's frescoes, too, have been designed to make an impact on the viewer as he enters the room. The central ceiling fresco is intended to bring together the themes of the two wall paintings, and to illustrate these in a generally allegorical form. On the right-hand side of the picture, which has been conceived as an illusionistic view of the skies, Apollo approaches in his chariot of the sun, together with the Burgundian bride, who he is leading towards a personification of the Holy Roman Empire of the German Nation, enthroned on a podium on the left-hand side. The symbolic figure of Franconia who kneels before a shield to the side of the podium can be seen as an allusion to the two wall frescoes. She represents the bestowing of the dukedom following Frederick's marriage to Beatrice of Burgundy, and the resulting re-integration of Burgundy into the empire. The dynamic effect of the fresco cannot be attributed solely to the dramatic movement of the sun god's horses as they come storming forward, but derives principally from the overall composition. Tiepolo contrasts the figure-filled areas along the bottom edge of the picture with the largely empty areas of sky in its

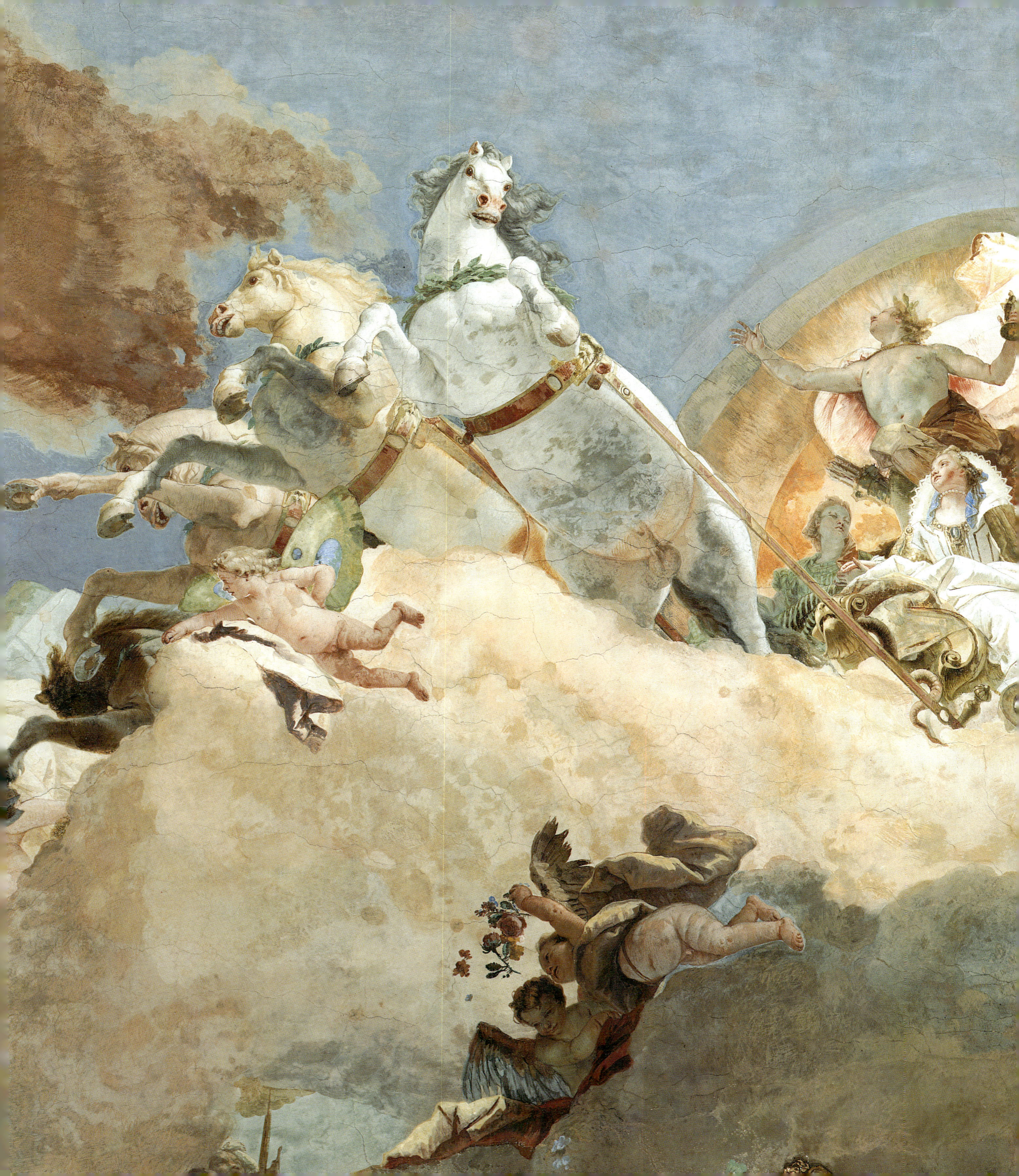

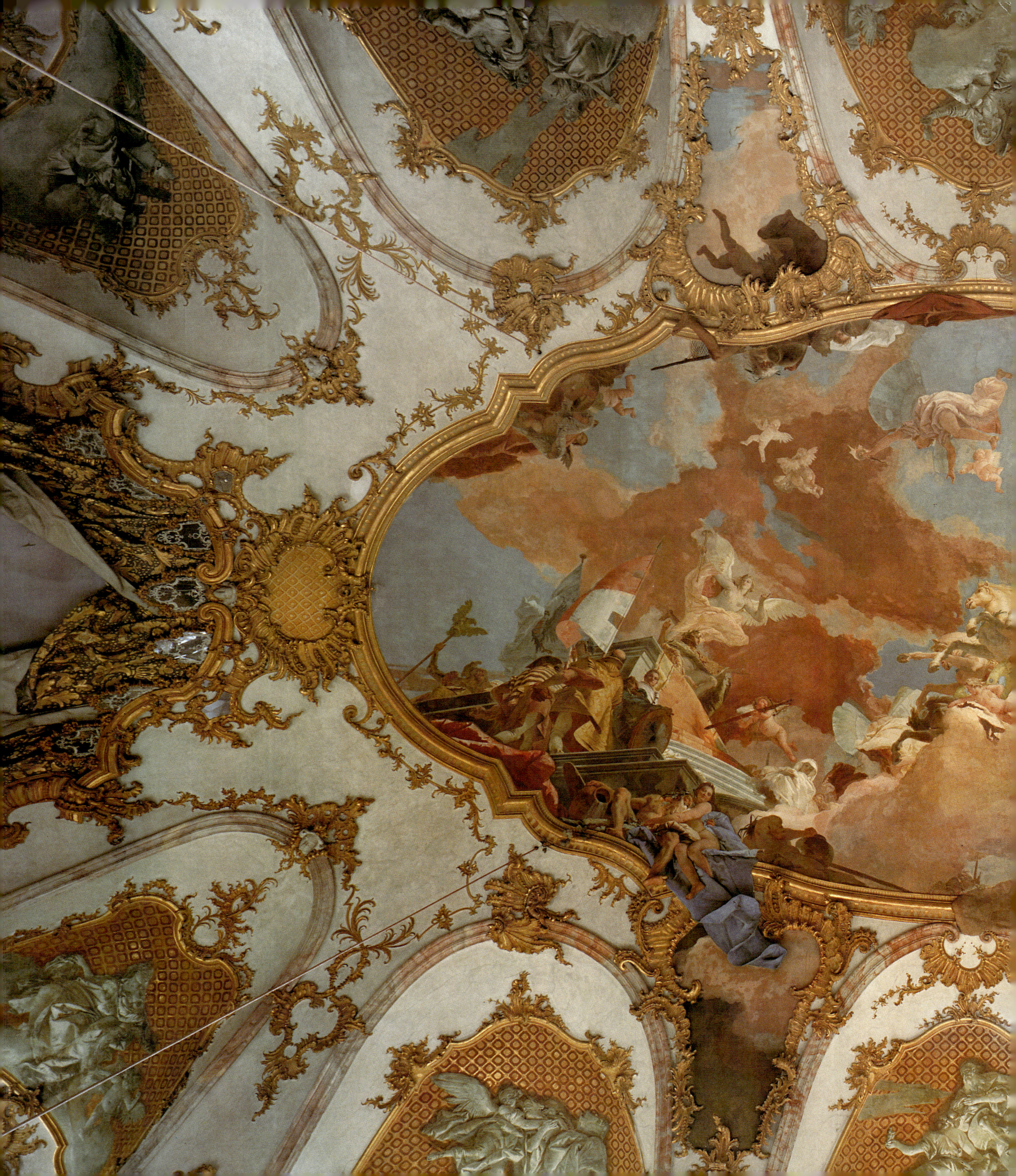

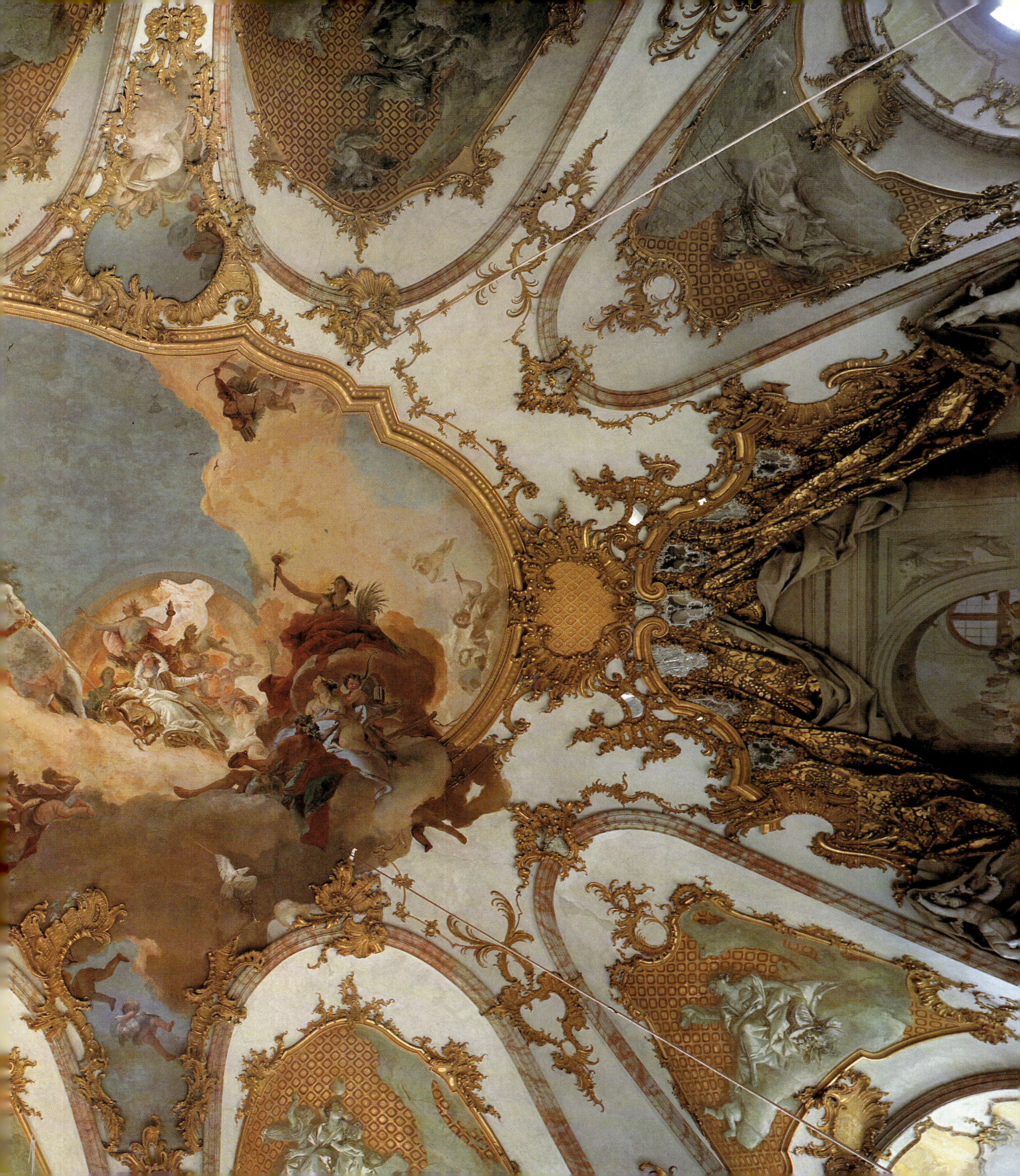

The foundation stone for this most important building of what is called the Southern German Baroque was laid by Prince-Bishop Johann Philipp Franz von Schönborn (1673–1724) in 1720. Immediately upon entering office, he had determined to move his headquarters from the Marienberg fortress to a brand new, modern residence within the Baroque city walls of Würzburg. The construction project benefited from his victory in legal proceedings which awarded him 600,000 florins of misappropriated funds. His uncle Lothar Franz von Schönborn (1655–1729), the Elector and Archbishop of Mainz and also First Chancellor of the Empire and Prince-Bishop of Bamberg, assisted with the planning. He involved the architects Maximilian von Welsch (1671–1745) and Johann Dientzenhofer (died 1726) at the planning stage. His brother, Friedrich Karl (1674–1746), sent from Vienna designs by the famous Viennese architect Lukas von Hildebrandt (1688–1745), who had already designed the palace of Schloß Pommersfelden together with Dientzenhofer.

The superior political connections of the Schönborns made it possible for them to employ first class architects. In Würzburg itself Johann Philipp Franz von Schönborn appointed the young architect Balthasar Neumann, who at first worked alongside the already aged Dientzenhofer, but who then went on to become chief architect and overseer of building works. The Prince-Bishop, however, was not to witness the completion of construction work. He died suddenly in 1724, with just half of the north side-wing standing. His successor, the thrifty Christoph Franz von Hutten, restricted himself to roofing the sections which had been constructed so far, but he too was to die only five years later.

With Friedrich Carl von Schönborn as the new Prince-Bishop, work on the building, whose size and demands proved greater than thought, was once again driven vigorously forward. The south wing was the next to be built – as a symmetrical counterpart to the already existing building. Only then did work begin on the central building, which houses the most important rooms, the main staircase and the garden façade. The shell was completed in 1744. Its homogenous appearance – in spite of the several different planning phases – is the work of Balthasar Neumann. He had adopted ideas from his older colleagues Welsch, Dientzenhofer and Hildebrandt, and was inspired by Robert de Cotte (1656–1735) and Germain Boffrand (1667–1754) on a study trip to Paris. In the meantime, his talent had matured and he had made a name for himself as an eminent contemporary architect with his designs for the

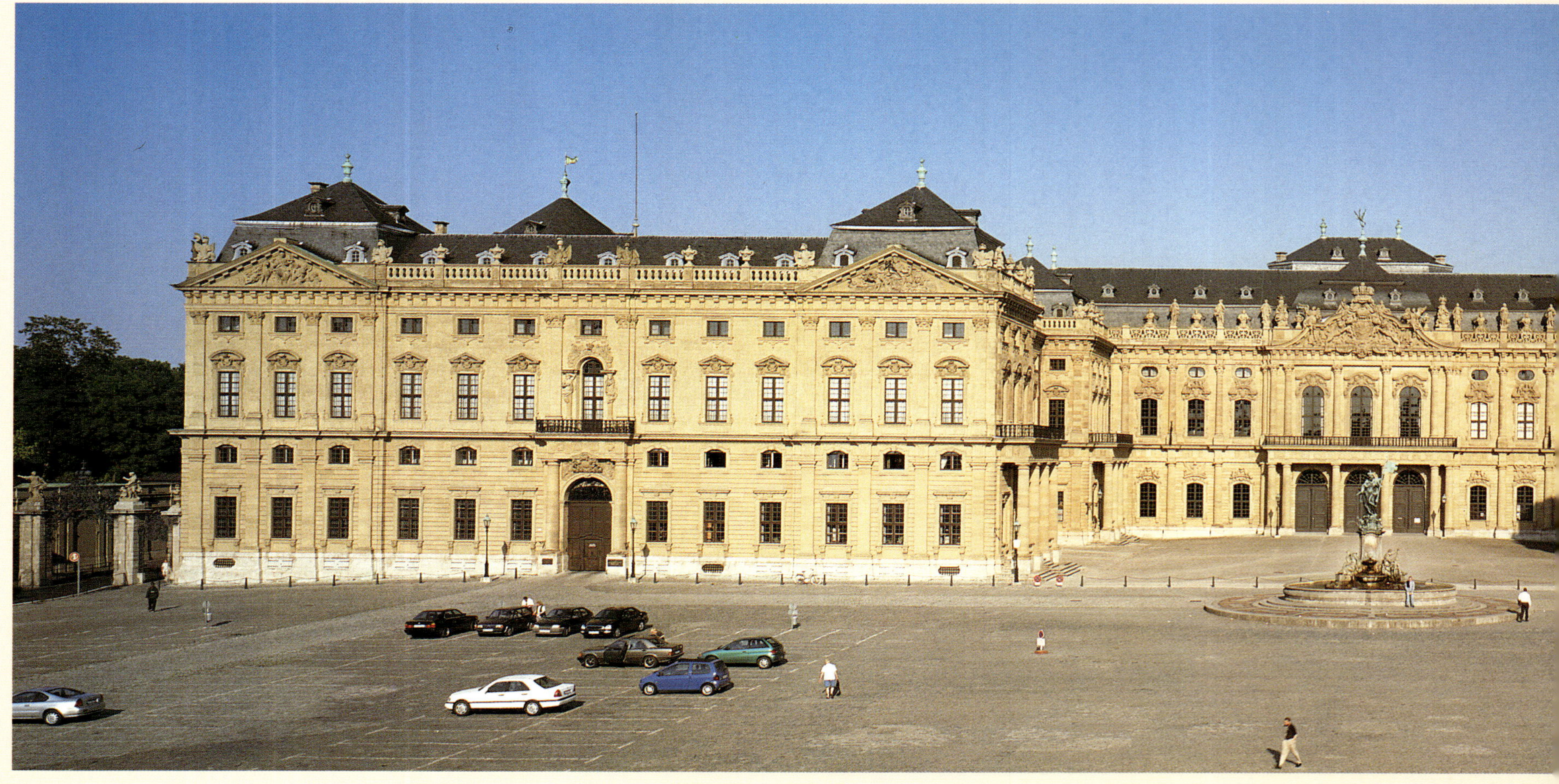

78 General view of the façade, construction commenced 1720
Residenz, Würzburg

The many windows, the divisions of columns and pilasters, and the ornamentation of the tympana on the imposing *cour d'honneur* façade overwhelm the approaching visitor. The middle wing, which sits back slightly, is particularly emphasized by its architectural-sculptural ornamentation, since this is where the ceremonial rooms are situated.

palaces at Würzburg, Bruchsal, Werneck and Brühl, as well as the churches at Vierzehnheiligen and Neresheim.

He built the Würzburg Residenz over a rectangular plan as a completely symmetrical complex of buildings consisting of three wings which encompass a *cour d'honneur* on the West side (ill. 79). The corner pavilions, emphasized by pilasters, triangular pediments and mansard roofs, frame a portal axis flanked by columns. In the *cour d'honneur*, Classical elements give way to Baroque columns, while the tympana are characterized by extravagant Rococo (ill. 78). Prince-Bishop Friedrich Carl died in 1746 while work on completion of the interiors was still in full swing. Since his successor had no interest in finishing it, and even dismissed Balthasar Neumann as architect, work came to a halt yet again. It was not until after his death in 1749, when Carl Philipp von Greiffenclau was elected, that Neumann was re-engaged and the fitting-out work continued. We also have him to thank for the decision to award the interior decoration to Tiepolo, which helped to bring about a most felicitous outcome: the creation of a true synthesis of the arts in the Würzburg Residenz through the congenial combination of architecture and painting.

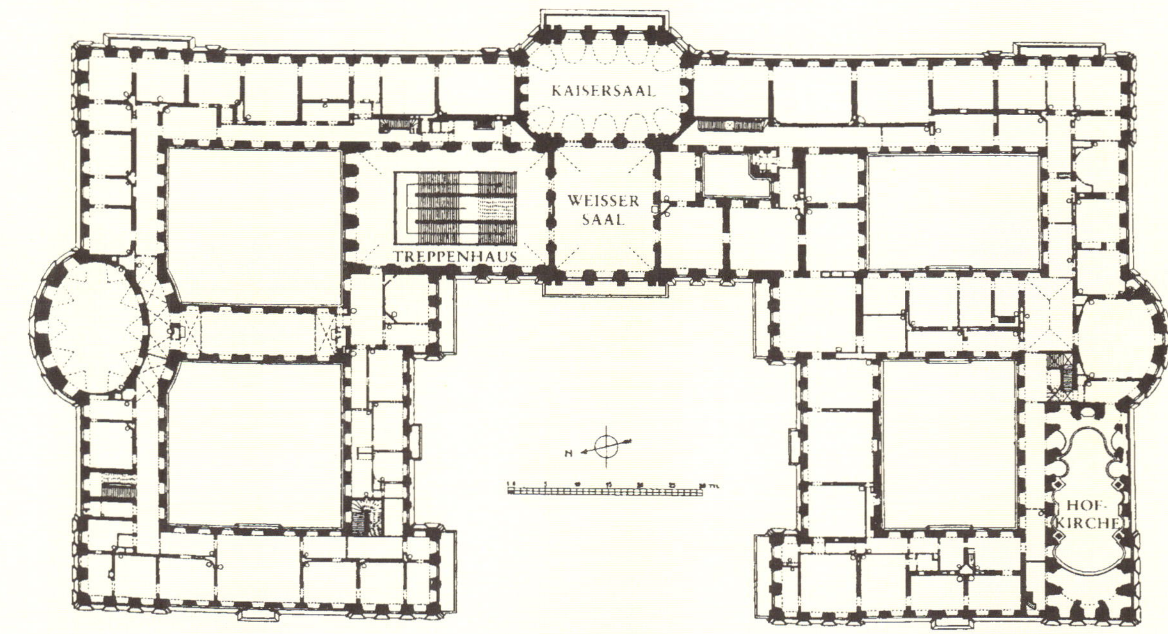

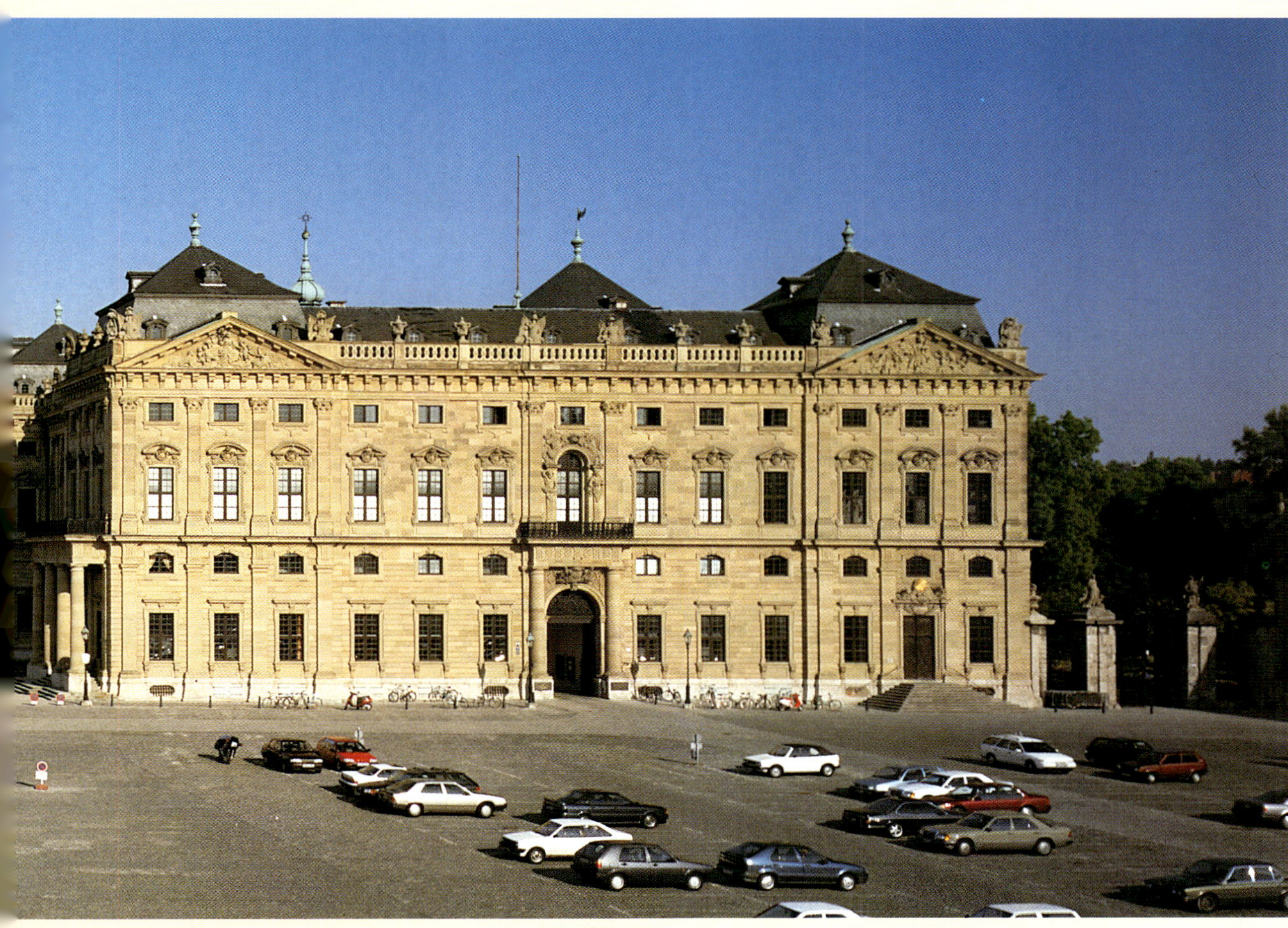

79 (above) Ground plan of the first floor
Residenz, Würzburg

The ground plan illustrates the ceremonial path followed by the visitor: entering from the vestibule on the left, he climbs the grand staircase and reaches the Kaisersaal (Imperial Hall) by way of the Weißer Saal (White Room).

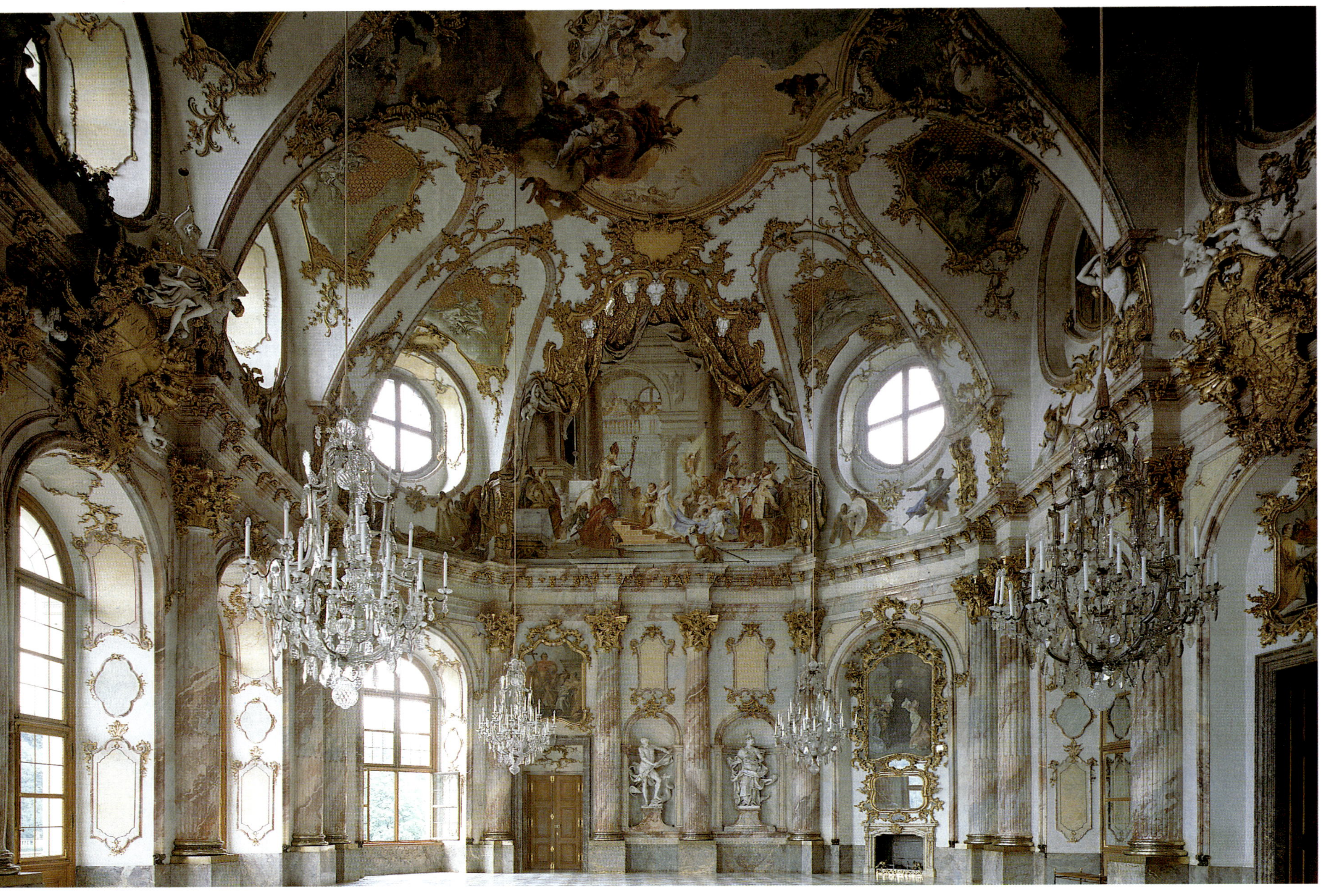

80 View of the Imperial Hall
Residenz, Würzburg

This picture shows the view towards the south end of the Imperial Hall and the portrayal of the marriage of Barbarossa and Beatrice of Burgundy, and shows how the fresco is incorporated into the opulence of the overall decoration.

upper portion. The multicolored, brightly-lit and dramatically-shadowed cloud formations create a dramatic composition.

The wall fresco *The Marriage of the Emperor Frederick Barbarossa to Beatrice of Burgundy* (ill. 81) illustrates the historical events surrounding the marriage which took place in Würzburg in 1156. It does so with reference to the particular relationship between the prince-bishops and the emperor. Furthermore, the portrayal of the emperor kneeling before the bishop is a clear symbol of the claims to power of the Church, according to which the emperor must bow to the Church in ecclesiastical matters. As with his paintings in the Palazzo Labia in Venice, Tiepolo succeeds in establishing a connection between the historical subject matter and the world of the viewer, and in freeing the historical picture from the overblown gravity so typical of the genre, by adding everyday motifs from courtly life, such as the balcony filled with musicians in the architectural backdrop, or the dwarf in the foreground whose ceremonial rod juts illusionistically out into the viewer's space.

On the opposite wall of the room is a representation which ignores the actual historical course of events and combines the investiture of Bishop Herold of Würzburg (1156) with the confirmation by Frederick Barbarossa of all privileges previously conferred upon the Würzburg bishops (ill. 82), which did not actually take place until 1168. This time, the emperor is presented as the supreme secular authority. The fact that the kneeling bishop bears the features of the client, Prince-Bishop von Greiffenklau, makes the historical event topical. In a departure from the strict formal observances of the court, Tiepolo has set the scene outdoors in front of an architectural backdrop and has ordered the figures in loose groupings. The addition of secondary figures, sword bearers or page boys, who detract from the main action, or the ironic positioning of the dog in the foreground, who almost seems to be really sitting on the

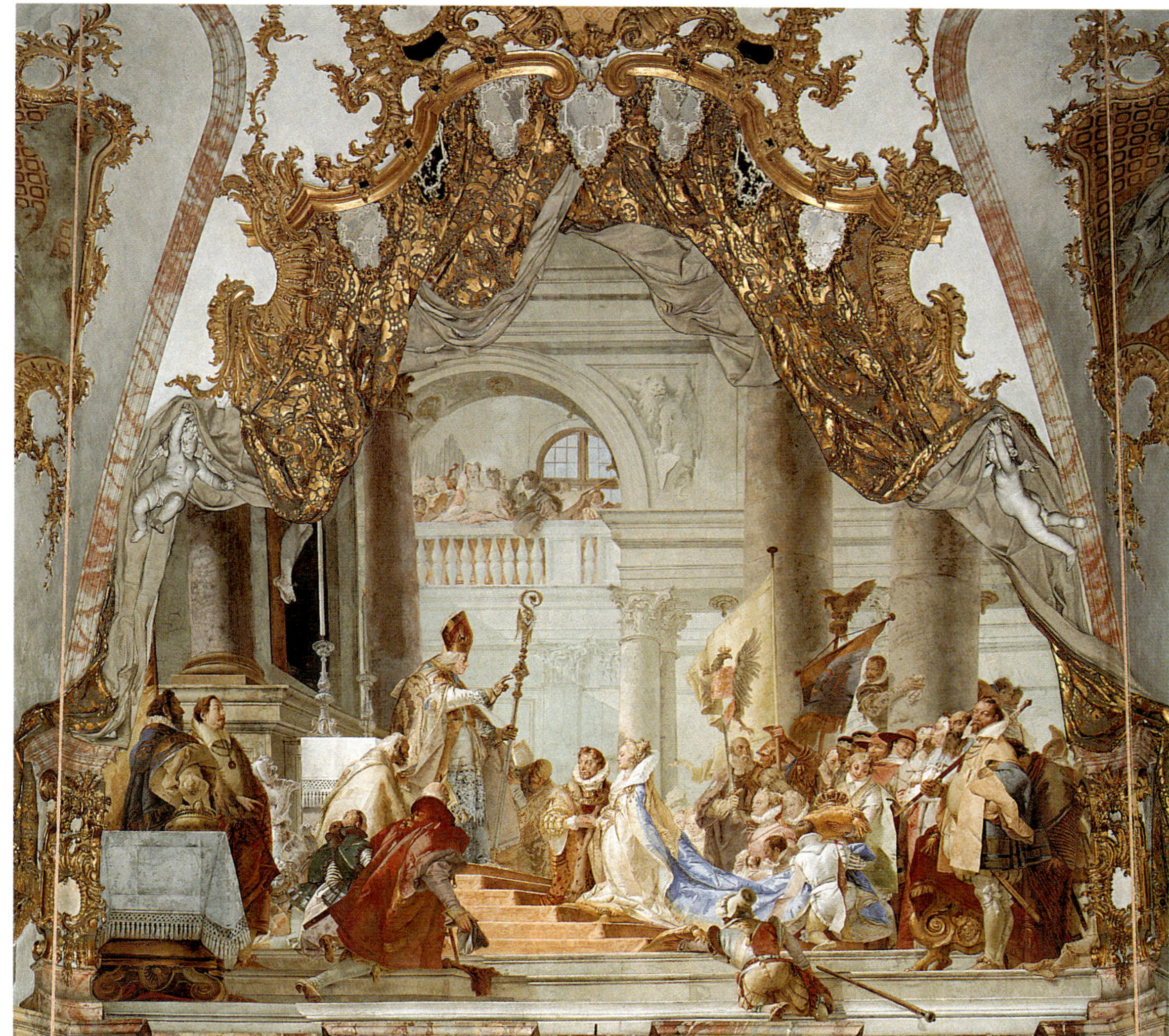

81 *The Marriage of the Emperor Frederick Barbarossa to Beatrice of Burgundy*, 1751
Fresco, 400 x 500 cm
Imperial Hall of the Residenz, Würzburg

The Emperor Frederick Barbarossa and his wife Beatrice kneel before Gebhard, Bishop of Würzburg. On the right of the picture, the royal household and dignitaries of empire are gathered, while the father of the bride, Count Raynald of Burgundy, kneels on the steps to the left of the altar, accompanied by two pageboys. The court jester, seen from behind, occupies a prominent position in the foreground at the foot of the steps to the altar, an example of Tiepolo's penchant for introducing witty and frivolous ideas to the agreed pictorial subject matter. The steps to the altar lead us into the picture and, along with the colossal background architecture, create great spatial depth. The musicians on the balcony in the background are a favorite motif of Tiepolo, which he uses to help make the historical subject matter topical.

cornice, is once again typical of Tiepolo's style of execution.

On the whole, the highly segmented stucco decoration of the Imperial Hall strongly restricted the space available for Tiepolo's decorative art. The figures who constantly breach the borders of the picture and illusionistically jut out into the viewer's space, along with the representations of mercenaries and courtiers who seem to rest on the ledges underneath the windows, demonstrate the efforts made by the artist to break out of the strict corset imposed by the setting. The frescoes on the side walls also create the illusion that the room has opened out: they are conceived as if the scenes were taking place behind curtains, lifted up by angels.

The Prince-Bishop was so pleased with the finished decoration of the Imperial Hall that, in 1752, he also invited Tiepolo to fresco the ceiling of the stairwell. In April of that year, Tiepolo presented the Prince-Bishop with an oil sketch, now in the Metropolitan Museum of Art in New York. The sketch outlines the basic essentials of the themes of the work, which would later be realized: the four known parts of the world (Europe, Asia, Africa and America) are arranged along the sides of the picture, with Apollo and the deities of Olympus at its center, representing the sun rising over the world. Nevertheless, the realized version differs from the sketch in essential points, and shows to what extent the artist was prepared to adapt his design to suit the location and in accordance with the requirements of his patron (ills. 83, 84). The changes affected the repertory of figures on the one hand, and the overall composition itself on the other. The whole area of the heavens was rotated through 180° and the ascension of a medallion bearing the portrait of Prince-Bishop von Greiffenklau was added above the depiction of Europe. This measure not only represents an additional tribute to the patron, but is significant, above all, in terms of composition, since a second center has now been created in the heavens alongside Apollo, thus increasing the drama of the scene. The changes mainly take into account the many viewpoints available

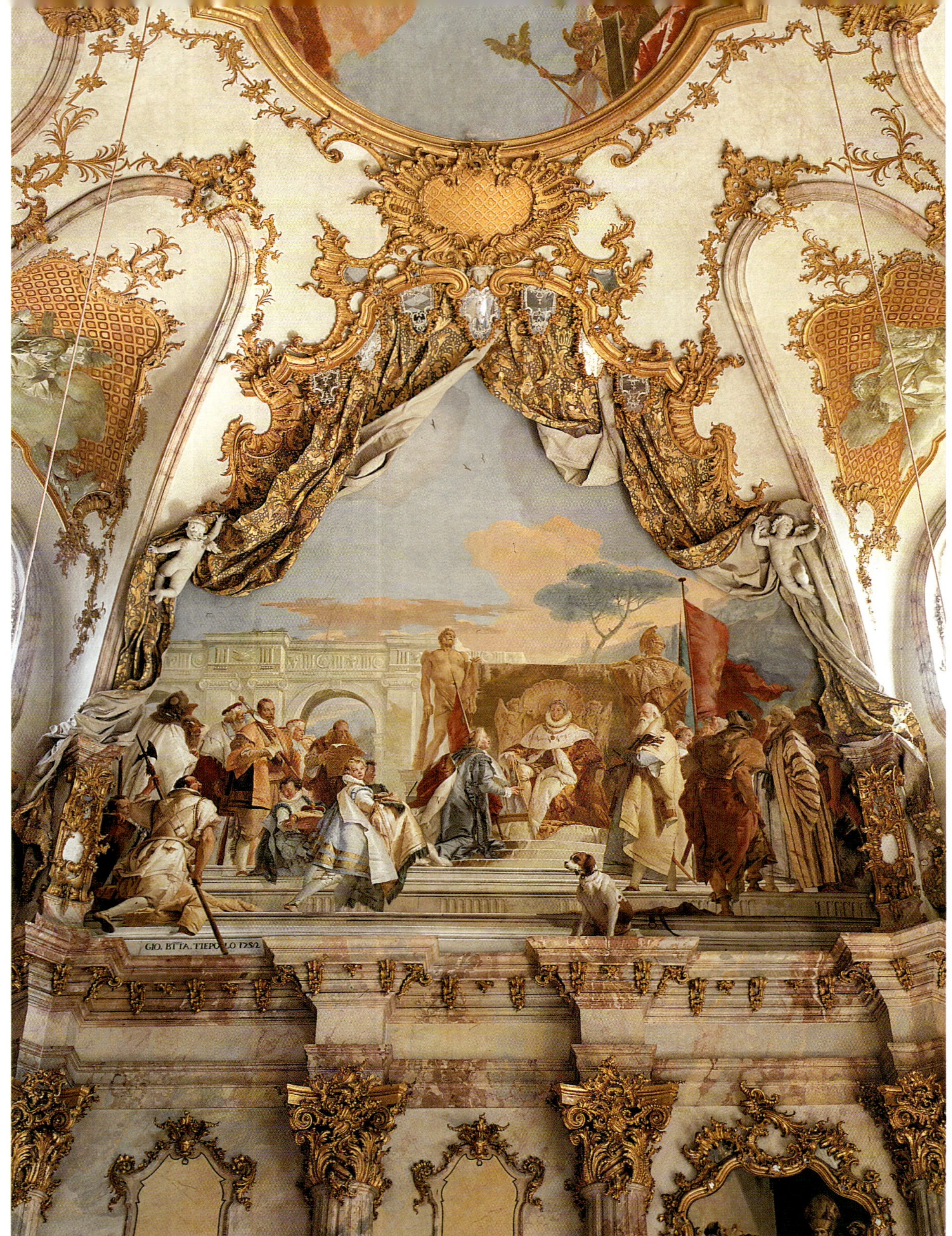

82 *The Investiture of Herold as Duke of Franconia*, 1751
Fresco, 400 x 500 cm
Imperial Hall of the Residenz, Würzburg

The Emperor sits on a golden throne, flanked by statues of Hercules and Minerva, and holds his scepter out towards Bishop Herold, who touches it with his fingers as he takes the oath. To the left and right of the throne, secular and ecclesiastical dignitaries are represented in ceremonial dress, including the Imperial Chancellor, who reads aloud the deed of Investiture, and the Imperial Marshall, who holds up his unsheathed sword. The architecture in the background conforms to a pictorial motif inspired by Veronese and often used by Tiepolo in his paintings in order to give the scene a festive setting.

to the visitor, who changes direction several times during his climb up the stairs, and who cannot take in the whole fresco at a glance.

The splendid staircase is itself an architectural masterpiece by the designer Balthasar Neumann, and provides an artistic setting for the ceremonial path followed by the visitor from the entrance to the Residence up to the Imperial Hall on the first floor. The visitor arrives at the foot of the stairs by way of a dimly-lit vestibule, whose shallow vault creates an impression of heaviness. Here, he catches his first glimpse of the brighter area of the upper storeys overhead. The first flight of stairs brings him to a mezzanine landing, where he must change direction and take either of the two sets of stairs, to the left or to the right, which ascend to the next level. Having arrived on the upper floor, he is overwhelmed by the enormous extent of a great room which is spanned by a single giant cove vault, without further supports. The stairwell, whose large, uninterrupted ceiling surface stood entirely at Tiepolo's disposal, is a technically brilliant achievement for its time (ill. 85).

Tiepolo's achievements in composing this fresco are twofold: he takes into consideration the way in which only parts of the fresco are visible to the viewer as he climbs, and he presents independent pieces which nevertheless fuse into a harmonic whole. From the foot of the stairs the viewer first sees the continent of

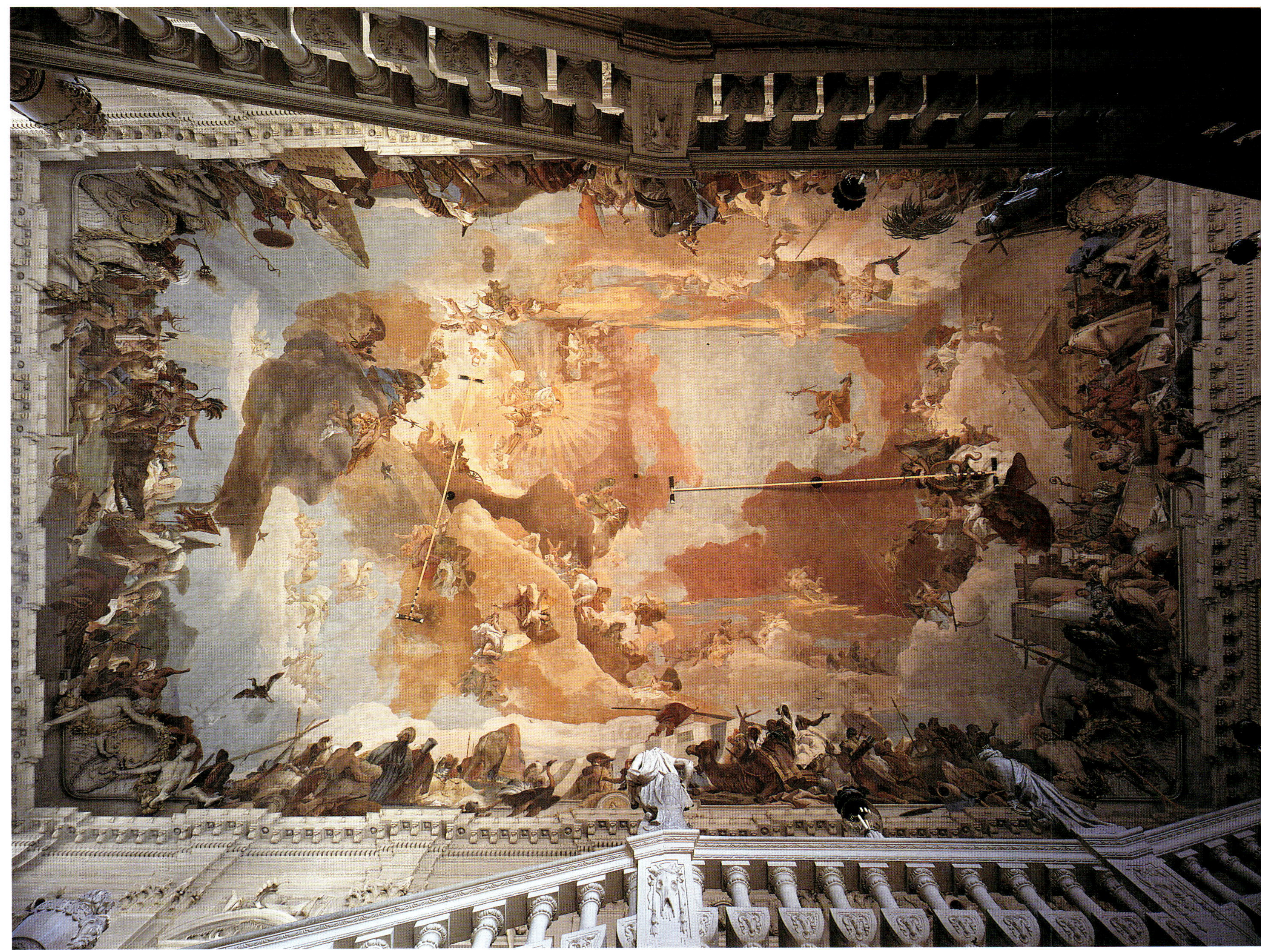

America, whose personification points with outstretched arm to a banner showing the mythical creature the griffin, a first allusion to the client (ills. 86, 87). On entering the stairwell, a wider picture is revealed, giving a view of the dramatic cloud formations which push open the skies, and of the figure of Apollo, bathed in radiant light. Halfway up the first flight of stairs, more of the long sides of the fresco are revealed, with Africa on the right (ills. 88, 89) and Asia on the left (ills. 90, 91). The groups of figures await the visitor almost like a court society. After this first flight, the viewer must change direction and now sees the portrayal of Europe for the first time on the short side opposite (ill. 92). The flourishing arts are symbolized here, partly personified by the artists involved in the construction of the Residence (ill. 93). Above them, the Prince-Bishop's portrait medallion is borne aloft through the heavens by geni and allegorical figures. Like Apollo, who cannot be seen from here, it too lets its light shine forth over the world (ill. 94). In comparison to the other Continents, the Europa fresco is statically conceived. This, and the sometimes frontal arrangement of its figures, causes the viewer to pause and so constitutes a first high point on the way to the Imperial Hall. The fresco was, therefore, never laid out with an overall view in mind, and the criticisms of the largely empty areas of sky at its center which were later to be frequently voiced, are thus unfounded. Instead we are captivated by the harmonic

83 *Apollo and the Continents*, 1752/53
(overall view, photographed from below)
Fresco, 1900 x 3050 cm
Stairwell of the Residenz, Würzburg

The perspectival distortion at the edges of the overall view of the ceiling fresco tell us that this was never intended as a vantage point for the visitor. Instead, the fresco was to open out to the viewer as he ascended the staircase. Apollo is portrayed in the center of the heavens, Venus and Mars rest on a cloud below him, while the zodiac appears on a band behind them with the four seasons to the left. The Horae can be recognized by their butterfly wings. The upper part of the fresco is meant to be viewed from the opposite angle and shows Mercury and, a little below him, the gods Diana, Jupiter and Saturn.

84 *Apollo and the Continents* (detail ill. 83), 1752/53

Apollo has left his palace and is floating slowly downward, accompanied by two of the Horae, while the rising sun shines out behind him. This is a mythological representation of the sun rising over the Earth, which is symbolized by the surrounding Continents. The sun appears as a life-giving force which determines the course of the days, months and years.

perfection through which both architecture and painted decoration serve the same purpose: the magnificent staging of the ceremonial path through the Residence. Leaving that aside, we again find Tiepolo's customary methods of portrayal: the addition of secondary figures and ironic episodes to the main action, and the toying with image and reality through the breaching of the picture's borders. This is added to by the illusionistic portrayal of the figures who rest on the cornice and jut out into the viewer's space. It is not without reason that the Würzburg frescoes are considered the high point of Tiepolo's artistic career. This can be attributed to the particularly happy conditions in which he worked, to the genial architectural surroundings, to the successful collaboration between the different artists and, above all, to the licence which the patron granted Tiepolo with respect to his highly imaginative creations, which the latter was finally able to realize here, away from the traditional ties of his native city.

However, the decoration of the Residence was not the only work to engage Tiepolo during his stay in Würzburg. Especially in the winter months, when work on the frescoes stopped due to the weather, he painted numerous pictures of outstanding quality for the court and various other clients; pictures which have undeservedly been overshadowed by the frescoes. In the winter of 1751/52, Tiepolo delivered two altarpieces to the court church in Würzburg: *The Assumption of the Virgin Mary* and *The Fall of the Rebel Angels*. In 1753, he completed *The Adoration of the Magi* (ill. 96), now in the Alte Pinakothek in Munich, for the former abbey church at Münsterschwarzach. Tiepolo's tightly-packed and two-dimensional composition offers an individual and highly effective re-enactment of the subject-matter. The different pictorial motifs, which appear unconnected, are, in part, truncated and take on the character of props. The figures are presented in magnificent costumes, as if they were actors on a stage. The emphasis lies less on what is actually happening and more on the Epiphany, the manifestation of Christ, which is particularly emphasized by the special management of light around the brightly-lit Virgin and Child.

Alongside these religious commissions, Tiepolo also painted works with a secular subject matter. He executed two oil paintings after Tasso's "Gerusalemme liberata" for Adam Friedrich von Seinsheim, the then Court Chamberlain, thus returning to a literary subject, which he had already painted once ten years before. *Rinaldo enchanted by Armida* and *Rinaldo abandoning Armida* belong to the most important paintings of the Würzburg period. The coloring is stronger and somewhat darker than in the Venetian version, but it is still the arcadian and pastoral elements of the epic which are prominent. Two further small-scale pictures depicting *Rinaldo parting from Armida* and *Rinaldo and Armida in the Enchanted Garden, observed by Carlo and Ubaldo* in the Gemäldegalerie, Berlin, have been connected with the two Würzburg pictures. Some hold them to be sketches, others to be *ricordi* or original works.

The mythological oil painting *The Death of Hyacinth* (ill. 95), executed in the period 1752/53 for Count Bückeburg, bears stylistic comparison with the Würzburg Tasso-cycle. The picture shows Apollo lamenting his friend Hyacinth, who – according to Ovid's "Metamorphoses" – he has killed during a discus-throwing contest. The latter has here been replaced by a ball game, based on a 16th century Italian translation of Ovid. The inherent tragedy of the scene, reflected in Apollo's sweeping gestures and in the alarmed faces of the bystanders, is undermined by the grinning statue of Pan, which towers directly behind Apollo, and by the parrot, a traditional symbol of lasciviousness and a hidden allusion to the illicit relationship between Apollo and Hyacinth.

Four history pictures with representations from Roman history – *Mucius Scaevola before Porsenna* and *Coriolanus before the Walls of Rome*, presumably commissioned by Balthasar Neumann – and from the Old Testament – *Esther before Ahasveros* and *David and Abigail* – conclude Tiepolo's creative years in Würzburg.

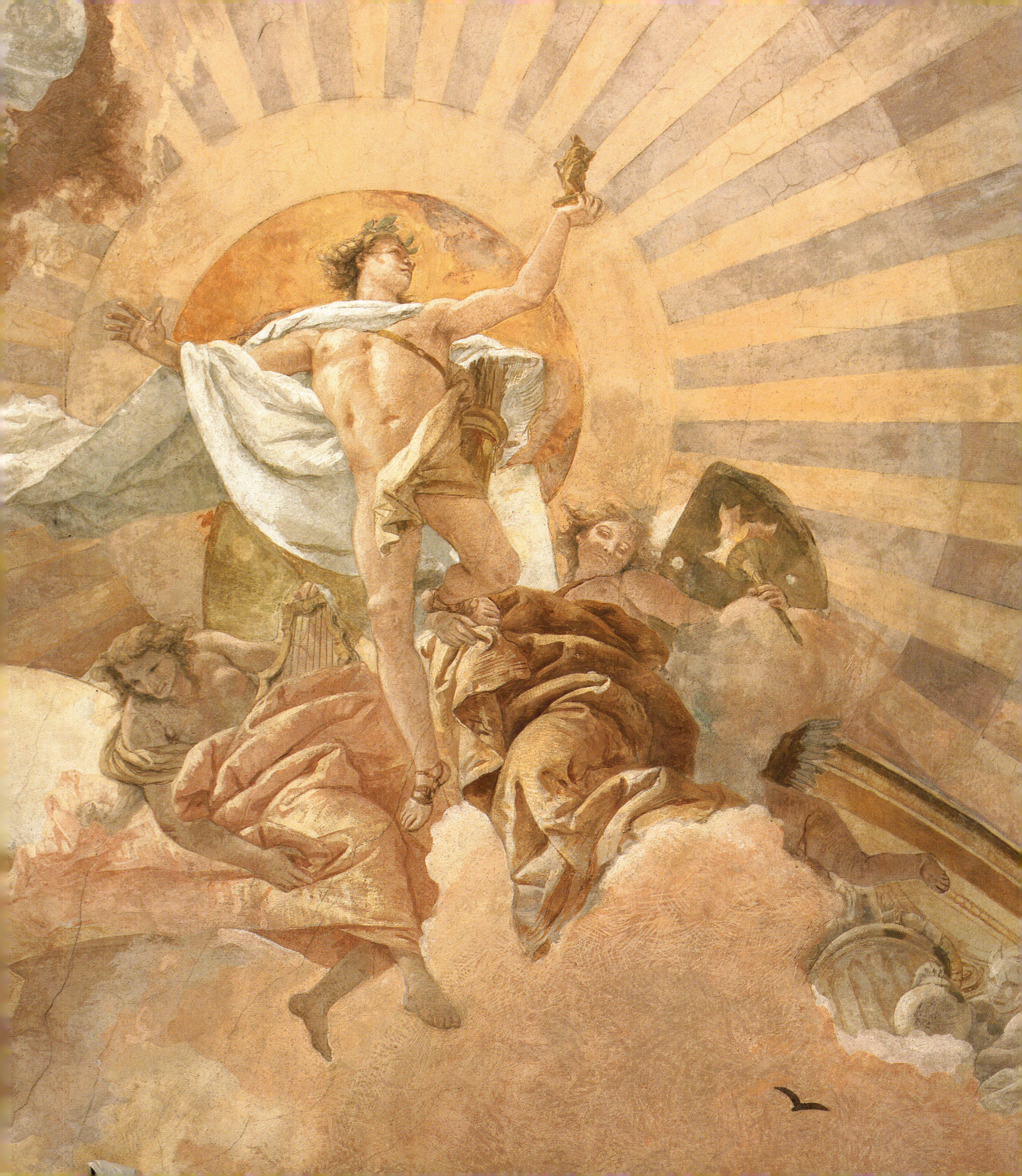

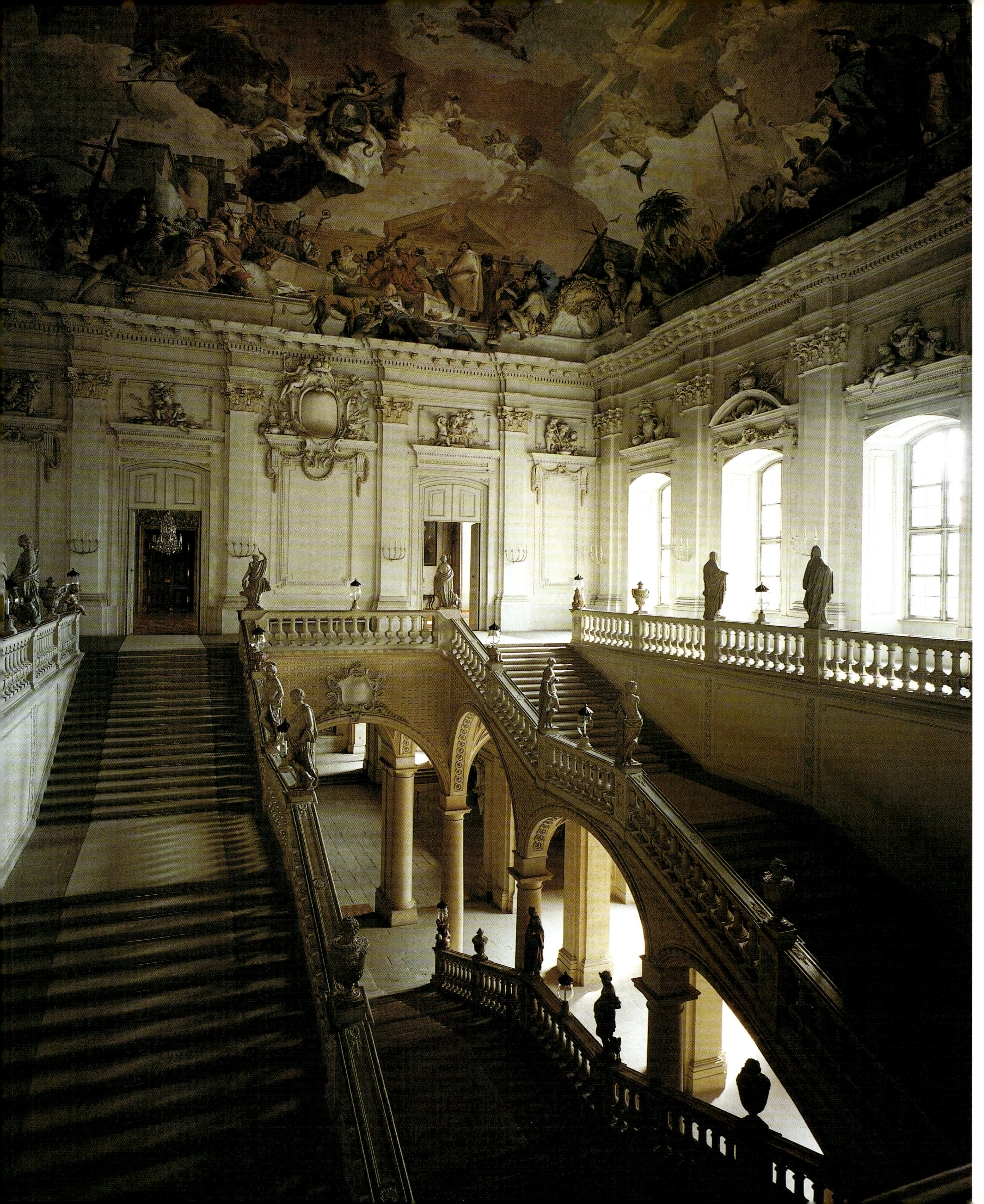

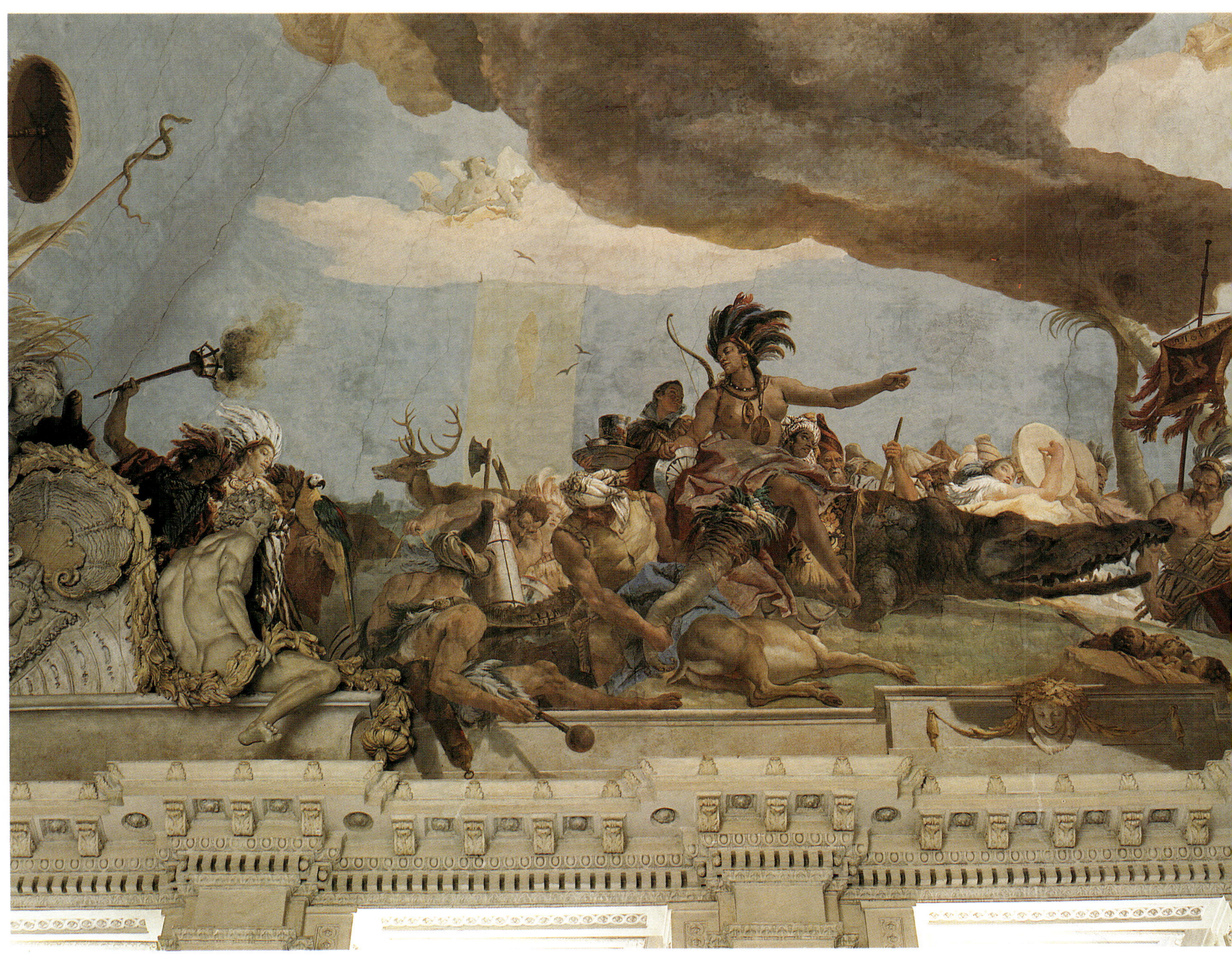

85 (opposite) Stairwell seen from the gallery,
looking south-east
Residenz, Würzburg

The photo shows the staircase rising from the ground-floor vestibule to the brightly lit, spacious hall at the top of the stairwell. We can see the enormous scale on which it has been built and the way in which it harmonizes with Tiepolo's ceiling fresco.

86 (above) *Apollo and the Continents* (detail ill. 83, *America*, left-hand side), 1752/53

The personification of the American Continent rides on a huge crocodile. With her naked upper torso and feathered head-dress, she represents the uncivilized world. She is surrounded by people characterized as wild creatures, who hunt with bow and arrow. The figure reclining below her holds a horn of plenty as a symbol of the riches and fertility of this part of the world, which was of the greatest interest to the Europeans.

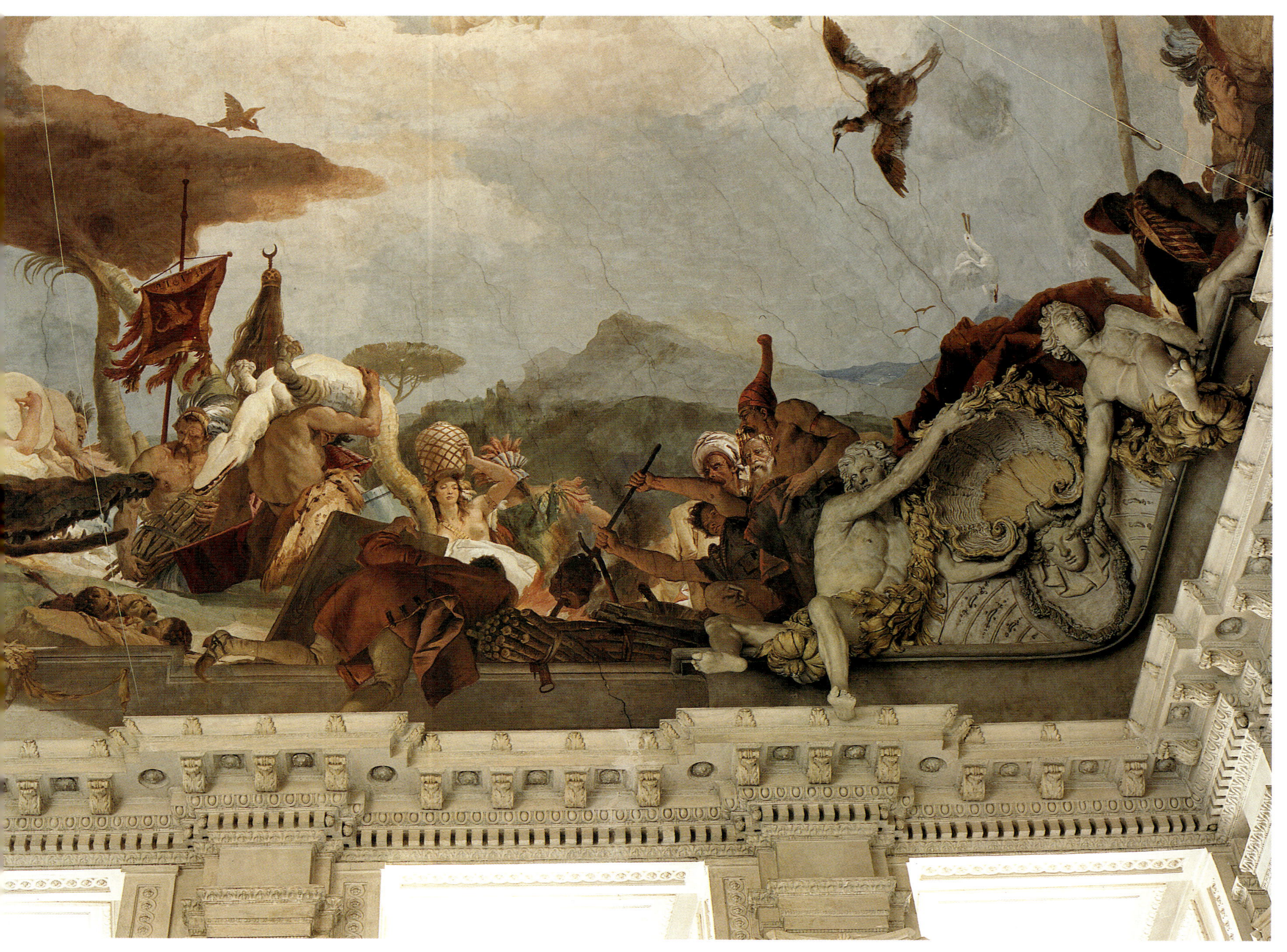

87 *Apollo and the Continents* (detail ill. 83, *America*, right-hand side), 1752/53

The Europeans of Tiepolo's day imagined the inhabitants of the continent of America to be barely civilized, a belief symbolized in his depiction of human beings who look to nature for sustenance and who eat their meals in the open air. It was assumed that cannibalism was practised in this part of the world, and the heads which lie around in the foreground allude to this. As a *capriccio*, Tiepolo has placed in the foreground the portrayal of a European, who hides behind a stone slab and secretly observes the continent.

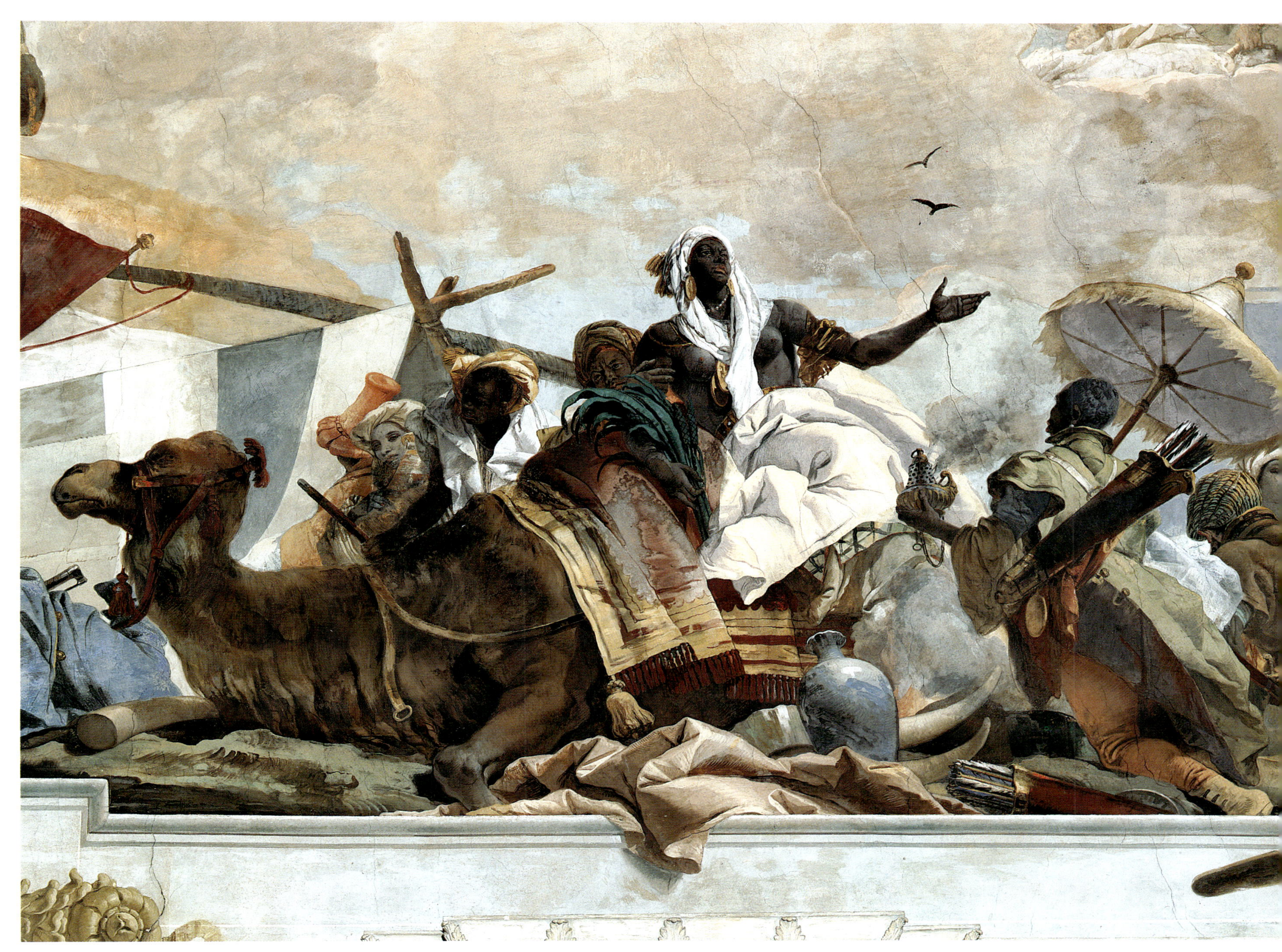

88 *Apollo and the Continents*, (detail ill. 83, *Africa*, right-hand side),1752/53

The personification of Africa sits astride a dromedary in the hustle and bustle of a market scene, surrounded by Negroes, Orientals and Europeans. She is being offered an incense burner, which, along with other vessels on magnificent cloths and the tusks of ivory, symbolize the goods and the riches of the continent, so coveted by the Europeans. Africa is clearly depicted as a much more civilized place than America.

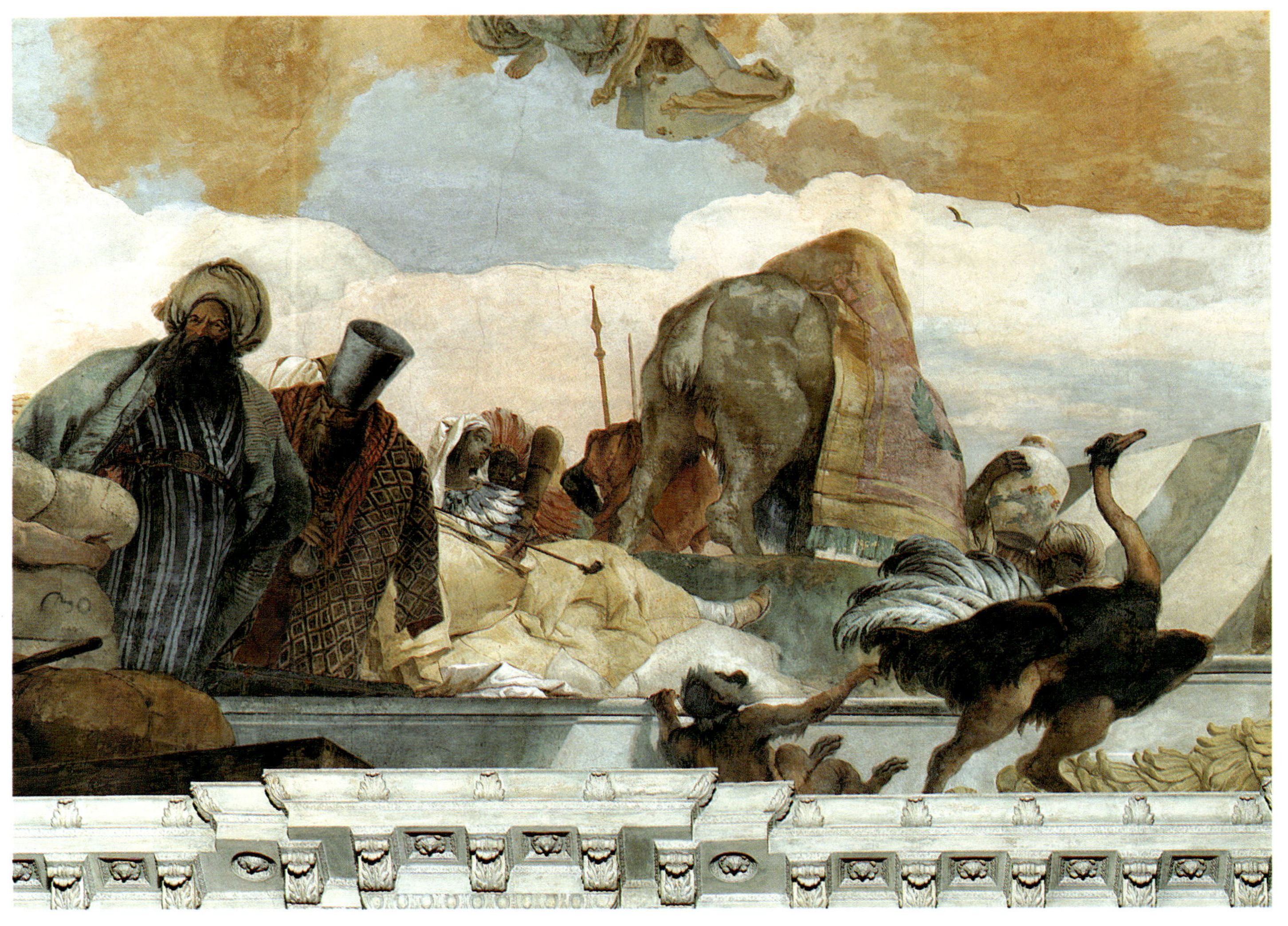

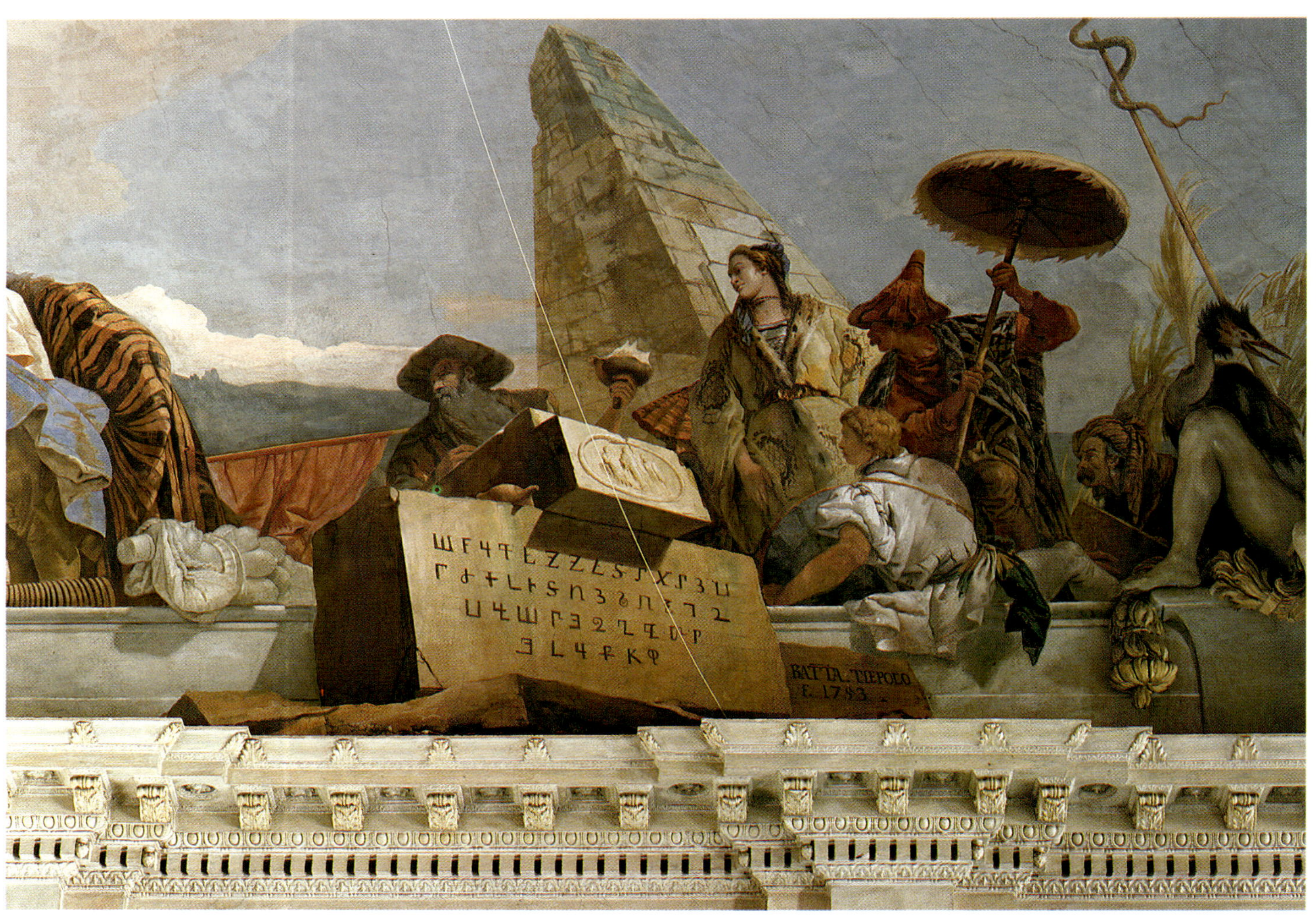
BAT.TA TIEPOLO

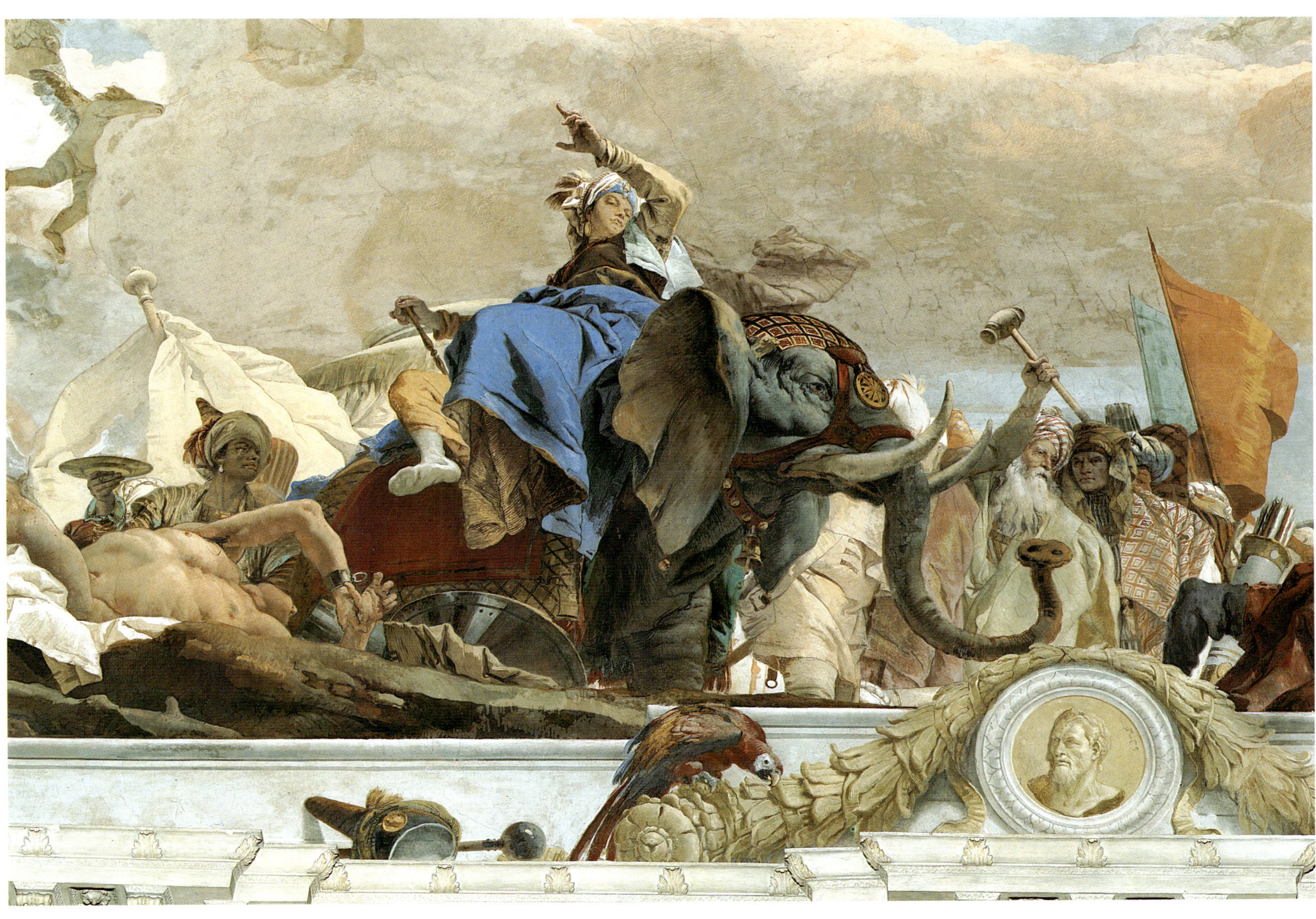

89 (opposite, above) *Apollo and the Continents* (detail ill. 83, *Africa*, left-hand side), 1752/53

Here, too, it is Africa's flourishing trade which is the focus of the representation, in which portly merchants are occupied with their wares, stored in large bales and barrels. The monkey and the ostrich in the foreground, like the dromedary, were considered animals characteristic of Africa, but here they are intended more as playful additions to the portrayal.

90 (opposite, below) *Apollo and the Continents* (detail ill. 83, *Asia*, obelisk group), 1752/53

The meaning of the various individual figures in the so-called obelisk group, which conceals a complex symbolic language, has not yet been sufficiently explained. The female figure in the yellow coat in front of the pyramid is often interpreted as the personification of Princedom, while the old man with the hat behind the hieroglyphic stone seems to be a sage. The symbol of the snake entwined around a rod reminds us of the staff of Aesculapius and refers to the art of medicine. The composition of the scene is highly reminiscent of Tiepolo's *Capricci* series of prints of 1743, or of the *Scherzi di fantasia*, which followed a few years later.

91 (above) *Apollo and the Continents* (detail ill. 83, *Asia*, figure of Asia), 1752/53

The magnificently costumed personification of Asia rides on a splendidly adorned elephant in the midst of scenes which are meant to distinguish the continent as the birthplace of writing, of science and of kingship. The prisoners lying on the ground and the army of soldiers behind them allude to the military importance of the continent; the parrot stands for the animal kingdom.

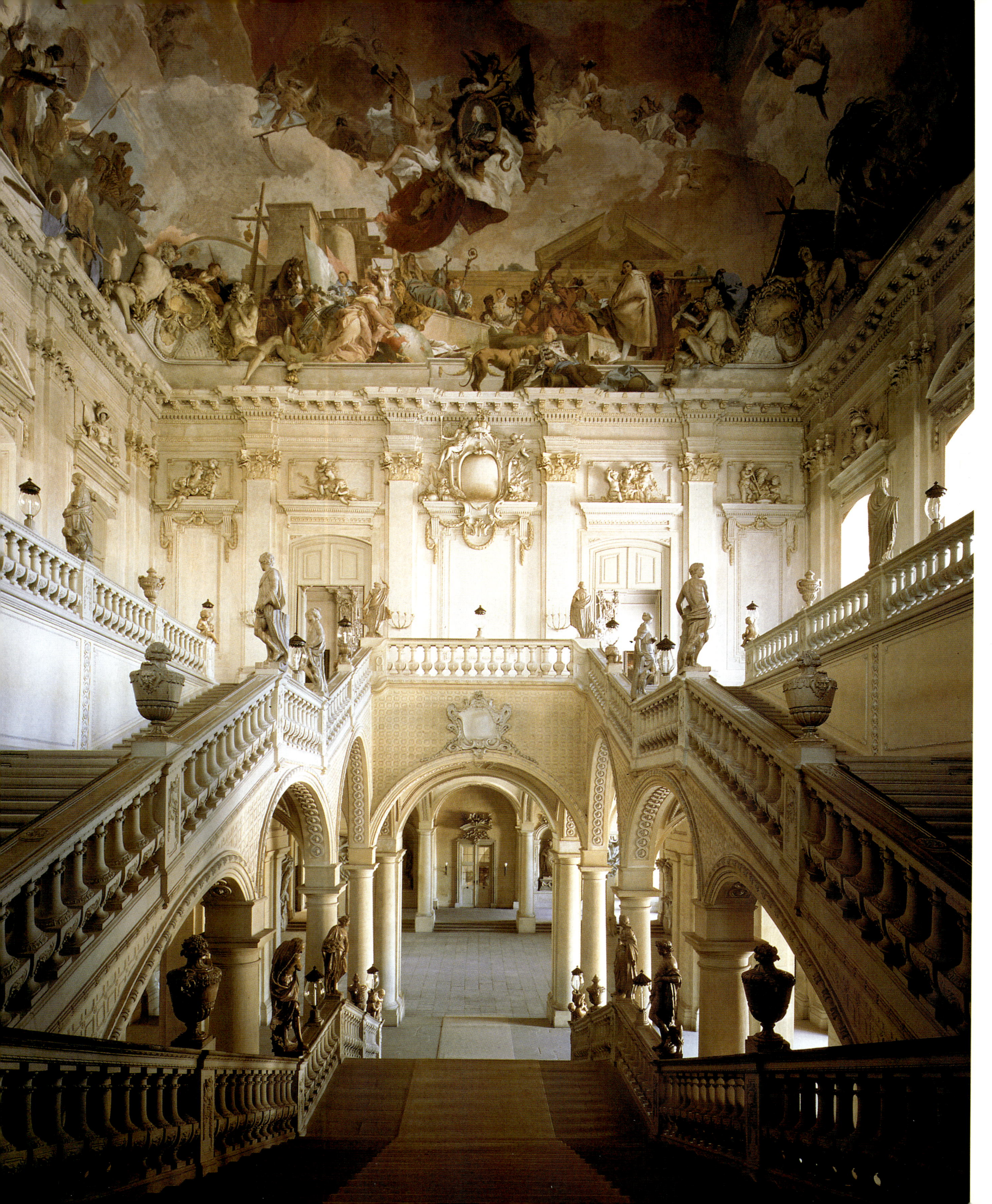

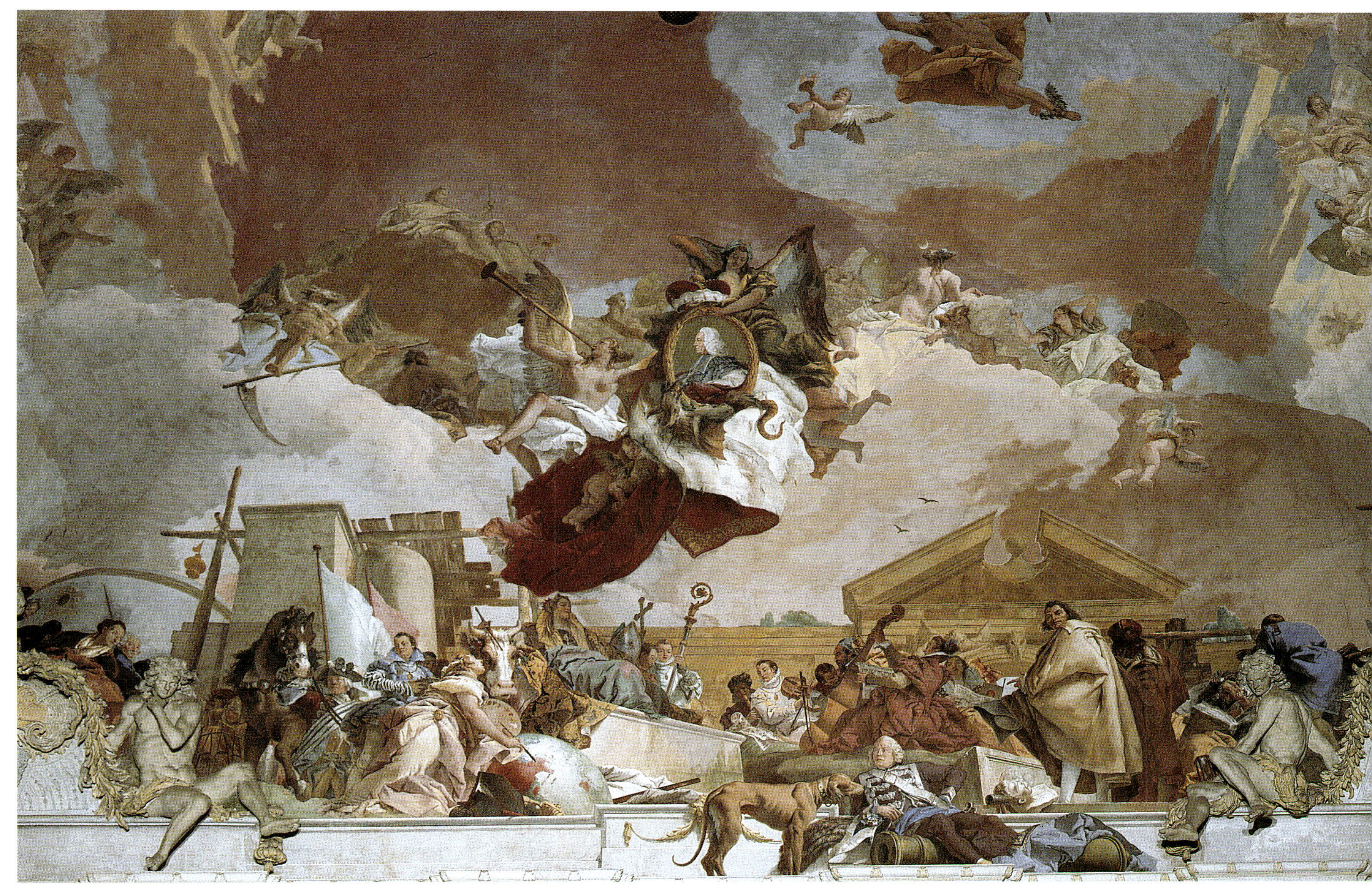

92 (opposite) View of the stairwell
Residenz, Würzburg

From this vantage point the viewer sees the representation of the personification of Europe for the first time, whereas the other Continents and the center of the heavens cannot be seen. Neither can the actual dimensions of the hall be recognized until higher up.

93 (above) *Apollo and the Continents* (detail ill. 83, *Europe*, overall view), 1752/53

The personification of Europe, enthroned on a stone podium and resting against a bull, is surrounded by figures who are meant to refer to the importance of religion and the visual arts on this continent. In the left foreground, a figure symbolizing Painting kneels over a globe, palette and brush in hand. A musician on the right-hand side symbolizes Music, while the man facing the viewer and surrounded by the attributes of sculpture represents that branch of the arts. Tiepolo has lent him the features of the stucco artist Antonio Bossi. The figure reclining in the foreground is a portrait of Balthasar Neumann, who designed the Residence. His uniform refers to his rank as colonel in the Artillery. On the extreme left, Tiepolo portrayed himself and his son Giandomenico along with the painter Franz Ignaz Roth.

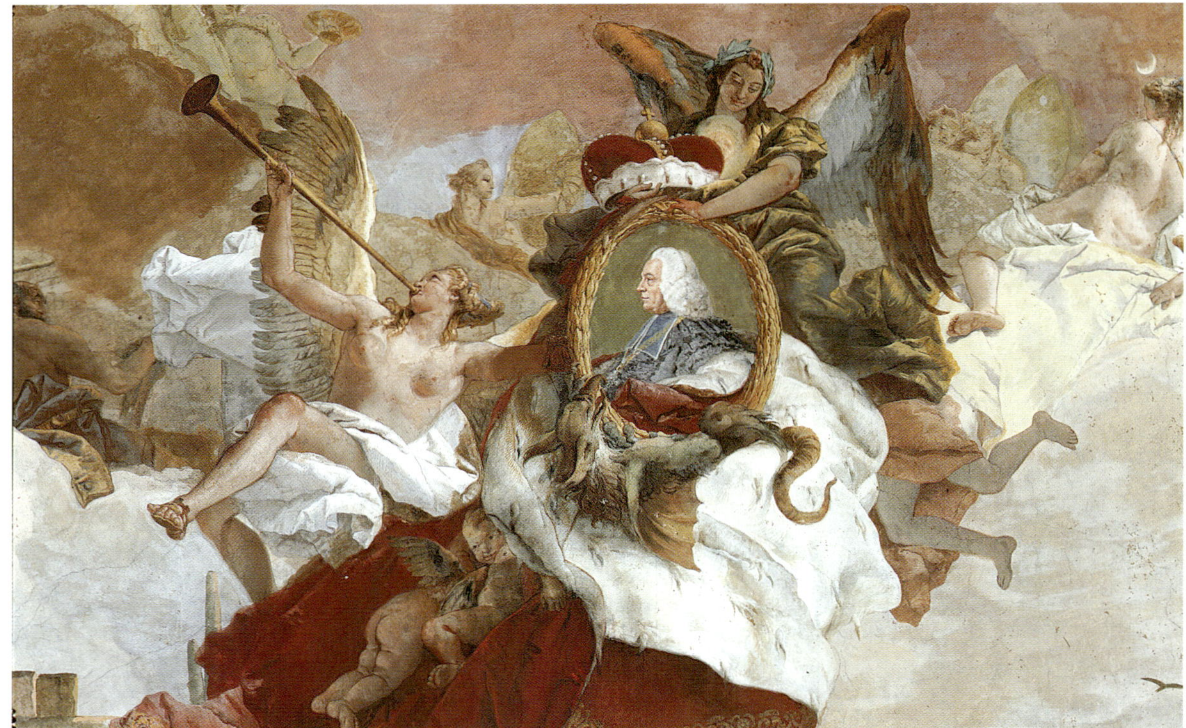

94 (right) *Apollo and the Continents* (detail ill. 83, *Europe*, Prince-Bishop von Greiffenclau), 1752/53

The portrait medallion of Carl Philipp von Greiffenclau is borne aloft above the personification of Europe. To the left, the goddess Fame sounds her trumpet and supports the likeness, while the winged personification of Virtue holds a crown over it. A griffin, the heraldic animal of the Greiffenclau family, can be seen at the bottom edge of the medallion. The flapping red imperial mantle, trimmed with ermine, emphasizes the ascension and the glory of the Prince-Bishop, as he soars up to the deities of Olympus visible in the background.

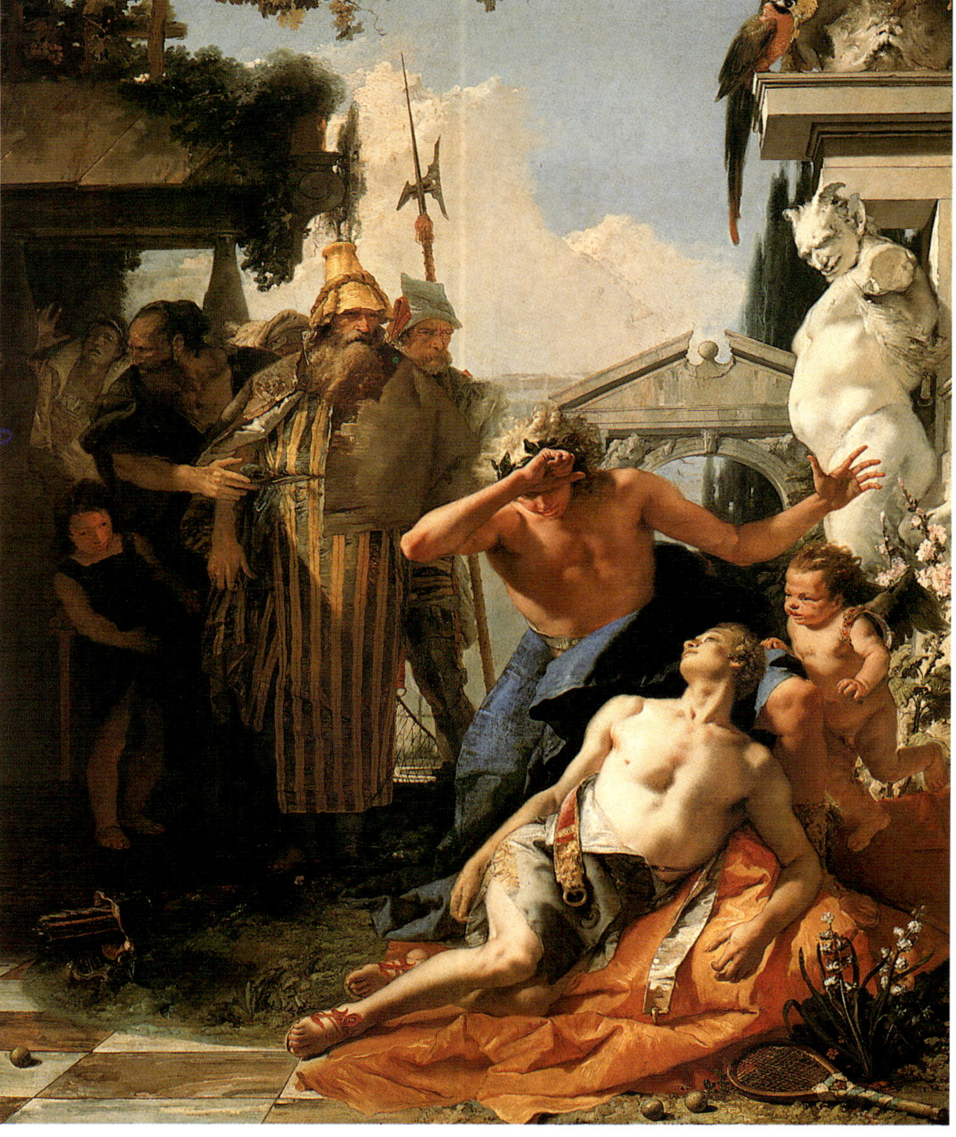

95 (left) *The Death of Hyacinth*, ca. 1752/53
Oil on canvas, 287 x 235 cm
Museo Thyssen-Bornemisza, Madrid

In the foreground, accompanied by a *putto*, and with a sweeping gesture, Apollo laments Hyacinth, who he accidentally killed during a ball game, and whose body is impressively laid out on a red cloth. Behind them to the left, and somewhat distanced, is a group of onlookers included as staffage, while a grinning statue of Pan and a parrot, on the right, act as a third center in the composition, their presence turning the tragedy of the scene to irony.

96 (opposite) *The Adoration of the Magi*, 1753
Oil on canvas, 405 x 211 cm
Bayerische Staatsgemäldesammlungen, Alte Pinakothek, Munich

In the center of the picture, the brightly-lit group with the Virgin Mary and Child and the oldest of the three kings, who approaches the Child with a gesture of heartfelt adoration, is striking in contrast to the darker shades around them. The composition of the picture, with its elements arranged in tiers, is unusual. So too is the combination of architectonal elements, such as the steps with the wooden hut behind, the two figures of the Moorish King and the pageboy, who are seen from behind and cut off at the sides, as well as the objects strewn, apparently randomly, in the foreground.

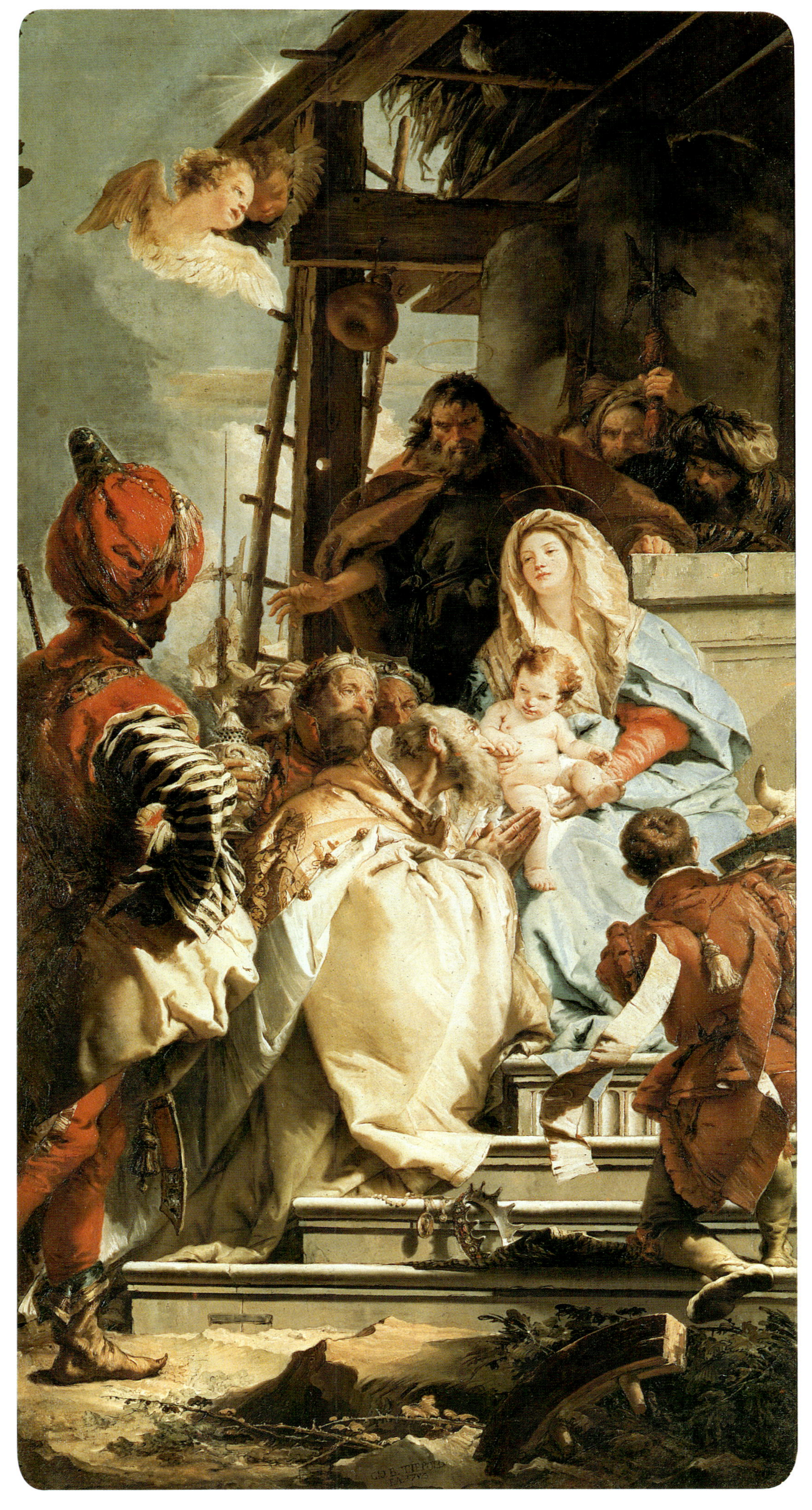

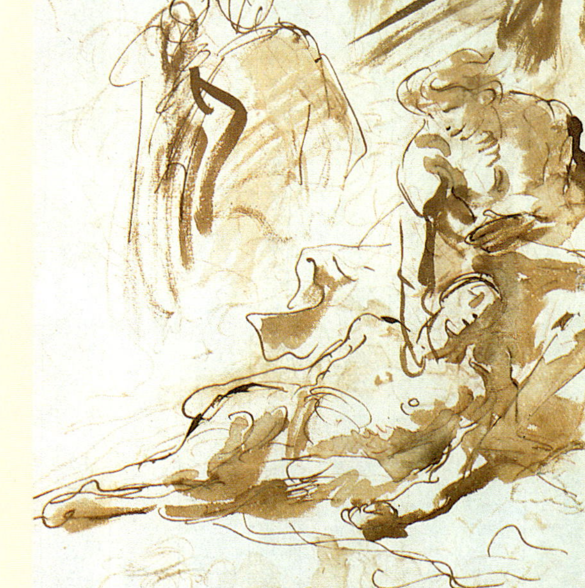

97 Studies for *The Death of Hyacinth*, ca. 1752/53
Bister over red-chalk underdrawing on linen paper, 32.4 x 22.2 cm
Victoria and Albert Museum, London

The drawings on the front and back of the sheet illustrate how Tiepolo arrived at the finished composition. While Hyacinth is still portrayed in the upper part of the drawing on the recto side as sitting half upright, the smaller sketch in the lower half already shows him reclining. This was then executed the other way round on the back of the page (not visible here) and already displays the essential elements of the finished version.

Tiepolo's talent for painting, the much-lauded impression of virtuosity and facility which his works convey, was in reality the result of his ability as a draftsman and of his thorough preparation. The drawings were produced mainly as studies for large, or even smaller, commissions. A few, however, were executed as cabinet pieces and stood as works of art in their own right. Only a few of the early drawings were copied from life models. In these, Tiepolo used many different drawing techniques. Most were pencil and wash, or pen-and-ink drawings on white paper, while others were drawings executed in red or black chalk and highlighted in white on blue or white paper (ills. 97–99). He used washes to convey spatial depth, and the physical appearance of the figures, as well as to shade objects.

Apart from his early style, it is difficult to establish a chronological order for the more than 3,000 surviving drawings, which he never dated. In the 1740s he had begun to develop a more shorthand style of drawing, to which he remained faithful until the 1760s. He used several styles and techniques at the same time, fell back on earlier work, made stylistic leaps, and modified whichever technique he happened to be using, making it scarcely possible to date individual drawings. The drawings also confirm his economical way of working, and present us with a homogenous canon of forms, sketches of figures and motifs, that he used again and again in different contexts.

He prepared the large decorative projects, such as the fresco cycle in the Würzburg Residence, through an impressively large number of designs and studies, which document his astonishing work procedures. The at times very dissimilar compositional studies often contained various alternatives for just the one scene. They illustrate the fertile imagination and the spontaneity with which Tiepolo approached his decorative commissions.

The artist was also an expert printmaker, although he seldom worked in the medium. Along with two early sheets and his masterpiece the *Adoration of the Magi*, the two main works, the *Vari Capricci* and *Scherzi di fantasia* cycles, are of prime importance. Their date of origin is disputed, the *Capricci* series first appeared in 1749 as an appendix to the *chiaroscuro* woodcuts of Antonio Maria Zanetti (1680–1757) and comprised ten etchings. They were not published independently, and given their current title, until after Tiepolo's death in 1785 (ill. 100). The *Scherzi di fantasia* series of 23 etchings was produced in the 1740s and published by Giandomenico as a complete cycle in 1773 (ills. 101, 102). Since neither series had been commissioned, and Tiepolo himself did not set great store in having them circulated, it has been assumed that he was simply fooling around, creating meaningless exercises for his own pleasure.

Both cycles show a brightly-lit Arcadian world in which the principle of variation is applied to a particular repertory of figures, objects and motifs, which appear over and over in new form. Yet neither the scene of the action, the identity of the figures or the symbolism of the objects, which often brings to mind the theme of transitoriness, can be exactly determined. Instead, the bringing together of unusual and contradictory objects challenges the viewer as he searches in vain to find some meaning. The incomprehensibility of the scenes violates all known rules of pictorial convention. For this reason they were judged to be *capricci*: scenes representing the free play of the imagination, in which the artist could indulge freely and without criticism in this medium. But if we look at the commissioned works, such as the obelisk group in the Asia fresco in the Würzburg Residence, then we notice that the same principle of the *capriccio* also shaped the pictorial conception of his monumental fresco cycles, where it has just the same confusing effect of blurring the pictorial themes, thus clarifying the programmatic importance of the two series of etchings to his overall output.

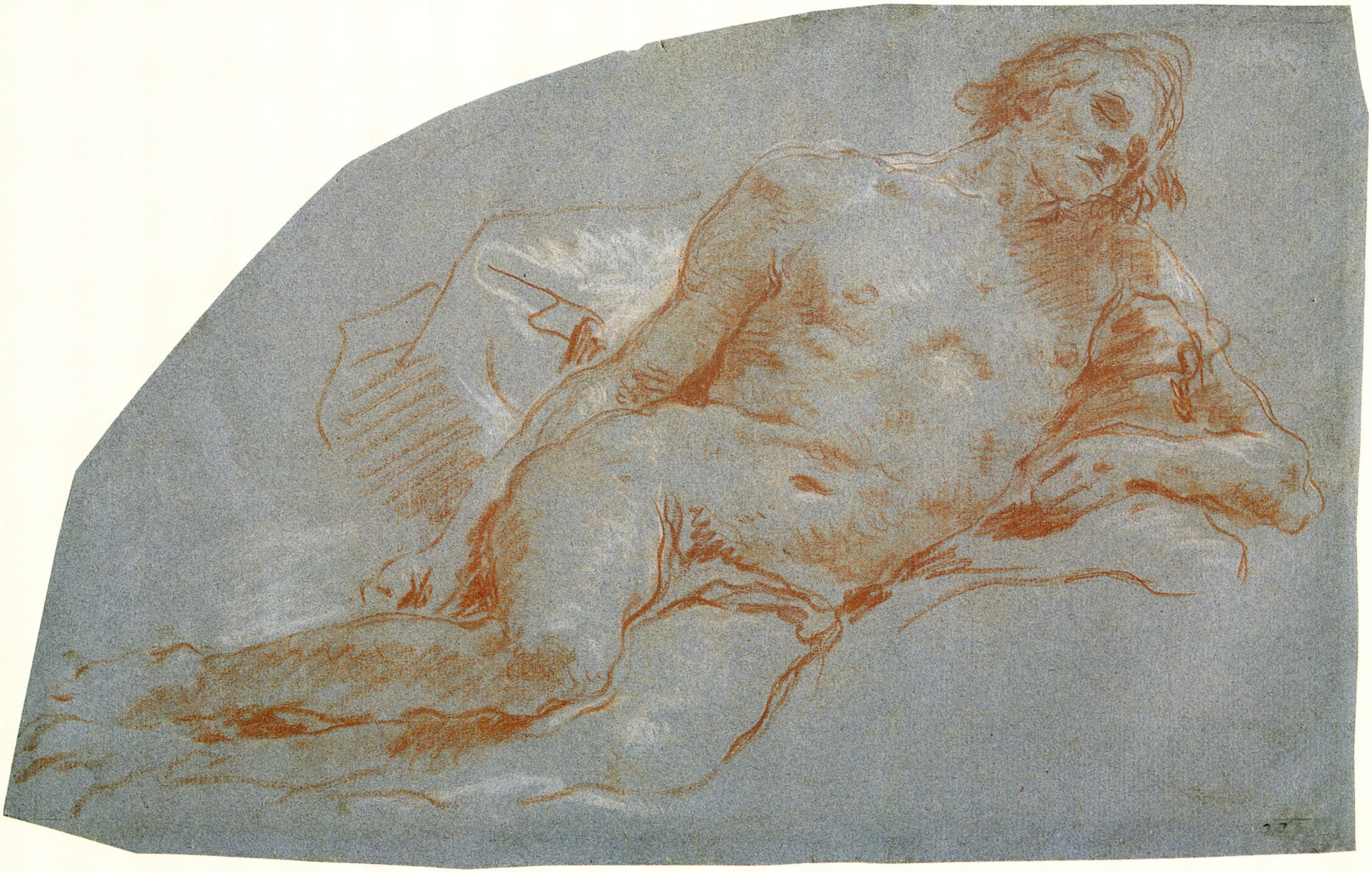

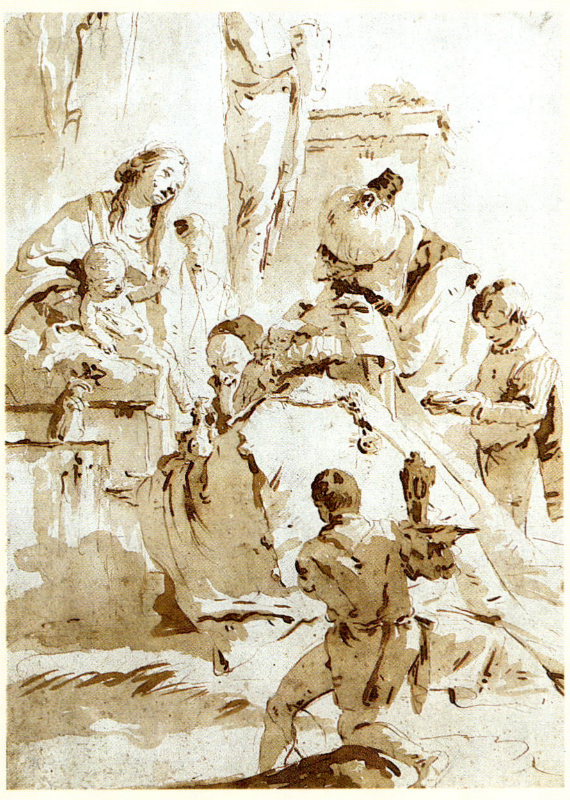

99 (left) *The Adoration of the Magi*, ca. 1753
Brown pen and ink, with a brown wash, over an underdrawing in black pencil,
42 x 29.5cm
Staatliche Museen zu Berlin – Preußischer Kulturbesitz, Kupferstichkabinett, Berlin

This wonderful compositional drawing has a great deal in common with the altarpiece of the same title for the convent church at Schwarzach, although the scene is the other way round here. The corrections to the position of the leg of the boy in the foreground show that Tiepolo used his drawings to experiment.

98 (above) *Male Nude, reclining to the left*, ca. 1752/53
Red chalk, heightened with white, on blue paper,
22.5 x 34.5 cm
Staatsgalerie, Graphische Sammlung, Stuttgart

This drawing is a study from life for the body of Hyacinth, which has been modelled here mainly by means of various parallel hatchings. In contrast to the finished work, the man portrayed here appears older and less athletic. He reminds us more of a study for a "dead Christ" than of the dying Hyacinth.

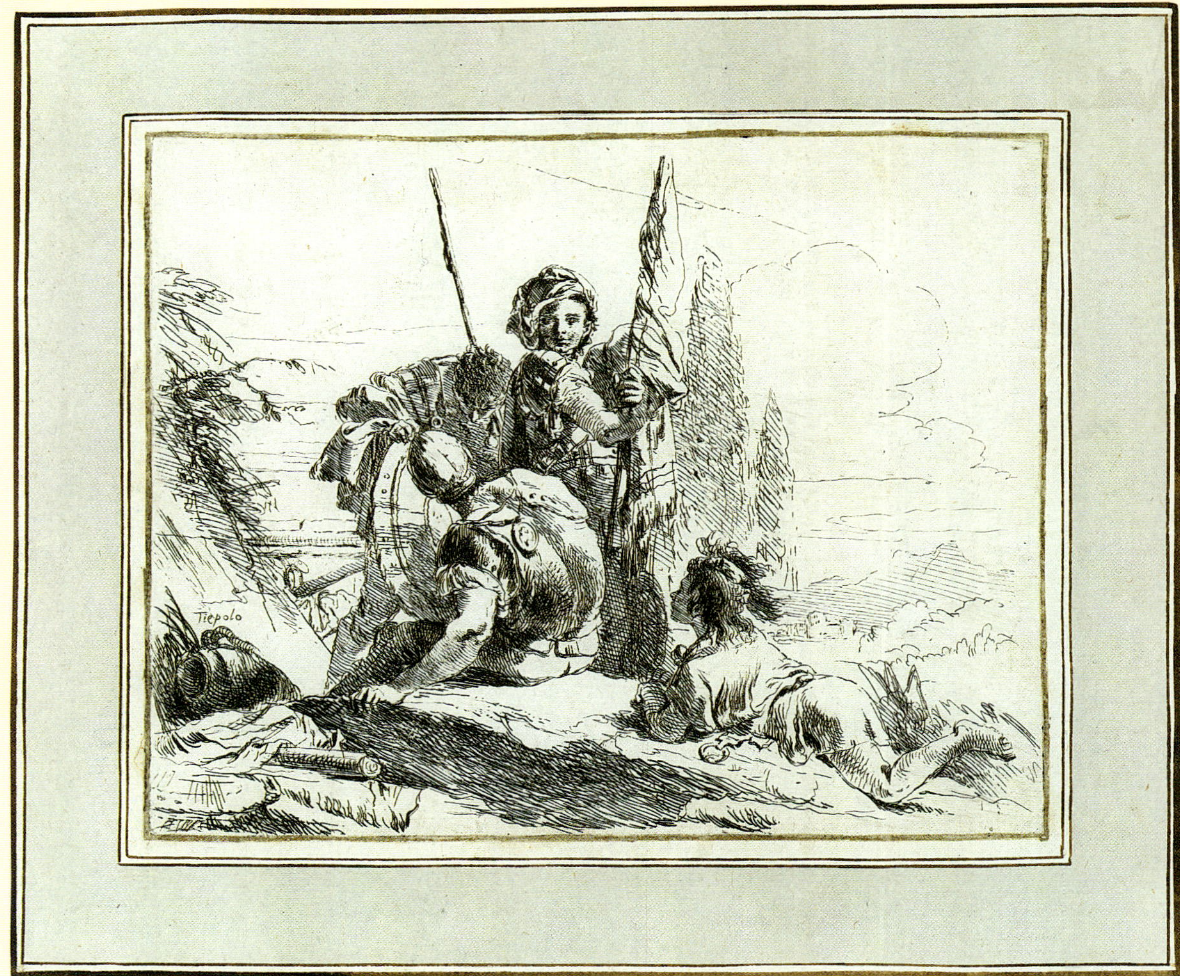

100 *Soldiers and Boy in a Landscape*, ca. 1743
Etching, 14.2 x 17.5 cm
The Metropolitan Museum of Art, Harris Brisbane Dick Fund, New York

A group of three soldiers is depicted in the center of the picture, in a deftly sketched landscape. A boy lies on his stomach in the grass in front of them, and observes them. While two of the soldiers appear to be examining a shield, the third, standing upright in the very center of the picture, holding a banner, looks straight at the viewer with his youthful features. Like the other scenes from the *Capricci*, this is a combination of various enigmatic elements which defy explanation.

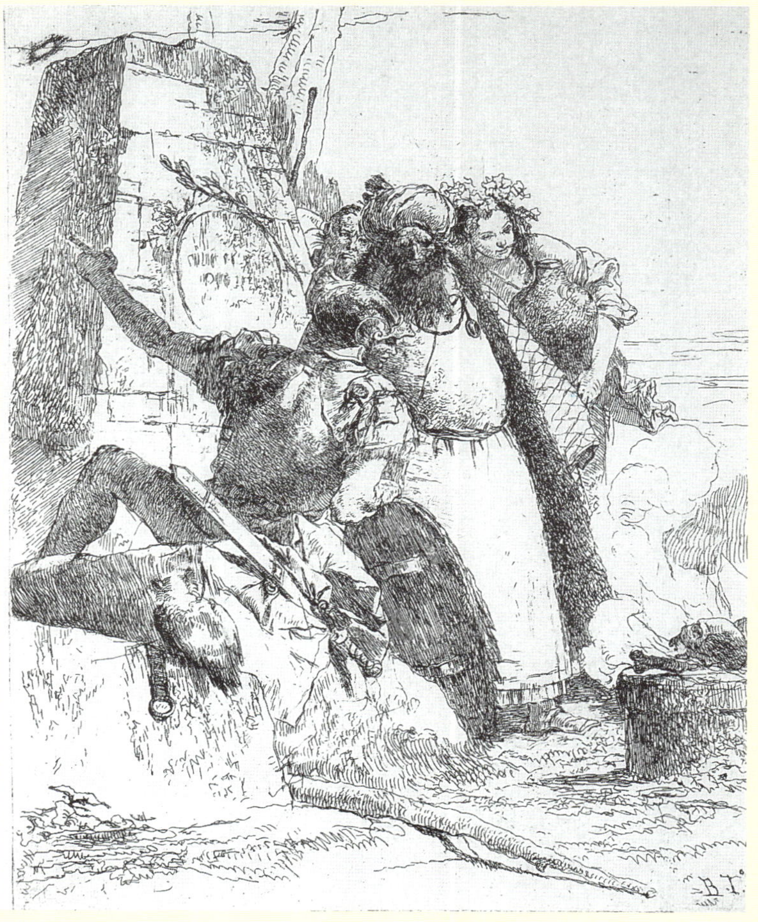

101 *A Warrior, a Sage and a Bacchante look at a burning Skull*, ca.1778
Etching, 22.2 x 17.8 cm
Museum der Bildenden Künste, Graphische Sammlung, Leipzig

In front of a stone pyramid, which brings to mind a monument, stand the sage, in Oriental costume, and the bacchante, while the warrior is seated next to them, pointing towards the background. All three are looking at the burning skull on the bottom right edge of the picture. Once again the various pictorial elements are derived from different contexts with different meanings. No deeper meaning is intended – it is the bizarre, elaborate composition which is given prominence.

102 *Oriental Peasant and his Family*, ca.1778
Etching, 22.2 x 17.3 cm
Museum der Bildenden Künste, Graphische Sammlung, Leipzig

An Oriental peasant and his wife sit at the foot of a tree, next to a block of stone resembling a sarcophagus, their son seated on his mother's lap. Behind them we see the head of a cow, an owl sits on a rotting branch overhead, various objects and a quiver full of arrows are scattered in the foreground. Yet again, the bringing together of objects laden with symbolism is enigmatic.

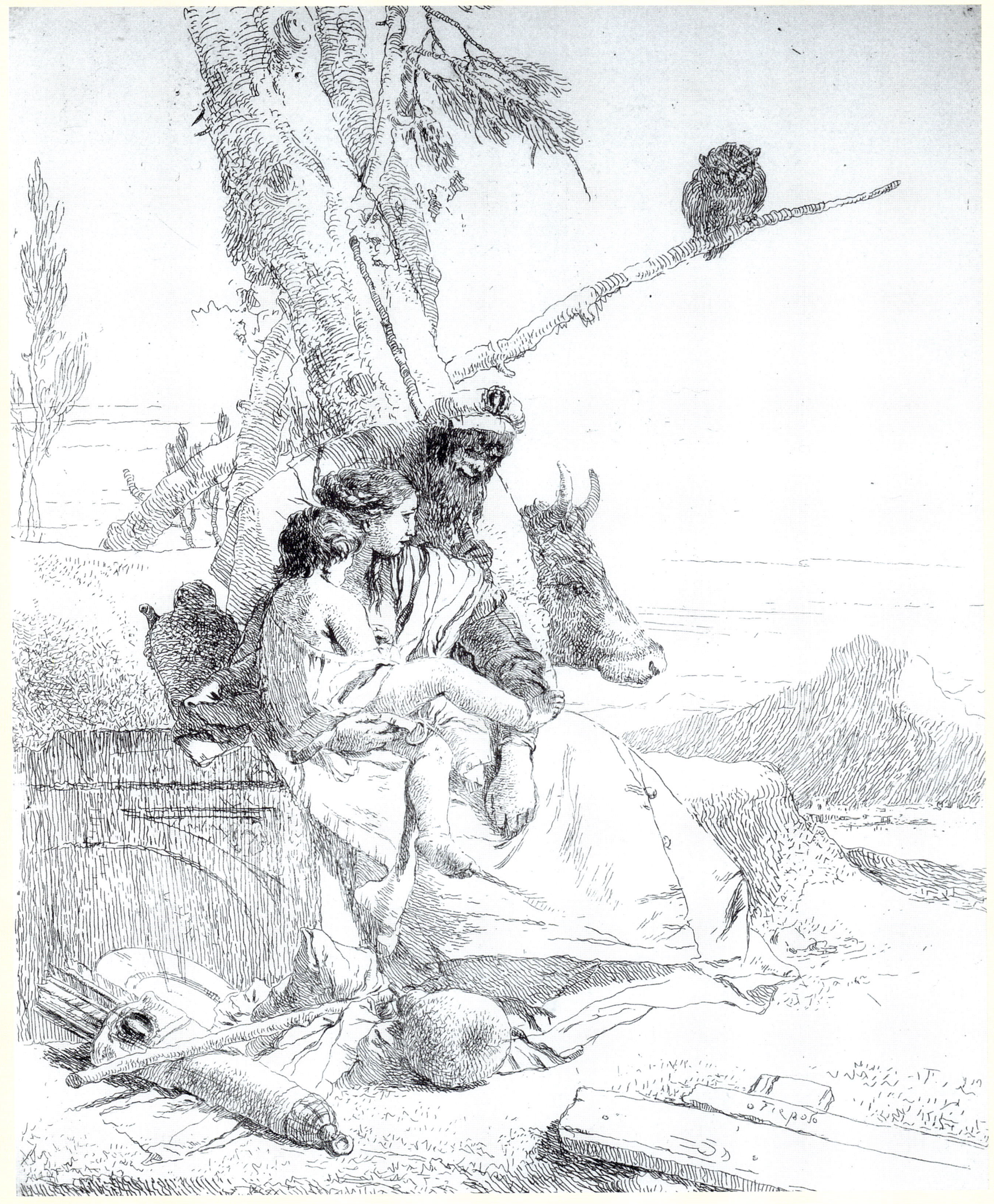
o Tiepolo

Activities in Venice and the Surrounding Area 1754–1761

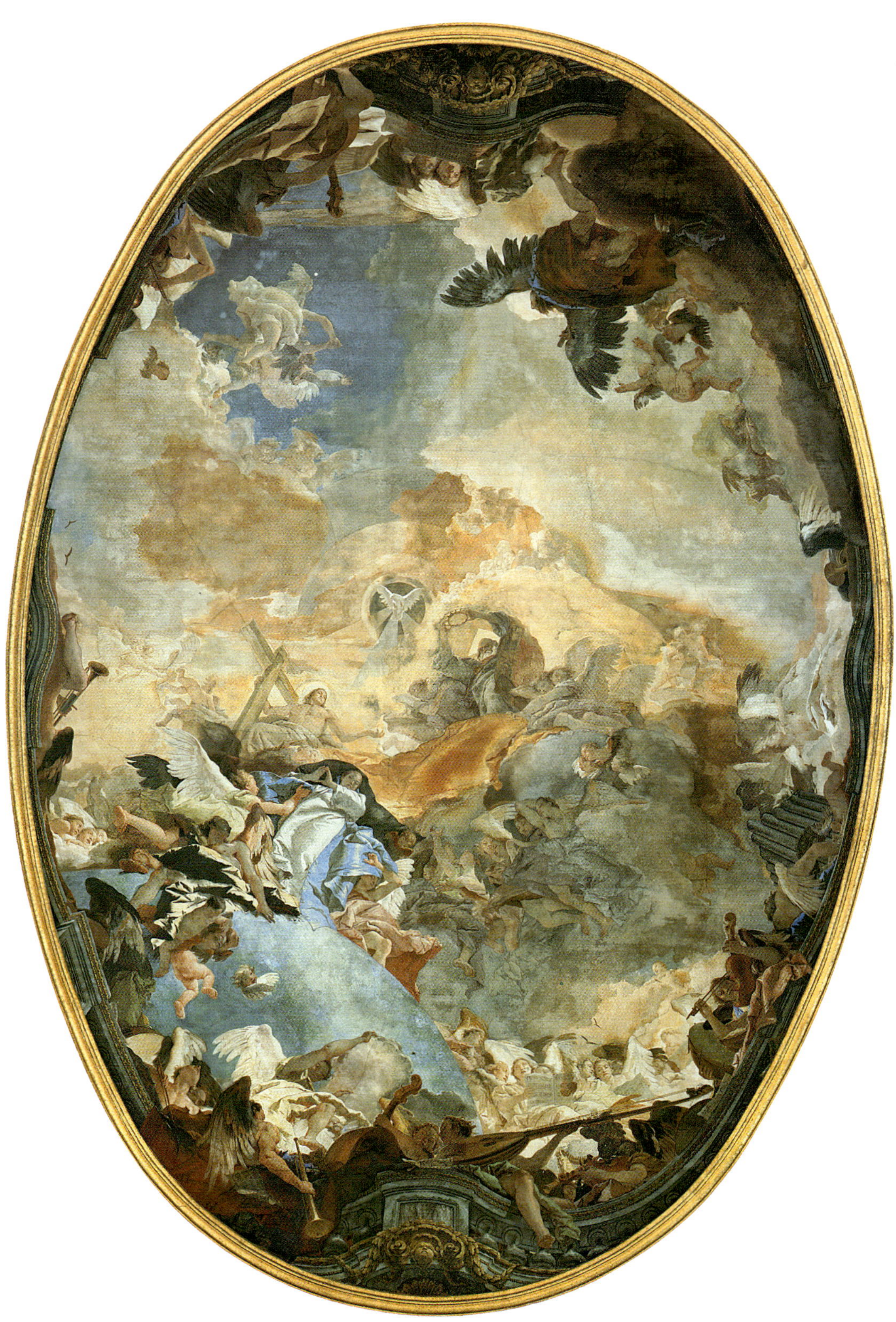

On his return to La Serenissima, Tiepolo immediately received several new commissions. In 1754, he unveiled the altarpiece *The Virgin Mary appearing to St. John Nepomuk* in the church of San Polo in Venice. The work is characteristic of the period which followed his stay in Würzburg. Here, Tiepolo dispensed with the background architecture which he normally used to stabilize his compositions and presented the figures floating in space, as if weightless. It is assumed that the unusually solid and dark-colored clouds in this picture are a tribute to the artist Piazzetta, who had died shortly before on the Feast Day of St. John Nepomuk. The portrayal of the Virgin Mary alludes to the famous *Sistine Madonna* of Raphael (1483–1520), which had decorated the altar in San Polo from 1740 until 1754, when it was acquired by Augustus III of Saxony for the royal art collection in Dresden.

The greatest artistic project of the period, which was also the last major ecclesiastical commission Tiepolo would receive in Venice, was the decoration of the Church of the Pietà, built by Giorgio Massari in 1745. In the course of 1754, Tiepolo painted the monumental ceiling fresco *The Coronation of the Blessed Virgin* (ill. 103) along with three smaller frescos *The ecclesiastical Virtues, David and the Angel* and *Strength and Peace* (now destroyed). The central ceiling fresco of the coronation of the Virgin Mary has a large number of angels playing musical instruments disposed around its edges, and probably served as a paean to music and so as an allusion to the concerts held in the church by a famous local musical institute.

In 1755 Tiepolo and several of his colleagues were involved in drafting the statutes for the Academy of the Arts in Padua, whose first President he was to become from 1756 to 1758.

In 1757, Tiepolo and his son Giandomenico were invited to Vicenza to fresco rooms in the Villa Valmarana and in the adjoining guest quarters, the so-called *foresteria*. Their patron was Count Giustino Valmarana, a scholar and theater enthusiast who was also a distant relative of Niccolò Loschi, in whose villa Tiepolo had worked in 1734. At Villa Valmarana, Tiepolo frescoed the vestibule and four ground-floor rooms, while his son Giandomenico executed the

Giovanni Domenico Tiepolo was born on 30 August 1727, in Venice, the son of Giambattista Tiepolo and his wife Cecilia Guardi. At the beginning of the 1740s he joined his father's workshop, where he began by making copies of the latter's drawings and engravings. In 1747, the twenty-year old painted his own cycle of 14 pictures, known as the *Stations of the Cross*, for the Oratory of the Crucifix in the church of San Polo in Venice, where they are still housed today. He avoided any trace of the grandiloquent style which often characterizes the theatrical re-enactments of his father. Instead, he executed quiet, intimate scenes which portray the suffering of Christ, the grief of his Disciples, and the cold objectivity of the onlookers.

In the period 1750–1770, Giandomenico was his father's closest collaborator. Without him, Giambattista would never have been able to complete the large number of commissions so quickly. At the same time, Giandomenico also worked as an independent artist, although a strict separation of the two roles was not always possible. From 1750–1753, he was heavily involved in the execution of the frescos in the Würzburg Residence, but also produced a large number of independent works. Examples include: *An Encampment* (ill. 107), now in the Mittelrheinisches Landesmuseum in Mainz, or *The Last Supper* (ill. 106), now in the Staatsgalerie at the Residenz, Würzburg. His works are characterized by a simple and direct style of painting, as regards both the subject matter – see, for example, *The Minuet* (now in the Louvre in Paris), which illustrates pleasure in a country dance (ill. 104) – and the composition, since the pictures often contain very simple constellations of figures.

The collaboration with his father at the Villa Valmarana in 1757 demonstrates how successfully Giandomenico could function both as Giambattista's assistant and as an artist in his own right. While he was able to illustrate simple, lyrical scenes of distant lands, courtly excursions and rustic pleasures in the guests' quarters at the villa (ill. 105), known as the *foresteria*, he obviously had no trouble in also executing his father's great themes of epic poetry in the villa. Although he had long since developed his own style in his own pictures, it is often difficult to tell which parts of their collaborations were painted by the father and which by the son. In Spain, to where he had accompanied his father in 1762, he was mainly active as Tiepolo's associate.

The most distinguished of Giandomenico's works were produced once he returned to Venice following his father's death. *Abraham and the three Angels* (1773) and the large work *The Building of the Trojan Horse* (1773/74) show him continuing the tradition of Venetian monumental painting. From 1780 to 1783, he was president of the Venetian Academy. In 1785 he painted the fresco *The Apotheosis of the Giustiniani Family* on the ceiling of the Sala del Maggior Consiglio in the Doge's Palace. Genre scenes and portraits of clowns, which ranging from light ironic undertones to bizarre satire, were to play an ever more important role in his œuvre.

His work found its most personal expression in the late 1790s in the fresco decorations for his own country house in Zianigo, now in the Ca' Rezzonico in Venice. The dancing, tumbling and romping *pulcinelli* demonstrate his talent for studies in movement and for theatrical effects. Alongside painting, Giandomenico was also an eminent draftsman and engraver. One of his first series was of engravings after the *Stations of the Cross* in San Polo in Venice. In 1749, he produced the series *The Flight into Egypt* and, in 1770, the *Raccolta di teste* with 60 portraits of heads, patriarchal in style, based on images by Giambattista. In the 1790s, he executed more than twenty scenes from everyday life, in which he contrasted comic figures with commonplace occurrences, and burlesque episodes with touching and convincing depictions of ordinary life. He died on 3 March 1804 in Venice.

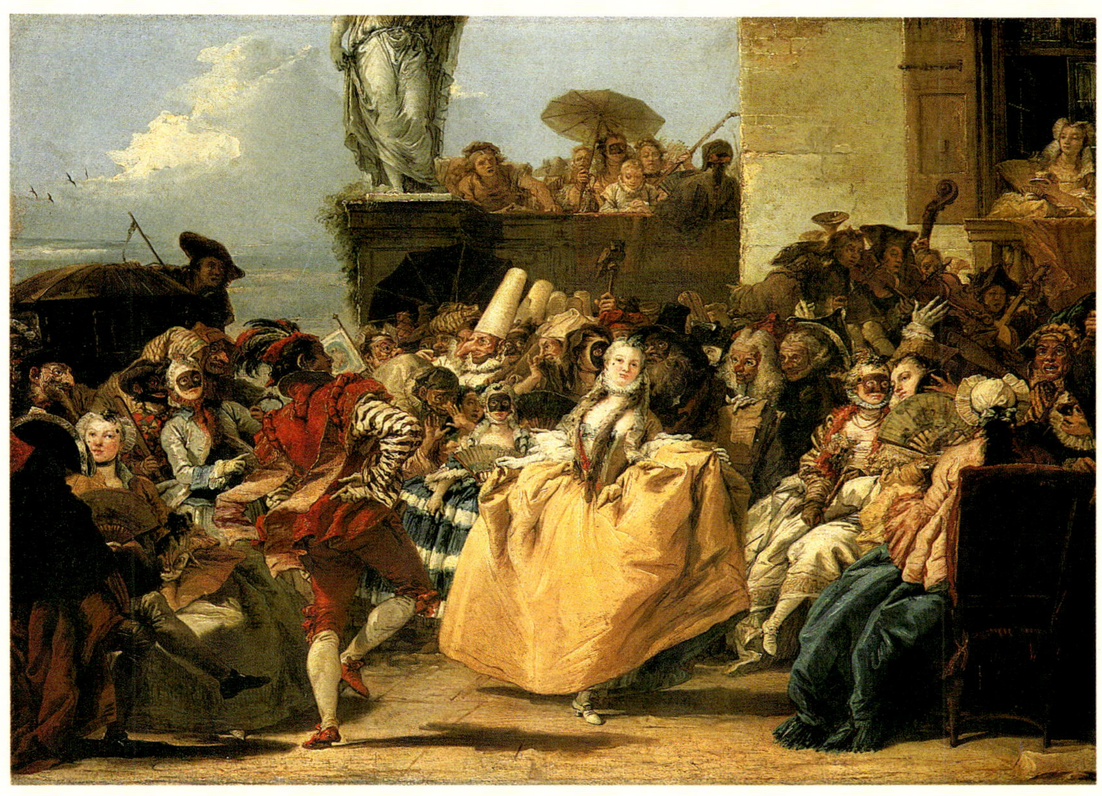

104 (above) Giovanni Domenico Tiepolo
The Minuet, ca. 1765
Oil on canvas, 75.5 x 120 cm
Musée du Louvre, Paris

This rustic festival is one of Giandomenico's masterpieces. It shows people, in a variety of costumes, who have gathered in the open air, in front of an architectural setting which cannot be more closely identified. Near the center of the picture we see a man, his back towards us. He has just begun to dance with a finely dressed lady. It is probably this scene which gives the picture its title, which otherwise only vaguely refers to what we actually see happening. The theme is not intended to carry a deeper meaning, but merely to portray a happy zest for life.

103 (opposite) *The Coronation of the Blessed Virgin*, 1754
Fresco, 1320 x 700 cm
Santa Maria della Visitazione (Pietà), Venice

That this fresco impresses is due mainly to the host of figures portrayed, to the way the light is handled, from the darkness around the edges to the radiance at the center, and to the impression of great depth conveyed. Mary is seen, strongly foreshortened from below, standing on the globe. To the left above her, Christ sits with the Cross, while God the Father, on the right, holds the crown in readiness. The dove, the symbol of the Holy Ghost, has been positioned slightly left of center. In view of the extraordinary number of music-making angels, the subject of the Coronation of the Virgin almost takes second place in the picture to the theme of music – a reference to the church as a venue for important concerts.

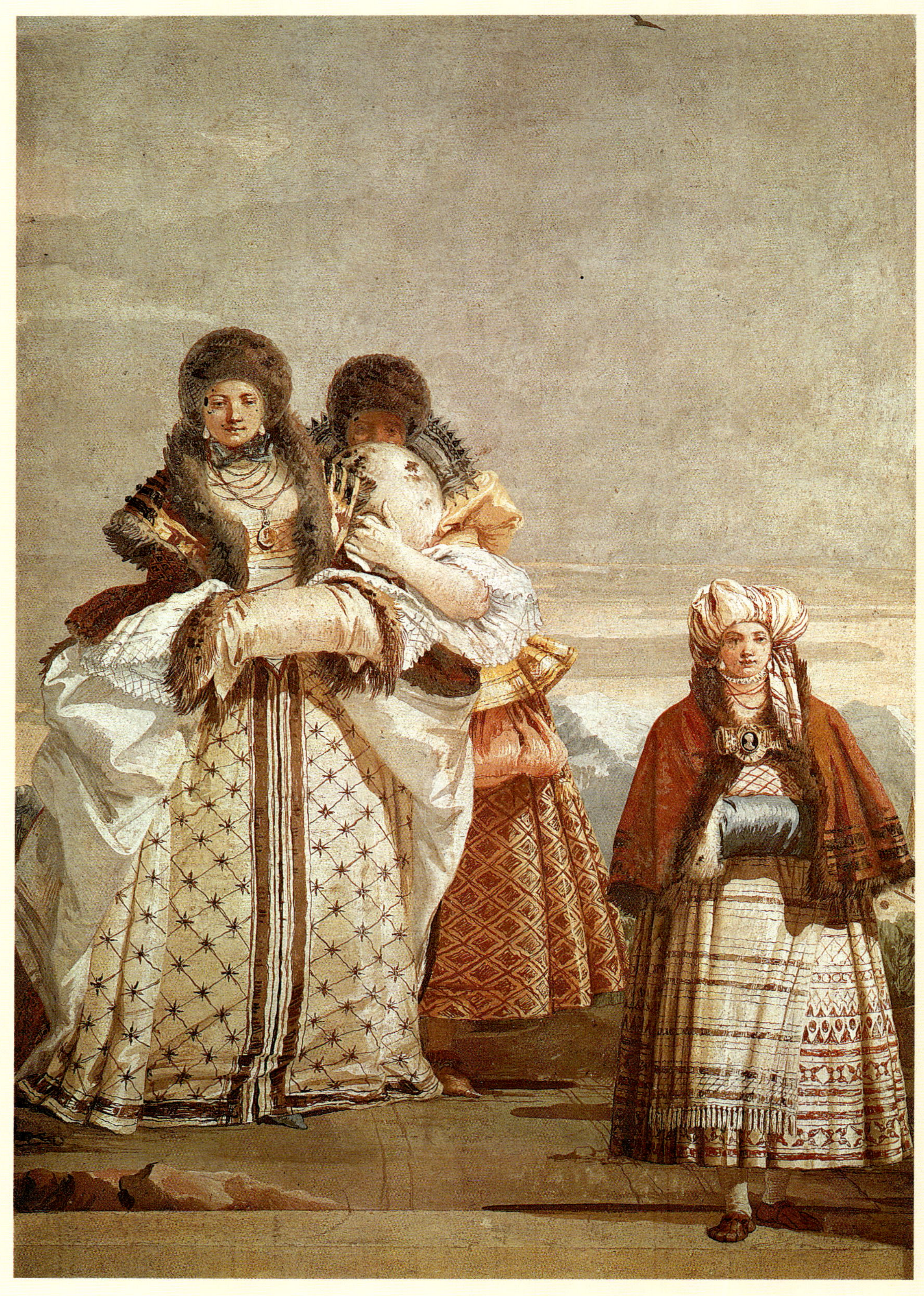

105 Giovanni Domenico Tiepolo
Winter Promenade, 1757
Fresco
Foresteria of the Villa Valmarana, Vicenza

This scene is in the Gothic Pavilion in the *foresteria* of the Villa Valmarana, so-called in reference to the feigned Gothic architectural elements of its setting, designed by Mengozzi (known as Colonna). The fresco is painted as an illusionistic view out into the open countryside, and displays a strongly simplified composition in which three handsomely dressed women walk frontally towards the viewer. Apart from the few mountains suggested on the distant horizon, and the several birds silhouetted in the upper half of the picture, the background consists only of an empty expanse of sky.

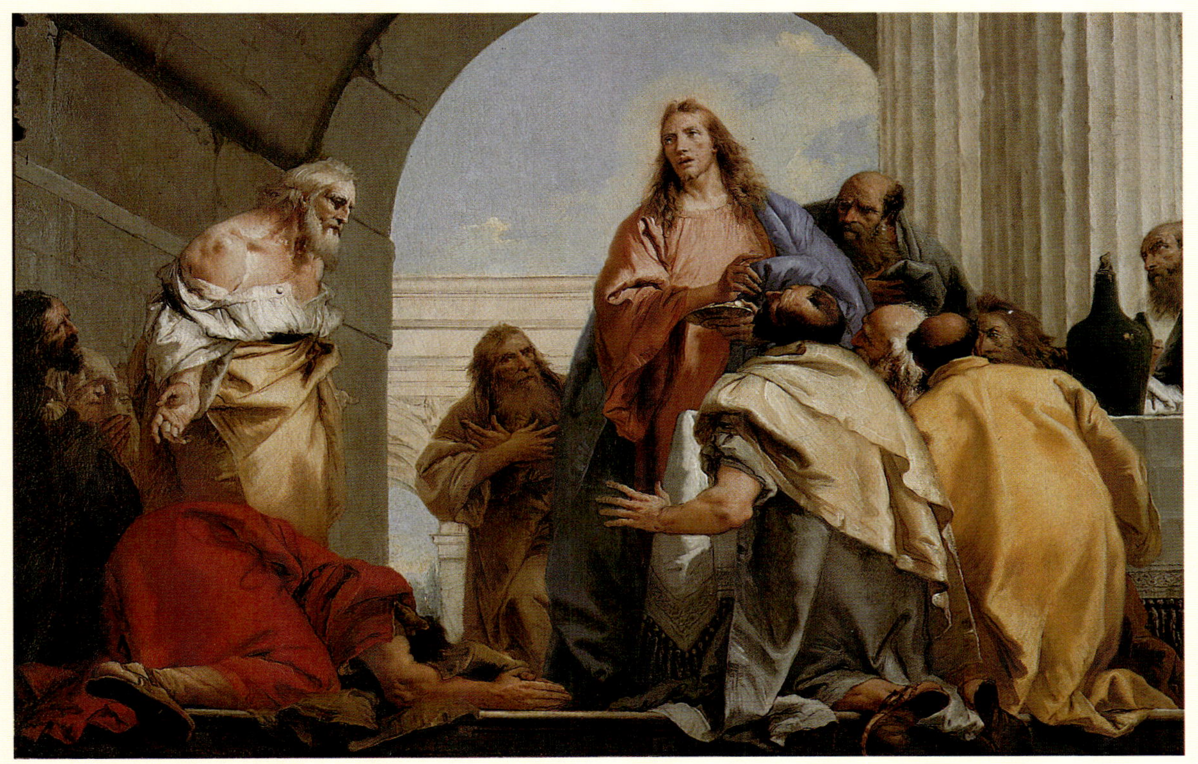

106 Giovanni Domenico Tiepolo
The Last Supper, 1752
Oil on canvas, 99.2 x 150 cm
Bayerische Staatsgemäldesammlungen, Staatsgalerie in der Residenz, Würzburg

The subject is the Last Supper before the death of Christ. Christ, in the center of the picture, is blessing the man who kneels before him, having already offered him bread. The scene clearly refers to the transubstantiation of bread into the body of Christ which takes place during the celebration of the Mass, and symbolizes the sacrament of the Eucharist. The figure lying on the floor symbolizes the sympathy and emotion of the participating disciples, of whom only James, on the left edge of the picture, is identified by his attribute, the shell. The figure in white robes who stands on the left is most likely Peter, while the bearded man to the right, behind Christ, conforms to the standardized portrayal of Paul.

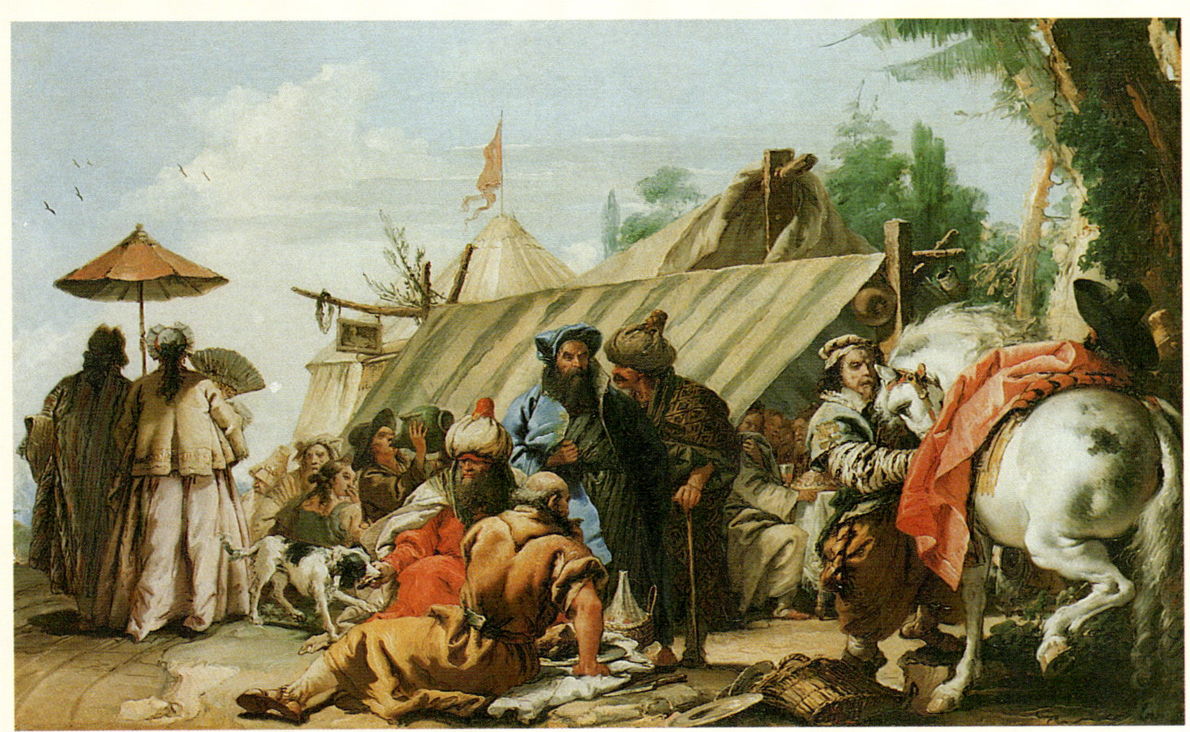

107 Giovanni Domenico Tiepolo
An Encampment, ca. 1752
Oil on canvas, 76 x 120 cm
Mittelrheinisches Landesmuseum, Mainz

This picture is the earliest known "fantasy piece" by Giandomenico. It shows a variety of people from different cultural and thematic circles, dressed in the fashions of various centuries. We simply cannot determine what event has brought them together. He had found the stimulus for themes which are no longer related to mythological, historical or Christian pictorial subjects in his father's *Capricci* and *Scherzi*. The combination of figures is based on various sources, and uses several motifs borrowed from Giambattista's repertory.

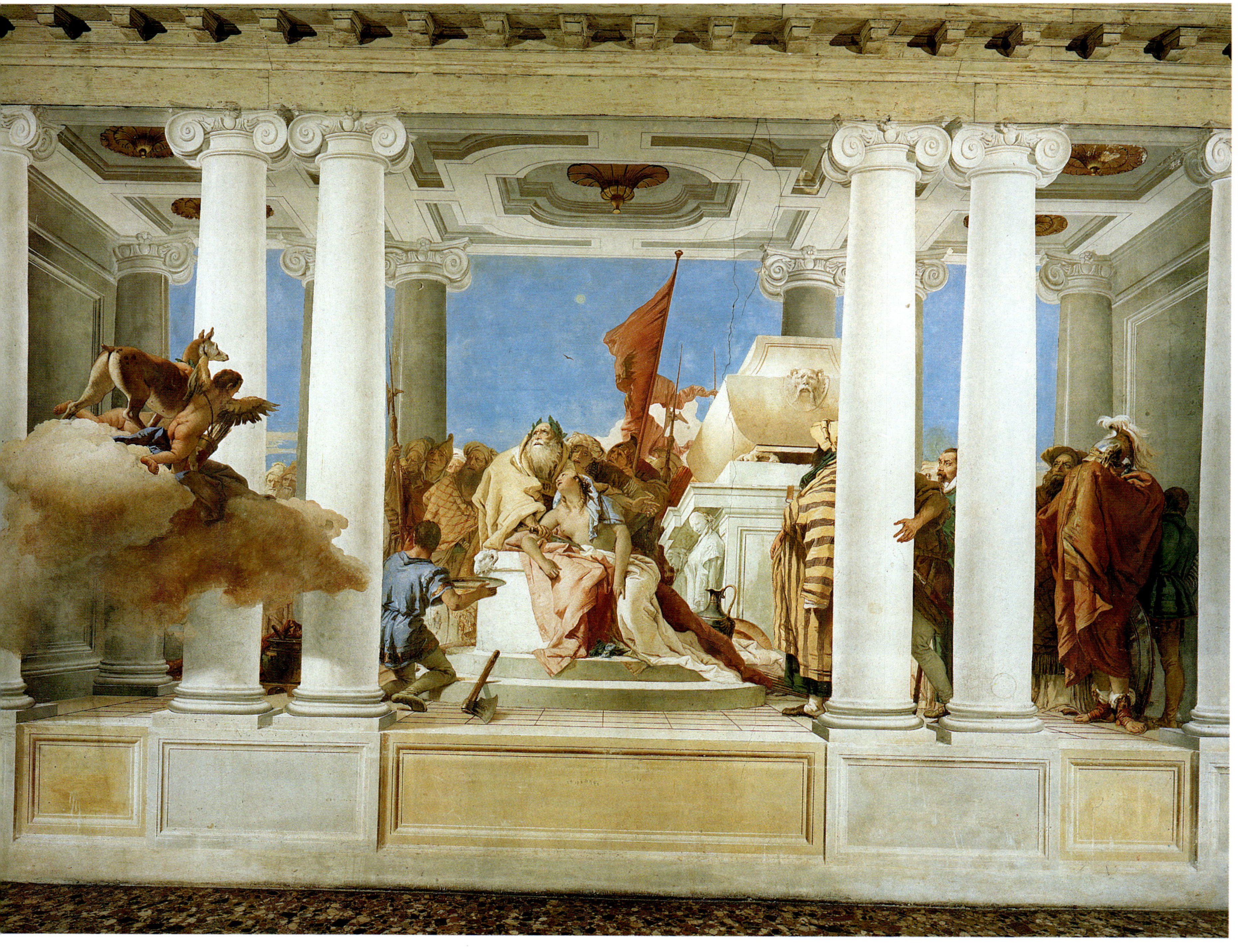

108 *The Sacrifice of Iphigenia*, 1757
Fresco, 350 x 700 cm
Villa Valmarana, Vicenza

The sacrifice of Iphigenia takes place in an illusionistic hall of columns, which partially block the spectator's view of the scene. In the center of the picture, Iphigenia lies on the altar, the priest ready to apply the knife. However, the deer hind sent by Diana to save Iphigenia is already descending on a cloud, accompanied by two *putti*, from the left towards the altar. Agamemnon stands somewhat isolated, on the very right of the picture, covering his face in order not to have to witness the death of his daughter. As onlookers, Tiepolo has gathered together warriors and Orientals, one of whom has placed his arm around a column, adding a perfect touch to the illusionism of the simulated architecture.

decoration in the adjacent guest house. Giandomenico's lively genre scenes featuring peasants and merchants were intended to form a marked contrast with Giambattista's noble and tragic themes in the Villa, borrowed from famous works of Greek, Roman and Italian literature. The "Iliad" of Homer (ca. 750–650 BC), the "Aeneid" of Virgil (70–19 BC), "Orlando furioso" by Ariosto (1474–1533) and "Gerusalemme liberata" by Tasso (1544–1595) were the sources for the different scenes which, because of the small, almost intimate proportions of the rooms, are narrated with a certain simplicity and using a limited number of figures.

Visitors to the Villa first enter the vestibule and are surprised by the illusionistic opening up of the right-hand wall through an impressive portico, behind which is the scene portraying the sacrifice of Iphigenia (ill. 108). In order to appease the gods and be granted wind to carry his ships to Troy, Agamemnon was forced to sacrifice his daughter, who kneels before the altar of the high priest in the center of the fresco. The right-hand side shows Agamemnon covering his face in order not to have to watch the terrible scene. For this reason he does not see the deer hind standing atop a descending cloud on the left-hand side, which has been sent by the goddess Diana – portrayed on the ceiling of the room alongside the wind-god Aeolus – out of sympathy for Iphigenia, to be sacrificed in the girl's place. The soldiers and ships represented on the walls to either side of the entrance allude to the departure of the Greek fleet (ills. 110, 111). Four monochrome allegories of rivers complete the decoration of the vestibule.

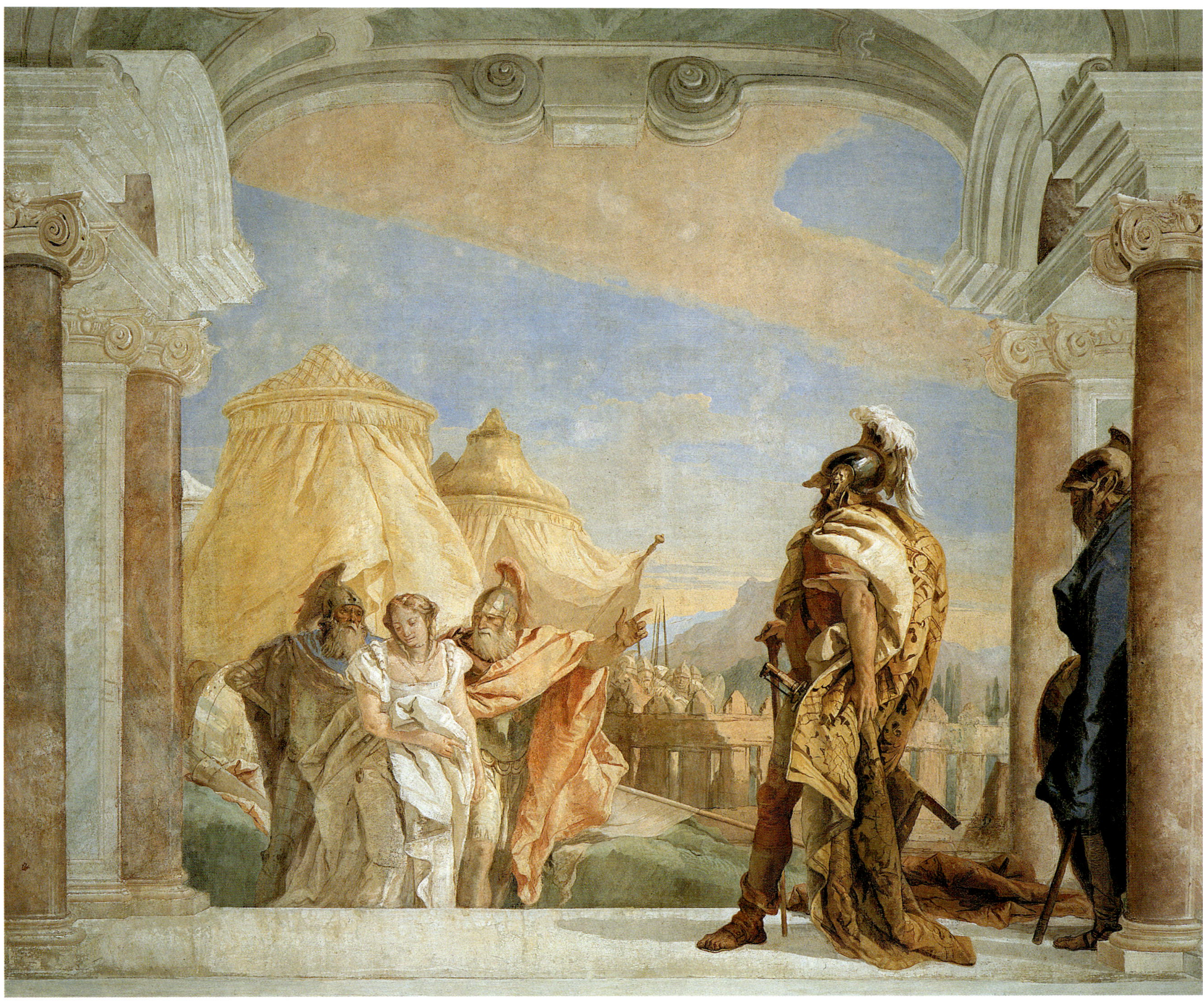

Love, fulfilled and unrequited, provides the subject matter of the frescos in the four adjoining rooms. The walls in the Homer room tell the story of Achilles' unfortunate love for the slave girl Briseis (ills. 109, 112, 114), while the goddess Minerva appears on the central ceiling fresco surrounded by *putti*. The scenes on the walls again unfold in a kind of simulated loggia-architecture, which gives the impression of the room leading directly outdoors and in which the protagonists appear like actors on a stage.

The requited love between Angelica and Medoro, with the addition of a scene in which Ruggero frees Angelica, is the subject of the Ariosto room (ills. 113, 116). On the ceiling is a depiction of Amor, the god of Love, riding blindfold in his chariot drawn by *putti*. This time Tiepolo has foregone illusionistic openings in the wall scenes in favour of a curved framing.

In the Virgil room, too, the scenes are contained within a definite framework. Three episodes from the life of Aeneas adorn the walls (ills. 117, 119, 120). A representation of *Vulcan's Forge* on the fireplace wall was most likely executed by Giandomenico, along with the medallions of scenes from antiquity and two *supra porte* paintings of allegorical figures. The fresco *The Triumph of Venus*, destroyed in 1944, occupied the ceiling.

The remaining room is decorated with episodes from the love story of Rinaldo and Armida, now Tiepolo's third version of this subject (ill. 118). The four scenes are once more enclosed within definite frames and one of their remarkable features is the extremely simplified composition made necessary by their closeness to the

109 *Eurybates and Talthybios lead Briseis to Agamemnon*, 1757
Fresco, 300 x 280 cm
Villa Valmarana, Vicenza

Agamemnon had Achilles' favorite slave, Briseis, handed over to him, in return for having been forced to surrender Chryseis, the daughter of a priest of Apollo. The representation shows an imperious-looking Agamemnon, in a kind of loggia in the foreground, awaiting the slave girl, who is being brought to him by two soldiers. The tents of the Greek army appear in the background. The panoramic landscape completes the scenery.

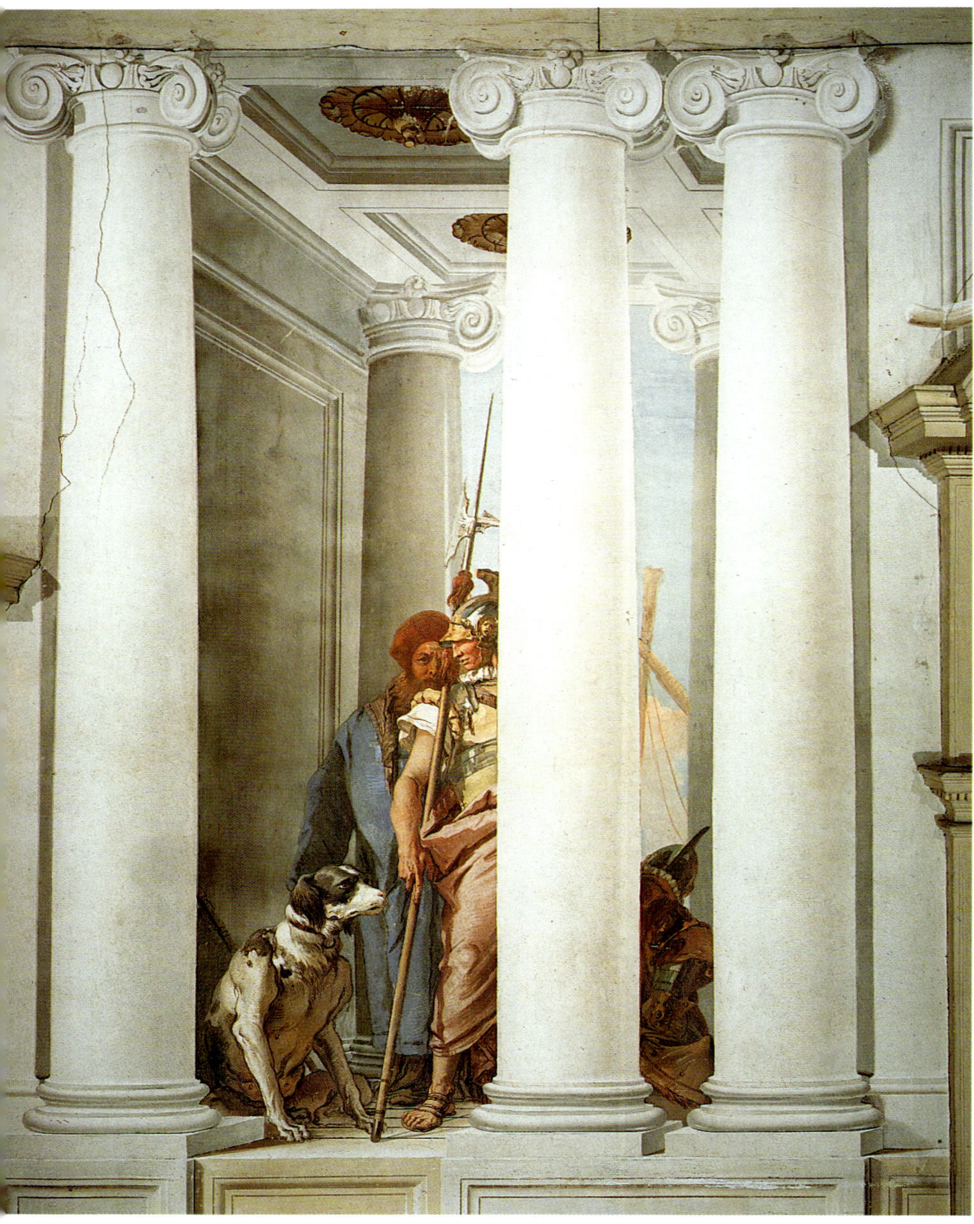

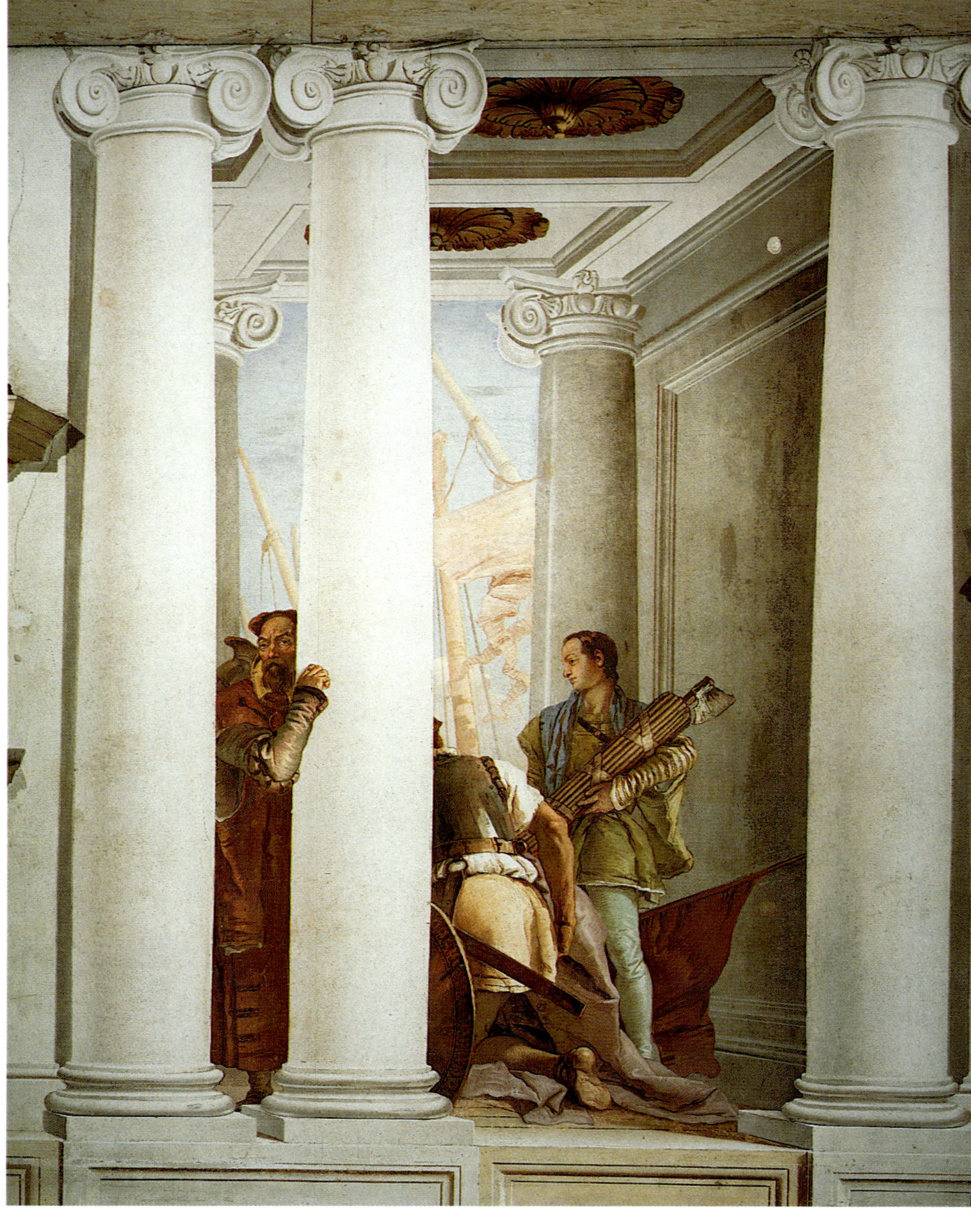

110 (above left) Detail of *The Greek fleet in Aulis*, 1757
Fresco, 350 x 115 cm
Villa Valmarana, Vicenza

To the right of the entrance, almost hidden by the columns of the imitation architecture, we see the soldiers of the Greek fleet, in the process of packing up their weapons in order to take them aboard ship, whose sails can be made out in the background. However, the scene is more important for its decorative qualities than for its content. Another game is being played with the different levels of reality, especially in the figure of the man who stands behind the pillar and looks at the viewer.

111 (above right) Detail of *The Greek Fleet in Aulis*, 1757
Fresco, 350 x 115 cm
Villa Valmarana, Vicenza

The two men differ in their dress from the soldiers on the right-hand side. They obviously hold a higher rank and are waiting for the ships to be loaded up. This scene, too, is of no particular importance to the overall content, but is intended to enrich the decoration of the room by playing illusionistic games with reality.

112 (opposite) *The Rage of Achilles*, 1757
Fresco, 300 x 300 cm
Villa Valmarana, Vicenza

Outraged at having lost his beloved, Achilles draws his sword to kill Agamemnon. The sudden appearance of the goddess Minerva, who, in this fresco, has grabbed Achilles by the hair, prevents the act of violence. Agamemnon stands to the left and tries to shield himself with his cloak, while in the background, in front of a rounded temple, a huddled row of Greek soldiers observes the scene. What stands out in this fresco, is the facial expression of Achilles, almost contorted by rage into a grimace, something seldom found in Tiepolo.

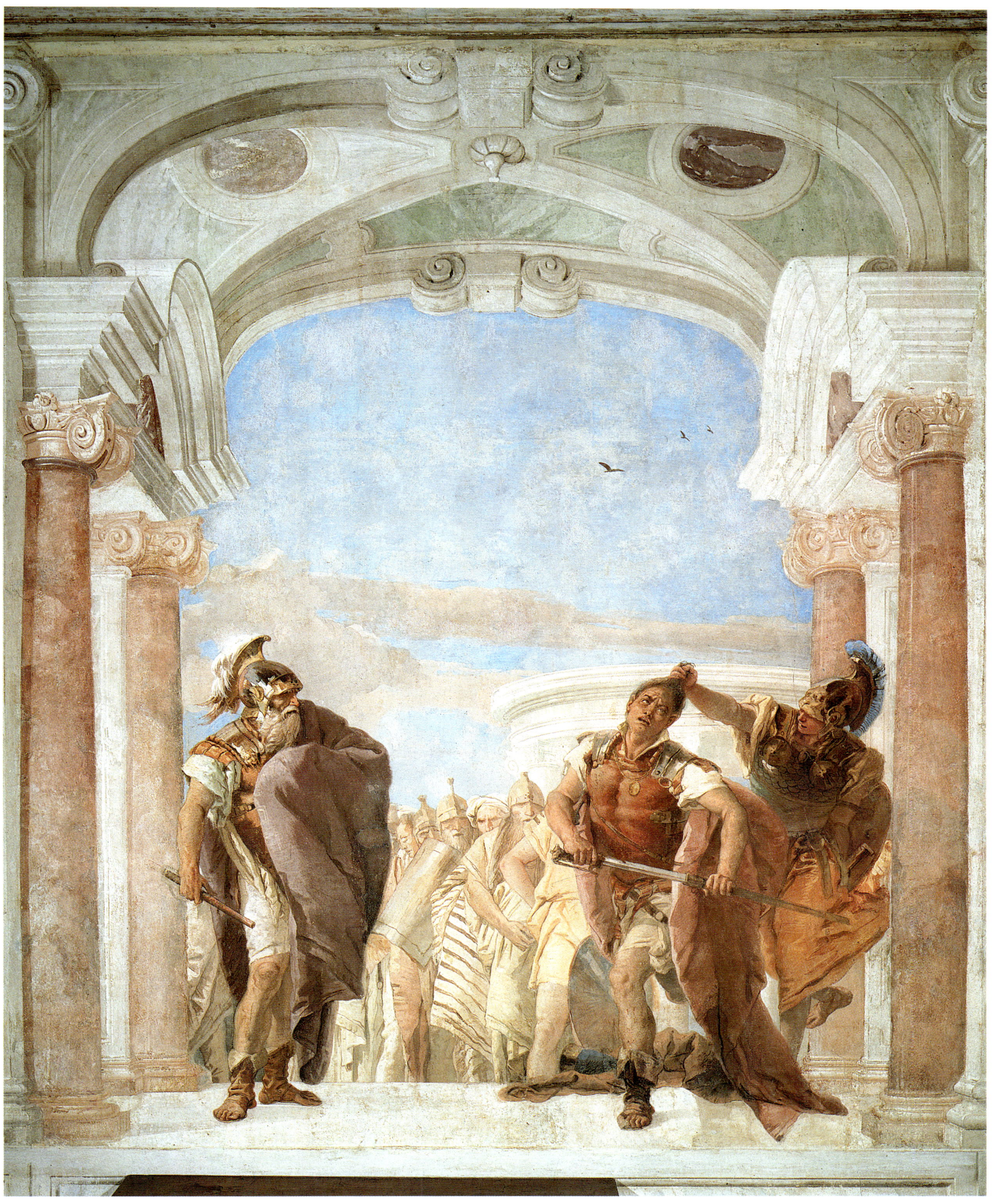

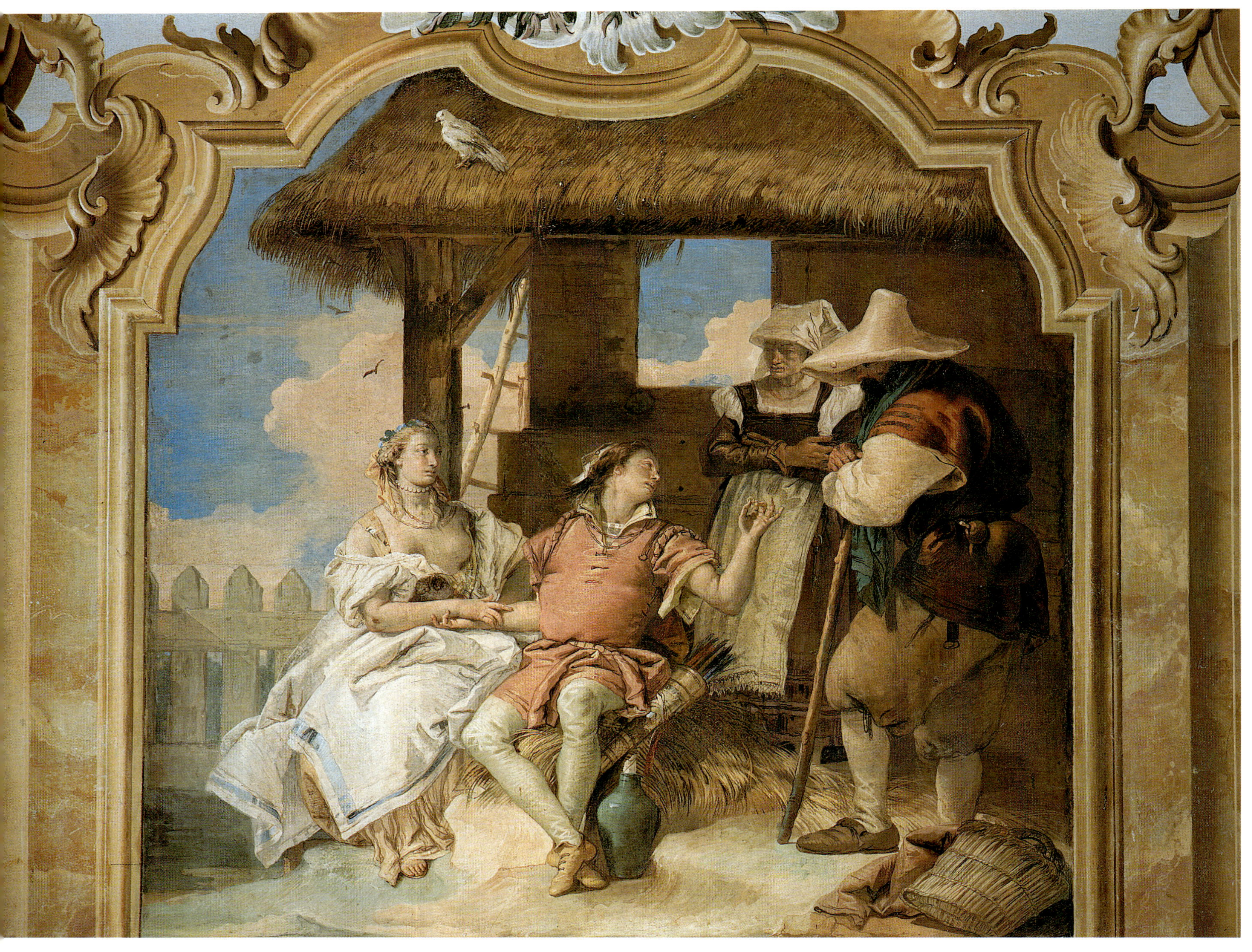

113 *Angelico and Medoro with the Shepherds*, 1757
Fresco, 250 x 250 cm
Villa Valmarana, Vicenza

The fresco portrays a scene from the love story of the young knight and the maiden Angelica from Ariosto's "Orlando furioso". The two are given temporary shelter by a shepherd couple, once Angelica has found and cared for the wounded Medoro. As a way of thanking them for their hospitality, Medoro gives them the ring which Angelica had previously received from Orlando. The simple depiction of the peasants brings to mind Giandomenico's country scenes in the *foresteria*.

viewer in the confined room. The ceiling picture *The Triumph of Light over Darkness* (ills. 121, 122) is often attributed to Giandomenico Tiepolo.

The characteristic element of the frescos in the Villa Valmarana is surely the way in which the representations have been conceived as theatrical scenes, in which the various heroes act as if on the stage. However, the new quality which Tiepolo invests in the portrayal of emotional tension is far more impressive than the illusionism of the frescos, developed in collaboration with Mengozzi Colonna, and which establishes a relationship between the world of the paintings and the world of the viewer. This is evident in the moving portrayal of the grieving Agamemnon, of the weeping Thetis and her long-suffering son or in Armida's plaintive gesture.

Having completed work in Vicenza, Tiepolo returned to Venice and began decorating the Palazzo Rezzonico (known as the Ca'Rezzonico) for his clients, Lodovico Rezzonico and his wife Faustina Savorgan. To celebrate their marriage, he painted two ceiling frescos, an *Allegory of Marriage* and an *Allegory of Merit accompanied by Nobility and Virtue* (ill. 123), in collaboration with Giandomenico and Girolamo Mengozzi Colonna. In portraying the *Allegory of the Marriage*, Tiepolo returned to the theme of the married couple sitting in Apollo's horse-drawn Chariot of the Sun, to which he added the usual round of triumphal allegories (Grace, Fame, Wisdom, Merit, etc). The whole setting is dominated by bright light and extremely clear color management. In the second fresco, Nobility

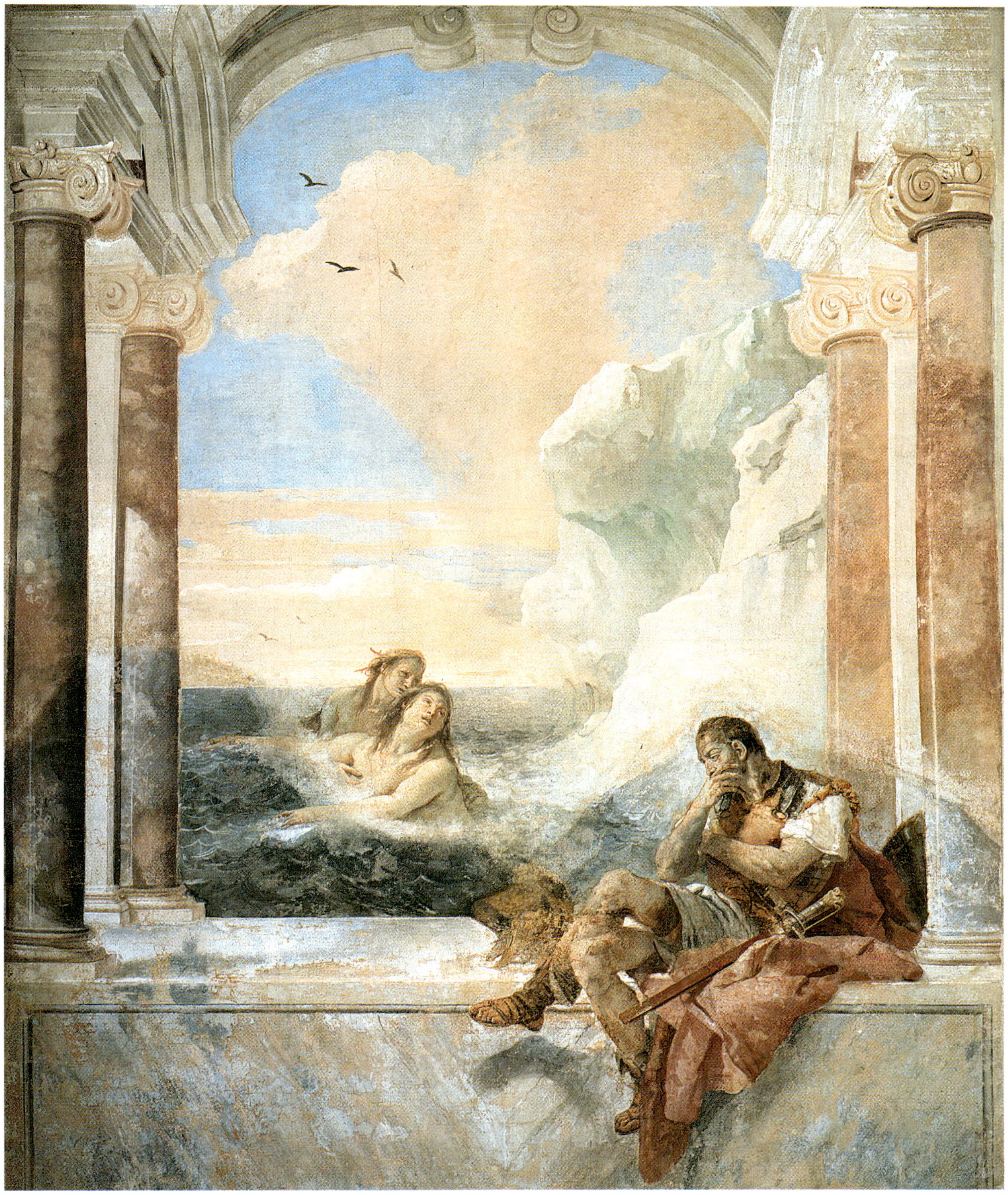

114 (left) *Thetis consoling Achilles*, 1757
Fresco, 300 x 200 cm
Villa Valmarana, Vicenza

Achilles sits on the balustrade of a balcony in a loggia on the seashore, his legs dangling illusionistically down into the viewer's space, and bemoans his fate. Out in the water, his mother, the sea-goddess Thetis, appears in the company of a Nereid, and attempts to console him. The picture, largely bereft of figures, with its expansive view of the sea attempts to capture the sad mood of the hero.

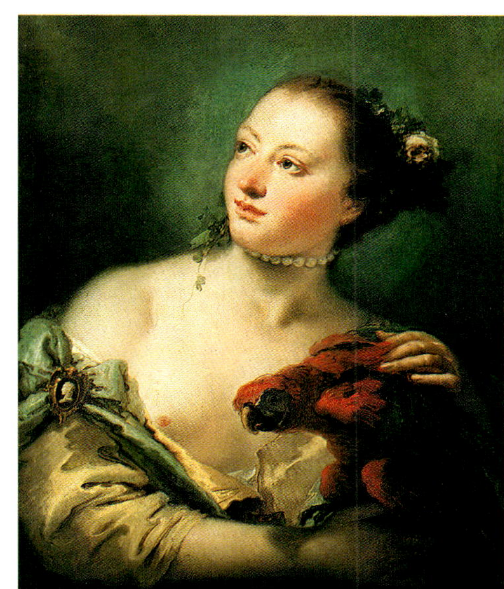

115 (above) *Young Woman with Parrot*, 1758–1760
Oil on canvas, 70 x 52 cm
Ashmolean Museum of Art and Archaeology, Oxford

The brightly-lit half-length portrait of *a Young Woman with Parrot* is set in front of a dark green background. She gazes out of the picture to the left. Executed with very smooth brushstrokes, the portrait differs from Tiepolo's usual physiognomies, and is more reminiscent of works of the French Rococo. The bare décolleté and the parrot, a symbol of lasciviousness, refer to the long Italian tradition of pictures of female courtiers and courtesans.

and Virtue accompany Merit to the temple of Glory. The group of figures floating on a cloud illusionistically overlaps the picture frame and so creates a connection between the world of the viewer and the eternal kingdom of Glory depicted in the fresco. The decoration of the Ca' Rezzonico was Tiepolo's last fresco cycle in his native city of Venice. These works would later frequently be criticised for the supposedly superficial treatment of the subject matter and a lack of intensity in the portrayal. However, following recent restoration, these criticisms have proved to be unfounded. On the contrary: the frescos belong to the late-period masterpieces, particularly on account of their light coloring and the rendering of even the smallest details, such as the allegorical figures around the picture frame.

The allegorical canvas *Neptune paying Homage to Venice* (ill. 125) was painted, probably in 1758, for the Doges' Palace in Venice, where it was hung in the Sala delle quattro porte in place of a fresco by Tintoretto. As an allegory of state, it represents a genre very seldom employed in the 18th century, and which properly derives from the Renaissance period in art, to which Tiepolo refers in the way he depicts the figures and the costumes. Stylistically, it is related to the oil painting *Time revealing Truth* (now in the Museum of Fine Arts in Boston) and the ceiling picture *Venus entrusting a Son to Time* (now in the National Gallery in London), which were also executed during this period.

In 1759, Tiepolo created the large altarpiece showing *St. Thecla liberating the City of Este from the Plague* (ills.

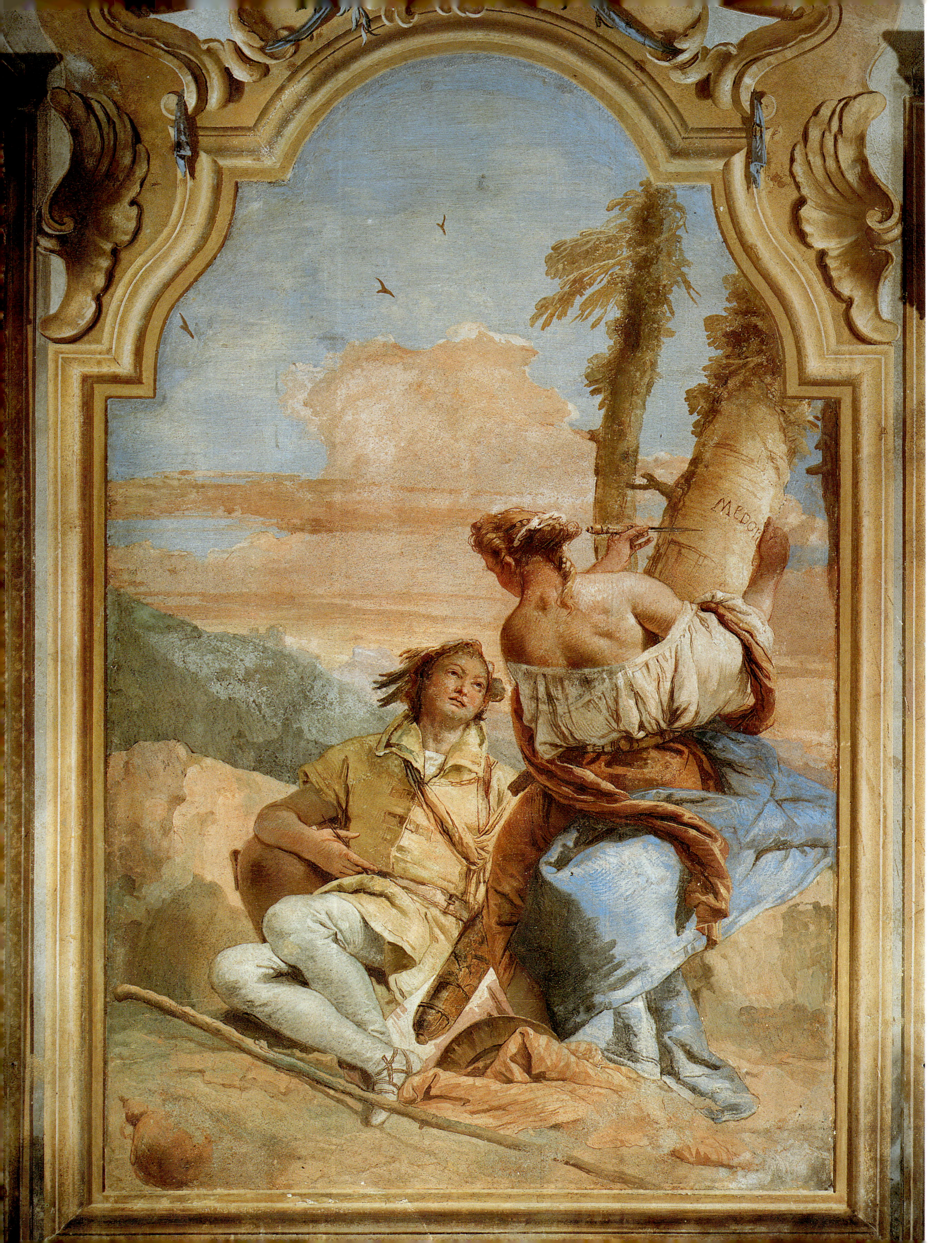
MEDOR

116 (opposite) *Angelica carving Medoro's Name on a Tree*, 1757
Fresco, 250 x 160 cm
Villa Valmarana, Vicenza

In front of an extensive, yet barely-developed landscape, Angelica carves the name of her beloved onto a tree. She has her back to the viewer and is looking down at Medoro, who sits to her left.

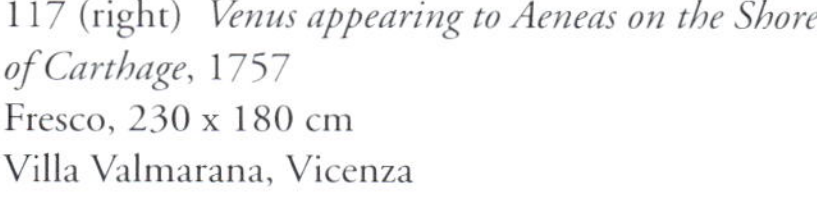

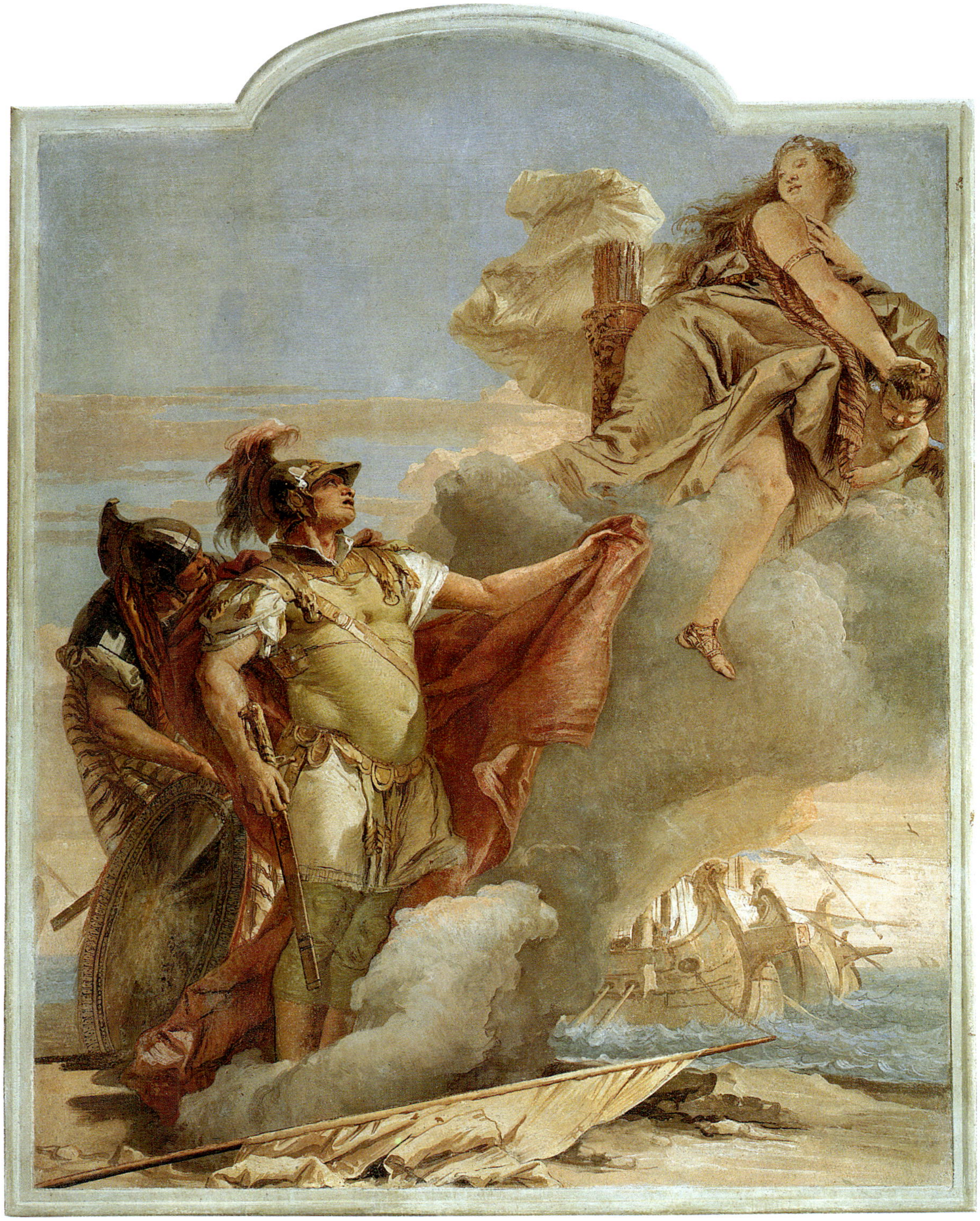

117 (right) *Venus appearing to Aeneas on the Shores of Carthage*, 1757
Fresco, 230 x 180 cm
Villa Valmarana, Vicenza

During the destruction of Troy, Aeneas flees the city, at the order of the gods, to establish a new city in Italy. A storm drives him to the shores of Carthage. Accompanied by Achates, he makes his way to Dido, the queen of Carthage. His mother Venus appears to him along the way and carries the two men, enveloped in a cloud, unscathed to Carthage. Aeneas and Achates stand on the left of the picture, while Venus, accompanied by Amor, hovers above them to the right, and is in the act of transporting them on a cloud. Ships lie at anchor in the background.

126, 127) for Este cathedral. The subject matter refers to the great plague epidemic of 1630 in the Veneto, which hit the city of Este particularly hard. The altarpiece was commissioned over a hundred years later to celebrate the reconstruction of the city and its economic recovery. In the foreground, we see the cathedral's titular saint, Thecla, interceding on behalf of the inhabitants of the city, which is visible in the background, while in heaven God the Father, with an impressive gesture, banishes the plague, personified by a dark figure. One of the astonishing things about this work is the strong coloring of the main protagonists, who thus stand out from the dark grey world of the mortal victims of the plague.

That same year, Tiepolo visited Udine for the last time and, with his son Giandomenico, decorated the Oratory of the Purità with a fresco-cycle *The Assumption of the Virgin Mary* and representations of putti, angels and cherubs, as well as the altarpiece *The Immaculate Conception*.

The portrait of the *Young Woman with Parrot*, painted at around the same time, and now in the Ashmolean Museum in Oxford (ill. 115), is probably one of a series of fantasy portraits, to which the *Young Woman with Mandolin* in the Institute of Arts in Detroit and the *Young Woman with Three-Cornered Hat* (now in the National Gallery in Washington) also belong. These were commissioned by the Russian Czarina. These portraits belong

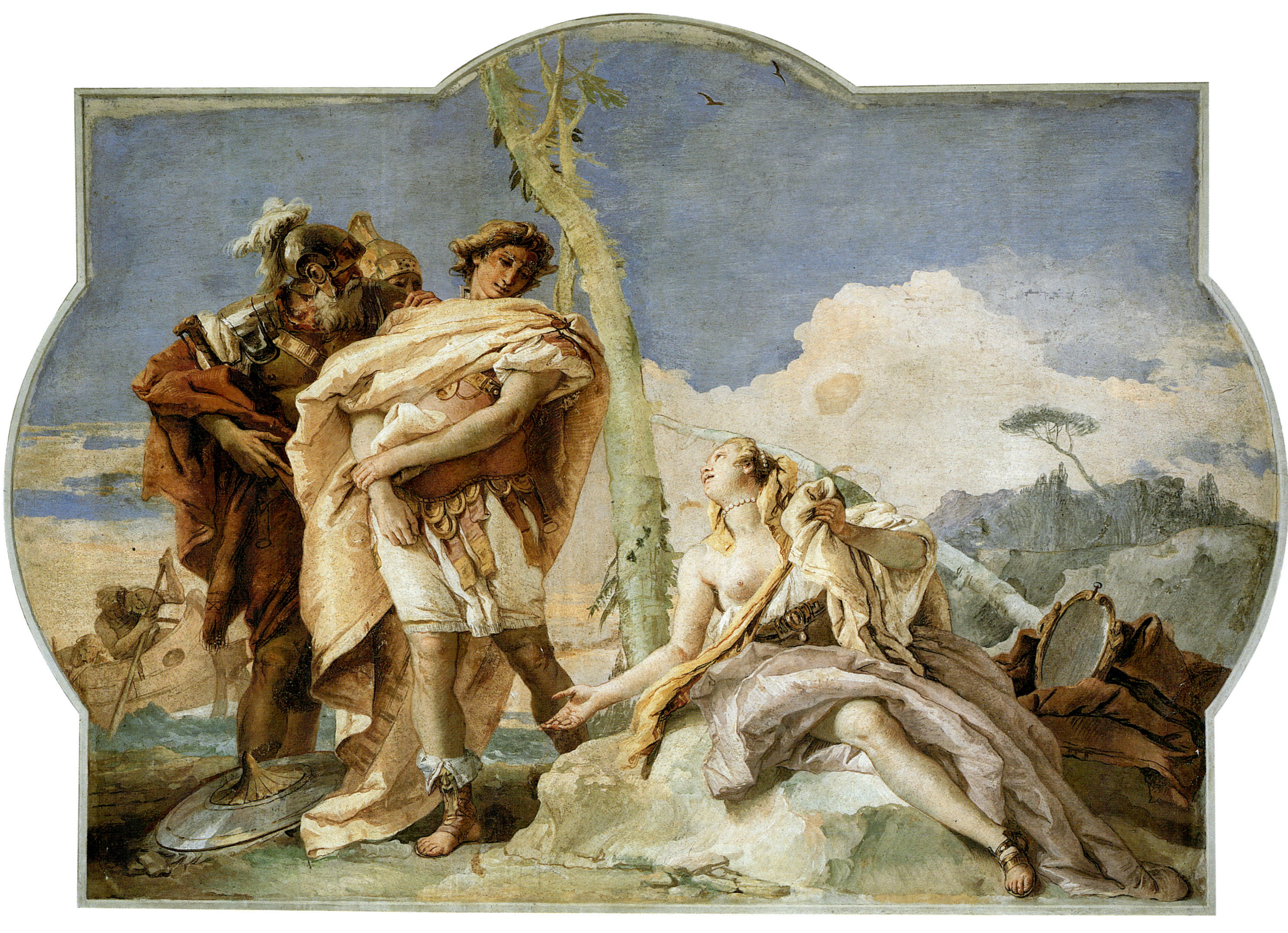

118 *Rinaldo abandoning Armida*, 1757
Fresco, 220 x 310 cm
Villa Valmarana, Vicenza

During the crusades, Rinaldo, who had allowed himself to be carried off to an island by the sorceress Armida, stayed away from the fighting. Two warriors were sent to bring him back. They discover him in Armida's enchanted garden and hold up to him a shield, as a mirror in which he recognizes that he has neglected his duties. He abandons the sorceress and returns to the battle. The scene is divided down the middle by a tree. Armida sits to its right and attempts to make Rinaldo stay. He is preparing to depart with his companions on the left. A ship awaits him in the background.

to the long tradition of half-length representations of beautiful women, female courtiers and courtesans, such as those by Veronese and Titian, which were especially popular in Venice from the 16th century onwards.

The two mythological paintings *Venus and Vulcan* and *Apollo and Daphne* (now in the Museum of Art, Johnson Collection in Philadelphia and in the National Gallery in Washington) can also be dated to the latter half of the 1750s. They were probably conceived as *supra porte* paintings, but nothing further is known about their origins. In spite of their small size, they are two of the most important and most beautiful examples of works executed for private and cultured patrons.

Although Tiepolo was now an old man of sixty-four, who in the meantime suffered from attacks of gout, he accepted a commission from the Pisani family in May 1760 to fresco the ceiling of the main salon in their noble villa on the Brenta canal in Stra. *The Apotheosis of the Pisani Family* was to be not only the grandest fresco decoration ever carried out by him in a private residence, but also the last project he would complete in his native country before leaving for Spain. The fresco, surrounded by an impressive architectural frame – painted by Pietro Visconti, a *quadratura* specialist from Milan –, shows the usual fusion of allegorical personifications and real portraiture (ills. 128–130).

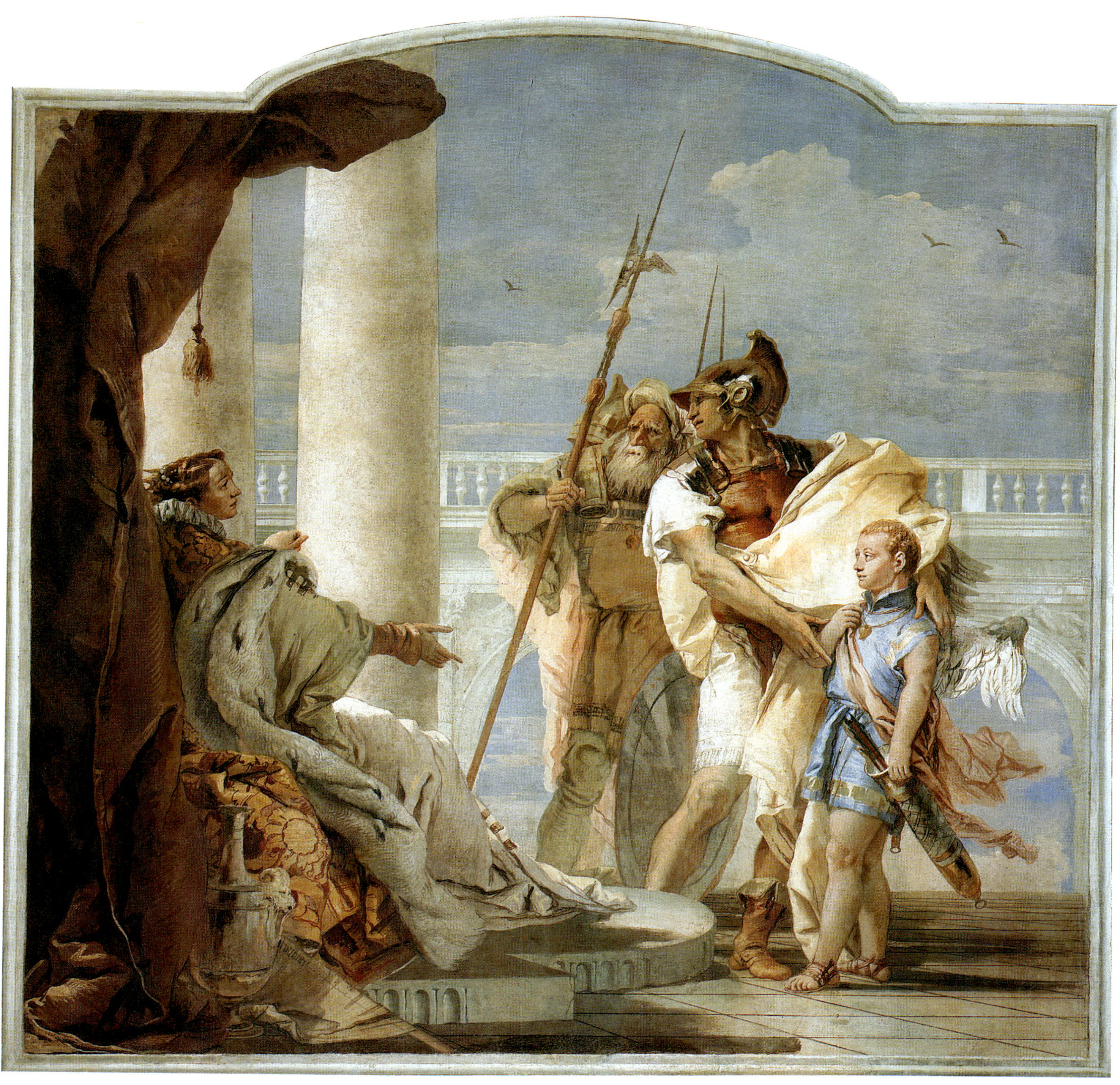

The Pisani family float on clouds alongside the liberal arts and the Virtues. Above them, the allegorical figure of Fame sounds her trumpet, putting the figure symbolizing Heresy to flight further down the picture. Giandomenico Tiepolo created feigned classical reliefs on mythological and allegorical themes on the walls above a balcony. However, the confidence with which Tiepolo symbolized the glorious future of the Pisani family and their standing in Venice did not turn out to be justified. The Venetian Republic was conquered by Napoleon's troops in 1797, and the Italian Viceroy appointed by him took up residence in the Villa Pisani.

As he revealed in a letter to Algarotti, Tiepolo had originally estimated that the decoration of the Villa Pisani would take three to four years to complete. This period of time would allow him to carry out other commissions in tandem with this, and he did in fact interrupt work at Stra in 1760 to execute the ceiling fresco, *The Triumph of Hercules*, in the Palazzo Canossa in Verona. In designing this work, which was destroyed in a bombing raid in 1945, Tiepolo fell back on tried-and-tested decorative models. The temple of glory and the horse-drawn triumphal chariot bring to mind the frescos in the Ca' Rezzonico in Venice. Tiepolo and his colleagues could not possibly have executed the large

119 *Aeneas introducing Cupid dressed as Ascanius to Dido*, 1757
Fresco, 230 x 240 cm
Villa Valmarana, Vicenza

Queen Dido of Carthage has welcomed Aeneas. By way of thanks, the latter has his son Ascanius brought from the ship with gifts for the hostess. Venus swaps him for Amor underway, which leads to Aeneas and Dido falling in love. The subject matter of the fresco is the presentation of Aeneas' son, but the wings and the quiver of arrows point to the true identity of the god of Love. On the left, Dido, in splendid robes, sits enthroned underneath a kind of baldachin. The scene is furnished with an architectural backdrop typical of Tiepolo.

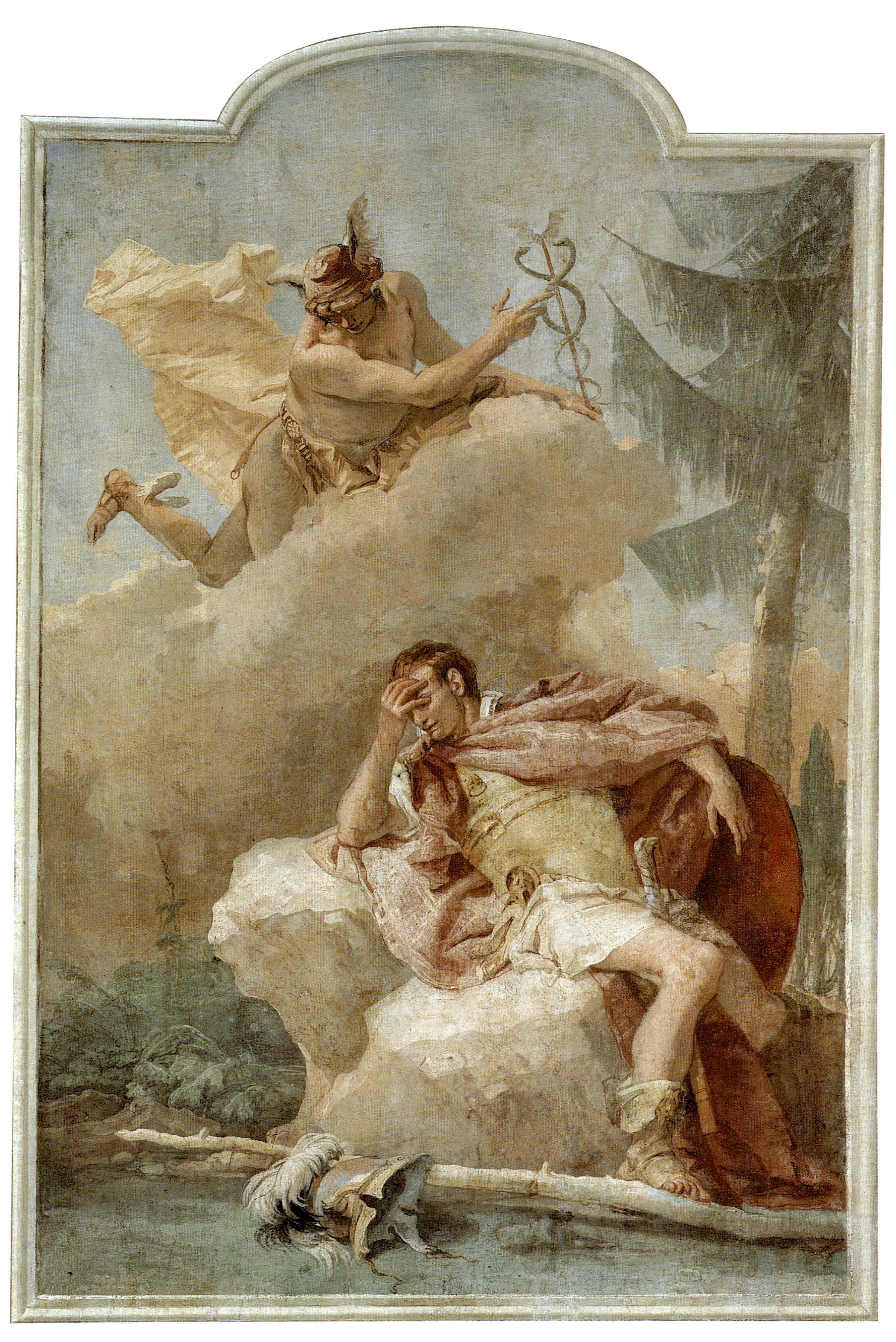

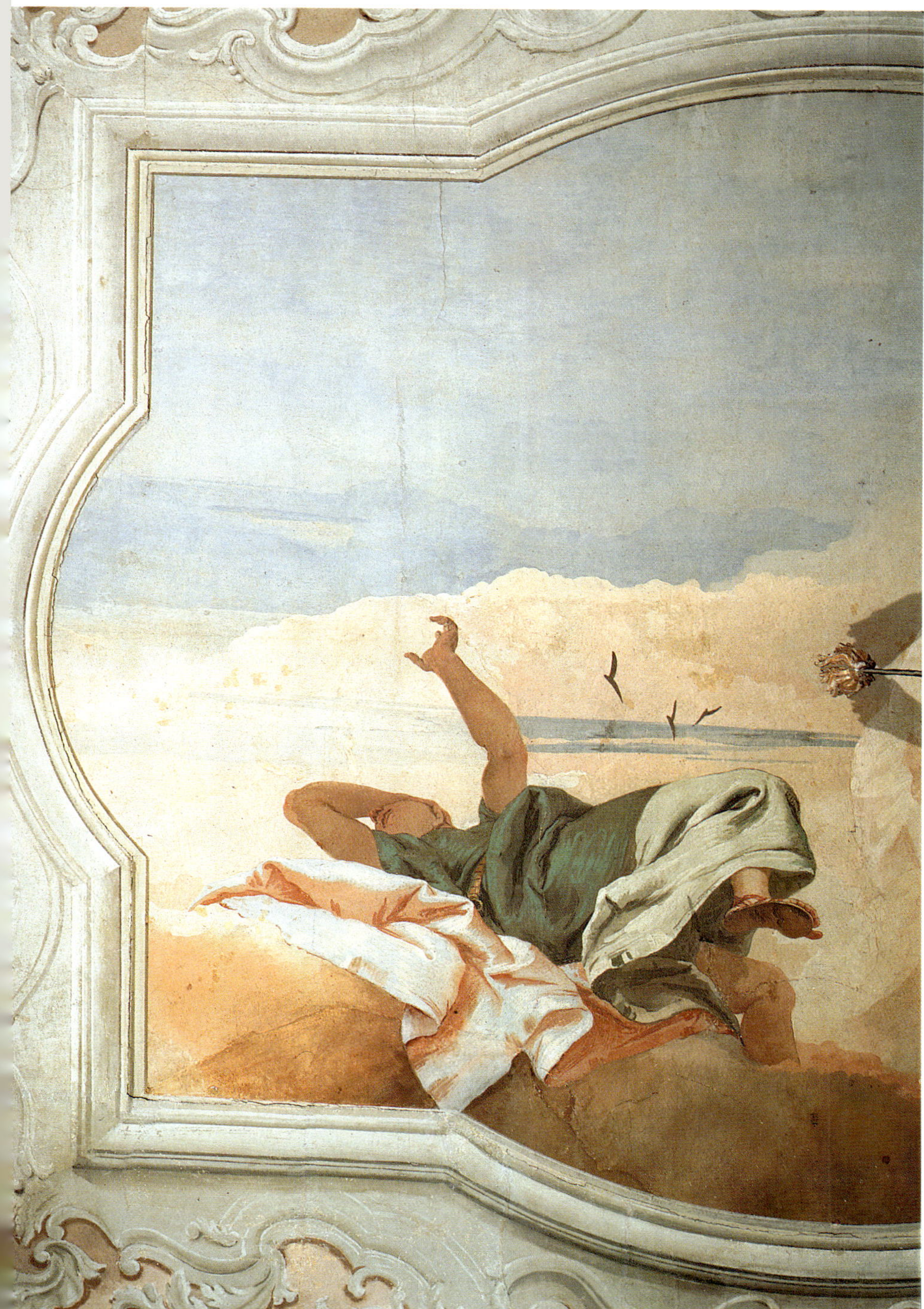

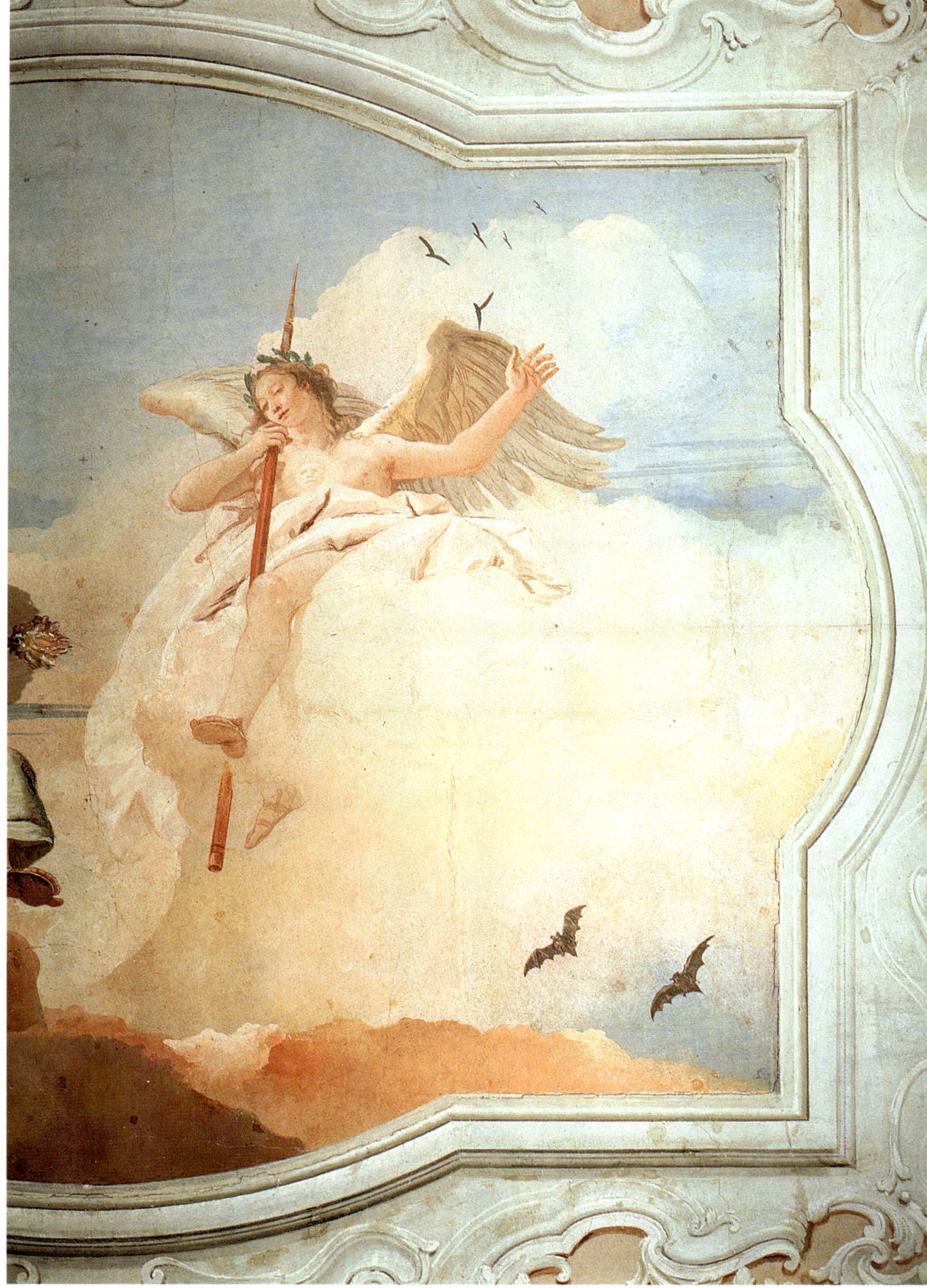

120 (opposite) *Mercury appearing to Aeneas*, 1757
Fresco, 230 x 145 cm
Villa Valmarana, Vicenza

Mercury, sent by Zeus, appears to the sleeping Aeneas in a dream and reminds him of his orders to establish a city in Italy. Aeneas consequently abandons Dido. The fresco shows the hero asleep on a rock in front of an unidentified landscape, while Mercury floats on a cloud above him. His hand points out of the picture, and so indicates the imminent departure of Aeneas from Carthage.

121 (above left) Detail of *The Triumph of Light over Darkness*, 1757
Fresco
Villa Valmarana, Vicenza

Darkness is represented by a contorted figure in dark clothes, who reclines on a brownish cloud, shielding his face with one hand, and stretching out the other to block out the light. The fact that even this half of the picture is brightly-lit makes it clear that Light has triumphed over Darkness.

122 (above right) Detail of *The Triumph of Light over Darkness*, 1757
Fresco
Villa Valmarana, Vicenza

The detail shows Light, personified by a winged figure in white robes and crowned with a laurel wreath, hovering on a bright cloud in the upper half of the picture, and holding a lance. Above her, a number of birds fly, alluding to the dawning day, while the bats on the lower edge of the picture belong to the kingdom of Darkness.

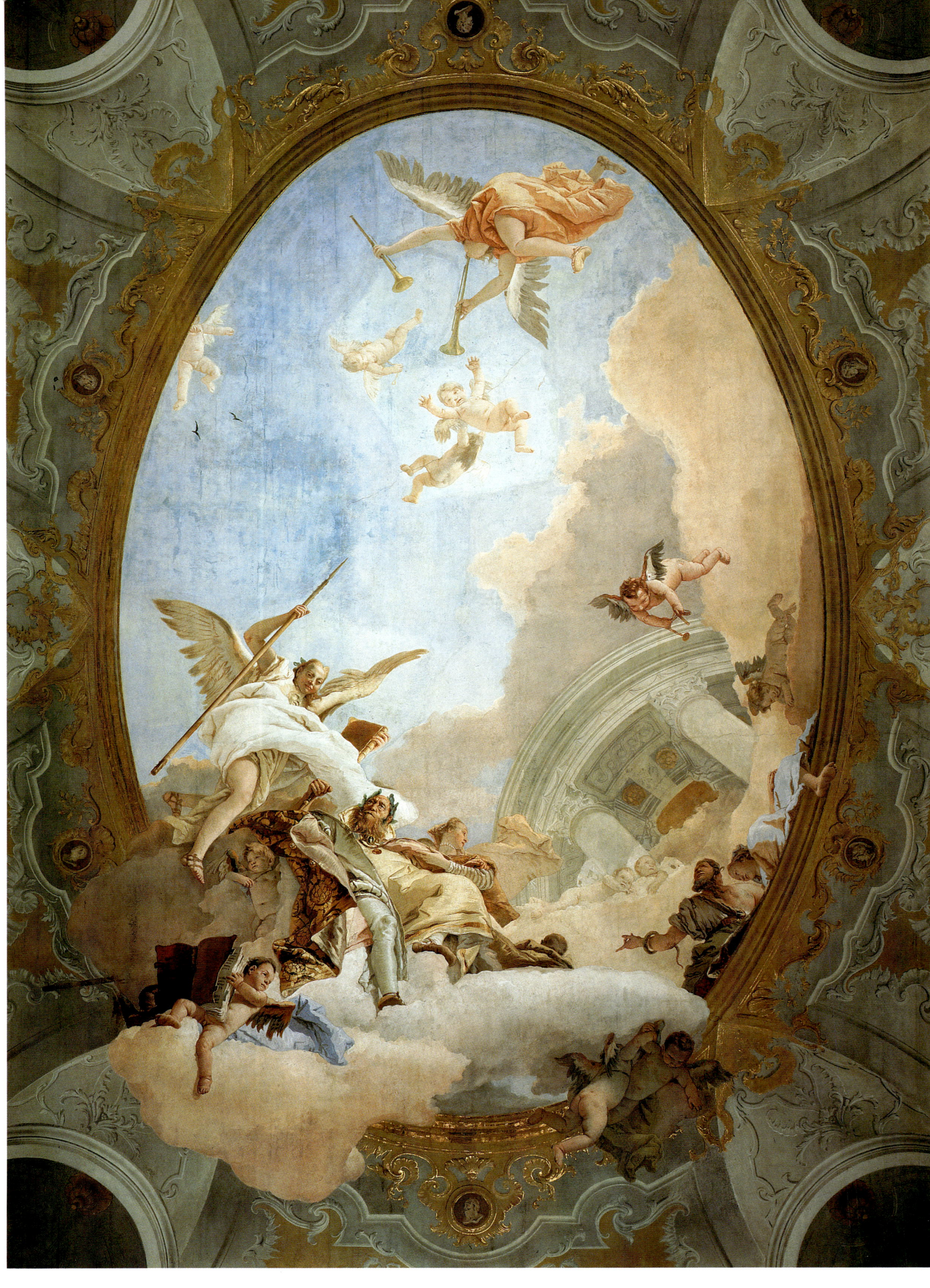

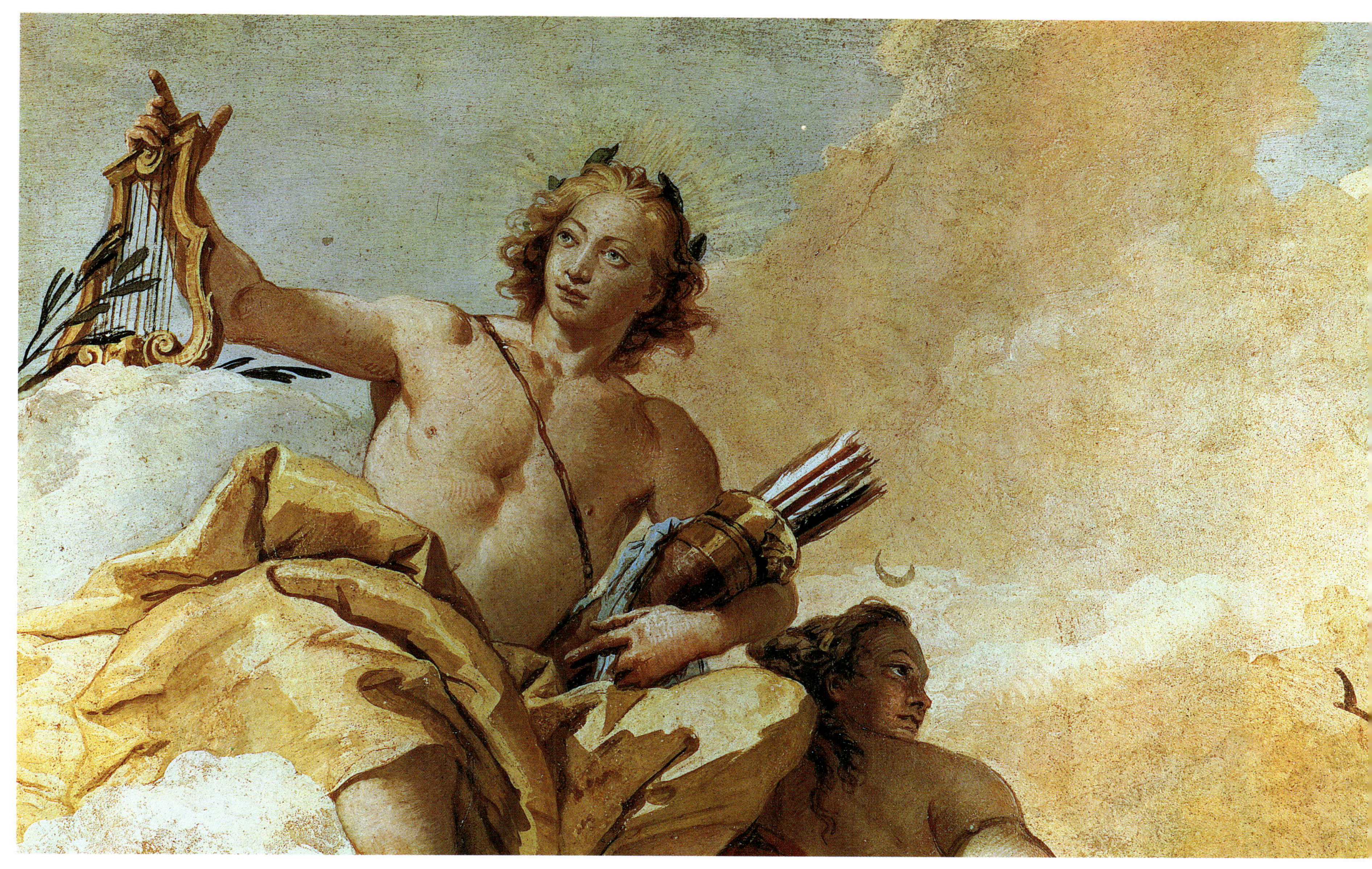

123 (opposite) *Allegory of Merit accompanied by Nobility and Virtue*, 1757/58
Fresco, 1000 x 600 cm
Museo del Settecento Veneziano di Ca' Rezzonico, Venice

The oval-shaped ceiling fresco shows the allegory of Merit on the left-hand side, personified by an elderly, bearded man wearing a laurel wreath. Accompanied by Nobility and the winged figure of Virtue, dressed in white, he rises up on a cloud populated by *putti* towards the temple of Glory. On the upper edge of the picture, Fame announces the glory of Merit by sounding her trumpets. The mostly empty skies in the center of the fresco contain only clouds and several *putti*.

124 (above) Detail of *Apollo and Diana*, 1757
Fresco, 200 x 185 cm
Villa Valmarana, Vicenza

Giambattista chose to decorate only one of the rooms in the *foresteria* at the Villa Valmarana. In the so-called Olympus Room he frescoed Mars, Venus and Amor; Mercury; Time; Jupiter; and Apollo and Diana. This last fresco shows the two deities sitting on a cloud. Apollo, who faces the viewer, holds his lyre in his right hand and his quiver of arrows in his left, while Diana, partly concealed and with her back to the viewer, reclines to his right. Apollo's golden yellow robe and the yellowish color of the clouds are meant to allude to his office as Sun God.

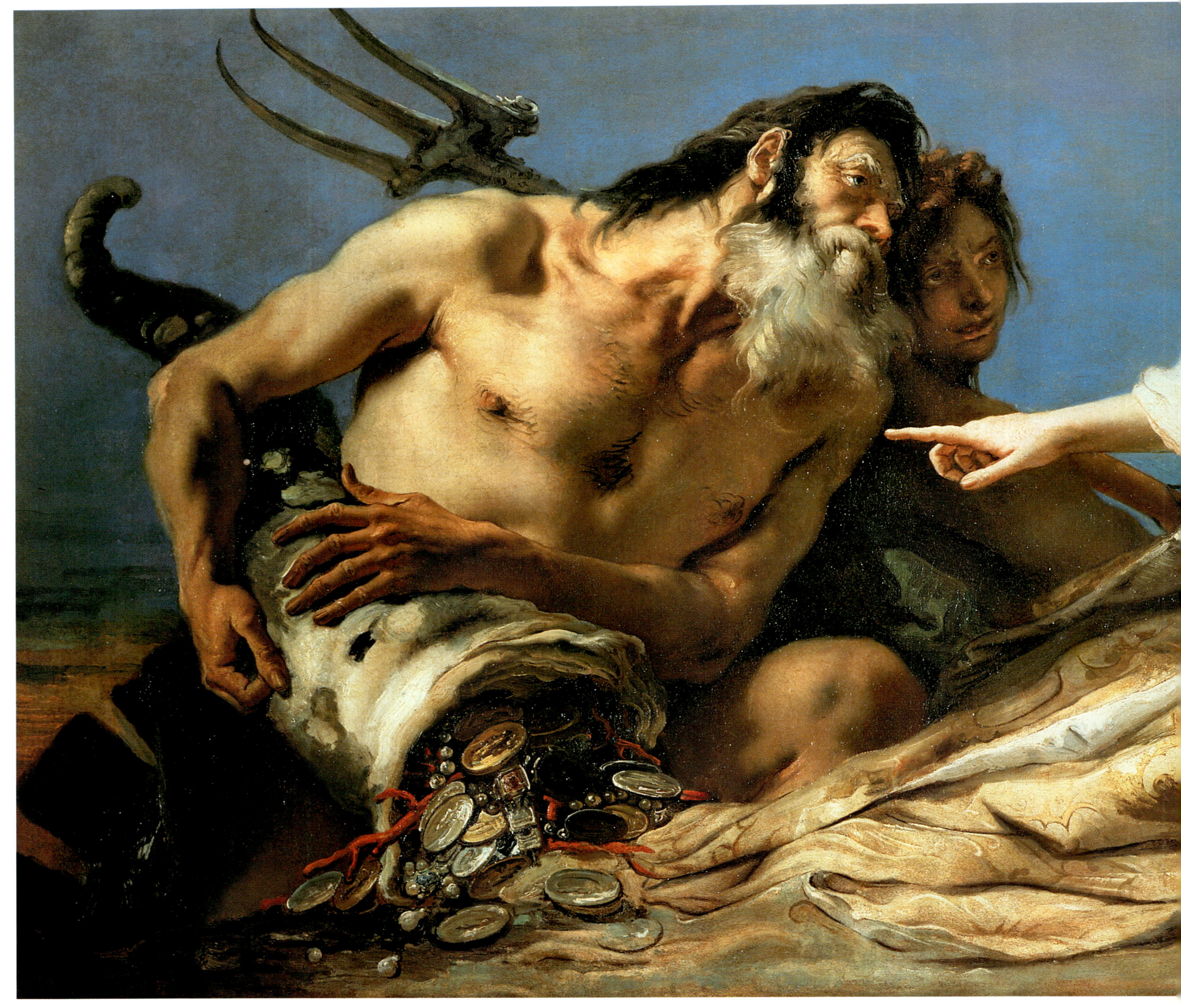

125 *Neptune paying Homage to Venice*, ca. 1758
Oil on canvas, 135 x 275 cm
Palazzo Ducale, Venice

Serenissima, or Venice, appears in the shape of a handsomely dressed young woman, wearing an ermine cape, a crown inlaid with gems and other valuable adornments. In her left hand she holds a scepter, as a symbol of power. The lion at her side is an allusion to the heraldic animal of Venice, the lion of St. Mark. She reclines in front of a curtain on the seashore. Symbolizing the sea, the god Neptune, accompanied by a Triton, empties out before her an amphora filled with jewels, corals and coins. The picture is an allegory of the wealth acquired by Venice as a sea power.

number of commissions they received without falling back on such models.

King Charles III of Spain (1716–1788) was determined to win the services of Tiepolo to decorate the Royal Palace in Madrid and he used the office of the Spanish ambassador in Venice to exert pressure on the city government. Tiepolo thus saw himself forced to complete the ceiling of the Villa Pisani in just one and a half years instead of the planned four. The breathtaking speed with which he and his colleagues worked, and the outstanding nature of their technical achievements, is revealed by the number of days they spent working on the fresco: 32 on the center of the ceiling, 12 on the figures within the *quadratura* painting, and 32 days on Visconti's architectural surround and ornamentation, which, all in all, adds up to less than three months actual work on the fresco. Under these circumstances, it is not surprising that this time the oil sketch housed in the Musée des Beaux Arts in Angers hardly differs at all from the finished fresco. The original conception was essentially adhered to since there was no time to make substantial changes. The

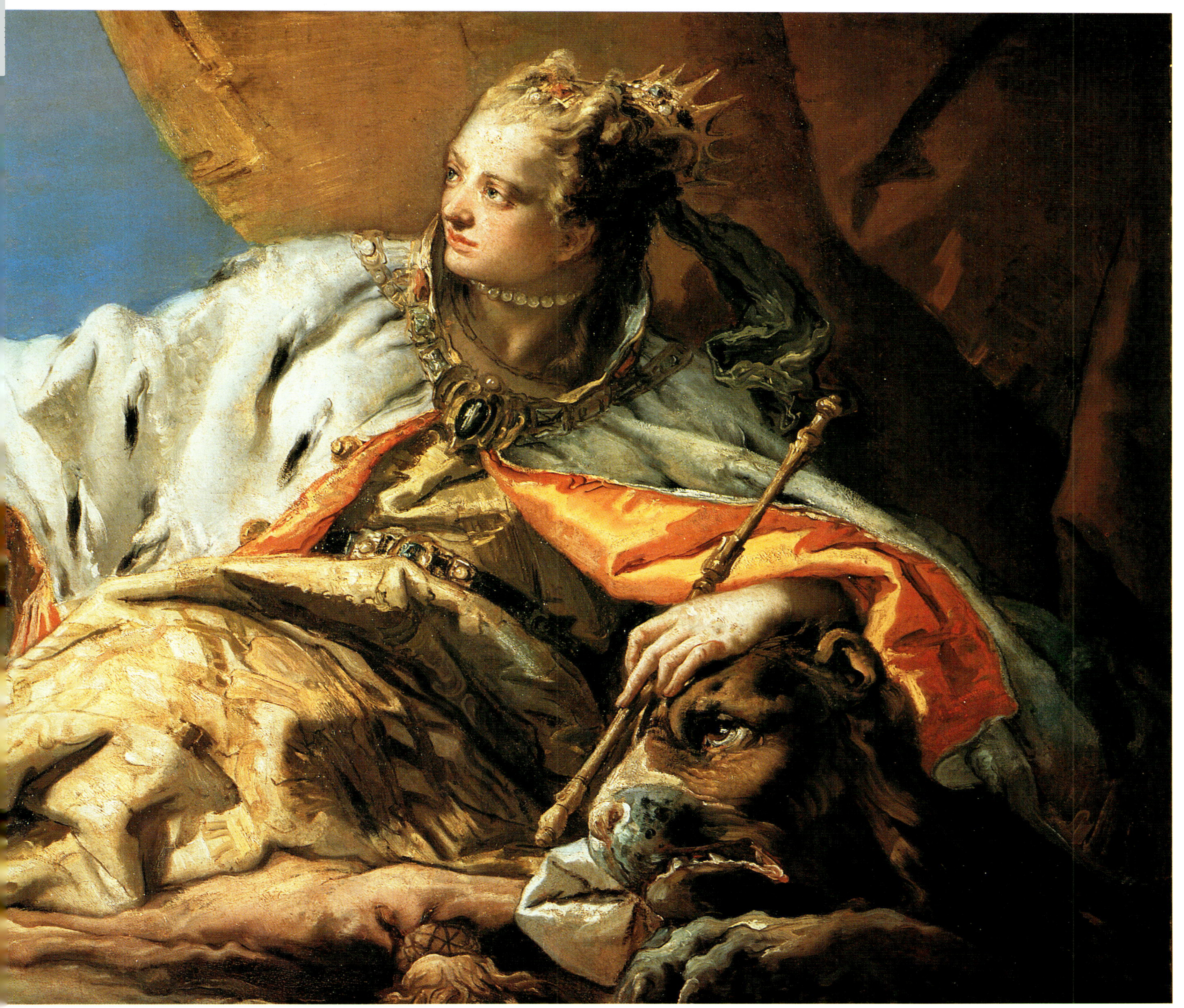

creation of a completely open space, whose endless depths are populated by figures bathed in light, heralds a new phase in Tiepolo's œuvre, which was later to culminate, on a completely different scale and in a different genre, in the *Mariancapricci* in Spain. It must be asked, to what extent Giandomenico Tiepolo might have been involved in this development – he was in a position to offer his ageing father far much more than just technical support in the realisation of these large projects; and his own works are staged in a less theatrical fashion, and so are more easily accessible. In the oil sketch for the ceiling fresco in the Villa Pisani Tiepolo already conjures up a universe which is far too spacious to be filled by the physical presence of the figures. This lends the work a special, fragile spatial structure, characteristic of his late period as a whole. The completion of the wall decorations in the Villa Pisana was entrusted to other artists, since Tiepolo and his two sons Giandomenico and Lorenzo set off on their journey to Spain on 31 March 1762. Tiepolo had left his native soil for ever.

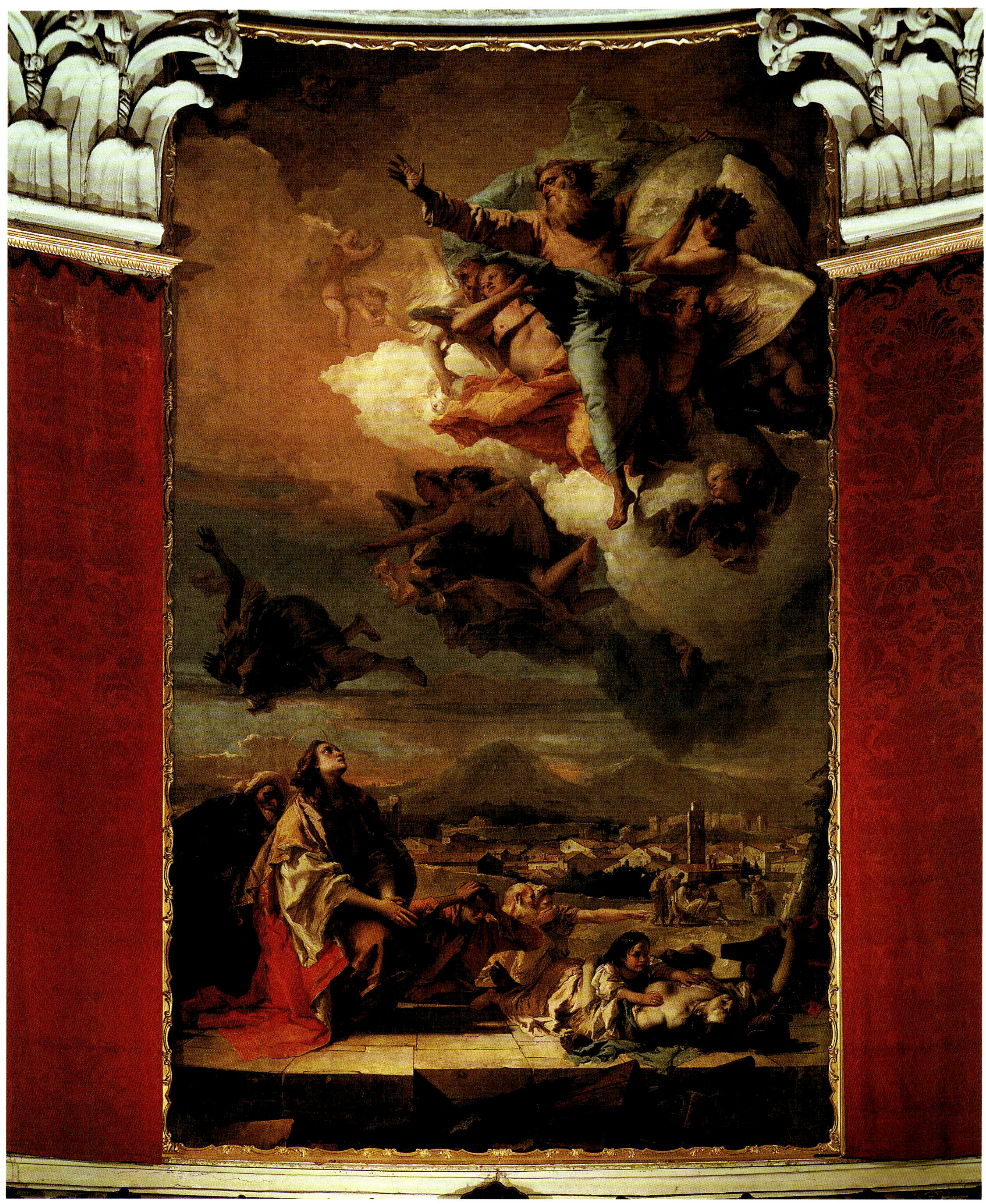

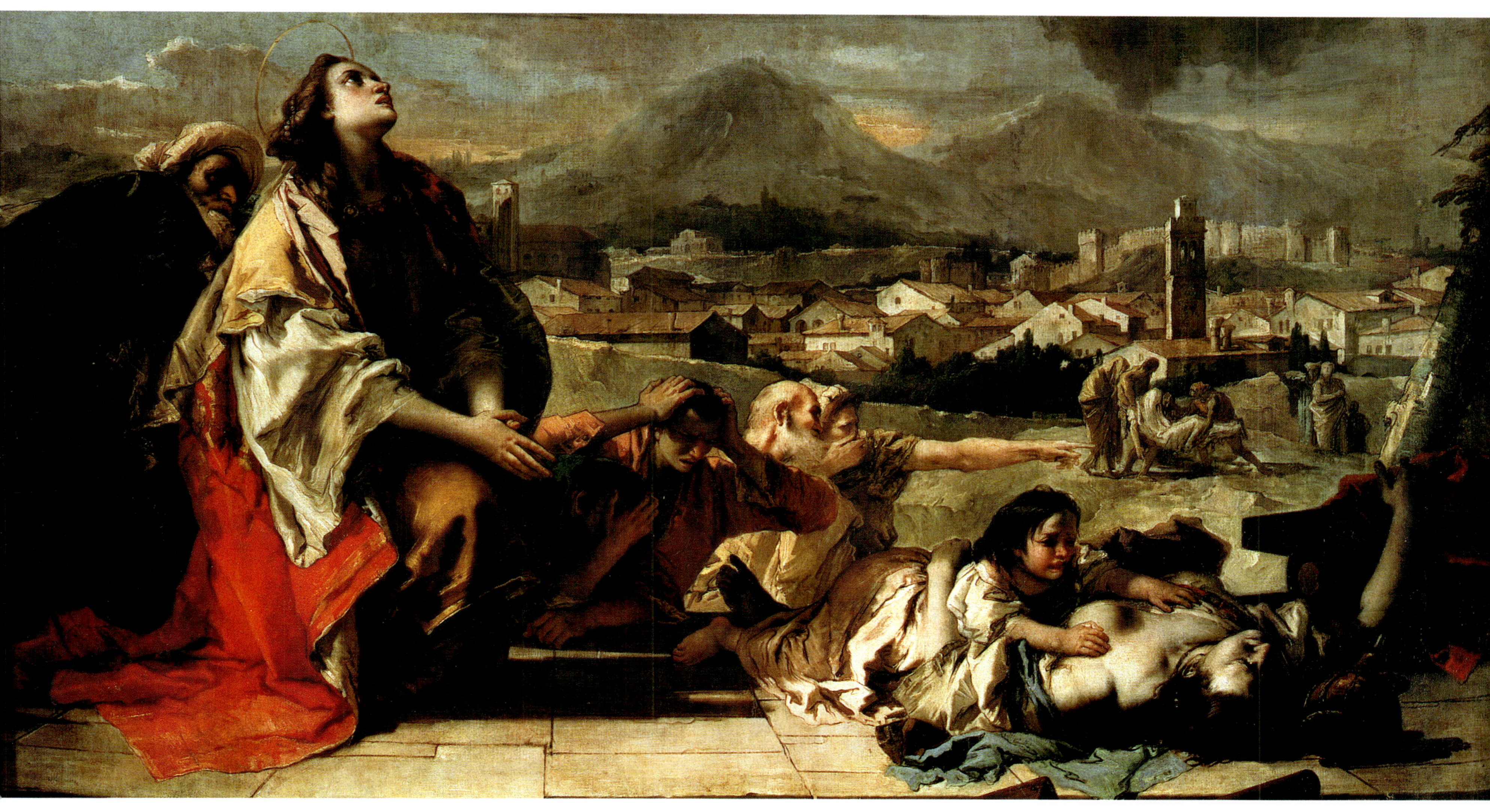

126 (opposite) *St. Thecla liberating the City of Este from the Plague*, 1759
Oil on canvas, 675 x 390 cm
Duomo, Este

Accompanied by several angels, God the Father hovers on a cloud over the city of Este and, with a powerful gesture of his hands, orders the plague, personified by a dark figure, out of the city. St. Thecla appears at the bottom edge of the picture and beseeches deliverance for the city, whose inhabitants next to her react with despairing gestures to the discovery of new victims of the plague. The successful connection between the upper and lower portions of the picture, and the contrast between the gloomy colors of the plague-ridden area and the brilliant colors of the divine manifestation, make the picture one of the highlights of Tiepolo's late period.

127 *St. Thecla liberating the City of Este from the Plague* (detail ill. 126), 1759

This detail makes it plain that the lower half of the picture was conceived autonomously and can almost be viewed independently of the upper half. The spacious background shows Este, lying at the feet of a chain of mountains. The inhabitants carry the dead out of the city to bury them outside its walls. The most moving scenes, presented with dramatic realism, take place in the foreground where a crying child lies in the arms of its dead mother.

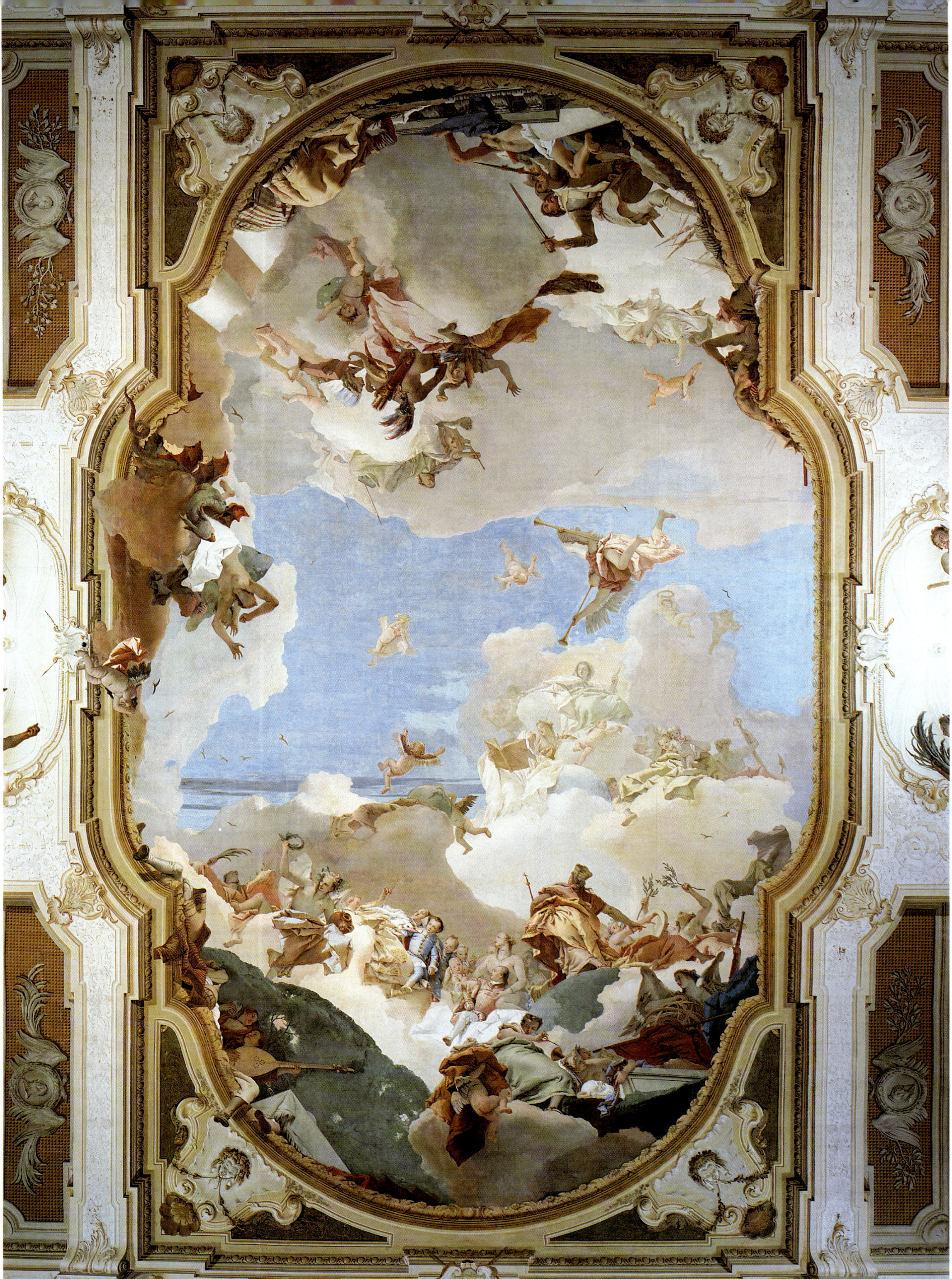

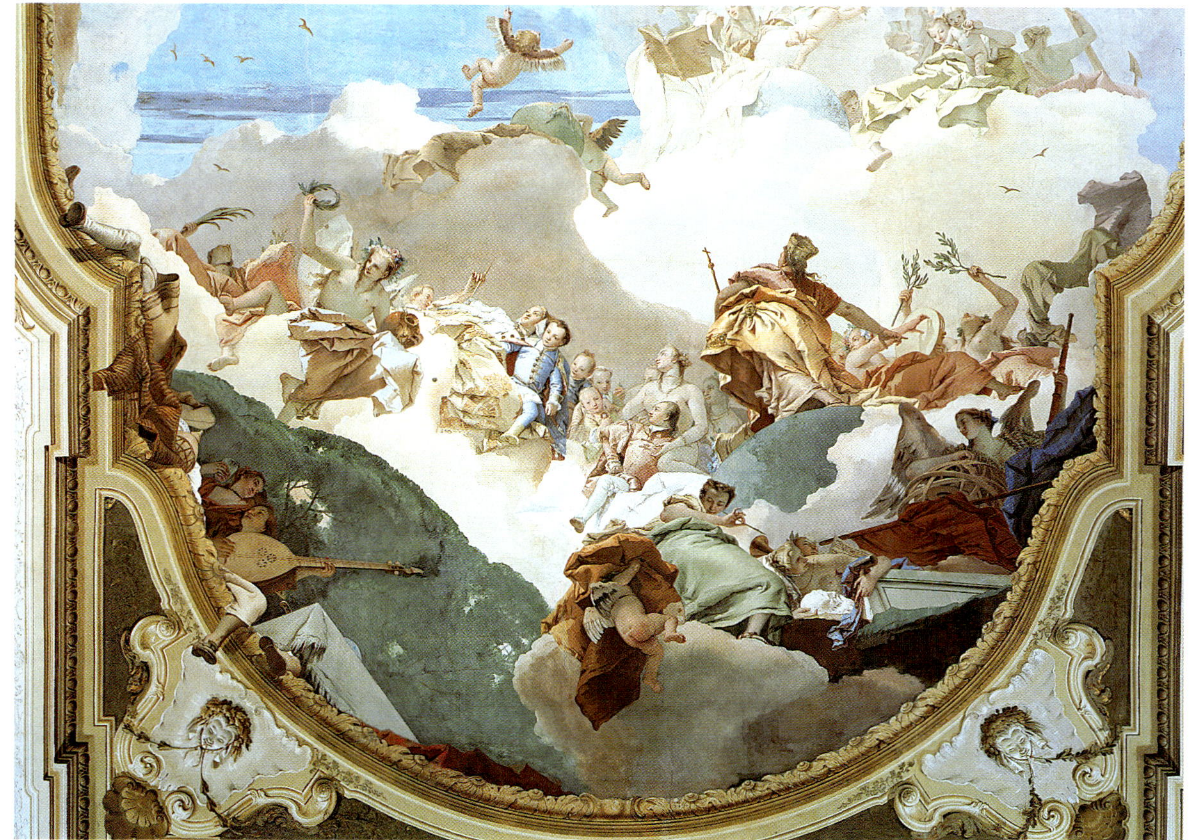

129 (left) *The Apotheosis of the Pisani family* (detail ill. 128), 1761/62

The various members of the Pisani family are surrounded by several allegorical figures. Truth appears as a naked woman, the crowned woman atop the globe and seen from behind personifies Italy, while the various arts are represented at her feet: Astronomy with telescope and globe, Music with horn and score, Sculpture with block of marble and bust, as well as Painting with brush. The allegories of Peace with palm leaves, and of Plenty with amphora and floral crown complete the scene on the left-hand side.

130 (below) *The Apotheosis of the Pisani family* (detail ill. 128), 1761/62

This section shows the known continents of Asia, America, and Africa on a cloud, while Europe is portrayed above them, on a bull, to express the greater degree of civilization she was thought to possess. A battle scene appears along the lower edge of the picture and obviously refers to the subjugation of the Turks, symbolized by the two figures in long coats, who have thrown themselves down in front of the invaders.

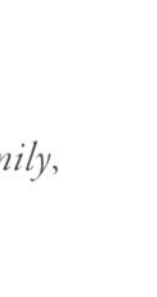

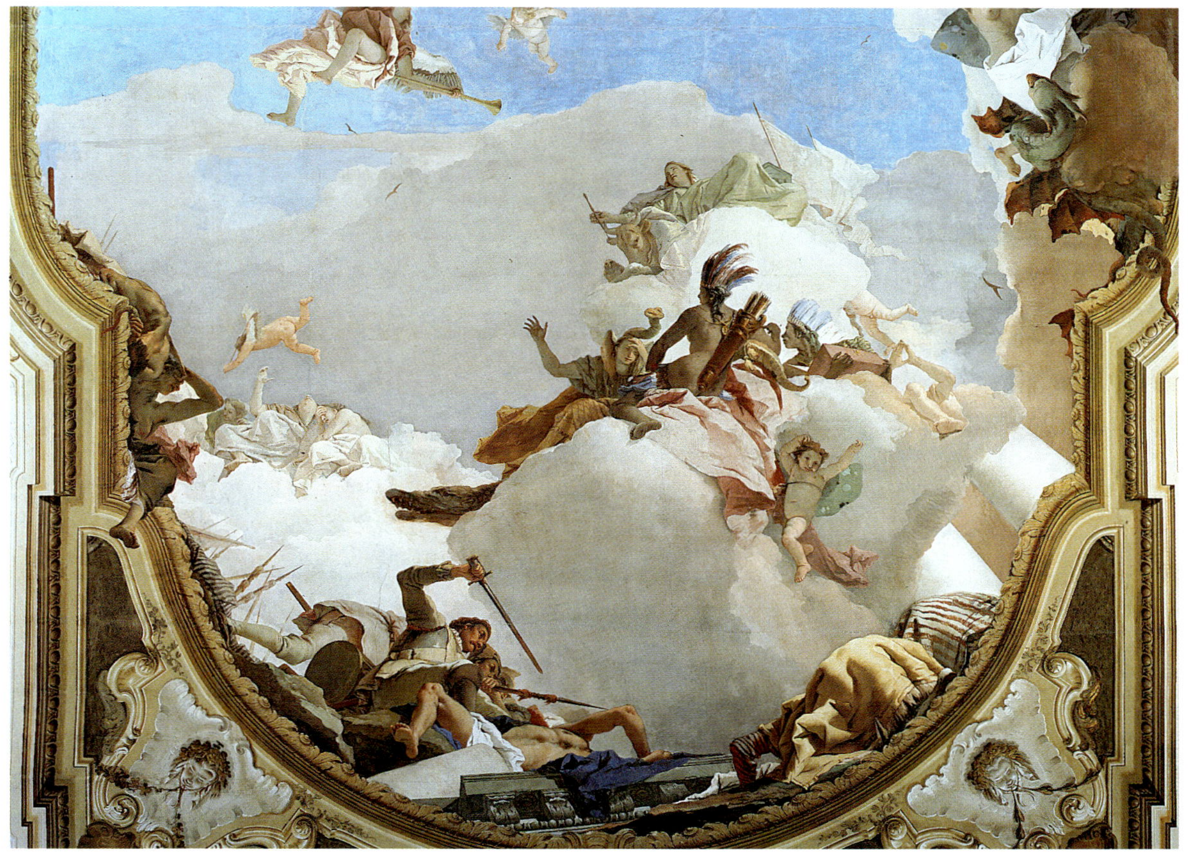

128 (opposite) *The Apotheosis of the Pisani family*, 1761/62
Fresco, 2350 x 1350 cm
Villa Pisani, Stra

The ceiling fresco is conceived as a *trompe-l'œil* opening onto a silvery-blue sky, whose endless depths are defined by various towering cloud formations. The composition consists of two sections which exist independently of one another: the portrayal of the Pisani family and various allegorical figures in the lower portion, and the Contintents in the upper portion. The figure of Fame, sounding her trumpets in either direction, connects the two. Below her, Divine Wisdom is enthroned and reigns over a harmonious empire. The Virtues Faith, Justice, Love, Hope and Strength appear at her feet.

The final years in Madrid 1762–1770

131 Detail of *The Glory of Spain*, 1762–1766
Fresco, 2700 x 1000 cm
Palacio Real, Throne Room, Madrid

This section shows the personification of Princely Glory next to a pyramid, the symbol of Eternity. The lion indicates strength, and the *putto* with the cornucopia the wealth of the dynasty, while the crown refers in general to the royal line of descent. The remaining three figures most likely represent the virtues Generosity, Kindness and Hope. Higher up, the personification of Faith appears as a woman dressed in white, with raised chalice and cross. Venus and Amor, and two other goddesses, can be seen at the top of the picture.

After a two-month long, strenuous journey via Genoa and Barcelona, Tiepolo and his sons arrived in Madrid on 4 June 1762. In spite of his advanced age, he was extremely productive in the remaining eight years of his life, creating an impressive number of large frescos and altarpieces in Madrid. There has been a great deal of speculation about the reasons behind the now sixty-six year-old-artist's decision to leave his homeland for ever and to embark on the adventure of this arduous journey and of working in an unknown environment. On the one hand, he was surely tempted by the opportunity to once again execute a grand, painted decorative project in a royal residence – especially where that residence was also the seat of one of the oldest and most eminent monarchies in Europe. On the other hand, he appears to have been very well aware of the fact that the time for his art, in which he portrayed triumphal apotheoses and the glorification of the virtues of his clients by means of illusionistic settings, was well and truly over. Enlightenment ideas imported from France had, in the meantime, firmly taken root in Venice. The new concepts based on scientific knowledge and reason were incompatible with the fictitious worlds projected by illusionistic ceiling painting. It cannot be overlooked that Tiepolo had hardly received any significant commissions in Venice itself since the end of the 1750s, and was active only on the mainland. Rich patrons appeared to be less and less willing to invest their money in representations of themselves which had gone out of fashion.

And so Tiepolo was one of the few European painters still working on a monumental scale and able to realize extensive interior decorations. King Charles III of Spain had thus made the right choice in commissioning this artist to decorate the Throne Room of the Royal Palace in Madrid, only recently built to designs by Filippo Juvarra (1676–1736) by his pupil Sacchetti (died 1764). Charles III also employed other artists in the palace, such as Corrado Giaquinto (1699–1765) from Naples, who, however, returned to his native city shortly before Tiepolo's arrival in Madrid. Anton Raphael Mengs (1728–1779) arrived at the same time as Tiepolo, and he worked on the decoration of the palace along with the Spanish painter Francisco Bayeu (1734–1795) and various other native artists.

Tiepolo had already completed the oil sketch for the ceiling fresco in the Throne Room, *The Glory of Spain*, in Venice. The subject portrayed is the glorification of the Spanish nation, which in the course of the 16th and 17th centuries had developed into one of the leading European powers, politically, geographically and culturally. The sketch reflects both the new policies of the ruling house of Bourbon, which during the reign of Charles III (1759–88) was considered one of the most enlightenened monarchies of the age, and historical events from the country's past, combining the two in a condensed presentation of Spain.

The fresco itself differs little from the sketch, but there has been a shift in content, which stresses the values of peace and wisdom instead of the achievements in battle of Spain as a military power which had been emphasized in the sketch (ills. 131–134). It is assumed that this was in reaction to changed political circumstances, since Spain had only recently (1763) been forced to sign a humiliating peace treaty with England. As a result, attempts were made to give the martial themes in the fresco less prominence.

The compositional scheme of the ceiling fresco in the Throne Room is a brilliant synthesis of decorative elements from Tiepolo's earlier works, such as those in the Villa Cordellina in Montecchio Maggiore, or in the Residence in Würzburg and the Villa Pisani in Stra. Tiepolo reproduces his previous work in a new setting without compromizing the original character of the fresco or giving the impression of its being a copy. In the center of the picture, which has been shifted slightly downwards, the Spanish Monarchy is enthroned on a globe between Minerva and Apollo. Above her, the allegory of Fame sounds her trumpets, while the personifications of Justice, Clemency, Abundance and Moderation appear below her. Traditional representations of the deities of Olympus and allegorical figures familiar from Cesare Ripa's "Iconologia", including the personification of Christian Faith, enliven the remaining free space between the clouds. The personification of the territories conquered by Spain, and a depiction of the figures of Terror and Rage being

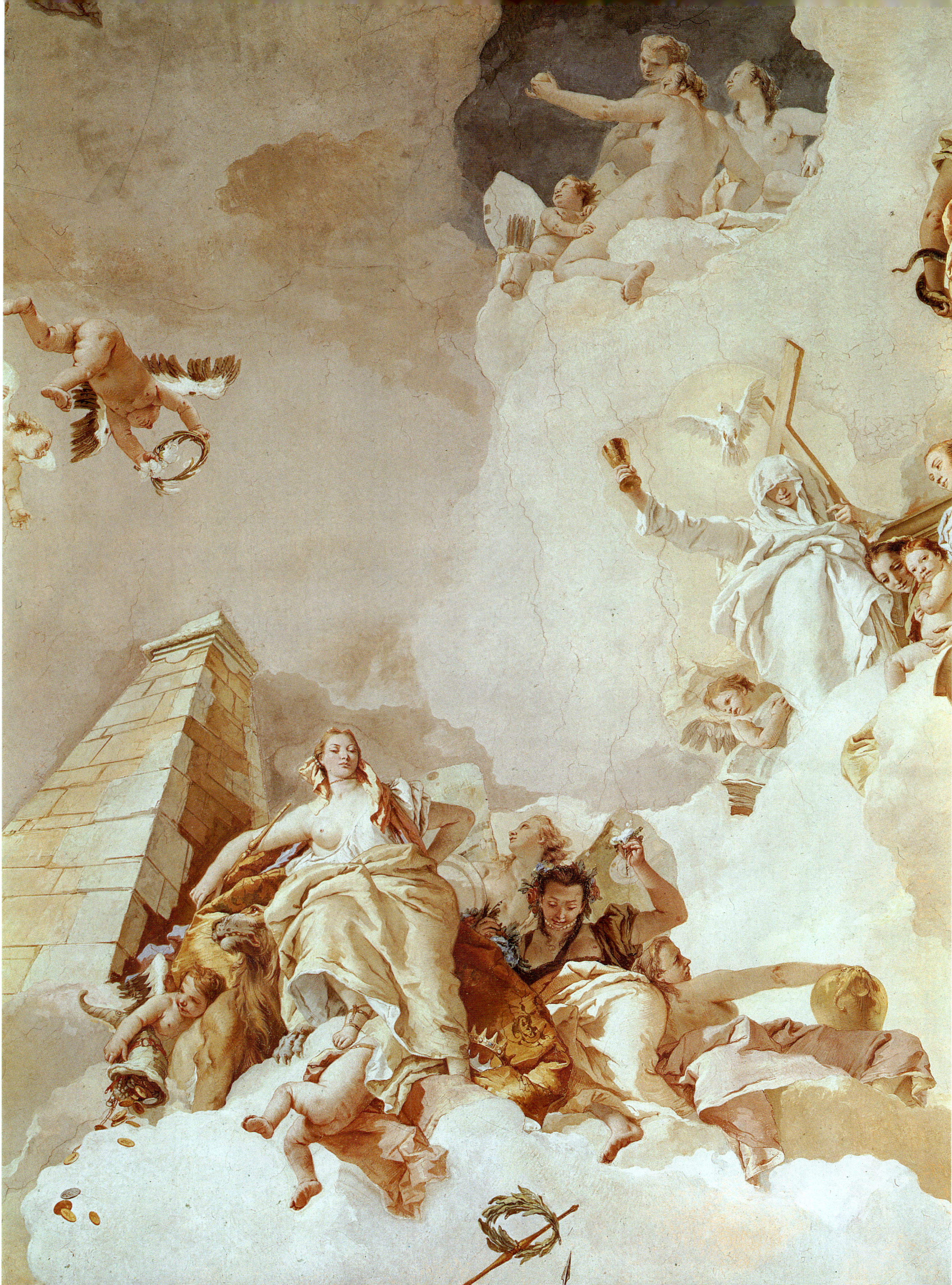

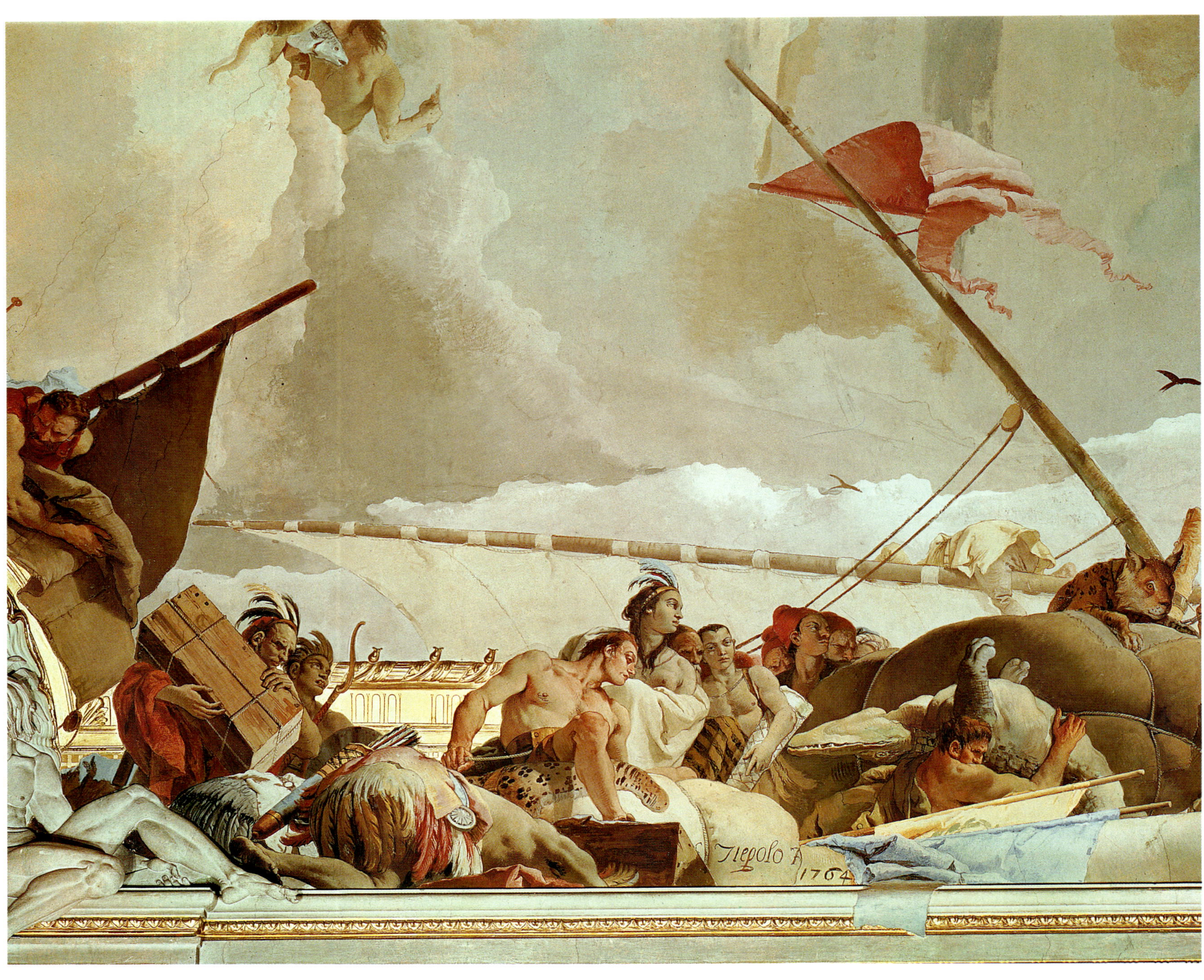

132 Detail of *The Glory of Spain*, 1762–1766
Fresco, 2700 x 1000 cm
Palacio Real, Throne Room, Madrid

The loading of a European ship with the treasures of the American continent is depicted in a direct allusion to the discovery of America by Christopher Columbus and to the Spanish conquest of the New World in the 16th century. The two Red Indians in the foreground, who throw themselves to the ground in front of the ship, symbolize the Europeans' victory over the natives.

banished by the light of the French Enlightenment, run round the edges of the frame. In spite of the complex structure of the numerous figural elements and the intricate meaning of its content, and thanks to the largely empty expanse of sky, the fresco appears to be one of the airiest Tiepolo ever created.

In evaluating this fresco, and in comparison with the earlier works, we are left with a feeling of disappointment which stems not so much from the fresco itself as from the low ceiling, the lack of architectural design in the room, the weak lighting and the strict framework. Where Tiepolo's early compositions had been able to not only decorate a room, but to bring it alive through illusionistic games, the ceiling painting in the Royal Palace in Madrid is constrained within a rigid framework, where it cannot achieve its effects unhindered. The treatment of the subject matter, too, is less poetic here, and is intended rather to illustrate the iconography of the nation, which is, of course, in keeping with the function of the room as Throne Room.

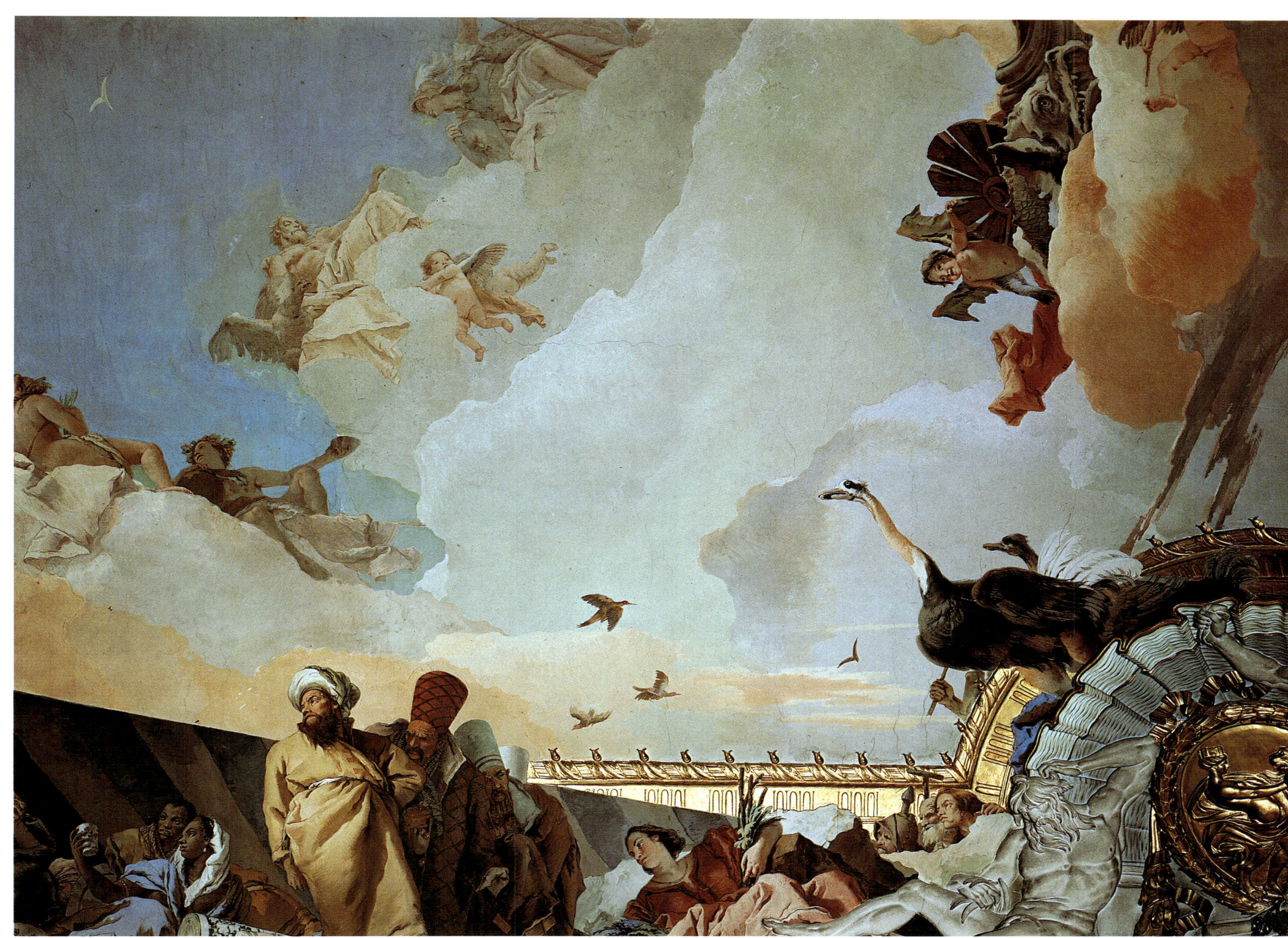

Work on the Throne Room was completed in 1764. The King was pleased with the result and asked Tiepolo to carry out further decorative work within the palace. The painting of a ceiling fresco in the Guard Room followed. *The Apotheosis of Aeneas* alludes to the legend that the Spanish monarchy is descended from Aeneas and his divine mother Venus. In the fresco, Aeneas appears as a warrior-hero on clouds, with Venus awaiting him higher up. She holds the weapons made for him by Vulcan, whose forge is portrayed at the bottom of the picture. Aeneas, who is ascending towards the Temple of Glory (the latter barely visible behind the clouds) has, in his striving for immortality, literally overtaken Time, personified by a dark figure on the right-hand edge of the picture.

The astonishing thing about the artistic design of the fresco is the way in which it largely eschews illusionistic foreshortening, the relatively clear ordering of the figures, who are all too easy to read, and the composition of a clear perspective with a definite vanishing point.

133 Detail of *The Glory of Spain*, 1762–1766
Fresco, 2700 x 1000 cm
Palacio Real, Throne Room, Madrid

A part of the African Continent appears at the lower edge of the picture, characterized by the ostrich. In the clouds, we see Jupiter and his eagle, Minerva, Bacchus, and another divinity. From this angle we can again see that scenes and figural groupings, which, in his other fresco cycles, Tiepolo linked together in an organic fashion, are here divided up and separated from one another in spite of the *trompe-l'œil* breaching of the framework.

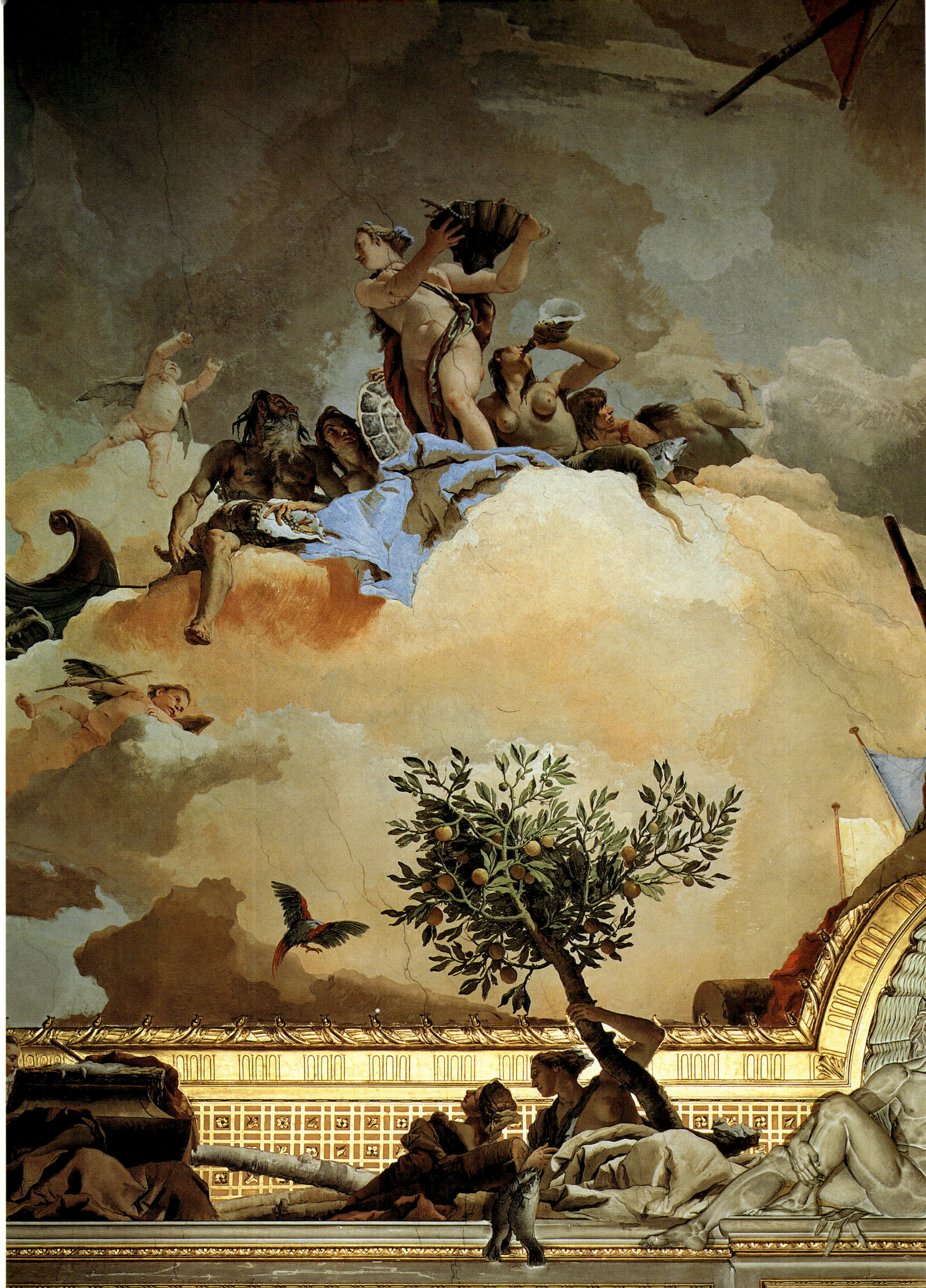

134 (opposite) Detail of *The Glory of Spain*, 1762–1766
Fresco, 2700 x 1000 cm
Palacio Real, Throne Room, Madrid

The sea-goddess Thetis hovers on a cloud, together with her spouse Oceanus, and holds aloft a shell filled with treasures. Tritons and Nereids, who are meant to symbolize the riches of the sea, accompany the scene. The attempt to bridge the austere Classical golden frame using the group of figures and the orange tree at the lower edge of the picture (possibly a personification of the Province of Aragon), and to create the typical connection between the fresco and the space occupied by the viewer does not succeed here.

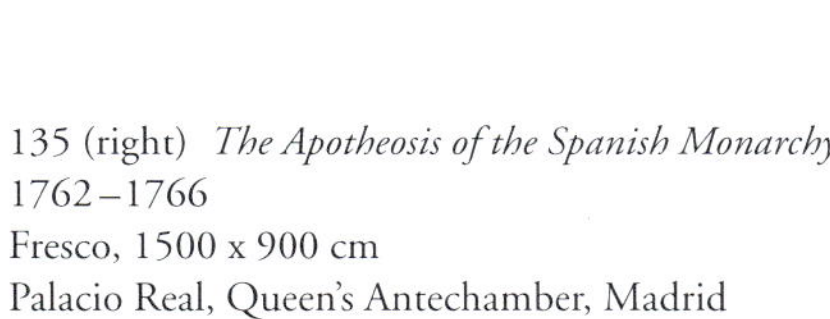

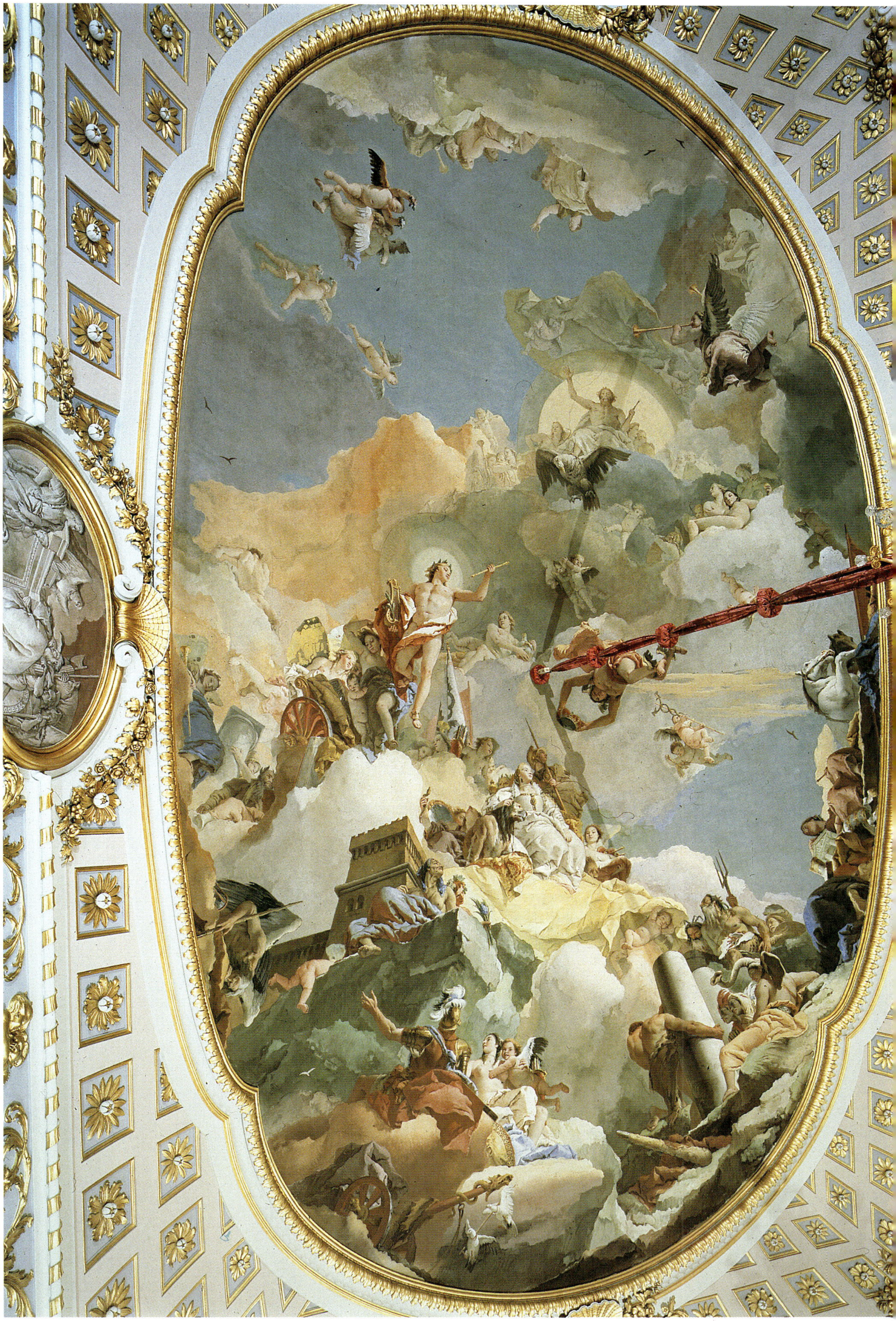

135 (right) *The Apotheosis of the Spanish Monarchy*, 1762–1766
Fresco, 1500 x 900 cm
Palacio Real, Queen's Antechamber, Madrid

The lower half of the oval ceiling fresco displays the personification of the Spanish Monarchy, enthroned among the clouds and crowned by Mercury. To the right above her, Apollo stands in front of his sun-chariot, while in the upper half of the picture we see Jupiter on his throne, Fame with trumpets, as well as *putti* and other divinities. Below the Spanish monarchy, the personification of Ancient Castilia, the most important Spanish province, appears with a tower, below that are Venus and Mars, while the meeting of the Continents Europe and Africa at Spanish Gibraltar is symbolized at the bottom left by the pillars of Hercules.

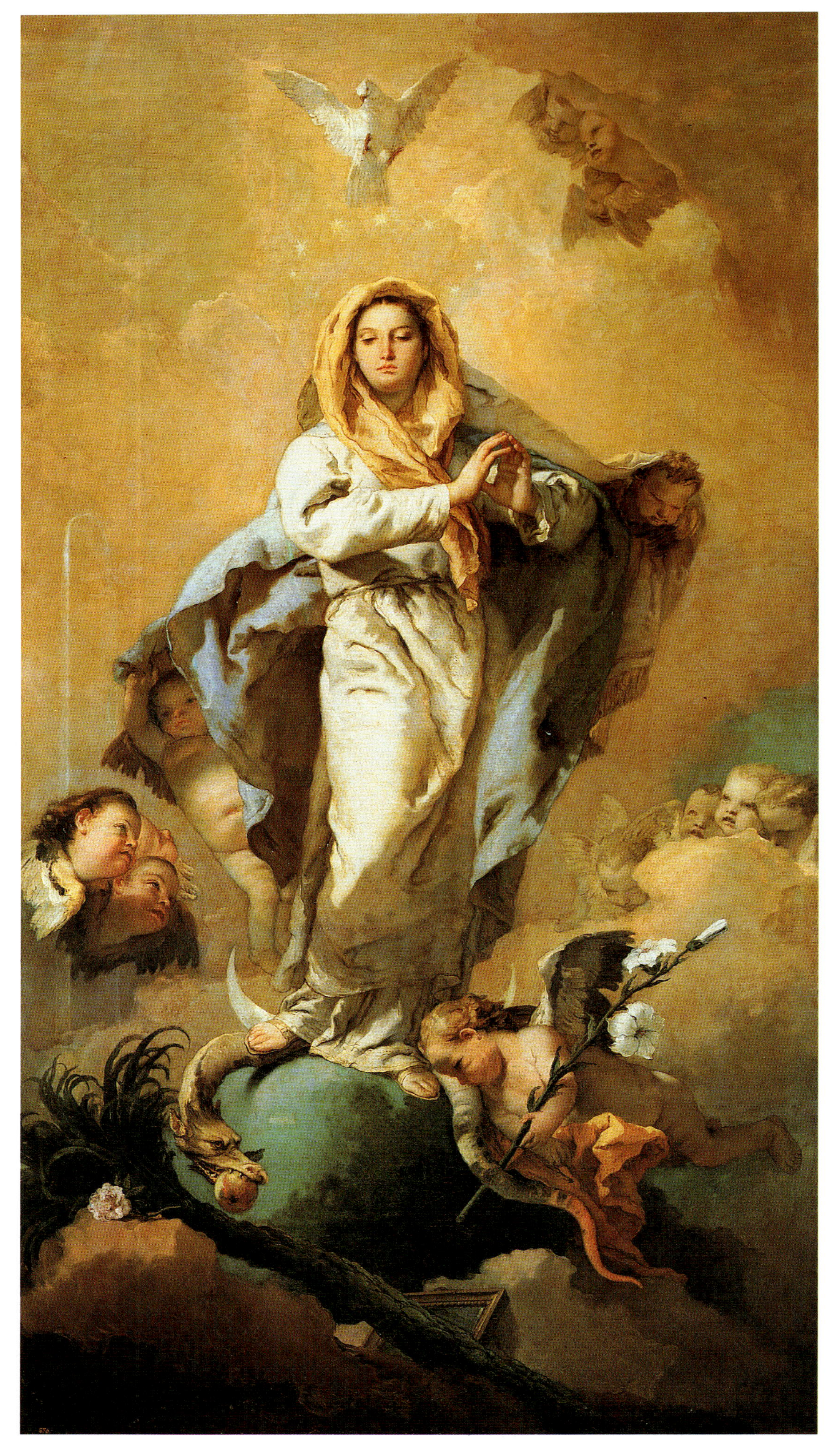

These radical changes, compared to his earlier works, are a response to the Neoclassical tendencies he had already encountered in Italy, and to which he was once again exposed in Spain – particularly through the influence of Anton Raphael Mengs. Mengs, one of the most eminent representatives of early Classicism, was mainly sponsored by the influential Franciscan monk and personal confessor to King Charles III, Joaquin de Eleta, a great admirer of the German artitst who disseminated his style at the court. The supposition that Tiepolo fell out of favour with his royal client belongs in the realm of fiction. He was entrusted with large decorative projects right up to his death.

In the Queen's antechamber, a small room adjoining the Throne Room, Tiepolo created the ceiling fresco *The Apotheosis of the Spanish Monarchy* (ill. 135), for which two oil sketches – now in the Metropolitan Museum in New York – survive. The two very different designs have been combined in the finished fresco, and further elements have been added. It depicts Jupiter, seated on his Olympian throne, his hand raised to receive the personification of the Spanish Monarchy, who is crowned by Mercury and accompanied by Apollo. Further mythological and allegorical figures appear, including Neptune, with whose wealth Spain is supposedly blessed.

Having completed work in the Royal Palace in Madrid in 1766, Tiepolo made the final decision not to return to Venice, but to continue to work for the Spanish king. In a letter to the king's Secretary in 1767, he applied for the task of decorating the newly-completed royal Chapel of San Pasquale Baylon in Aranjuez, for which seven canvases were to be executed to be hung above the altars. This difficult undertaking, overseen by Father Joaquin de Eleta, was the last royal project, and also the last major work, Tiepolo would ever carry out in Spain. In just two years he completed the seven canvases: *St. Pascal Babylon adoring the Sacrament*, *The Immaculate Conception* (ill. 136), *The Stigmatization of St. Francis of Assisi*, *St. Anthony of Padua with the Christ Child*, *St. Peter of Alcantara*, *St. Joseph with the Christ Child* and *St. Charles Borromeus meditating on the Crucifix*. However, only the first six pictures were installed in 1770 – almost a year after Tiepolo's death. The cycle of pictures celebrated famous Franciscan saints and the Immaculate Conception, a belief strongly championed by the Franciscan order. The demanding task of furnishing a church with seven individual paintings was new to Tiepolo and represented a challenge, since it differed from the programme of the more usual fresco decorations. The subjects to be depicted, predominately male saints, ascetics meditating or in a state of ecstasy, were also new to this painter of religious scenes whose normal interests lay in narrative diversity and in the character and emotions of his figures. The pictures were removed again in 1775 and replaced by early Classicist works by Anton Raphael Mengs, Francisco Bayeu and Mariano Salvador de Maellas (1739–1819), which conformed more to the change in taste in favour of academic art and to the traditional ideas of the Spanish court as to how saints should be portrayed.

From an artistic point of view, the grand fresco decorations in the Spanish Royal Palace are surpassed by a group of small-scale devotional pictures, painted by Tiepolo during the last years of his life for private clients, most likely members of the Spanish court. Variations on the subject of *The Flight into Egypt* (ill. 137), now in the Museu Nacional de Arte Antigua in Lisbon, the Staatsgalerie in Stuttgart, a private collection in New York and in the Torre and Tasso Collection in Bellagio, a series of four pictures identical in format and stylistic treatment, are particularly noteworthy. The subject matter itself is a commonly portrayed theme in Christian art, and one which Tiepolo had also depicted many times in the course of his career.

In 1753, Tiepolo's son Giandomenico had also published a series of 27 engravings, executed during his stay in Würzburg, entitled *Idee pittoresche sopra la Fuga in Egitto*. The pictures show the Holy Family on their way through the wilderness accompanied by angels and stopping in strange cities. The intimacy of the representations, which impress upon the viewer the fate of a family forced to leave its homeland, may have inspired Tiepolo's own highly individual series, executed in the manner of *capricci*.

Nevertheless, the Spanish version of this theme differs fundamentally from anything that Tiepolo or his son had previously created. In the sketch in the Staatsgalerie in Stuttgart especially, the actual subject matter appears to have been pushed into the background – the exhausted figures of the Holy Family no longer appear able to cover the immense distances and, from the point of view of the pictorial narrative, play only a secondary role to the overpowering landscape. We are left with a moving scene in which man is at the mercy of nature, and the only remaining hope lies in divine mercy. The rapid, uneasy brushstrokes, the nervous contours, the dull colours and the economical treatment of the objects portrayed, a style of painting which has often been compared with the later works of Titian, underline the meditative calm and resignation expressed by the pictures. It is difficult not to see these works as an autobiographical statement by the artist, now over seventy years old, thinking shortly before his death of the home to which he would never return and of the family he had left behind.

Two other small-scale works *The Lamentation of Christ* and *The Entombment* (now in private collections) have been executed in the same style. These are in turn comparable to the two representations of *The Angels appearing to Abraham* and *The Annunciation*, now in the collection of the Duchess of Vilhermosa in Pedrola, which belong to the characteristic late-period works of the artist.

In spite of the tone of resignation in these very personal works, Giambattista Tiepolo had the strength to accept another large commission from King Charles III at the end of 1769: that of frescoing the collegiate church of San Ildefonso in La Granja. The designs for the decoration included several scenes within a stucco framework. However, Tiepolo was only able to complete the oil sketch *The Allegory of the Immaculate Conception*, now in Dublin, before his sudden death on

136 *The Immaculate Conception*, 1767–1769
Oil on canvas, 279 x 152 cm
Museo Nacional del Prado, Madrid

In an awe-inspiring, powerful manifestation, the Virgin Mary hovers in the skies, atop a globe, and in front of a yellow background. Above her the dove appears, symbolizing the Holy Spirit. The palm tree in the foreground is a symbol of Mary's victory and superiority over evil in the world, the snake under her feet stands for original sin. The mirror, on the other hand, illustrates the belief that she is completely without blemish and that she herself is the mirror of all virtues. The crescent moon refers to the Woman of the Apocalypse in St. John's Gospel and is also a symbol of chastity.

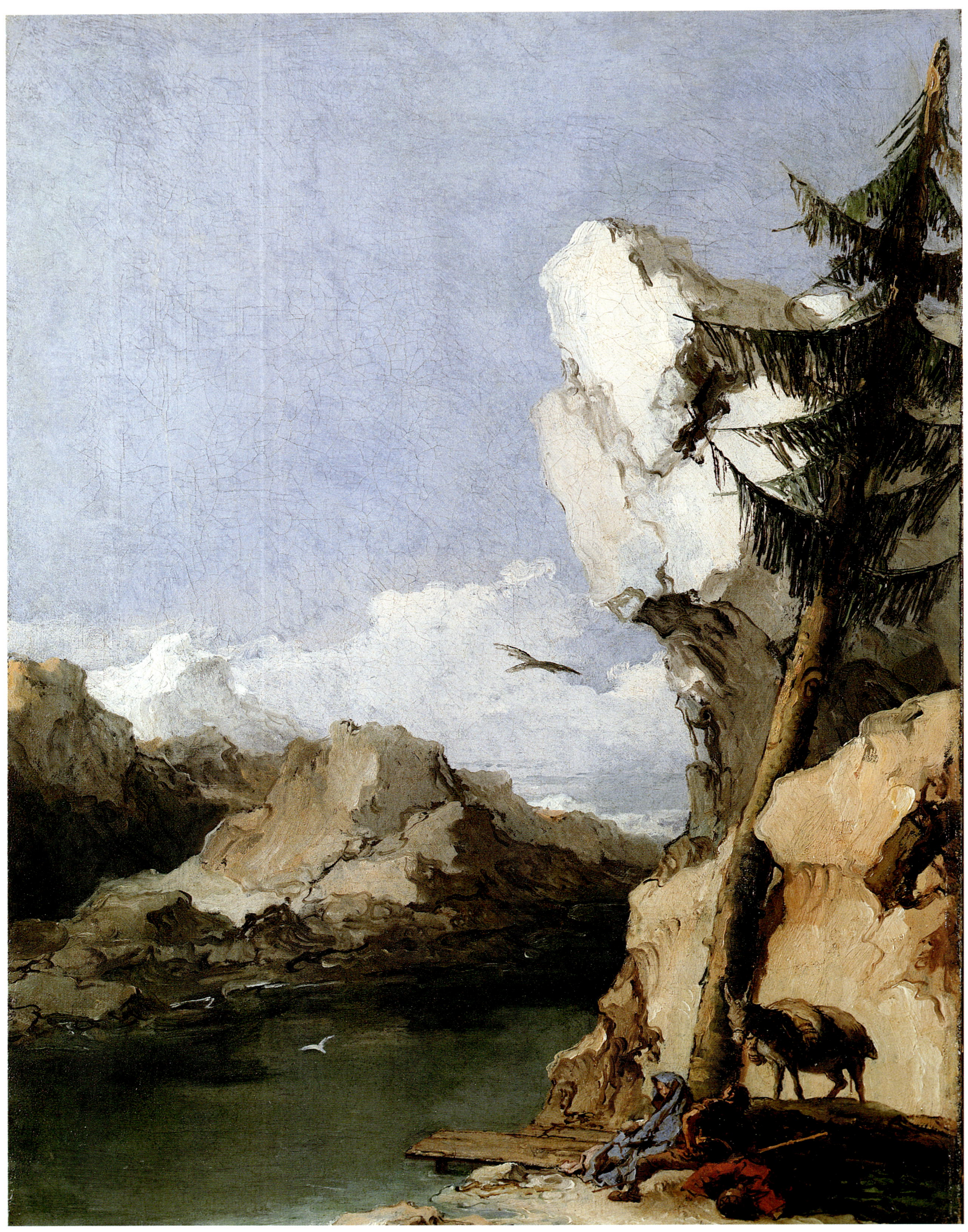

137 (opposite) *The Rest on the Flight to Egypt*, 1767–1769
Oil on canvas, 57 x 44 cm
Staatsgalerie Stuttgart

The theme of the rest on the flight to Egypt plays only a secondary role in this depiction. The scene is dominated by an isolated, precipitous-looking mountain landscape, through which a wide river flows, whose dark green color announces impassable depths. The white dove, which can be made out right in the middle of the river, is the only reference to any hope of salvation in this by and large desolate setting.

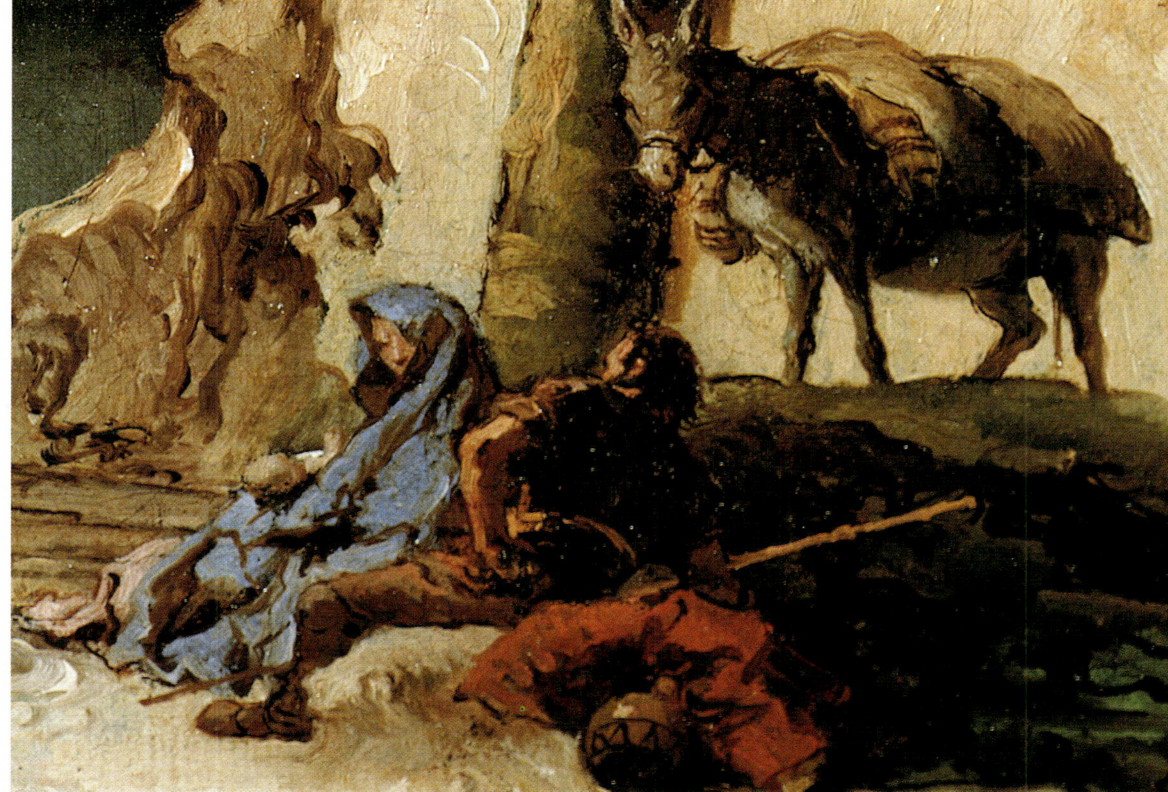

138 (right) *The Rest on the flight to Egypt* (detail ill. 137), 1767–1769

The figures of the Holy Family, who have come to a stop, exhausted, and rest in front of a tree in the foreground, look really tiny.

27 March 1770. He was laid to rest in the church of San Martin in Madrid. However, the building was later destroyed, and his grave is now unmarked. News of his death did not reach Venice until the following month, on 21 April 1770. Of his two sons, Giandomenico alone returned home, arriving in Venice on 12 November of that same year. Lorenzo, on the other hand, remained in Madrid and tried unsuccessfully to obtain the position of court painter.

After his death Tiepolo's art went out of fashion relatively quickly, as did Italian Baroque painting as a whole. Following the collapse of the Ancien Régime, there was no longer any interest in an art which served to glorify absolutist rulers. It was not until the 20th century that interest in Tiepolo was revived. Numerous studies of his work have recently contributed to establishing his importance as a painter of frescos and as a famous representative of the tradition of Italian painting.

CHRONOLOGY

1696 Giovanni Battista (Giambattista) Tiepolo is born on 5 March in Venice.

1697 His father dies on 10 March.

1710 Presumably the year of his entrance into Gregorio Lazzarini's workshop.

1715/16 Work on the *Apostle* series for the arches of Santa Maria dei Derelitti (the church of the Ospedaletto).

1716 On 16 August, the Feast Day of St. Roch, exhibits his painting *The Crossing of the Red Sea*.

1719 On 21 November, Tiepolo marries Cecilia Guardi, the sister of the painters Gian Antonio and Francesco Guardi.

1721 Commission for the altarpiece *Our Lady of Carmel* in the church of San Aponal.

1722 Commission for the *Martyrdom of Saint Bartholomew* for the church of San Stae.

1726 Visits Udine and decorates the chapel of the Holy Sacrament in the cathedral, as well as beginning work on the frescoes (1726–1729) in the Palazzo Patriarcale for Dionisio Dolfin.

1727 Birth of his son Giandomenico.

1730/31 Visit to Milan.

1732/33 Decoration of the Colleoni Chapel in the cathedral at Bergamo.

1734 Frescoes in Villa Loschi near Vicenza.

1736 Birth of his son Lorenzo.

1737 Three frescoes in the basilica of Sant'Ambrogio. Three altarpieces for the cathedral at Udine. Frescoes in Santa Maria del Rosario, which Tiepolo completes in 1739.

1740 Frescoes in the Palazzo Clerici in Milan. *The Virgin appearing to Saint Philip Neri* altarpiece for the church of San Filippo Neri in Camerino.

1743 *Apotheosis of the Admiral Vettor Pisani* in the Palazzo Pisani-Moretta.

1743/44 Frescoes in the Villa Cordellina in Montecchio Maggiore near Vicenza.

1744 Completion of the ceiling paintings for the Scuola Grande dei Carmini.

1744/45 Frescoes and canvases for the Palazzo Barbarigo.

1745 Ceiling fresco in the church of the Scalzi (destroyed in 1915). Consigns the altarpiece *The Martyrdom of Saint John* to the cathedral at Bergamo.

1746/47 Frescoes in the Palazzo Labia.

1748 Consigns the altarpiece *The Virgin Mary with Saints Catherine, Rose of Lima and Agnes of Montepulciano* to the church of the Gesuati.

1749 Delivers the central ceiling panel to the Scuola Grande dei Carmini.

1750 On 12 December leaves for Würzburg, accompanied by his sons.

1752 Completion of work on the frescoes in the Imperial Hall and commencement of the decoration of the stairwell.

1753 On 8 November departs from Würzburg and returns to Venice.

1754 Frescoes in Santa Maria della Visitazione (the church of the Pietà).

1757 Frescoes in the Villa Valmarana and in Ca' Rezzonico.

1759 Frescoes for the Oratorio della Purità in Udine. Consigns the altarpiece *Saint Thecla liberating the City of Este from the Plague* to the cathedral at Este.

1760 Works for Czarina Helena Petrovna.

1760/61 Work at the Villa Pisani in Stra and in the Palazzo Canossa in Verona.

1762 On 4 June arrives, accompanied by his sons Giandomenico and Lorenzo, at the court of Charles III in Madrid.

1767–1769 Seven altarpieces for San Pasquale Baylon in Aranjuez.

1769 Decorates the collegiate church of San Ildefonso in La Granja.

1770 Sudden death of Giambattista Tiepolo on 27 March. Burial in the church of San Martin in Madrid.

GLOSSARY

All Saints painting (Ger. *Allerheiligenbild*), a picture relating the Feast of All Saints (November 1). Such pictures show the adoration of the Holy Trinity (God the Father, the Holy Spirit, and the Lamb as a symbol of God the Son) by saints, patriarchs, prophets, and the Christian community on earth. The imagery is largely derived from the Book of Revelations.

altarpiece, a picture or sculpture that stands on or is set up behind an altar. Many altarpieces were very simple (a single panel painting), though some were huge and complex works. A few combined both painting and sculpture within a carved framework.

allegory (Gk. *allegorein*, "say differently"), a work of art which represents some abstract quality or idea, either by means of a single figure (personification) or by grouping objects and figures together. In addition to the Christian allegories of the Middle Ages, Renaissance allegories make frequent allusions to Greek and Roman legends and literature.

Ancien Régime (Fr. "old regime"), the social and political order in France before the French revolution of 1789.

arcade (Lat. *arcus,* "arch"), a series of arches supported by columns, piers or pillars. In a **blind arcade** the arches are built into a wall.

Arcadian, relating to Arcadia (a mountainous area of Greece), in Greek and Roman literature, a place where a contented life of rural simplicity is lived, an earthly paradise peopled by shepherds.

attribute (Lat. *attributum*, "added"), a symbolic object which is conventionally used to identify a particular person, usually a saint or mythological figure.

Augustinians, in the Roman Catholic Church, a mendicant order founded in 1256 under the rule of St. Augustine (AD 354 – 430). The order became widespread in the 14th and 15th centuries, renowned for its scholarship and teaching. Under the influence of humanism during the Renaissance, Augustinians played a leading role in seeking Church reform.

bacchante, a priestess or attendant at a festival in honor of Bacchus, in Greek and Roman mythology the god of wine and fertility.

baldachin, or **baldacchino** (It. "brocade"), originally a textile canopy supported on poles and carried by dignitaries and relics. Later, an architectural canopy of stone or wood set over a high altar or bishop's throne.

balustrade, a rail supported by a row of small posts or open-work panels.

Baroque (Port. *barocco*, "an irregular pearl or stone"), the period in art history from about 1600 to about 1750. In this sense the term covers a wide range of styles and artists. In painting and sculpture there were three main forms of Baroque: (1) sumptuous display, a style associated with the Catholic Counter Reformation and the absolutist courts of Europe (Bernini, Rubens); (2) dramatic realism (Caravaggio); and (3) everyday realism, a development seen in particular in Holland (Rembrandt, Vermeer). In architecture, there was an emphasis on expressiveness and grandeur, achieved through scale, the dramatic use of light and shadow, and increasingly elaborate decoration. In Germany and Austria, Baroque architecture and decoration acquired flamboyance and great opulence.

bust, a sculpted portrait consisting of the head and shoulders. Developed in ancient Greece and widely used in ancient Rome, the bust was revived in 15th-century Italy.

cabinet piece/picture, a small painting, originally (in the 17th century) one small enough to be kept in a "cabinet of curiosities", where collectors kept and displayed their collections of art works and curiosities.

caduceus (Gk. karux, "herald"), in Greek mythology, a winged herald's staff that has two serpents wound around it. It is usually carried by Hermes.

capriccio pl. ***capricci*** (It. "caprice"), a painting or drawing of a city or landscape that combines real and imaginary (often mythological) elements; a picture full of imaginary elements.

Carmelites (Lat. *Ordo Fratrum Beatae Mariae Virginis de Monte Carmelo*, Brothers of Our Blessed Lady of Mount Carmel), a Roman Catholic order of contempletive mendicant friars. Founded in Palestine in the 12th century, the Carmelites were originally a group of hermits. In the 13th century, the order was refounded as an order resembling the Dominicans and Franciscans. An order of Carmelite Sisters was founded in the 15th century, and reforms introduced by St. Teresa of Ávila in the 16th century led to the creation of the Barefoot (Discalced) Carmelites.

chiaroscuro (It. "light dark"), in painting, the modelling of form (the creation of a sense of three-dimensionality in objects) through the use of light and shade. The introduction of oil paints in the 15th century, replacing tempera, encouraged the development of chiaroscuro, for oil paint allowed a far greater range and control of tone. The term chiaroscuro is used in particular for the dramatic contrasts of light and dark introduced by Caravaggio. When the contrast of light and dark is strong, chiaroscuro becomes an important element of composition.

choir (Gk. *khoros,* "area for dancing; chorus"), in a Christian church, the areas set aside for singers and the clergy, generally the area between the crossing and the high altar.

Classicism, a return to the style, motifs, or values of the art of ancient Greece and Rome (**classical Antiquity**). There have been several periods of Classicism, which is characterized by restraint, harmony, balance, and moral seriousness, the subjects depicted often being taken from the history or mythology of classical Antiquity. French art played a leading role in 17th-century Classicism, its leading figure being Nicolas Poussin (1594–1665). Classicism became the "official" French style through the French Academie Royale de Peinture et Sculpture, founded in 1648 under the directorship of the artist Charles Lebrun.

cornice, in architecture, a projecting molding that runs around the top of a building or the wall of a room.

Counter Reformation, 16th- and 17th-century reform movement in the Roman Catholic Church. Prompted initially by internal criticism, it was given greater momentum by the emergence of Protestantism. The Counter Reformation led to a new emphasis on teaching, missionary work, and the suppression of heresy. In Catholic countries there was the deliberate cultivation of the arts in supporting the Church's message, with works both explicitly illustrating doctrine and also aiming to make a direct appeal to the emotions. Among the major artists of the Counter Reformation were Bernini, Rubens, and Caravaggio.

cour d'honneur (Fr. "court of honor"), the front courtyard of a palace or mansion, where important guests were received.

crosier, a staff with a crook or cross at the end carried by a bishop or archbishop as a symbol of office.

décolleté (Fr.), having a very low neckline.

Doge (Lat. *dux,* "leader"), the elected head of the Venetian state. The office was in existence from 697 to 1797.

Dominicans (Lat. *Ordo Praedictatorum,* Order of Preachers), a Roman Catholic order of mendicant friars founded by St. Dominic in 1216 to spread the faith through preaching and teaching. The Dominicans were one of the most influential religious orders in the later Middle Ages, their intellectual authority being established by such figures as Albertus Magnus and St.Thomas Aquinas. The Dominicans played the leading role in the Inquisition.

Enlightenment, intellectual movement dominating Europe in the 18th century. It was broadly characterized by a new confidence in the power of human reason, and an optimism about human progress. In politics, the Enlightenment saw the development of liberalism, and so prepared the way for the American and French Revolutions. Philosophy was strongly influenced by science, and the arts drew increasingly on classical Greek and Roman models.

exempla virtutis (Lat. "examples of manliness"), depictions of famous men, usually figures from Greek and Roman history and also the Bible, as examples of specific virtues.

Franciscans, a Roman Catholic order of mendicant friars founded by St. Francis of Assisi (given papal approval in 1223). Committed to charitable and missionary work, they stressed the veneration of the Holy Virgin, a fact that was highly significant in the development of images of the Madonna in Italian art. In time, the absolute poverty of the early Franciscans gave way to a far more relaxed view of property and wealth, and the Franciscans became some of the most important patrons of art in the early Renaissance.

fresco (It. "fresh"), wall painting technique in which pigments are applied to wet (fresh) plaster (*intonaco*). The pigments bind with the drying plaster to form a very durable image. Only a small area can be painted in a day, and these areas, drying to a slightly different tint, can in time be seen. Small amounts of retouching and detail work could be carried out on the dry plaster, a technique known as *a secco* fresco.

grisaille (Fr. *gris,* "gray"), a painting done entirely in one color, usually gray. Grisaille paintings were often intended to imitate sculptures.

grotto (It. *grotta*), a small cave or cavern, particularly one created in a garden for aesthetic effect and decorated with shells or statues.

hatching, in a drawing, print or painting, a series of close parallel lines that create the effect of shadow, and therefore contour and three-dimensionality.

iconography (Gk. "description of images"), the systematic study and identification of the subject-matter and symbolism of art works, as opposed to their style; the set of symbolic forms on which a given work is based. Originally, the study and identification of classical portraits. Renaissance art drew heavily on two **iconographical** traditions: Christianity, and ancient Greek and Roman art, thought and literature.

Jesuits (the **Society of Jesus**), a Roman Catholic teaching order founded by St. Ignatius Loyola in 1534. The express purpose of the Jesuits was to fight heresy within the Church (they played a leading role in the Counter Reformation), and to spread the faith through missionary work in the many parts of the world recently discovered by Western explorers and colonists.

loggia (It.), a gallery or room open on one or more sides, its roof supported by columns. Loggias in Italian Renaissance buildings were generally on the upper levels. Renaissance loggias were also separate structures, often standing in markets and town squares, that could be used for public ceremonies.

lunette (Fr. "little moon"), in architecture, a semicircular space, such as that over a door or window or in a vaulted roof, that may contain a window, painting or sculptural decoration.

medallion, in architecture, a large ornamental plaque or disc.

modello (It. "model"), a drawing of a proposed painting, often executed for the patron's approval. They were often highly finished and the design could be transferred to the canvas or wall by means of a grid drawn over the *modello* (**squared *modello***) and then scaled up.

monochrome (Gk. *monokhromatos,* "one color"), painted in a single color; a painting executed in a single color.

Neo-classicism, a style in European art and architecture from the mid 18th century until the end of the 19th century. Based as it was on the use of ancient Greek and Roman models and motifs, its development was greatly influenced by the excavations at Pompeii and Herculaneum, and by the theories of the German art historian Johann Joachim Winckelmann (1717–1768). Intellectually and politically it was closely linked to the Enlightenment rejection of the aristocratic frivolity of **Rococo**, the style of the Ancien Régime. Among Neo-classicism's leading figures were the French painter Jacques-Louis David (1744–1825), the German painter Anton Raffael Mengs (1728–1729), and the Italian sculptor Antonio Canova (1757–1822).

Nereids, in Greek mythology, sea nymphs, the daughters of the sea god Nereus.

obelisk (Gk. *obeliskos,* "slender, pointed implement"), an upright column with four sides tapering the top to a pyramid or cone,

Oratorians (or **Congregation of the Oratory**), in the Catholic Church, an order of secular priests who live in independent communities, prayer and preaching being central to their mission. The Oratorians was founded by St Philip Neri (1515–1595).

Palladian, in architecture, in the style of the Italian architect Andrea Palladio (1508–1580), who developed an austere form of classicism derived from ancient Roman architecture.

pastoral (Lat. *pastor*, "shepherd"), relating to a romantic or idealized image of rural life; in classical literature, to a world peopled by shepherds, nymphs, and satyrs.

pavilion (Lat. *papilio*, "butterfly, hence tent"), a lightly constructed, ornamental building, such as a garden summerhouse; a small, ornamental structure built onto a palace or château; a prominent section of a monumental façade, projecting either centrally or at both ends.

pediment, in classical architecture, the triangular end of a low-pitched roof, sometimes filled with relief sculptures; especially in Renaissance and Baroque architecture, a decorative architectural element over a door or window, usually triangular (broad and low), but sometimes segmental.

pilaster (Lat. *pilastrum*, "pillar"), a rectangular column set into a wall, usually as a decorative feature.

podium (Gk. *pous*, "foot"), an elevated platform.

Poor Clares, in the Roman Catholic Church, a contemplative order of nuns founded by St. Clare and St. Francis of Assisi about 1214. The order was one of the most austere.

portico (Lat. *porticus*, "porch"), a roofed space in front of an entrance, the roof often supported by columns.

presbytery (Gk. *presbuteros*, "priest"), in a church, the area reserved for the clergy, usually between the choir and the high altar.

putti sing. **putto** (It. "boys"), plump naked little children, usually boys, most commonly found in late Renaissance and Baroque works. They can be either sacred (angels) or secular (the attendants of Venus).

quadratura, wall and ceiling painting consisting of illusionistic architectural details that create the impression a room has been extended.

ricordo pl. ***ricordi*** (It.), a drawing or sketch of an existing work.

Rococo, a style of design, painting, and architecture dominating the 18th century, often considered the last stage of the Baroque. Developing in the Paris townhouses of the French aristocracy at the turn of the 18th century, Rococo was elegant and ornately decorative, its mood lighthearted and witty. Louis XV furniture, richly decorated with organic forms, is a typical product. Leading exponents of the Rococo style included the French painters Antoine Watteau (1684–1721) and Jean-Honoré Fragonard (1732–1806), and the German architect Johann Balthasar Neumann (1687–1753). Rococo gave way to **Neo-classicism**.

Sacra Conversazione (It. "holy conversation"), a representation of the Virgin and Child attended by saints. There is seldom a literal conversation depicted, though as the theme developed the interaction between the participants – expressed through gesture, glance and movement – greatly increased. The saints depicted usually include saint to whom church or altar is dedicated, local saints, or those chosen by the patron who commissioned the work.

sarcophagus, pl. **sarcophagi** (Gk. "flesh eating"), a coffin or tomb, made of stone, wood or terracotta, and sometimes (especially among the Greeks and Romans) carved with inscriptions and reliefs.

scapular (Lat. *scapula*, "shoulder"), a loose, sleeveless garment worn over the shoulders.

(di) sotto in sù (It. "up from under"), perspective in which people and objects are seen from below and shown with extreme foreshortening.

stucco (It.), a protective coat of coarse plaster applied to external walls; plaster decorations, usually interior. During the Renaissance, stucco decorative work, often employing classical motifs, achieved a high degree of artistry.

supra porte or **sopraporta**, (It."over the door"), painting or relief sculpture over a door. Accentuating the whole door area, they were particularly popular in Baroque and Rococo rooms. Sopraporta paintings were often *capricci*, and generally formed an integral part of the architectural ensemble.

Tenebrism, in painting, the use of large areas of deep shadow together with strong contrasts between light and shadow. Tenebrism developed during the Baroque, the **Tenebrists** being followers of the Italian artist Caravaggio.

tiara (Lat. "triple crown"), dome-shaped triple crown worn by a pope.

triptych (Gk. *triptukhos*, "threefold"), a painting in three sections, usually an altarpiece, consisting of a central panel and two outer panels, or wings. In many medieval triptychs the two outer wings were hinged so that they could be closed over the center panel.

trompe-l'œil (Fr. "deceives the eye"), a painting which, through various naturalistic devices, creates the illusion that the objects depicted are actually there in front of us. Dating from classical times, trompe-l'œil was revived in the 15th century.

tympanum, pl. **tympana** (Lat. "drum"), in classical architecture, the triangular area enclosed by a pediment, often decorated with sculptures. In medieval architecture, the semi-circular area over a door's lintel, enclosed by an arch, often decorated with sculptures or mosaics.

vedutà, pl. **vedute** (It. "view"), a painting or drawing of a city, a "view".

wash, a layer of thin watercolor or ink painted on a drawing.

SELECTED BIBLIOGRAPHY

Aikema, Bernard: "Early Tiepolo Studies, 1: The Ospedaletto Problem", in: *Mitteilungen des Kunsthistorischen Instituts in Florenz*, 26 (1982), pp. 339–382

Alpers, Svetlana and Michael Baxandall: Tiepolo and the Pictorial Intelligence, New Haven 1994

Ashton, Mark: "Allegory, Fact and Meaning in Giambattista Tiepolo's Four Continents in Würzburg", in: *Art Bulletin*, 60 (1978), pp. 109–125

Barcham, William L.: The Religious Paintings of Giambattista Tiepolo: Piety and Tradition in Eighteenth-Century Venice, Oxford 1989

Barcham, William L.: Giambattista Tiepolo, New York 1992

Büttner, Frank: Giovanni Battista Tiepolo: Die Fresken in der Residenz zu Würzburg, Würzburg 1980

Exhibition catalogue Cambridge, Mass.: Tiepolo, a Bicentenary Exhibition, 1770–1970: Drawings, Mainly from American Collections, by Giambattista Tiepolo and the Members of his Circle, George Knox (ed.), Cambridge, Mass: Fogg Art Museum, Harvard University 1970

Exhibition catalogue Fort Worth: Giambattista Tiepolo: Master of the Oil Sketch, Beverly L. Brown (ed.), Kimbell Art Museum, Fort Worth 1993

Exhibition catalogue London: The Glory of Venice: Art in the Eighteenth Century, Jane Martineau and Andrew Robinson (eds.), Royal Academy of Arts, London 1994

Exhibition catalogue Ottawa: Etchings by the Tiepolos: Domenico Tiepolo's Collection of the Family Etchings, George Knox and Elaine Dee (eds.), National Gallery of Canada, Ottawa 1976

Exhibition catalogue Venice: Giambattista Tiepolo 1696–1996, Milan 1996

Exhibition catalogue Würzburg: Der Himmel auf Erden: Tiepolo in Würzburg, Peter O. Krückmann (ed.), 2 vols., Residenz, Würzburg 1996

Fehl, Philipp P.: Decorum and Wit: The Poetry of Venetian Painting Essays in the History of the Classical Tradition, Vienna 1992

Gemin, Massimo and Filippo Pedrocco: Giambattista Tiepolo: I dipinti, opera completa, Venice 1993

Howard, Deborah: "Giambattista Tiepolo's Frescoes for the Church of the Pietà in Venice", in: *Oxford Art Journal*, 9 (1986) Nr. 1, pp. 11–28

Knox, George: Giambattista and DomenicoTiepolo: A Study and Catalogue Raisonné of the Chalk Drawings, 2 vols., Oxford 1980

Levey, Michael: Giambattista Tiepolo: His Life and Art, 2nd ed., New Haven 1994

Morassi, Antonio: A Complete Catalogue of the Paintings of G. B. Tiepolo, Including Pictures by his Pupils and Followers Wrongly Attributed to Him, London 1962

Sánchez Cantón, Francisco J.: J. B. Tiepolo en España, Madrid 1953

Urbani de Gheltof, Giuseppe M.: Tiepolo e la sua famiglia; note e documenti inedeti, Venice 1879

Whistler, Catherine: Giambattista Tiepolo in Spain: The Late Religious Paintings, Ph.D. dissertation, University College Dublin, National University of Ireland 1984

PHOTOGRAPHIC CREDITS

The publishers would like to thank the museums, collectors, archives and photographers for permission to reproduce the works in this book. Particular thanks go to the Scala photographic archives for their productive cooperation.

Archiv für Kunst und Geschichte, Berlin (105 below); © Archivio Osvaldo Böhm, Venezia (8, 9, 10); Archivio Fotografico dell'Amministrazione Provinciale di Vicenza, Vicenza – Photo: Vajenti (56); Photograph © 1998, The Art Institute of Chicago, Illinois, All Rights Reserved (57); Artothek, Peissenberg – Photo: Gundermann (105 above), Photo: Joachim Blauel (37); © The Ashmolean Museum, Oxford (111 right); Mit Genehmigung der Bayerischen Verwaltung der Staatlichen Schlösser, Gärten und Seen, München – Photo: Achim Bednorz (77, 78/79, 80/81, 84, 85, 87, 89, 90, 92 below), Photo: Wolf – Christian von der Mülbe (82, 83, 88, 91, 92 above, 93, 94, 95, 96 above); Bildarchiv Preußischer Kulturbesitz, Berlin – Photo: Jörg P. Anders (99 below); Cappella Colleoni, Bergamo (30, 31); © Fundación Colección Thyssen-Bornemisza, Madrid (96 below); Galleria dell'Accademia su concessione del Ministero dei Beni Culturali e Ambientali, Venezia (52); Museum der Bildenden Künste, Leipzig – Photo: Gerstenberger (100 below, 101); Photograph © 1996 By The Metropolitan Museum of Art, New York, New York (32.12.1): Harris Brisbane Dick Fund, 1932 (100 above); © National Gallery of Victoria, Melbourne (53); Reproduced by courtesy of the Trustees, The National Gallery, London (55); © RMN, Paris – Photo: Jean Schormans (103); © R. P. M., Patrimonio Nacional, Madrid (131); Scala, Istituto Fotografico Editoriale, Antella/Firenze (2, 7, 11, 12, 13, 14, 15, 16, 17, 18, 19, 20, 21, 22, 23, 24, 26, 27, 28, 29, 32, 33, 34, 35, 36, 41, 42, 43, 44, 45, 46, 47, 48, 49, 50, 51, 54, 58, 59, 60, 63, 64, 65, 68, 70, 71, 72, 73, 74, 75, 97, 102, 104, 106, 107, 108, 109, 110, 111 left, 112, 113, 114, 115, 116, 117, 118, 119, 120/121, 122, 123, 124, 127, 128, 129, 130, 132); Staatsgalerie Stuttgart, Stuttgart (99 above, 134); Stockholm University Art Collection, Stockholm (38/39); Courtesy of the Trustees, Victoria and Albert Museum, Picture Library, London – Photo: P. de Bay (98).